MAN *and* GOD

MAN
and
GOD

Studies in Biblical Theology

by ELIEZER BERKOVITS

Hebrew Theological College
Skokie, Illinois

Wayne State University Press

DETROIT, 1969

17649

Contents

Preface

THE chief concern of this study is theological. What is the faith, what is the message of the Bible in the area of our investigation? What is the biblical teaching and testimony about God? We believe that one may dispense with the methods of higher criticism to establish the faith and the message. No matter what one's opinion may be regarding the literary sources of the Bible, it would be sheer irresponsibility to maintain that the biblical text represents an accidental and haphazard conglomeration of pieces of writings without much unity and consistency between the various parts. It may be well worthwhile recalling some pertinent words by N. H. Snaith in *The Distinctive Ideas of the Old Testament* (London, 1955):

The literary criticism (Higher Criticism) of the Old Testament has often forgotten that those who pieced the Old Testament together, pieced it together as we have it now. They chose the order we have. The analysis of the sources is but the first step in literary criticism. The editors had the final say, and they used all the material from its varied sources in order to teach their particular message. This message, that of Scripture as a whole, can never be found so long as we think of the Bible only with respect to its literary sources. (p. 89)

Snaith's insight has been anticipated by several decades by Rosenzweig and Buber in their significant translation of the

7

Bible into German. About one aspect of their joint endeavor Franz Rosenzweig wrote that for them the "R," which for German higher criticism stands for *Redakteur,* had the inspiring meaning of the Hebrew *Rabbenu,* our teacher. Indeed, he who does not find the teacher and master in the Bible has no Bible. No matter what the literary origins, *Rabbenu* had the final say. The final say of *Rabbenu,* or of the "Editors," is the Bible. It establishes the intrinsic unity of the message and the teaching.

The theological and religious interest in the Bible is not concerned with history or literature but exclusively with the faith and the testimony of *Rabbenu.* But this can only be established if one is able to discover the unity and consistency implanted by *Rabbenu.* His inspiration, his faith, his testimony make the Bible one. To find this oneness of the message, "the message of the Scripture as a whole," is the theological and religious concern.

Who is *Rabbenu?* For many, and this author is among them, he is the prophets and teachers who, under divine inspiration, proclaimed the message and the teaching. Others may have different opinions. The theological and religious concern is with the wholeness of the testimony, no matter whether such wholeness is the work of the "Editors" or of *"Moshe Rabbenu."*

While this author believes in the theological unity of the Bible, he did not go out to prove it. In fact, he did not go out to prove anything. He let the Bible speak to him, but in its entirety and wholeness. He found a surprising consistency in the usage of the basic ideas which he has investigated.

What has impressed him most painfully has been the realization that all translations have been misrepresentations of essential biblical teaching. Who is not familiar with the phrase, "the Lord He is our God"? The words have been responsible for a great deal of misunderstanding about the biblical teaching regarding God. We have shown that the expression occurs nowhere in the Hebrew Bible. "Y He is our *Elohim*" has specific biblical meaning which is completely lost in the translation. Similarly, ideas like *mishpat, emeth, emunah, sedeq,* etc. have their unique biblical significance. The accepted translations are, in fact, misrepresentations.

In our analysis we have had to contend with the difficulty that often, in discussing one term, we could not anticipate the results of the discussions of other terms which also occur in the same context. In such cases we either let the old translation stand, even though it had to be later rejected, or let the not-yet analyzed Hebrew concepts stand in the original.

The tetragrammaton as well as the term *Elohim* caused a problem of translation of their own. We have resolved it by letting the Hebrew stand wherever an appreciation of the original was necessary for the understanding of an idea or a passage. Otherwise, we followed the not very satisfactory habit of translating the words as "the Lord, God." We abbreviate the tetragrammaton with Y, which corresponds to the Hebrew *Yod,* rather than with the customary I.

Our study is based entirely on the Masoretic text. The English translation we use is in general the Jewish Publication Society edition of 1916 and, occasionally, the Revised Version. Where we depart from these translations, as is often the case, we usually indicate our reasons for our disagreement.

For technical reasons it was impossible to employ any of the usual methods for the transliteration of Hebrew words. Wherever practical the transliteration was put on a phonetic basis without seeking or achieving complete consistency.

Since our interest is completely theological, there was no need for us to follow the division of the books of the Bible as has become customary among Bible scholars whose main interest is literary and historical.

E. B.

The Knowledge of God

THAT HE IS Y

THE Bible speaks of man's knowledge of God mainly in four different phrases. There is, for instance, the expression: that they may know that I am YHVH.[1] Often, however, the word *Elohim* is added and we have, that they may know that I am YHVH, their God. A further variation we find in the phrase, that they may know that YHVH is the God. Finally, there is also the form in which, instead of a subordinate clause, the more direct accusative is used, as for instance, thou shalt know YHVH. The question we wish to discuss in this chapter is: are these terms about man's knowledge of God used indiscriminately, or has each one of these phrases a specific meaning of its own? When the Bible says that you may know that I am YHVH, could it just as well have added the word, *Elohekha*, your God? Or in cases where the word is found, would the meaning of the text be in any way affected, had the phrase, your God, been omitted? Again, when the accusative is used, could the thought have been expressed by the more frequent propositional clause and, instead of thou shalt know YHVH, could the text just as well have read, thou shalt know that I am YHVH? Is there some principle that determines when to use one, when the other, of these phrases about knowing God?

Let us look at a number of passages in which to know God means to know that He is YHVH. Let us see whether we may discern some one feature which they have in common. Most of

11

these passages occur in Ezekiel, but they are also found in many of the other books of the Bible. We shall quote them at random:

I will lay My hand upon Egypt, and bring forth My hosts, My people the children of Israel, out of the land of Egypt by great judgments. And the Egyptians shall know that I am YHVH, when I stretch forth My hand upon Egypt, and bring out the children of Israel from among them. (Exod. 7:4–5)

And I will harden Pharaoh's heart, and he shall follow after them; and I will get Me honour upon Pharaoh, and upon all his host; and the Egyptians shall know that I am YHVH. (Exod. 14:4)

For I have hardened his heart, and the heart of his servants, that I might show these My signs in the midst of them; and that thou mayest tell in the ears of thy son, and of thy son's son, what I have wrought upon Egypt, and My signs which I have done among them; that ye may know that I am YHVH. (Exod. 10:1–2)

And behold, a prophet came near unto Ahab king of Israel, and said: Thus saith YHVH: Hast thou seen all this great multitude? behold, I will deliver it into thy hand this day; and thou shalt know that I am YHVH. (I Kings 20:13; see also vs. 28)

Already these few passages seem to reveal a common pattern. God will be known by his mighty deed, by the signs and miracles which he performs in Egypt, by the destruction of the enemies of Israel. In the passages quoted, the Egyptians, the children of Israel, or King Ahab will know that He is YHVH by the convincing revelation of his supernatural might and power. This is expressed with clear emphasis on the occasion when Moses foretells Pharaoh the miracle of the turning of the waters of the Nile into blood. The words we read there are:

Thus saith YHVH: *In this* thou shalt know that I am YHVH— behold, I will smite with the rod that is in my hand upon the waters which are in the river, and they shall be turned to blood. And the fish that are in the river shall die, and the river shall become foul; and the Egyptians shall loathe to drink water from the river [italics added]. (Exod. 7:17)

The supernatural mightiness of God, which is revealed in the miracle, makes it known to all that He is YHVH. Most emphatic are numerous passages in Ezekiel which also show that YHVH makes himself known in this manner by what he performs on Jew or gentile alike. A terrible judgment, which is pronounced over Jerusalem, and in which God declares that he will have no pity with her inhabitants, concludes with the words:

Thus shall Mine anger spend itself, and I will satisfy My fury upon them, and I will be eased; and they shall know that I am YHVH.[2] I have spoken in My zeal, when I have spent My fury upon them. (Ezek. 5:13)

Consulting any reliable Bible concordance, anyone may find the many passages in Ezekiel that express the same idea. We shall let a few more stand here to make the point.

Another terrible judgment over Israel reads:

And I will . . . deliver you into the hands of strangers, and will execute judgments among you. Ye shall fall by the sword; I will judge you upon the border of Israel; and ye shall know that I am YHVH. Though this city shall not be your caldron, you shall be the flesh in the midst thereof; I will judge you upon the border of Israel; and ye shall know that I am YHVH. (Ezek. 11:9–11)

When God draws his sword against the land of Israel to cut from it the righteous and the wicked, it is said:

And all flesh shall know that I am YHVH.[3] I have drawn forth My sword out of its sheath. (Ezek. 21:10)

In the context of the punishment meted out to Seir it is said:

I will make thee perpetual desolations, and thy cities shall not return; and ye shall know that I am YHVH. (Ezek. 35:9)

The more passages one examines, the more clear does it become that they all have a common denominator: God becomes known through the manifestation of his power and his judgment over men and nations, over nature and history.

What does a similar analysis of the contexts reveal about the meaning of the phrase, according to which the knowledge acquired teaches one that He is YHVH our God? Once again we shall list some of the passages side by side.

Right at the beginning of Moses' mission of redemption, he is sent by God to the children of Israel with a message that contains the following words:

And I will take you to Me for a people, and I will be to you a God; and ye shall know that I am YHVH your God, who brought you out from under the burdens of the Egyptians. (Exod. 6:7)

When the children of Israel were murmuring in the desert, asking for food, Moses conveyed to them the words of God:

At dusk ye shall eat flesh, and in the morning ye shall be filled with bread; and ye shall know that I am YHVH your God. (Exod. 16:12)

About the service in the Tent of Meeting God says:

And I will dwell among the children of Israel, and will be their God. And they shall know that I am YHVH their God, that brought them forth out of the land of Egypt, that I may dwell among them. (Exod. 29:45–46)

Once again a pattern is noticeable. Significantly, however, it is rather different from the one, which we have found analyzing the term, to know that He is YHVH. In fact, it seems to be its very opposite. One can hardly think of a greater contrast than between the grim passages of Ezekiel, in which the prophet describes the manner of fury in which the knowledge reaches man that He is YHVH, and the tender words of loving care in which God assures the children of Israel that he will take them for a people unto himself, that he brought them out of Egypt so that he might dwell in their midst, that they may know that He is YHVH their God. Even when in their pusillanimity the children of Israel murmur

14

against Moses and, by implication, against God, God fulfills their wish, granting them the manna and the meat of quails so that they may know that He is YHVH their God. We would then be justified in saying that when God makes manifest his power, when he reveals himself as the sovereign ruler or judge, when he thus is above man and nature, removed from them and transcending them, he makes himself known as YHVH. On the other hand, when he reveals his caring concern for man, when he shows his providential intervention on behalf of man, when he is near man, in the midst of men, he communicates knowledge that He is "YHVH your God." The idea is greatly strengthened by a passage in Deuteronomy, in which the providential care is recalled by which the children of Israel were guided in the wilderness:

And I have led you forty years in the wilderness; your clothes are not waxen old upon you, and thy shoe is not waxen old upon thy foot. Ye have not eaten bread, neither have ye drunk wine or strong drink; that ye might know that I am YHVH your God.

(Deut. 29:4–5)

The fact that they were sustained in the wilderness by the miracles of providence gave them knowledge of God; however, not the knowledge that He was YHVH, but that He was YHVH their God.

Most interesting is the exactitude with which, for instance, Ezekiel uses the two phrases under discussion. In chapter 36, God, speaking of the restoration of Israel, says:

And the land that was desolate shall be tilled, whereas it was a desolation in the sight of all that passed by. And they shall say: This land that was desolate is become like the garden of Eden; and the waste and desolate and ruined cities are fortified and inhabited. Then the nations I have left round about you shall know that I am YHVH! I have builded the ruined places, and planted that which was desolate. (vss. 34–36)

Another passage, dealing also with the theme of Israel's future redemption tells of the prophetic vision of the feast of

God on the mountains of Israel. The birds of prey and the beasts of the field are invited to feed on "the flesh of the mighty" and to drink "the blood of the princes." They are promised that they will be filled at God's table "with horses and horsemen, with mighty men, and with all men of war." Continuing the theme, it is said:

And I will set My glory among the nations, and all the nations shall see My judgment that I have executed, and My hand that I have laid upon them. So the house of Israel shall know that I am YHVH their God, from that day and forward. (Ezek. 39:21–22)

The two passages are rather different in tone. The one draws the idyllic picture of restoration and rebirth, the other speaks of wrath and judgment. The first describes the impact that God's redemptive act on behalf of Israel has on the nations. In the second example, on the other hand, the stress is on the significance for Israel of God's judgment over the nations. God's providential intervention in history is a revelation that He is YHVH when the providential act is for the sake of Israel and is viewed by the nations. In such an act only Israel could recognize that He is YHVH their God; the nations will see in it only the revelation of divine sovereignty. The one who redeems Israel is for them too YHVH, but it is not "their God." For "my God" means the one who cares for me providentially. On the other hand, in the act of judgment performed upon the nations, Israel recognizes that He is YHVH their God, if what happens to the nations takes place on "the mountains of Israel" for the sake of Israel's preservation. The differing meanings of the manifestation of the same divine act, when looked upon from differing points of interest, may be discerned in biblical books as apart from each other as Joshua and Isaiah. Concerning the twelve stones that were set up at Gilgal, after the crossing of the Jordan, Joshua said to the people:

For YHVH your God dried up the waters of Jordan from before you, until ye were passed over, as YHVH your God did to the Red Sea,

which He dried up from before us, until we were passed over, that
all the peoples of the earth may know the hand of YHVH, that it
is mighty; that ye may fear YHVH your God for ever. (Josh.
4:23–24)

A divine miracle is here described in its significance for the
peoples and for Israel, for whose salvation it was performed.
For the peoples it meant the knowledge of the power of
YHVH; for Israel it communicated something YHVH their
God did for them. A similar formulation we find in the opening
verses of chapter 45 of Isaiah. The prophetic words are addressed to God's anointed Cyrus, before whom God subdues
nations. It is promised to him that:

I will go before thee, and make the crooked places straight; I will
break in pieces the doors of brass, and cut in sunder the bars of
iron; and I will give thee the treasures of darkness, and hidden
riches of secret places, that thou mayest know that I am YHVH,
who call thee by thy name, even the God of Israel. For the sake of
Jacob My servant and Israel Mine elect, I have called thee by thy
name.

Cyrus is allocated a task within a divine plan. That he may
perform his task, God subdues the nations before him and
defeats his enemies. Thus, Cyrus beholds the revelation of
divine might and learns to know that He is YHVH. But since
what happens is done for the sake of Israel and not for the
sake of Cyrus, it is also made known to him that He who is
YHVH for all is "the God of Israel."

There are two significant passages in Ezekiel in which the
prophet, in relationship to Israel, changes the two terms, I am
YHVH and I am YHVH their God, in the same context because of the change in the point of emphasis. Toward the end
of chapter 34 in Ezekiel we read a moving prophecy of the
future redemption of Israel:

And the tree of the field shall yield its fruit, and the earth shall
yield her produce, and they shall be safe in their land; and they
shall know that I am YHVH, when I have broken the bars of their

17

yoke, and have delivered them out of the hand of those that made bondmen of them. . . . but they shall dwell safely, and none shall make them afraid. And I will raise up unto them a plantation for renown, and they shall be no more consumed with hunger in the land, neither bear the shame of the nations any more. And *they shall know that I am YHVH their God*[4] am with them, and that they, the house of Israel, are My people [italics added].

In the first part of this quotation occurs the phrase, I am YHVH; in the second part, the words are added, their God. However, there is an obvious change in emphasis. In the context in which the first formula occurs, the stress is laid on the revelation of divine might. This is underlined by the conjunction, *when*. They shall know that He is YHVH, *when* God breaks the bars of their yoke. But when God reveals to them his nearness, that he is the one who is with them, then they will learn that He is YHVH their God.[5]

Most revealing in this respect is a passage in chapter 20 of Ezekiel. God reminds the children of Israel of the commandments he gave them in the wilderness, when he enjoined them saying:

I am YHVH your God; walk in My statutes, and keep Mine ordinances, and do them; and hallow My sabbaths, and they shall be a sign between Me and you, that *ye may know that I am YHVH your God* [italics added]. (vss. 19–20)

This is what God told them in the wilderness. But they did not listen. They rebelled against God. They did not keep the commandments and desecrated the sabbaths of God. Speaking in the name of God, the prophet continues:

Wherefore I gave them also statutes that were not good, and ordinances whereby they should not live; and I polluted them in their own gifts, in that they set apart all that openeth the womb, that I might destroy them, to the end *that they may know that I am YHVH* [italics added]. (vss. 25–26)

In itself, this is a somewhat difficult passage to understand and one may do well to consult the various commentaries.

However, the distinction between the previous quotation and this one offers no difficulty. The very statutes and commandments, the law concerning the sabbath and the holy days are themselves "the sign" between God and Israel; they themselves are a visible manifestation of providential care for Israel. The children of Israel were given this "sign" that they may live and know that YHVH is their God. However, those other ordinances, which are not good, and are given to them as a punishment for their sins so that they should not live and might be destroyed, bring it about that they might know that He is YHVH. The change in the usage of the two phrases in such close proximity is determined by the change in the theme and emphasis.

There is hardly an exception to the rule that the manifestation of divine transcendence, of God's supernatural mastery over men and nature, makes known to the one who experiences it that He is YHVH; whereas the experience of divine immanence, of God's providence and nearness, is responsible for the knowledge that He is YHVH, one's God. Occasionally, a passage may contradict the rule. A careful analysis, however, shows that what, at first sight, appears to be an exception rather than being a contradiction confirms the principle that we have discovered. A point in case is a passage in the same chapter of Ezekiel from which we have taken the above two quotations. The concluding verses in chapter 20 read:

And ye shall know that I am YHVH, when I shall bring you into the land of Israel, into the country which I lifted up My hand to give unto your fathers. And there shall ye remember your ways, and all your doings, wherein ye have polluted yourselves; and ye shall loathe yourselves in your own sight for all your evils that ye have committed. And ye shall know that I am YHVH, when I have wrought with you for My name's sake, not according to your evil ways, nor according to your corrupt doings, O ye house of Israel saith the Lord YHVH.

Leading the children of Israel back into the land that God promised to their fathers is, of course, an act of providence.

19

One might, therefore, have expected the phrase, and ye shall know that I am YHVH your God. One must, however, note that according to the context the return to the promised land does not occur in a condition of reconciliation between God and the people. The relation between Israel and God is still severed because of their "evil ways" and "corrupt doings." Yet return they will to the land even without returning to God, because God will act for His name's sake. God's own "name" in the world has become involved in the destiny of Israel. He will lead them back to their own land not because of his concern for them at that moment, but because of his concern for his own "name" in the sight of the nations. While the divine deed is providential in its effect, it is not undertaken with providential motivation. Most interesting is the point made in the text that the children of Israel will understand this. They will remember their wrongdoings. They will know that what is being done by God is not done for their sake, which they would not deserve, but for the sake of God's name. Their return to the land of their fathers is, therefore, not a manifestation of divine concern with their own destiny, thus they will know that He is YHVH, but not that he is "their God."

The only other passage of this kind is found at the end of chapter 16 in Ezekiel. In conclusion of a chastising address to the people of Israel, in which their utter corruption was held up before them, we read:

For thus saith the Lord YHVH: I will even deal with thee as thou hast done, who hast despised the oath in breaking the covenant. Nevertheless I will remember My covenant with thee in the days of thy youth, and I will establish unto thee an everlasting covenant. Then shalt thou remember thy ways, and be ashamed, when thou shalt receive thy sisters, thine elder sisters and thy younger; and I will give them unto thee for daughters, but not because of *thy* covenant. And I will establish *My* covenant with thee, and thou shalt know that I am YHVH; that thou mayest remember, and be confounded, and never open thy mouth any more because of thy shame; when I have forgiven thee all that thou hast done, saith the Lord YHVH [italics added].

Here too, the divine deed is providential in its effect. The supremacy of Jerusalem over her sisters, Sodom and Samaria, will be restored. God will establish with Israel an eternal covenant. At the same time Israel is reminded that it has broken the covenant. What is done for them is not because of *their* covenant, which they have not kept, but because of God's covenant with them. God acts for them not because of them, but because of his covenant with them. The motivation of the divine action is the same as in the passage in chapter 20. God acts in their behalf for his name's sake. Even God's forgiving their sins has the nature of a psychological punishment, for it will put them to shame so that they will not open their mouth because of their dishonor. The very act of God's goodness toward them will humiliate them, causing them to recall their evil ways. In a situation of this kind God is not really near. He does what he does because of what he is and not because of what he is for man. What is revealed to Israel on this occasion is that He is YHVH, not that He is YHVH their God.

Most significant is the use of the phrase "I am YHVH" in the well-known chapter 37 of Ezekiel. It occurs in the prophet's vision of the valley of the bones. Ezekiel is called upon to prophesy in the name of God concerning the dry bones. In this prophecy the phrase "and ye shall know that I am YHVH" occurs three times. Let us see how it is being used. These are the relevant words of the prophecy.

Thus saith the Lord YHVH unto these bones: Behold I will cause breath to enter into you, and ye shall live. And I will lay sinews upon you, and will bring up flesh upon you, and cover you with skin, and put breath in you, and ye shall live; and ye *shall know that I am YHVH.*

Thus saith the Lord Y: Behold, I will open your graves, and cause you to come up out of your graves, O My people; and I will bring you into the land of Israel. *And ye shall know that I am Y,* when

I have opened your graves, and caused you to come up out of your graves, O my people. And I will put My spirit in you, and ye shall live, and I will place you in your own land: *And ye shall know that I am Y; I have spoken, and performed it* [italics added]. (vss. 5–6; 12–14)

Surely, in this case, the tender reference to *ammi*, My people, which is repeated twice, suggests a relationship of intimacy between God and Israel. To God's "My people" would appropriately correspond the knowledge that he is their God. Yet the words are not found here. This, however, is a unique vision. The miracle is not that Israel will be brought back to their land but that the dry bones will come to life again. It is not God's providential concern that is revealed in the miracle of resurrection—dry bones are in no need of providence—but his sovereignty over life and death. The vision of resurrection makes manifest how God transcends all creation and how, as the creator of all life, he may transform even death into life. The emphasis here is not in his relation to the living but on his majestic power even over death. Therefore, the resurrected will know that He is Y.[6]

THAT HE IS Y ELOHIM

There remains, however, one question which requires further elucidation. If the manifestation of God's sovereignty over nature and history conveys the knowledge that He is Y, what is the reason for the retention of the name that indicates divine transcendence when he reveals himself to men through his acts of providence and caring attention? By such acts he reveals himself as "our God" or "their God." Why then is it necessary to state in such cases: that they may know that I am Y their God? Why would it not suffice to say: that they may know that I am their God? Two contradictory aspects of divine self-revelation seem to be combined in the phrase, that He is Y our, or your, *Elohim*. We shall gain an insight into the significance of this strange combination of opposites from the third biblical formulation that deals with man's acquisition of knowledge of God, the knowledge *ki Y hu ha–Elohim,* that Y He is the *Elohim.*[7]

In our opinion it is chapter 18 in I Kings that throws most light on the meaning of this phrase. We are referring of course to the confrontation between Elijah, the people, and the prophets of Baal. Turning to the people, Elijah addresses to them the well-known words: "How long halt ye between two opinions? If Y be the *Elohim,* follow Him; but if Baal, follow him" (vs. 21). We depart here from the accepted translation that renders, if Y be God. As we shall see presently, the term *Elohim* in this context has a specific connotation which is completely obscured by the English translation. If, at least, the translators would have retained the definite article in front of *Elohim* and read, if Y be the God! this might have been awkward, but not as misleading as the current translation. It might have alerted the reader that the word God was used in a specific sense. The incorrect translation in this place, as well as in all the other passages where the same phrase occurs, is a serious mistranslation that completely distorts the meaning of the original and is responsible for a host of misconceptions about the biblical teaching concerning God. The English, if Y be God! suggests that the people of Israel were doubting whether Y was God or not. There is nothing of it in the Hebrew text. The very style of the question proves that the people knew very well who Y was, they knew that he existed. He was, indeed, very real to them. They knew very well that he was God, as the term is understood in English parlance. What they did not know or, rather, concerning which they were "halting between two opinions," was the question whether Y was also *ha–Elohim,* the God in a specific sense. In what specific sense? The answer to this question is given in Elijah's formulation of the challenge to the people: if Y is the God, follow him! *Ha–Elohim* is the one whom one may follow. The God whom one may follow is the one who leads. He who leads is near; he leads because he is concerned. He is "our" God.

23

The performance of the prophet Elijah on this occasion should be understood in the context of Judaism's struggle for the purification of the God idea in the establishment of a strict monotheism. As is well known, many of the primitive people perceived the concept of a Supreme Deity that dwelt beyond time and space. But he was a God who was aloof, who could not be reached by man and for whom the affairs and lives of men were too insignificant to deserve his attention. The people called for a God who was accessible. Mediating deities between the Supreme God and little man were required. Such were the ideas of many of the early Jews. The long addiction to the Baal service, the toleration of the sacrifices on the *bamot,* existed side by side with their faith in Y as the Supreme God who was the ultimate source of all life, all-powerful and all-mighty, but just because of that far removed; as we would say today, transcendent. This became already clear in the story of the Golden Calf. When the idol was made, the people exclaimed: "This is thy *Elohim,* O Israel, which brought thee up out of the land of Egypt." Yet, Aaron was able to say to them: "Tomorrow shall be a feast to Y."[8] The acceptance of an *Elohim* does not involve the rejection of Y. On the contrary, the feast in honor of the *Elohim* is a feast to Y. The *Elohim* is the mediator, he is the deputy of Y on earth. Y is above him; but even the *Elohim* derives his power and existence from Y. The *Elohim,* however, is the one who is near, he is the one who is immediately concerned with Israel. "This is thy *Elohim,* O Israel, which brought thee up out of the land of Egypt"; this, indeed, is the function of an *Elohim;* this is not the immediate concern of the Supreme God, Y—such was their way of thinking. Moses was teaching them that there were no mediating divinities between Y and man. Y was dealing with man directly. This was exemplified for them by the figure of Moses itself. But the people came to look upon Moses as the mediator. And when Moses was delayed to come down from the mountain, they spoke to Aaron: "Up, make us an *Elohim* who shall go before us; for as for this Moses, the man that brought us up out of the land of Egypt, we know not what is become of him."[9] According to their understanding, it was not Y who brought them out of Egypt, but his representative, through whom he acted, Moses. But the new idea does not work. This Moses, the *man* who led us out of Egypt—and note the emphasis on man—has disappeared. A mere man will never do. Give us an *Elohim*, who shall go before us. As in the challenge of Elijah to the people, the *Elohim* is the one whom one follows, so already in the story of the Golden Calf, the *Elohim* is the one whom one can follow because he goes before one. He is the God who is near, but under Y, who is aloof. This is also the significance of the golden calves that were set up by Jerobeam at Beth-el and at Dan. There too, we encounter the very same words that were uttered by the people on the occasion of the first golden calf: "Behold thy *Elohim*, O Israel, which brought thee up out of the land of Egypt."[10] It could be done so easily, because the calves did not mean to replace Y, but only to mediate between him and Israel.

We return now to a careful examination of the story of Elijah's confrontation with the prophets of Baal on the Carmel. The people were wavering. They were not sure whether Y was the *Elohim*, the one who leads and whom one may follow or was there, perhaps, a need for an *Elohim* to stand between Y and man, to be concerned about man directly. It is important to pay attention to the carefully chosen words of Elijah. Speaking to the priests of Baal, he says: "And call ye on the name of your *Elohim*." However, he does not continue saying: and I will call on the name of my *Elohim*, but: "and I will call on the name of Y." He could not say, my *Elohim*; that was exactly the point under discussion. Was Y also *Elohim*, the one who is near and accessible? Thus he completes his statement to the Baal's priests: "And the God that answereth by fire, let him be the *Elohim*."[11] The answer will be the proof. It is the characteristic of a God who is near and concerned about man that he answers man's plea. If Y answers, then he is not only the Supreme God, but also the near one; he is then not only the Creator but also the Sustainer;

then Y is, notwithstanding his transcendence, also the *Elohim*, who walks before man and whom man may follow.

Let us now turn our attention to the prayer of Elijah. When the sacrifice had been offered, Elijah came near and spoke:

O Y, *Elohim* of Abraham, of Isaac, and of Israel, let it be known this day that thou art *Elohim* in Israel, and that I am Thy servant, and that I have done all these things at Thy word. Answer me, O Y, answer me,[12] that this people may know that thou, Y, art the *Elohim*, for thou didst turn their heart backward.

The prayer is addressed to Y who is also *Elohim*. He is the same who, even though he is Y, was the *Elohim* of Abraham, Isaac, and Jacob; he guided them, he exercised his providence over them. The God who is far, he is also near; he transcends all, yet he is near all. But the people of Israel do not know it. They separate between Y and *Elohim*. Let it be known that thou art *Elohim* in Israel, that there is no separation of functions within God. Noteworthy also is the phrase: that I am Thy servant, and that I have done all these things at Thy word. If Y is not also *Elohim*, then no human being may be his servant, his messenger to man; then no one may do anything at his word. Y, if he is not also *Elohim*, has no word for man. That he has a servant, a prophet, a word to communicate, proves that Y is *Elohim*. Finally, there is the plea for an answer that this people may know that thou Y are the *Elohim*. *Elohim* is the Answerer; and if Y answers, then he is *Elohim*. When the answer came and all the people saw it, they fell on their faces and exclaimed: "Y, He is the *Elohim*; Y, He is the *Elohim*."[13]

The same phrase occurs also in Deuteronomy as well as in another place in I Kings, where it is given added emphasis. In chapter 4 of Deuteronomy the children of Israel are reminded of "the great thing" that God did for them, of the voice of God that they heard speaking to them, the miracles and the signs that God performed for their sake. The significance of it all is summed up in the words: "Unto thee it was shown, that thou mightest know that Y, He is the *Elohim*; there is none else beside Him." The theme is elaborated further in the words: "Out of heaven He made thee hear His voice, that He might instruct thee . . . and because He loved thy fathers, and chose their seed after them, and brought thee out with His presence, with His great power, out of Egypt, to drive out nations before thee greater and mightier than thou." Once again the significance of that experience is grasped in the words: "Know this day, and lay it to thy heart, that Y, He is the *Elohim* in heaven above and upon the earth beneath; there is none else."[14]

The knowledge that reached the people was communicated to them through the revelation of divine might as well as divine providence. In keeping with our analysis this taught them that He was Y and that Y was the *Elohim*. However, in these two passages the words are added: "There is none else beside Him" and "There is none else." But how was it shown to them that there was none else beside Him? The answer seems to be that there never was a question whether there could be another Y beside Y, i.e., a God of equal status, power, and dignity. The question was: was there an *Elohim*, a mediating deity, beside Him? Once, however, it was shown to the people of Israel that Y Himself was the *Elohim*,[15] it was also established that there was no one else beside Him.

We may now read with better understanding the first words of the Decalogue. The usual translation reads:

I am the Lord thy God, who brought thee out of the land of Egypt, out of the house of bondage. Thou shalt have no other gods before me.[16]

This is not the Bible. The Lord thy God is meaningless repetition. The words "before me" are not only superfluous in this translation but seem to be empty of all significance. Our rendering is:

I am Y your *Elohim*, who brought thee out of the land of Egypt, out of the house of bondage. Thou shalt have no other *Elohim* before me [more literally: added to my presence].

We may recall that when the children of Israel made the Golden Calf, they said: This is thy *Elohim*, Israel, who brought thee up out of the land of Egypt, and they proceeded to celebrate a feast unto Y. Y was the Supreme God, but his was not the menial task of leading people out of the house of bondage. That task he delegated to an *Elohim*. To counter such ideas the Decalogue commences with the majestic statement: I the omnipotent and transcendent Y am also yours, your *Elohim*, I am the very same that has brought thee out of Egypt. To bring people out of the house of bondage is also one of my functions. For Y He is *Elohim*. Therefore, thou shalt have no other *Elohim* "before me," in addition to my presence, an *Elohim* to mediate between me and my creation, between me and man. The phrase, no other *Elohim* before me, conforms to the phrase, which we have discussed earlier, there is none else beside me.

Hosea put it this way:

> Yet I am Y your *Elohim*
> From the land of Egypt;
> And thou knowest no *Elohim* but Me,
> And beside Me there is no saviour. (13:4)

The passage brings to clear expression the identity between *Elohim* and the savior. However, there is no savior beside Y, for Y is *Elohim*. Israel should have known that since the days of its liberation from Egypt.[17]

Even the message of Jephtah to the king of Ammon is consistent with this terminology.[18] The reference in that message to "the Lord, the God of Israel," who had "dispossessed the Amorites from before His people Israel," as the English translation has it, may easily be misunderstood as being the counterpart to Chemosh, the god of Ammon. As Chemosh was Ammon's tribal deity, so was—in Jephtah's understanding—Y Israel's. However, if this were so, Jephtah's plea, also addressed to the king of Ammon, that "Y, the Judge, be judge this day between the children of Israel and the children of

Ammon" would be meaningless. The passage suggests that the concept, Y, the Judge, was intelligible to the Ammonite to whom it was addressed. One could call on him to judge impartially between the children of Israel and the children of Ammon. It is significant that, when Jephtah speaks of what God did for Israel, he calls him, Y the *Elohim* of Israel; but when he calls upon him to judge between Israel and Ammon, he refers to "Y, the Judge." It was meaningful to speak to the Ammonites about Y, the Judge, because they, too, knew of a Supreme God who ruled over all men. Chemosh for them was the *Elohim* that was mediating between the Supreme God, the *El Elyon*, and the Ammonites. For Jephtah, however, Y and the *Elohim* of Israel were identical. The concept that Y, He is *Elohim*, does not tolerate any tribal deity beside Y, as it rejects categorically the idea of any mediating divinity between God and man.

We are now able to interpret more meaningfully the basic affirmation of the faith of Judaism. In English translation it reads: "Hear, O Israel, the Lord our God, the Lord is one."[19] Only the Lord knows what this means, if it has meaning at all. Of course, the statement that God is one does make good sense. But why is it not stated so? Why not simply: Hear, O Israel, our God is one. Or, if one insists on the tautology, the Lord our God, why not: Hear, O Israel, the Lord our God is one. We render it: "Hear, O Israel, Y is our *Elohim;* Y is one." This is a vital statement about God in which every word counts. Hear, O Israel, Y is identical with "our" *Elohim*. The transcendent Creator is also the immanent Preserver. God who in his absoluteness is far removed is also near; the King and Ruler is also the Father and Sustainer. But notwithstanding that Y is also *Elohim*, Y is yet One.

The phrase, which we have found in Deuteronomy and in I Kings, to know that Y He is *Elohim*, occurs also in the dedicatory prayer of King Solomon, where it deserves special attention. Whereas in the other places the knowledge that Y He is *Elohim* is limited to the people of Israel, Solomon prays that it may be granted to all the peoples. The words are found at the conclusion of the king's prayer:

And let these my words, wherewith I have made supplication before Y, be nigh unto Y our *Elohim* day and night, that He maintain the cause of His servant, and the cause of His people Israel, as every day shall require; that all the peoples of the earth may know that Y, He is the *Elohim;* there is none else.[20]

Naturally, the fact that Y maintains the cause of his people Israel does not reveal that he is *Elohim* for the nations. These concluding words refer to the entire contents of the supplication of Solomon. But the king prayed also for the nations, pleading:

Moreover concerning the stranger that is not of Thy people Israel, when he shall come out of a far country for Thy name's sake . . . when he shall come and pray toward this house; hear Thou in heaven Thy dwelling-place, and do according to all that the stranger calleth to Thee for; that all the peoples of the earth may know Thy name, to fear Thee, as doth Thy people Israel.[21]

By seeing the prayer of the stranger, "not of Thy people Israel," answered, all the peoples of the earth will know that Y He is also *Elohim* and there is none else beside Him. The idea is the same as in the story of Elijah. By "answering" Y reveals that he is the *Elohim*. Certainly, if all the peoples of the earth are to fear God as his people Israel, then they too must become his people. This, however, is only possible if, to them too, Y is revealed as being one and the same as the *Elohim*.

It is in chapter 45 of Isaiah that we find the theme stated in its most comprehensive universal terms. We have already made reference to the words in the opening phase of the chapter: "that thou mayest know that I am Y, who call thee by thy name, even the *Elohim* of Israel." The handing over of the nations into the hand of Cyrus, revealing God's might, make known to Cyrus that He is Y. But God uses Cyrus as an instrument in order to save Israel. Therefore, it is Israel's *Elohim* who calls Cyrus. He calls him "for the sake of Jacob My servant, and Israel Mine elect." It is, however, not left at that. God is not to remain unknown as *Elohim* to the rest of the world. The words further addressed to Cyrus are:

I have called thee by thy name,
I have surnamed thee, though thou hast not known Me.
I am Y, and there is none else,
Beside Me there is no *Elohim;*
I have girded thee, though thou hast not known Me;
That they may know from the rising of the sun, and
 from the west,
That there is none beside Me;
I am Y, and there is none else;
I form the light, and create darkness;
I make peace, and create evil;
I am Y that doeth all these things.

It is the theme of Y being *Elohim* elaborated in a universal context. Originally, it is the one who is Y for Cyrus, as he is for all creation, and Israel's *Elohim* who calls Cyrus. The ultimate purpose of it, however, is that it be known to all that he is Y, beside whom no mediating *Elohim* may be placed. There is only Y and nothing else. For Y is *Elohim* and Y is one. He alone is the source of light and darkness, of peace and even of evil. He alone is the One who does all these things.

The idea is propounded further in verse 18 of the same chapter:

For thus saith Y:
The Creator of the heavens, He is the *Elohim;*
He who formed the earth and made it, He established it,
He created it not a waste, He formed it to be inhabited:
I am Y, and there is none else.[22]

The Creator of the heavens is, of course, Y. The first line of the statement affirms that Y He is the *Elohim.* But the rhythmic balance of the entire verse teaches us a great deal more. It explains the significance of the affirmation that Y is the *Elohim*. "He who formed the earth and made it" corresponds to "the Creator of the heavens." The former and maker of the earth is, of course, the same as the Creator of the heavens. If so, then "He is the *Elohim*" holds the balance to, "He established it." In other words, if we did not know that Y was also *Elohim*, we should only know that he created heaven and earth, but not that he also "established" it. He established it because Y He is the *Elohim*. But what is the significance of the activity of establishing in this context? Again we may elicit the meaning from the parallelism in the verse. The concepts the Creator and the Former of the first and second lines are taken up again in the third line. He created it, but not a waste. "Not a waste" parallels: He is the *Elohim*. He formed it that it be inhabited. "To be inhabited" is then the meaning of "He established it." What is the meaning of all this? If one separates *Elohim* from Y, the Creator becomes the omnipotent supreme power in the universe, but utterly unconcerned about his creation. He might have created out of a super-abundance of vitality, remaining completely self-centered and apart from the consequences of his action. It would still be creation, but without any purpose as regards his creatures—a purposeless universe of waste, an earth not for the sake of habitation. This, however, is not the case. Y is the *Elohim*. He is purposefully related to his creation and to his creatures. In the very act of creation Y acted as Providence, for he created not for waste and formed an earth to be inhabited. The verse is appropriately concluded: "I am Y, there is none else." There is, indeed, none else, for Y He is the *Elohim*.

The theme reaches its climactic statement in the verses with which the chapter ends:

> Assemble yourselves and come and draw near together,
> Ye that are escaped of the nations;
> They have no knowledge that carry the wood of their
> graven image,
> And pray unto an *El* [singular for *Elohim*] that cannot
> save.

Declare ye, and bring them near.
Yea, let them take counsel together:
Who hath announced this from ancient time,
And declared it of old?
Am I not Y!
And there is no *Elohim* else beside Me;
A just *El* and savior;
There is none beside Me.
Look unto Me, and be ye saved,
All the ends of the earth;
For I am *El*, and there is none else
By Myself have I sworn,

. . . .

That unto Me every knee shall bow,
Every tongue shall swear,
Only in Y, shall one say of Me, is victory and strength;
Even to Him shall they come and will be ashamed,
All they that were incensed against Him.
In Y shall all the seed of Israel
Be justified, and shall glory.

The peoples, with their idols, are in search of *Elohim* to save them. Y, they imagine, is too mighty and aloof to be concerned with them. They want little gods to serve their little needs and interests. But their *El* cannot save, for Y alone is the *Elohim* and there is none else beside him. Y is the only *El* and Savior. The time will come when all men will realize it and will seek their strength and salvation in Y alone.[23]

We may now conclude this part of our discussion by taking up once again the question at the opening of this section. We have found in the previous section that the manifestation of divine omnipotence brings the knowledge that He is Y; whereas the revelation of divine providence teaches that He is Y our God. We would do well now to replace the words "our God" or "their God" with the terms "our *Elohim*" or "their *Elohim*," since *Elohim*—in this context—has the specific connotation that we have defined. We may very well find that

33

God manifests himself as the omnipotent sovereign and Judge. When this happens, people who witness such manifestation know that he is Y. It, however, never happens that he reveals himself in such a manner that people would know that he is *Elohim*. For Y is *Elohim*. One may know that he is Y or that he is Y our *Elohim*, but never that he is only *Elohim*. For Y is our *Elohim* and Y is One.[24]

THE DECLARATORY PHRASES

It is not our intention to define the rules for the use of the terms Y and *Elohim* in the whole of the Bible. Ours has been a limited task—to determine the meaning of the two names for God when they occur in contexts that speak of revelation of knowledge about God. It is quite conceivable that, since Y and *Elohim* are one, the terms may be used interchangeably in phrases like, thus saith Y, or, and *Elohim* said. However, our studies in some of the fundamental concepts of the Bible, which have shown us an impressive consistency of usage across the entire face of the Bible, lead us to believe that a comprehensive investigation would show that Y and *Elohim* are not interchangeable at random, but are used consistently in conformity with certain rules and principles. The work has yet to be done. In pursuance of our more limited objective we shall examine the two declaratory phrases when God himself refers to himself as, I am Y, and as, I am Y, your (or their) *Elohim*. If certain specific manifestations of divine activity reveal that He is Y, while others, that He is Y, who is *Elohim*, it is not unreasonable to expect the same differentiation of meaning when God refers to himself in the declaratory manner by one or the other expression. We have already found this to be the case in the opening words of the Decalogue as well as in the affirmation of faith beginning with the words, "Hear, O Israel." We shall now investigate the subject more comprehensively.

On a few occasions, "I am Y" is used as an introduction to a revelation as if the speaker were identifying himself.[25] This kind of introduction is justified, no matter what the contents of the revelation that follows may be. When such an identification is necessary, the expression is appropriate even when what is being revealed is an action which shows God in his capacity as *Elohim*. The phrase does not refer to the contents of the revelation; it eliminates in advance all possible misconception concerning the identity of the speaker. Independently of the contents of the revelation, it is Y who addresses Abraham or Moses. We have to deal with those passages in which the declaratory statements of our discussion are the concluding words of a biblical revelation, quite obviously referring to the contents preceding them. In all such cases the declaration reaffirms the contents of the revelation, as if to say: this is so because I am Y or because I am Y your *Elohim*. Looking at these passages, we find the rule, which we have analyzed, quite convincingly buttressed further in the majority of the cases.

When God announces the tenth plague, the death of the first-born, with which he will smite the land of Egypt, he concludes by saying: "and against all the gods of Egypt I will execute judgment: I am Y."[26] While the passage seems to be the only one of its kind in the Books of Moses, there is a whole group of them in the prophecies of Ezekiel. In Ezekiel, they usually conclude with the phrase: I am Y; I have spoken it and will do it. They may be quoted at random; they all show the same characteristics. In connection with the punishment that is to befall Jerusalem so that the people of Israel may *know* that He is Y, it is also said:

So it shall be a reproach and a taunt, an instruction and an astonishment unto the nations that are round about thee, when I shall execute judgments in thee in anger and in fury, and in furious rebukes; I am Y, I have spoken it.

The chapter concludes on the same terrible note and with the same affirmation:

And I will increase the famine upon you, and will break your staff of bread: and will send upon you famine and evil beasts, and they shall bereave thee; and pestilence and blood shall pass through thee; and I will bring the sword upon thee. I am Y; I have spoken it.

These, and all the other passages of the same nature,[27] confirm what we have found as regards the knowledge of God. "I am Y" indicates the manifestation of divine judgment and sovereignty over men and nature.

What, however, do the passages tell us that conclude with the declaration, I am your *Elohim,* or with some other appropriate phrase? Do they too confirm our expectations? One of the most striking confirmations of our thesis, we meet in chapter 26 of Leviticus. It is all the more convincing since it is preceded by one of the most awe-inspiring predictions of divine judgment in the entire Bible, with which the children of Israel were threatened in advance, "if they will not hearken to Him and not do all these commandments." It is the chapter traditionally known among Jews as the *Tokhaha.* After the most terrifying pictures having been drawn of the circumstances that will befall them should they betray their covenant with God, the tone of the divine words addressed to them is changed and the Bible concludes:

And yet for all that, when they are in the land of their enemies, I will not reject them, neither will I abhor them, to destroy them utterly, and to break My covenant with them; for I am Y their *Elohim.*[28]

The covenant is the reality of the actual relation between God and Israel. It represents the truth that Y, the Supreme Ruler of all the worlds, dwells in the midst of Israel, for Y is their *Elohim.* This bond between Y and Israel is never to be severed. In the midst of his very anger, when he acts towards Israel as the awe-inspiring Supreme Lord, he remembers the covenant. He is Y their *Elohim.*

According to the law of the jubilee, all Jewish slaves went free in the fiftieth year. The reason given in the Bible is:

For unto Me the children of Israel are servants; they are My servants whom I brought forth out of the land of Egypt: I am Y your *Elohim.*[29]

36

Here, too, the closeness and intimacy of the relationship between God and Israel is emphasized. The meaning of this relationship determines the status of the Jew in the world. The Jew is God's servant and God's servant is not the servant of any man. This is so, because He is Y, the *Elohim* of Israel.

When we turn to the prophets we find the same consistency in the use of the phrase: I am Y your (or their) *Elohim*. When God speaks through the mouth of Isaiah to Israel, "His servant," to Jacob, whom he "has chosen," to "the seed of Abraham His friend," comfortingly and encouragingly, he says to Israel:

> Thou art My servant,
> I have chosen thee and not cast thee away;
> Fear thou not, for I am with thee,
> Be not dismayed, for I am thy *Elohim;*
> I strengthen thee, yea, I help thee;
> Yea, I uphold thee with My victorious right hand.
>
> .   .   .   .
>
> They that warred against thee
> Shall be as nothing, and as a thing of nought.
> For I am Y thy *Elohim,*
> I hold thy right hand,
> Who say unto thee: "Fear not,
> I help thee."

As we read on in the same chapter, we come across the moving words of hope and promise:

> The poor and the needy seek water and there is
>   none,
> And their tongue faileth for thirst,
> I am Y, I will answer them,
> Elohim of Israel, I will not forsake them.[30]

The translation of *Elohim* as God, which occurs three times in this context, obscures completely the emphasis in the Hebrew original. The point is not that God is God, which of course is so and means little. Nor does Isaiah make the statement that God is Israel's God and not God over the nations and the universe. Such an interpretation could only be based on ignorance and foolishness. What is said here quite clearly is that Y, the Universal Creator, is "with thee;" that he acts as *Elohim,* providentially and caringly, toward the weak and the poor; that Y is the one who answers, for, notwithstanding his being Y, he is *Elohim* of Israel.

When Zechariah prophesies concerning the day when God remembers "His flock the house of Judah," he speaks for God saying:

> And I will strengthen the house of Judah,
> And I will save the house of Joseph,
> And I will bring them back, for I have compassion
> upon them,
> And they shall be as though I had not cast them off;
> For I am Y their *Elohim,* and I will hear them.[31]

When God shows his anger toward Israel, he appears as the removed and far away Lord of the Universe, but when he acts compassionately, it is because the Lord of the Universe is their *Elohim,* their compassionate shepherd and father.

There is a small group of three to four verses in the Bible which, though they deal with providential care for Israel, yet conclude with the declaration: I am Y, and not with, I am Y their *Elohim.* One we find in chapter 26 of Leviticus, from which we have quoted the passage that God will not break his covenant with Israel, because He is Y their *Elohim.* The statement there concludes with the words:

But I will for their sakes remember the covenant of their ancestors, whom I brought forth out of the land of Egypt in the sight of the nations, that I might be *Elohim* unto them:[32] I am Y.[33]

Other, even more important, statements of this kind we find in chapter 6 of Exodus. They occur in one of the earliest messages of God to the children of Israel, communicated to them by the mouth of Moses. They are, one might say, the very foundations on which God's eternal people exist and survive. In them God identifies himself and explains his relationship to the children of Israel. This is the message to Israel:

I am Y, and I will bring you out from under the burdens of the Egyptians, and I will deliver you from their bondage, and I will redeem you with an outstretched arm and with great judgments; and I will take you to Me for a people, and I will be to you *Elohim*; and ye shall know that I am Y your *Elohim,* who brought you out from under the burdens of the Egyptians. And I will bring you in unto the land, concerning which I lifted up My hand to give it to Abraham, to Isaac, and to Jacob; and I will give it to you for a heritage: I am Y.[34]

This second passage is particularly revealing. God introduces himself as Y. And that is sufficient. The people know very well what is meant when it is said to them: I am Y. What they do not know is that Y stands in a specific relation to them. Therefore, it is necessary to enlighten them concerning this relationship. Y is going to save them from the house of bondage and take them for a people unto himself. Y is *Elohim*. When all this happens they will know that this is so; they will learn that Y is their *Elohim*. Nevertheless, the passage concludes, as the previous one which we have quoted, with the declaration: I am Y, and not, I am Y their *Elohim*. However, both passages have something in common, in which they differ from the other passages of a providential content. In all the other passages the providential deed or care is the proof that Y is *Elohim*. The proof has to be deduced from the divine deed. In the two passages under discussion, however, beyond God's providential action it is *explicitly* promised that God will be an *Elohim* unto them. For reasons of style and logic of contents such a promise cannot be made in the name of Y who is their *Elohim*. The very forcefulness of the declaration lies in the fact that it is Y who promises to act toward Israel as *Elohim*. A related passage we may recognize in chapter 60 of Isaiah. The prophet treats the same theme in his own inimitable style. It is found at the close of the exalted prophecy that opens with the words:

"Arise, shine, for thy light is come, and the glory of Y is risen upon thee." It too is a promise, in the entire Bible the most magnificent promise made to Israel:

> Thy sun shall no more go down,
> Neither shall thy moon withdraw itself;
> For Y shall be thine everlasting light,
> And the days of thy mourning shall be ended.
> Thy people also shall be all righteous,
> They shall inherit the land for ever;
> The branch of My planting, the work of My hands,
> Wherein I glory.
> The smallest shall become a thousand,
> And the least a mighty nation;
> I am Y; I will hasten it in its time.[35]

This is, of course, the ultimate form of divine providence. But the promise is not only expressed in what God will do for Israel, but also in what he will be unto Israel. He will be their everlasting light. The imagery illustrates the closest intimacy between God and Israel. It is the poetic formulation of the thought, and I will be *Elohim* unto them, at its deepest. As in the previous two texts, it is the very essence of the emphasis that it is Y who makes such a promise: "I am Y; I will hasten it in its time."[36]

Thus far, our expectation that the declaratory phrases, "I am Y" and "I am Y your *Elohim*" will show the same distinction in usage as that between the revelational ones concerning our knowledge of God, has been confirmed. We encounter, however, some difficulties in certain chapters of Leviticus, where concluding declaratory phrases are used to impress upon the people the importance of some divine injunction or law. Some of the laws conclude with the affirmation, I am Y; others again, I am Y your *Elohim*. One may easily find the examples, especially in chapters 18 and 19. On the basis of internal textual evidence, it is practically impossible to discover a reason why the emphasis of either of the declaratory statements is attached only to some of the laws and is omitted from the majority of them. But are we able to discern some ordering principle or principles in those cases when either of the two formulas are used? We may readily agree that a divine commandment could well carry the concluding emphasis: I am Y. It would indicate the source of authority from which the law derives its validity. The reference to Y would be appropriate as an indication of God's function as the Supreme Lawgiver and Judge. But how come that in a number of cases the command for the observance of a law is reinforced by the reference to God as "Y your *Elohim*"?

It would seem that the general injunction to keep God's commandments is enjoined with the phrase: I am Y. "And ye shall observe all My statutes, and all Mine ordinances, and do them: I am Y" seems to be the formula in such cases.[37] This, however, seems to be the case only when no reason is given for the commandments, as if the Bible wished to say: do them because God commanded them. The usage changes whenever the reason for the commandments is explicitly elaborated. In chapter 18 of Leviticus, for instance, we read:

I am Y your Elohim. After the doings of the land of Egypt, wherein ye dwelt, shall ye not do; and after the doings of the land of Canaan, whither I bring you, shall ye not do; neither shall ye walk in their statutes. Mine ordinances shall ye do, and My statutes shall ye keep, to walk therein: I am Y your *Elohim*.[38]

In these words moral judgment is passed over "the doings" of Egypt and Canaan. The statutes of God are not the laws of an autocrat who derives pleasure from ordering his subjects around. The laws of God are intended to counteract the evil practices of the Egyptians and the Canaanites and to show the children of Israel another way. The Lawgiver acts out of concern for his people. The giving of the law itself is a manifestation of divine providence. For this reason the authority behind the law is not just I am Y, but, I am Y your *Elohim*. This is borne out by other passages where the thought comes to even clearer expression. In the very same chapter we read:

Defile not ye yourselves in any of these things; for in all these the nations are defiled, which I cast out from before you. And the land was defiled, therefore I did visit the iniquity thereof upon it, and the land vomited out her inhabitants. Ye therefore shall keep My statutes and Mine ordinances, and shall not do any of these abominations . . . that the land vomit not you out also, when ye defile it, as it vomited out the nation before you. For whosoever shall do any of these abominations, even the souls that do them shall be cut off from among their people. Therefore shall ye keep My charge, that ye do not any of these abominable customs, which were done before you, and ye defile not yourselves therein: I am Y your *Elohim*.[39]

God is deeply concerned about the moral quality of his people. The land that he promised them cannot carry a spiritually defiled nation. God's laws are given to them that they may endure. Because he is *Elohim* does Y insist that his laws be kept. The idea is fully clinched in chapter 20 in the words:

Ye shall therefore keep all My statutes, and all My ordinances, and do them, that the land, whither I bring you to dwell therein, vomit you not out. And ye shall not walk in the customs of the nations which I am casting out before you; for they did all these things, and therefore I abhorred them. But I have said unto you: Ye shall inherit their land, and I will give unto you to possess it, a land flowing with milk and honey. I am Y your *Elohim*, who have set you apart from the peoples.[40]

God has shown that he was their *Elohim* by setting them apart from the nations and entering into a covenant with them. This, however, was not vacuous favoritism. He desired a people that was different from those whom he had to reject because of their abominations. Israel is set apart by the statutes and the ordinances of God that alone can preserve it in moral and spiritual health. Out of providential concern Y set them apart; out of the same concern he gave them his laws, for Y is their *Elohim*.

In connection with the law concerning the fringes, which the children of Israel were commanded to make in the corners of their garments, they were also enjoined to do all God's commandments, of which the fringes would remind them as they contemplated them. There, too, the doing of all the commandments is reinforced by the concluding observation: I am Y your *Elohim*.[41] The passage shares in common with the previous ones of the same kind the fact that, like with them, the injunction is not issued with peremptory authority. A reason is given why this law of the fringes should be observed:

And it shall be unto you for a fringe, that ye may look upon it, and remember all the commandments of Y and do them; and that ye go not about after your own heart and your own eyes, after which ye use to go astray.

As in the earlier texts which we have just discussed, the law is prescribed out of divine concern with the moral and spiritual condition of the people. Something is given them to help them to remember and that, as a result, they may not go astray as was their wont. As compared to the previous passages, this one has a distinguishing feature. The demand is made upon the children of Israel that they keep God's commandments and be holy unto "their *Elohim*." This may well lead us to an examination of such texts in which a law is given in association with the injunction for holiness. We shall place two such passages side by side:

Ye shall not make yourselves detestable with any swarming thing that swarmeth, neither shall ye make yourselves unclean with them, that ye should be defiled thereby. For I am Y your *Elohim*; sanctify yourselves therefore, and be ye holy; for I am holy. . . . For I am Y that brought you up out of the land of Egypt, to be your *Elohim*; ye shall therefore be holy, for I am holy.

Sanctify yourselves therefore, and be ye holy; for I am Y your *Elohim*. And keep my statutes, and do them: I am Y who sanctify you.[42]

The contexts in both places show clearly divine concern for the spiritual welfare of Israel. Worth noting, however, is the reason given for the command to be holy: to be holy because holy is also Y their *Elohim*. We do not find in the Bible a call to holiness because Y is holy, but because Y your *Elohim* is holy.[43] Y, the omnipotent, transcendent God, cannot be imitated. No one may be asked to be holy because Y is holy. Only because Y is *Elohim*, because notwithstanding his absoluteness, he relates himself to man and reveals himself as the providential father, is *imitatio dei* possible; only because of that may one say to a mere man: be thou holy, for God too is holy.

As we now proceed in our investigation of the individual commandments, we may not be able to discover clear and unambiguous rules, but some interesting features may yet emerge. Let us bear in mind that our question is not really why a law is occasionally underlined with the declaration, I am Y, but rather, why at times the longer formula is used, I am Y your *Elohim*. We note that when reference is made to the Exodus the emphasis is, I am Y your *Elohim*. For instance:

And if a stranger sojourn with thee in your land, ye shall not do him wrong. The stranger that sojourneth with you shall be unto you as the home born among you, and thou shalt love him as Thyself; for ye were strangers in the land of Egypt: I am Y your *Elohim*. Ye shall do no unrighteousness in judgment. . . . Just balance, just weights, a just ephah, and a just hin, shall ye have: I am Y your *Elohim*, who brought you out of the land of Egypt.[44]

The mentioning of Exodus calls for the affirmative phrase, I am Y your *Elohim*. The Exodus is the classical manifestation of divine providence over Israel. Anywhere God is mentioned in connection with it, he is called Y your *Elohim*.

We also observe that laws which are directed against idol worship are usually enjoined with the emphasis, I am Y your *Elohim*, but never with, I am Y. So we read, for instance: "Ye shall make you no idols, neither shall ye rear you up a graven image, or a pillar, neither shall ye place any figured stone in your land, to bow down unto it; for I am Y your *Elohim*."[45] This is all the more significant since the words that follow immediately are: "Ye shall keep My sabbaths, and reverence

My sanctuary: I am Y." Quite obviously, the change in phraseology intends to make a point. It would seem to us that what is emphasized is in keeping with our thesis. The danger was not that the idols may usurp the place of Y. They were meant to be the approachable connecting deities between Y and man. They were usurping the place of *Elohim*. The laws against idol worship pointedly conclude, I am Y your *Elohim*; once again the idea being: there is none else beside me.[46]

Our quote of the sabbath law, too, deserves some further attention. Exactly the same wording occurs once more in chapter 19 of Leviticus. But Ezekiel writes: "And hallow My sabbaths, and they shall be a sign between Me and you, that ye may know that I am Y your *Elohim*."[47] Is it unreasonable to assume that the prophet underlines the sabbath law with the *Elohim* phrase *because* he makes mention of the sign that the sabbath is between God and Israel? A sign *between* God and man means that Y is man's *Elohim*. The parallel to Ezekiel's formulation we find in Exodus where we read: "Verily ye shall keep My sabbaths, for it is a sign between Me and you throughout your generations, that ye may know that I am Y who sanctify you."[48] As in Ezekiel, the sabbath is designated as a sign between God and the children of Israel. It is, therefore, not enough to state: that they may know that I am Y. It is true, neither does the completion of the phrase, your *Elohim*, occur here. However, as we have already noted earlier, Israel's duty for holiness is the direct consequence of their being set apart from among the peoples. The God who sanctifies them is the one who set them apart in order to sanctify them. He is their *Elohim*. "That ye may know that I am Y who sanctify you" is the equivalent of Ezekiel's "that ye may know that I am Y your *Elohim*."[49]

There is, however, one place where the sabbath commandment is followed by the declaration, I am Y your *Elohim*, even though no reference is made to it as a sign between God and man. It is found in the opening part of chapter 19 of Leviticus. Is it an exception or does it confirm the rule? The passage is exceptional in one other important aspect. Most surprisingly, the sabbath law there is linked to the injunction to respect one's parents. It reads as follows: "Ye shall fear every man his mother, and his father, and ye shall keep My sabbaths: I am Y your *Elohim.*" The connection between respecting one's father and mother and the observance of the sabbath is puzzling. We accept the rabbinical interpretation that explains the connection in the following manner. Since God commands a man to respect his parents, one might think that one should obey one's parents even if they should demand of one some deed which involves a desecration of the sabbath. To exclude such a possibility, the Bible combined the two commandments, as if to say: even though one should respect one's father and mother, yet keep ye my sabbaths. The commandment to honor one's parents does not overrule the sabbath law; for I am Y your *Elohim* and you as well as your parents are obligated to honor me.[50] Have we gained anything from this interpretation for the clarification of our own problem? Psychologists, occasionally, see in the idea of God nothing more than the projection of the father image. One might say with much greater justification that, at times, the God image is projected upon a father or a mother and parents become idolized. There are, indeed, entire cultures in which ancestral worship takes the place of religion and God is replaced by the ancestral image. Returning now to our text, one might say that if a parental command could suspend a divine law, one would literally have idolized father and mother and established them as *"Elohim,"* standing between man and God. It is for this reason that this specific combination of two commandments is underlined by the statement: I am Y your *Elohim.* Since the term *Elohim* expresses the providential aspect of divine nature, the phrase in this context carries the association that Y himself is the Father, the ultimate Parent. Our interpretation is born out by what follows immediately upon the combined parents-sabbath commandment. "Turn ye not unto the idols, nor make yourselves molten gods: I am Y your *Elohim.*" If a parental wish would overrule any divine law, it would be tantamount to turning unto an idol.

We are left with a number of individual laws, whose importance is emphasized by the statement, I am Y your *Elohim*. We shall list them side by side.

And ye shall not wrong one another; but thou shalt fear thy *Elohim*; for I am Y your *Elohim*. (Lev. 25:17)

And thou shalt not glean thy vineyard, neither shalt thou gather the fallen fruit of thy vineyard; thou shalt leave them for the poor and for the stranger: I am Y your *Elohim*. (ibid. 19:10)

And when ye shall come into the land, and shall have planted all manner of trees for food, then ye shall count the fruit thereof as forbidden; three years it shall be as forbidden unto you; it shall not be eaten. And in the fourth year all the fruit thereof shall be holy, for giving praise unto Y. But in the fifth year may ye eat of the fruit thereof, that it may yield unto you more rich by the increase thereof: I am Y your *Elohim*. (ibid. 19:23–25)

Is there anything that these laws have in common? One may readily discern the common feature between the second and the third. In both cases one is required to give up something that one considers one's own. The gleanings and the fallen fruits in one's vineyard are one's own property. They have to be surrendered to the poor and the stranger. The yield of one's fruit trees in the first years is one's own, but one has to surrender it at God's demand. In this latter command it is said, that it may yield unto you more richly the increase thereof. Once again we shall quote the perspicacity of talmudic interpretation. Rabbi Akiba explained: the Torah speaks here to counter the promptings of man's evil inclination. A man might say: for four years I have toiled in vain. It is for this reason that it is said: that it may yield unto you more richly the increase thereof.[51] In other words: let him not worry; he will not be the loser for observing this law. Might we not then say that the affirmation, I am Y your *Elohim*, is appropriate at the conclusion of this law? A man need not worry about the loss

47

which he is to incur by keeping this commandment. Let him trust in God, for "I am Y your *Elohim,* your Sustainer and Provider." But this interpretation applies very well to our second quotation. A small farmer, who is required to give up the gleanings and the fallen fruits of his vineyard, may himself be hard put to it to make a tolerable living and not be inclined to be that generous toward the poor and the needy. It is for this reason that he is reminded: I am Y your *Elohim;* all your sustenance comes from Y who is your Provider.

What however about the first of the three laws that we have listed above? Rabbi Akiba's interpretation takes us right to it. In fact, it is derived from the very context in which that law itself occurs. "And ye shall not wrong one another" is said there in connection with the year of the Jubilee. Almost immediately after it, and in the same connection, we read:

And the land shall yield her fruit, and ye shall eat until ye have enough, and dwell therein in safety. And if ye shall say: "What shall we eat the seventh year? behold, we may not sow, nor gather in our increase; then I will command My blessing upon you in the sixth year, and it shall bring forth produce for the three years. (Lev. 25:19–20)

The same human anxiety about which this passage speaks applies to the entire institution of the Jubilee. The slaves were to go free, agricultural properties returned free to their original owners. One did not sell land, but only the crops according to the number of the years left to the Jubilee. All arrangements were only temporary; prices for land varied accordingly. The people were required to treat what they considered their property as if it were not their own. For, indeed "the land is Mine; for ye are strangers and settlers with Me." For reasons of economic anxiety and concern for their livelihood, it would be natural for some people not to be too conscientious in the observance of all the laws pertaining to the Jubilee. Here, too, the injunction: "And ye shall not wrong one another; but thou shalt fear thy *Elohim,*" is therefore properly concluded with the words: I am Y your *Elohim;* as to the future, trust in the one who is your Sustainer.

We may now sum up the results of our present discussion. The emphasis, I am Y, is appropriate when the source of authority is to be underlined. However, when reasons are given, which show that the laws themselves are a manifestation of divine care for the moral and spiritual health of Israel, the appropriate affirmation is: I am Y your *Elohim.* Whenever reference is made to the Exodus in connection with a particular law, the emphasis is: I am Y your *Elohim.* Laws that are directed against idol worship adequately emphasize that Y is Israel's *Elohim.* Finally, when a law requires surrender of possession, which may be the cause of economic anxiety, the reminder that Y is Israel's *Elohim* is a call to place one's trust in divine providence.

TO BECOME *ELOHIM* FOR SOMEONE

Another phrase which requires some elucidation and which has bearing on our immediate subject is the divine promise that God will be *l'Elohim* to some one person or to a people. The first time we encounter the expression in the Bible is in chapter 17 of Genesis where it occurs twice in the same context, in God's promise to Abraham.

And I will establish My covenant between Me and thee and thy seed after thee throughout their generations for an everlasting covenant, to become *Elohim* for thee and to thy seed after thee. And I will give unto thee, and to thy seed after thee, the land of thy sojournings, all the land of Canaan, for an everlasting possession; and I will become *Elohim* for them. (vss. 7–8)

For some mysterious reason in the Revised Version, followed here by the J.P.S. translation, the same Hebrew idiom, *lih'yot l'Elohim,* is changed in the translation. Accordingly, God promised Abraham to be a God unto him and to be the God of his children. Now, to say that God promises to be their

God is good English, but it is disregarding completely the Hebrew idiom. Regrettably, it also conveys an unbiblical meaning. For God, the Creator of all the worlds and the Absolute Sovereign over all his creation, as he is depicted in the Bible, is of course God. For him to *promise* that he *will* be someone's God in particular would be nonsensical. He is whatever he is. He *is* God and will not be anything in the future what he is not already now. He is God and as such, God over all. On the other hand, "to be a God unto thee," the promise regarding Abraham personally according to the adopted translation, is closer to the Hebrew original, but hardly very meaningful. What does it mean to be a God *to* someone? We believe that there is no one who has the slightest intelligible notion of it. It is not surprising that in this passage, as well as in all other passages in the entire Bible, the idiomatic quality of the Hebrew, *lih'yot l'Elohim,* was consistently overlooked. As long as the specific meaning of the term, *Elohim,* in this, and similar, context was not understood, the Hebrew idiom could not be appreciated. Nowhere does the phrase occur in the Bible: to be your God, or, to be their God. *"Lih'yot l"* does not mean: to be for, but, to become. Of course, to become God for you, would not do at all. What God promised Abraham was: I, God, will become *Elohim* for you and for your children. It makes excellent sense, if one realizes that the term *Elohim* indicates the providential attitude of God toward man, the manifestation of divine guidance and protection. "I shall become *Elohim* for you and for your children" does not mean that God will be his and his children's God, which is meaningless, but that God will enter into a providential relationship with them and will be *Elohim,* Leader, Protector, Savior, unto them. There is no passage in the Bible, where the term occurs, where it has not exactly this meaning. In the case of Abraham, to be *Elohim* for him and for his children is connected with the eternal covenant and the promise of the land. As in the case of Abraham, so at later times too the covenant between God and Israel is the manifestation that God becomes *Elohim* for Israel. We find it in Deuteronomy and in Jeremiah.[52] Often it is the Exodus which is mentioned to illustrate the point that God desires to be *Elohim* for the children of Israel. For instance: "For I am Y that brought you up out of the land of Egypt, to become *Elohim* for you.[53]

A most impressive passage is the one at the close of chapter 29 of Exodus. It illustrates, and—as it were—sums up, almost our entire discussion in this chapter. It runs as follows: "And I will dwell among the children of Israel, and I will become *Elohim* for them. And they shall know that I am Y their *Elohim,* that brought them forth out of the land of Egypt, that I may dwell among them. I am Y their *Elohim."* That the Divine Presence dwells among the children of Israel is due to God's desire to be *Elohim* for them. That the *Sh'khina* is in their midst gives Israel the knowledge that Y, the Far-One, is nevertheless, their *Elohim,* the one who is near. Y is, indeed, their *Elohim;* he acts toward them as *Elohim.*[54]

That *Elohim* stands for the manifestation of providential divine attitude toward man comes to clearest expression in some statements of the prophets. Jeremiah could never have said, as the translators would make us believe, that "at *that* time, saith the Lord, will I be the God of all the families of Israel." No matter when, and no matter what, God is God all the time. What God said to Israel through the prophet was a promise of divine providence. What he really said was: at that time, I shall become *Elohim* for Israel; I shall act toward them as *Elohim.*

Some of the most powerful prophecies of future redemption center around the theme that God will act as Elohim toward Israel. Jeremiah, for instance, declaimed in the name of God:

Behold, I will gather them out of all the countries, whither I have driven them in Mine anger, and in My fury, and in great wrath; and I will bring them back unto this place, and I will cause them to dwell safely; and they shall become a people for Me, and I shall become *Elohim* for them; and I will give them one heart and one way, that they may fear Me for ever; for the good of them and of their children after them; and I will make an everlasting covenant with them, that I will not turn away from them, to do them good; and I will put My fear in their hearts, that they shall not depart from Me.[55]

God is, of course, their God even when he punishes them in his anger; even in their Exile, he does not cease being God. But when he gathers them in from all the countries, he reveals himself as *Elohim* in redeeming action toward them; he becomes *Elohim* for them.

In discussing this passage, it may be advisable to pay some attention to the phrase often correlated to the one we have been discussing in this section of our study, i.e., *lih'yot li l'am*. Just as *lih'yot l'kha l'Elohim* does not mean, to be your God, neither does *lih'yot li l'am* mean, to be My people. Because of the idiomatic correspondence between the two phrases, we have translated: and they shall become a people for Me. We render all other passages containing the same idiomatic expression in the same manner. But what does it mean, to become a people for God? Just as "to become *Elohim* for them" indicates an attitude of divine concern toward Israel, so does "to become a people for Me" require an attitude of attachment to God on the part of Israel. As God is their *Elohim* by dwelling in their midst, so do they become his people by living in his presence. The everlasting covenant means, as Jeremiah puts it, that God will not turn from them, nor will they depart from him. God will give them "one heart and one way" that they may fear him for ever. God's providential care for them includes their spiritual salvation as well as their political redemption. This is in keeping with what we have established in the previous part of our discussion, i.e., that the giving of the Law itself is due to divine providence over Israel.

Jeremiah's theme is taken up again and sounded with even greater passion by Ezekiel.

Behold, I will take the children of Israel from among the nations, whither they are gone, and will gather them on every side, and bring them into their own land; and I will make them one nation in the land, upon the mountains of Israel . . . ; neither shall they defile themselves any more with their idols, nor with their detestable things, nor with any of their transgressions; but I will save them out of all their dwelling places, wherein they have sinned, and will cleanse them; so shall they become a people for Me and I shall become *Elohim* for them.[56]

By saving them from their Exile and by cleansing them from their sins will God become *Elohim* for them and they will become a people unto him because they will no longer defile themselves with their transgressions.[57] Not only will God cause them to dwell in their land, says Ezekiel, but he will also "sprinkle them with clean water" so that they be clean. He will also give them a "new heart" and a "new spirit"; he will put his own spirit in them and cause them to walk in his statutes and keep his commandments and do them. Thus, reconciliation will be established between God and Israel and the relationship of the covenant fulfilled, realized. Israel will become God's people and God will turn to Israel and become *Elohim* for them.[58]

At the close of this part of our discussion, it may be interesting to quote in full God's original message to Israel through the mouth of Moses, as they were launched into world history on their career as God's people.

> Wherefore say unto the children of Israel:
>> I am Y,
> and I will bring you out from under the burdens of
>> the Egyptians,
> and I will deliver you from their bondage, and I
>> will redeem you with an outstretched arm, and
>> with great judgments;
> and I will take you to Me for a people, and I will
>> become *Elohim* for you;
> and ye shall know that I am Y your *Elohim*, who
>> brought you out from under the burdens of the
>> Egyptians.

53

> And I will bring you in unto the land, concerning
>> which I lifted up My hand to give it to Abraham,
>> to Isaac, and to Jacob; and I will give it to
>> you for a heritage:
> I am Y. (Exod. 6:6–8)

We are now in a position to appreciate fully the exactness of the terminology used in this founding message to Israel. "I am Y" is the opening statement. Let there be no mistake about it. It is Y who is speaking and not some subsidiary deity under him, some mediating *Elohim* between God and man. And it is Y himself who will bring them out of the house of bondage and take them for a people unto himself, because Y will become *Elohim* for them. Then Israel will know that Y is their *Elohim*. He brought them out of Egypt and not some intermediary divine being. There is also the assurance that God will lead them to the land long promised to the patriarchs. Finally, we have the conclusion: I am Y, as if to say: I may be relied upon to keep my promise; I am the Creator and the Lord over all, I have the power to do as I plan.

Our examination has shown that there is in the entire Bible a remarkable consistency in the usage of some basic concepts, which originally defined the relationship between God and man, and in particular, that between God and Israel.

TO KNOW HIM

We come now to the final term indicating knowledge of God, which we set out to investigate. It is the expression: *lada'ath eth YHVH*. Practically at first glance we note that the concept has certain ethical implications, which at times are stated negatively, at others, positively. Of the sons of Eli, for instance, it is said that they were "base men, they knew not Y."[59] The passage conveys the idea that had they known Y, they would not have been base. We recall the bitter comment of Jeremiah:

O that I were in the wilderness,
In a lodging-place of wayfaring men,
That I might leave my people,
And go from them!
For they are all adulterers,
An assembly of treacherous men.
And they bend their tongue, their bow of falsehood;
And they are grown mighty in the land, but not for
     truth;
For they proceed from evil to evil,
And Me they know not,
Saith Y. (9:1–2)

The corresponding positive rendering of the thought is found in the famous chapter 11 of Isaiah where the vision of universal peace and harmony is concluded with the words:

They shall not hurt nor destroy
In all My holy mountain;
For the earth shall be full of the knowledge of Y,
As the waters cover the sea. (vs. 9)

Do these passages mean to say that the knowledge of God is identical with ethical action, that the two—perhaps—are interchangeable? We believe that what is indicated is a causal nexus between ethical and moral behavior and the knowledge of God. This is, in our mind, borne out by another passage in chapter 9 of Jeremiah. Verse 5 there says, concerning Israel:

Thy habitation is in the midst of deceit;
Through deceit they refuse to know Me,
Saith Y.

The rendering, "through deceit," obscures the meaning. In our opinion, the Hebrew *b'mirma* in the second line, is the equivalent of the two words *b'tokh mirma* in the first line. A better rendering would therefore be:

Thy habitation is in the midst of deceit;
In [the midst of] deceit they refuse to know Me.

55

The meaning is much clearer now. They dwell in the midst of deceit and in such a condition they, of course, refuse to know God. They hold on to their deceitfulness, which means that they refuse to know God. He who knows God cannot be deceitful.

What, however, may be the meaning of knowing God in the specific phrase under discussion? It seems to be different from the expressions that we have discussed earlier. It is not to know that he is Y, or, *that* he is Y our *Elohim*; but to know *him*. What is it that the sons of Eli did not know? Surely they must have known quite a great deal about God. They were priests in the sanctuary. They knew that he was Y, Israel's *Elohim*, who led them out of Egypt. The people of Israel, too, whom Jeremiah castigated without mercy, must have known a great deal about God. What kind of knowledge were they lacking? They knew about God, but they did not know Him. We may be led to an understanding of the term, if we recall what is said about Samuel, when God revealed himself to him for the first time. Samuel did not realize that God was calling him. The Bible says of him in this connection: "Now Samuel did not yet know Y, neither was the word of Y yet revealed to him."[60] No doubt, young Samuel must have known a great deal about God. He probably knew more than any one else of his generation. But, he did not yet know Y; the word of Y had not yet been revealed to him. In other words, as yet, he had had no experience of divine revelation. Like Job, Samuel too might have exclaimed: "I had heard of Thee by the hearing of the ear; but now mine eye seeth Thee." In the case of Samuel, to know Y certainly meant to have a personal experience of the Divine Presence, to confront God, and to be "face to face" to him as it were, and thus to know him. A person may know about another one a great deal; but one may actually know someone else, if one has entered into a real personal relationship with him. Such knowledge Samuel was lacking prior to his first experience of divine revelation. To know God, in this sense, would not mean intellectual knowledge or information, but what is understood by knowing a friend, someone beloved. One knows with one's whole being; the knowledge is a bond that unites. Such knowledge has no object but is an actual relation between two subjects. It is most intimate between God and his prophets, yet Hosea uses the same concept to describe the relation of love between God and all of Israel. It is a well-known passage, in which Israel is mystically symbolized as God's betrothed. Addressing Israel, God says:

> And I will betroth thee unto Me for ever;
> Yea, I will betroth thee unto Me in righteousness,
>   and in justice,
> And in lovingkindness, and in compassion.
> And I will betroth thee unto Me in faithfulness;
> And thou shalt know Y. (2:21–22)

If one bears in mind that, to know, in the Bible is also used to indicate the consummation of the union between husband and wife,[61] one might almost read instead of "thou shalt know Y," "thou shalt love Y." To know God means to stand in a personal relationship of love to him. It is a bold vision indeed, that Hosea carries to the people of Israel, maintaining that the relationship that is natural between God and his prophet is open for all Israel. Yet, he was building on an old tradition in Israel. In his last will and testament David said to Solomon:

And thou, Solomon my son, know thou the *Elohim* of thy father, and serve Him with a whole heart and with a willing mind; for Y searcheth all hearts, and understandeth all the imaginations of the thoughts; if thou seek Him, He will be found of thee. (1 Chron. 28:9)

That if one seeks God, God lets himself to be found means of course that one is able to find *him,* not just to learn *about* him. When one finds him, one knows him. And all may seek.

While this knowledge cannot always be as intimate as between God and the prophets or as in the mystical union between God and Israel in the vision of Hosea, it is always the expression of a personal intimacy of relationship between God and man. The idea found one of its finest expressions in one of the great passages of Jeremiah:

Behold, the days come, saith Y, that I will make a new covenant with the house of Israel, and with the house of Judah . . . this is the covenant that I will make with the house of Israel . . . I will put My law in their inward parts, and in their hearts will I write it; and I will become *Elohim* for them, and they will become a people for me; and they shall teach no more every man his neighbor, and every man his brother, saying: "Know Y"; for they shall all know Me, from the least of them unto the greatest of them, saith Y; for I will forgive their iniquity, and their sin will I remember no more. (31:31–34)

A superficial reading of the English translation will not reveal the logical connection between the two statements in the latter part of this quotation. How does Israel's knowledge of God depend on God's forgiving their sins? Only if to know him means to be at one with him, to enter into a relationship of intimacy with him, are the two ideas logically dependent on each other. For, as Isaiah would say, your iniquities separate between you and your God and your sins hide his face.[62] And when God's face is hidden one cannot "know" him, for the relationship has broken down. God forgives their sins, he removes the separation himself, he lets himself be found, that they may "know" him. Most interesting is the fact that Jeremiah singles them out individually for such knowledge of God, "from the least of them unto the greatest of them," as indeed such knowledge is the realization of a personal relationship between God and man. It will happen, when God's law will no longer have to be imposed upon them, but will become the inward law of their own nature. According to Isaiah, not even Egypt will be denied this immediate knowledge of God. For God will make himself known to Egypt too, "and the Egyptians shall know Y in that day." Yes, God will smite Egypt, but he will do it "smiting and healing"; and they shall return into Y and he will be entreated of them, and will heal them. It is this day, on which Egypt too will be called God's blessed people.[63]

Following Jeremiah, we may then say that to know God includes to carry God's law imprinted on one's "inward parts," to do his will out of love as a manifestation of one's own nature. To enter into the knowing relationship with God is the great transforming experience in human life, which changes human nature itself. This is the root of the causal connection between this knowledge of God and ethical conduct, which we noted at the beginning of our discussion. He who carries God's law inscribed on his heart cannot dwell in the midst of deceit. Thus, they shall not hurt nor destroy in all God's holy mountain, when the earth is full the knowledge of Y as the waters cover the sea.

In summation one may say that when God makes himself known through his actions one learns *about* him, either that he is Y or that he is Y our *Elohim*. But when man seeks him and he lets himself be found, then one knows *him* by a knowledge that is a bond of love between God and man.

Concluding Notes

Sigmund Mowinckel, in his study *Die Erkenntnis Gottes bei den Propheten* (Oslo, 1941), discusses the meaning only of the object phrase about the knowledge of God, *to know Y,* which we analyzed at the close of the chapter. His interpretation comes very close to our own. While it may not be quite correct to say, as he does, that in the Bible to know a person is always identical with a relationship of trust, friendship, with a sense of belonging to each other, often it is so. He is right in describing the knowledge of God as a personal, existential relation between God and man. On the whole, we agree with the main burden of his statements on this subject. He says, for instance:

Gotterkennen oder "kennen," das bedeutet für den Israeliten, in einem gegenseitigen, persönlichen Gemeinschaftsverhältnis zu ihm stehen, seinen Namen, sein Wesen, seinen Willen und seine Gefühle kennen, und zwar existentiell, so dasz man dadurch die Richtung, die Qualität, den Inhalt und die Direktive des eigenen Lebens erhält. . . . [p. 6] "Kennen" eben ein gegenseitiges, persönliches Gemeinschaftsverhältnis ist, innerhalb welcher der eine im Sinne und Geiste des Andern handeln kann und will—sei es "instinktiv" oder sei es, dasz er bewuszt seine Gedanken und seinen Willen darauf richtet. (pp. 39–40)

We feel, however, that Mowinckel does not fully realize the causal nexus between this kind of existential knowledge of God and the human attitude and action which follow from it. He is very close to it in calling the human deed that follows such knowledge of God instinctive. But he is not quite definite about it, as is seen from the end of our quotation. Thus, he also writes:

Die Erkenntnis Gottes ist nun aber, sehen wir, keine theoretisch-betrachtende Einsicht, sondern ein praktisches Verhalten und Tun. Darum, und nicht so sehr um den Gottesbegriff, handelt es sich in der Verkündigung der Propheten, wenn sie Gotteserkenntnis fordern und erwarten. . . . Wer Gott kennt, der musz es in seinem Tun zeigen. Das ist der Hauptpunkt in der prophetischen Auffassung der Gotteserkenntnis. (pp. 33–34)

He is quite right in stating that the knowledge of God is no theoretically contemplative insight and that the concern of the prophets is not with the philosophical concept of the idea of God. But one should not say that the prophetic interest is practical attitude and action. It is not. The knowledge of God is what Mowinckel himself said it was—an existential relation of mutuality of trust and confidence. The human attitude and the human deed are the outcome of such a personal relation. The knowledge of God has an existentially transforming influence upon the nature of men who participate in it. It is not that he who knows God *has* to show it in his behavior; he *will* show it because he cannot help showing it. He comes out of this "knowledge of God" another man. Since Mowinckel is not aware of this transfiguring effect of the knowledge of God, he is not able to appreciate fully Jeremiah's words about the new covenant, when God will write his law upon "their inward parts and in their hearts," so that there will be no more need for them to teach each other "saying: 'Know Y'; for they shall all know Me" (31:33–34). This is no new departure. As we have shown in our analysis of this text, Jeremiah elaborates what has been implicitly stated whenever the knowledge of God is mentioned, i.e., the transfiguring quality of the existential experience of this kind of knowledge.

Mowinckel discusses only one type of the biblical knowledge of God. He is not concerned with the phrases that speak of knowing God, using the formula with the subordinate clause: that they may know "that I am Y" or "that I am Y *Elohim*." G. Johannes Botterweck, in a dissertation entitled "Gott Erkennen: Im Sprachgebrauch des Alten Testaments" (Bonn, 1951), discusses these phrases too. As to the object phrase which is Mowinckel's subject, he leans completely on Mowinckel. As to the other two, he recognizes that they speak of a knowledge of God received through a manifestation of either His judgment or His salvation. However, he does not see the distinction between "that I am Y" and "that I am Y *Elohim*." Neither does he discuss the fourth phrase that we have noted, i.e., "to know that Y He is the *Elohim*." On the other hand, Walther Zimmerli in *Erkenntnis Gottes nach dem Buche Ezechiel, Eine theologische Studie* (Zurich, 1954), does analyze all the four formulas whose investigation has been our subject in this chapter. Unfortunately, we cannot agree with any of his conclusions. In our opinion he misses completely the significance of the object phrase which—as we have shown—is the most intimate form of knowing God. He is misled here by overlooking the distinction between "that I am Y" and "that I am Y *Elohim*." As a result, he overemphasizes "that I am Y," as an act of divine self-revelation in which God reveals his *Persongeheimnis* (the secret of his person) in the revelation of his name. Thus, this phrase stands for the highest form of man's knowledge of God, which leads Zimmerli to underrate the importance of the object phrase. In reality, as we have shown, the object phrase means knowledge of God, whereas the formula with the subordinate clause stands only for knowledge about God. Knowledge *of* God has the transfiguring effect; knowledge *about* God does not have it. Had he seen the distinction, he would have realized that this knowledge of God was not the communication of a supreme *Persongeheimnis* in the divine name, but a manifestation of divine involvement in human history through divine actions. Not seeing the distinction between the two versions of the subordinate clause, he can write:

Nun weisz ich, dasz Y Gott ist, wird die Antwort des Menschen vor dem ihm verkündeten und dann sich ereignenden Geschehnis sein müssen. In solcher Antwort wird er den, der sich in seinem Namen persönlich geoffenbart hat, als den Herrn Israels und damit auch den Herrn des einzelnen in Israel vor sich haben. (p. 67)

The fact is that this kind of responsive acknowledgment to the revelation never occurs when what is being revealed is that He is Y. We find such acknowledgement only as a human response to the revelation that Y is *Elohim,* as in the story of Elijah in I Kings 18 or in the prayer of Solomon in I Kings 8. The reason is simple. When God shows His sovereign might and authority over all creation, there was no need for any responsive acknowledgment. The people of the Bible never doubted His omnipotence. They were wavering only as regards the question whether Y himself acted also as the *Elohim* in the specific sense of providential care and guidance or were such tasks delegated to subordinate mediating deities. Only on this point was acknowledgment necessary. The answering exclamation is not that Y is God but that He is the *Elohim,* the term *Elohim* being used in the specific sense as we have indicated in our text.

Zimmerli is greatly puzzled by the fact that there seems to be no harmonizing formula in *Ezekiel* for the two types of divine action which are so far apart as "sein Gericht bis zum blutigen 'Ende,' sein Erwecken zu neuem Leben" (his judgment to the bitter end and his resurrection to a new life). Actually, we have found the unifying concept, and not only in *Ezekiel* but in the entire Bible, in the formula, Y He is *Elohim* or Y your *Elohim,* indicating that God, who is far removed is also near, that He who is transcendent is also immanent, that Y who is *Elohim* is One.

It seems to us that Bible scholars have overlooked the special meaning that *Elohim* has in all the texts that deal with the knowledge of God and the acknowledgement of Y as *Elohim.* It is usually assumed that *Elohim* is the general name for God and Y is the personal name that he has for Israel. We have shown that this is not so. The innumerable passages in which God exercises judgment over the nations that they may know that he is Y are in themselves sufficient to prove that Y is the biblical name for God in the universal sense, as the God of all creation, known as such by all nations. As we have seen, even the confrontation between Jephtah and the Ammonites, far from proving that Chemosh was seen as the counterpart to Y, proves the opposite, since in the end of his message to the king of Ammon he appeals to *Y the Judge* to judge between the children of Israel and the children of Ammon. Quite clearly, this was an appeal to a Supreme Judge whom the Ammonite would recognize too. A. B. Davidson, in *The Theology of the Old Testament* (New York, 1914), is right in saying that Y and *Elohim* are not parallel names; unfortunately he reverses the order. According to him, as with all Bible scholars, *Elohim* is the general term and Y the specific one. We have shown that, within the area of our specific subject matter in this chapter, the very opposite is the case. If Davidson and the others were right, the responsive formula of acknowledgment ought to be: *Elohim,* He is Y. Y, He is the *Elohim* cannot mean that Y is God, for that must already be known with the knowledge of the very name of Y. It would be homiletics to attach too much importance to the definite article in front of *Elohim* and interpret the phrase as, Y He is the God, meaning the supreme God, the one above all others. All the texts which we have analyzed in this connection prove that *Elohim* is to be understood in the specific sense, as the manifestation of Y, who notwithstanding his Sovereignty and aloofness, is yet near and providentially concerned.

Davidson makes the apt observation that there is "perhaps no more singular phenomenon in the history of Israel than the repeated outbreaks into idolatry. . . . These repeated falls into idol worship, exhibited throughout the whole history of Israel . . . require some explanation" (p. 86). Indeed, an explanation is required. But as long as one sees *Elohim* as the general idea of the deity and Y as the personal name of God for Israel, the explanation will not be forthcoming. Trying to understand the repeated backslidings of Israel into idolatry, one ought to bear in mind the words of Gerhard von Rad, *Old Testament Theology* (New York, 1962). On the subject of idol worship in Israel he writes:

In face of such misconceptions the theologian has to learn from the general science of religion what are the special properties of an image. It soon appears that images were only in the most exceptional cases actually identified with the deity concerned: at any rate this was not done in the cults with which Israel came into contact. Images made no claim to give an exhaustive representation of the being of the deity. The pagan religions knew as well as Israel did that deity is invisible, that it transcends all human ability to comprehend it, and that it cannot be captured by or comprised in a material object. But this did not deter them from consecrating cultic images to it. . . . The image has nothing to say about the being of the deity or the mode of its inner life. What it speaks about is rather how the deity is pleased to reveal himself, for the image is first and foremost the bearer of a revelation. (pp. 213–14)

This insight may well help us to explain the repeated falls of Israel into idolatry. The "calves" and the "baalim" were not meant to represent Y or to replace Y. They were symbols of His presence and His nearness by way of a mediating deity. Von Rad has been anticipated by Rabbi Yehuda Hallevi, the eleventh-century Jewish philosopher, who in his philosophical work, the *Kuzari,* uses the same insight in order to explain the sin of the "Golden Calf" (see part 1, par. 97). The average Israelite needed some visible symbol as a sign of the nearness of the invisible and remote Y. The Golden Calf, as also the calf of Samaria, had this mediating function. Our interpretation of the relevant passages was guided by Rabbi Yehuda Hallevi. One ought to appreciate the difficulty the average early Israelite must have encountered in making peace with the idea that Y had no mediators, that notwithstanding His omnipotent aloofness, He was yet near as Savior and Sustainer, that one had direct access to the awesome King who was also the loving Father. The prophets' struggle against religious syncretism is the struggle against the mediating deity, who as the Golden Calf or the Baal is always the *Elohim.* By affirming that Y is *Elohim* the statement is made that Y Himself is also the near one, notwithstanding His essential transcendence.

Bible scholars often maintain that the early prophets in Israel taught a practical monotheism but not a theoretical one. E. Sellin, for instance, sees clearly that Elijah's mocking of the Baal proves that he denied it every possible form of existence. But he continues, saying: "theoretischer Monotheismus ist das nicht . . . noch nicht, es fehlt . . . die positive Aussage, dasz Y der einzige Gott sei." (See *Theologie des Alten Testaments* [Leipzig, 1933], pp. 11–12.) He goes even as far as to say that not even the famous *Sh'ma* of the Jews contains such a statement of theoretical monotheism. It would seem, then, that all those generations of Jews who for more than two millenia have been living and dying with the *Sh'ma* on their lips, did not really know what they were saying. Sellin's mistake is unavoidable. As long as *Elohim,* in those contexts in which we have discussed the term, is understood as the general idea of God, it is impossible to gain a correct interpretation either of the first words of the Decalogue or of the *Sh'ma*. We have analyzed those passages. Once it is seen that *Elohim* is used in the specific sense, as outlined by us, the meaning of the *Sh'ma* becomes very plain and clear. Hear, O Israel, Y is our *Elohim*, i.e., He is the Judge and the Savior, the King and the Father, and yet: Y is One.

Such a statement is not a practically monotheistic statement, but a theoretically monotheistic one. And so are also all the other related statements, even the people's acknowledgment before the altar built by Elijah, exclaiming that Y He is the *Elohim*, Y He is the *Elohim*. Since Y was recognized as the Sovereign and Creator and since the *Elohim* of other religions had the function of subordinate deities under Y, the recognition that this was not true, that Y himself was also the *Elohim* and there were no mediators, was in fact a theoretically monotheistic affirmation.

CHAPTER 2

The Spirit of God

RUAH is probably one of the most difficult biblical ideas to define, if indeed there is one definition for it. Our concern here is with two of its combinations, *ruah Y* and *ruah Elohim*. While our chief interest is the investigation of such expressions that speak of the coming of the spirit of God upon a man, it may not be unadvisable to look carefully at those passages too where *ruah Y* and *ruah Elohim* occur not in that specific relationship to man.

Quite clearly, in a number of places in the Bible, notwithstanding the usual translations, *ruah Y* does not mean Spirit of Y, but is to be translated as a wind of Y, meaning, a wind caused by Y. When the sons of the prophets came to greet Elisha, after his master Elijah had been taken from him in a whirlwind, and offered to go and look for Elijah, they did not say, as the Revised Version has it: "lest peradventure the Spirit of the Lord hath taken him up, and cast him upon some mountain, or into some valley."[1] It is most unlikely that the Spirit of the Lord would ever engage in such antics. They were speaking of a very real wind of God, caused by him especially to carry Elijah away, that might have dropped the prophet at some distant spot in the mountain or in some valley. Similarly, when the trusted Obadiah hesitates to go on Elijah's errand to Ahab to announce the prophets reappearance, it is not that he fears that "the Spirit of the Lord" shall carry Elijah "whither I know not."[2] What Obadiah is afraid of is that Elijah might disappear again, carried away as if by a mighty wind from God. The experience with which the prophet Ezekiel was so familiar was not that he was carried by a spirit, but—as language and style prove—that he was taken up and put down again by an actual wind. Therefore, when the hand of God was upon him and—as we are told in the opening verse of chapter 37—he was "carried out" and "set down in the midst of the valley which was full of bones," this was not done "in the spirit of the Lord" but through the instrumentality of a wind brought on by God.[3]

The usage in these passages is not different from the one in Hosea,[4] that, announcing the punishment of Ephraim, makes mention of an east wind, which will come from the wilderness to dry up his fountain, and calls it, *ruah Y,* a wind of Y. The familiar passage in Isaiah, which declares all flesh to be grass and all its goodliness to be "as the flower of the field" also speaks of *ruah Y,* which blows upon it and causes the "grass" to wither and the "flower" to fade. Most definitely what is meant here is not the spirit of God. Neither is much gained here by rendering the phrase under discussion as the breath of the Lord.[5] Why should the breath of the Lord cause grass to wither and flower to fade? It is much simpler and more meaningful to understand the *ruah* here as a wind sent by God. This applies also to the way in which the phrase is used in chapter 59 of Isaiah. There, too, distress will not come in like a flood, "which the breath of the Lord driveth," but like one that is driven by a mighty wind, a wind of God.[6]

In all these passages, *ruah Y* is either a wind, miraculously caused by God, or simply a very powerful wind. It is to be noted that in contexts of this nature it is always *ruah Y* and never *ruah Elohim.* Only in the opening verses of Genesis do we find, *ruah Elohim,* where most certainly it does not mean a wind of *Elohim.* A hovering *ruah* is no wind. Once again the biblical usage here seems to agree with what we have found as we discussed the knowledge of God. There, the manifestation of divine power, of mastery over nature, or the execution of judgment, brought the knowledge that He was Y. Here, too, *ruah* that indicates might, or divine mastery over nature, or the power of punishing judgment is called *ruah Y* and not *ruah Elohim*. This is further supported by what we find as we turn to our main investigation in this chapter, to the passages that speak of the *ruah* of God that descends on a man. In that context, and in its simplest form, *ruah Y* stands for the infusion of supernatural physical strength into a mere man. As Samson was approaching the vineyards of Timnah and a young lion was charging at him, "the *ruah* of Y came mightily upon him and he rent him as one would have rent a kid, and he had nothing in his hand."[7] On another occasion, when Samson was delivered up into the hands of the Philistines bound and helpless and the Philistines were gleefully getting ready to avenge themselves on him, "the *ruah* of Y came mightily upon him, and the ropes that were upon his arms became as flax that was burnt with fire, and his bands dropped from off his hands."[8] In these cases *ruah Y* equipped an individual with great personal prowess and physical power in order to save himself in dangerous situations and from personal enemies. But *ruah Y* may accomplish much more than that. It may inspire a person with courage and authority of leadership to save an entire people. When the Midianites and the Amalekites and "the children of the east" pitched their tents in the valley of Jezreel in order to do battle against Israel, "the *ruah* of Y clothed Gideon" and he became the leader of his people against its enemies.[9] The same is said of Jephtah.[10] The nature of the effect of *ruah Y* on a person is made clearer in what is said about Othniel the son of Kenaz: "And the *ruah* of Y came upon him, and he judged Israel; and he went out to war, and Y delivered Cushan-rishatayim king of Aram into his hand."[11] *Ruah Y* inspires not only strength and courage for leading a people in war against an external enemy but also equips a man with the strength and authority of personality that are needed to head a people in the conduct of its internal domestic affairs. Not merely physical but also moral and spiritual strength that are inseparable from the office of a *shofet* in ancient Israel, the authority of leadership, were granted to a person by "the coming upon him" of *ruah Y.* This comes to expression even in the case of Samson. When the Bible says of him that "the *ruah* of Y began to move him in Mahaneh-Dan, between Zorah and Eshtaol,"[12] this—of course—does not mean some miraculous increase of bodily strength alone, but some divine inspiration that reached his entire personality to be God's chosen instrument in Israel's struggle against the Philistines. This is even clearer in the case of David. After his secret anointment to kingship by Samuel, the Bible says: "and the *ruah* of Y came mightily upon David from that day forward." And almost immediately afterward we read: "Now the *ruah* of Y departed from Saul."[13] The *ruah* of Y gave David intrinsic kingship, a strength and dignity of personality, a purposefulness of living, a sense of vocation that a man destined to be king needed. With the *ruah* of Y goes also success in enterprise and action. All this was taken from Saul. He still held on to the royal office but the *ruah* of Y had departed from him. The charisma of kingship was taken from him.

We may perhaps see an actual definition of *ruah Y* in what is said by Isaiah about the shoot that shall come forth out of the stock of Jesse.

> And the *ruah* of Y shall rest upon him,
> The spirit of wisdom and understanding,
> The spirit of counsel and might,
> The spirit of knowledge and of the fear of Y. (11:2)

The *ruah* of Y includes all this. However, it is most interesting to note that within *ruah Y* the spirit of wisdom and understanding, of knowledge and the fear of God, are not separated from the spirit of counsel and might. The one upon whom *ruah Y* descends unites within himself wisdom and might, the fear of God and effective counsel. But are not those exactly the qualities that the man of action, when he is the God-chosen leader, would have? And indeed, it is as such that the function of "the shoot out of the stock of Jesse" is described by Isaiah.

> And he shall not judge after the sight of his eyes,
> Neither decide after the hearing of his ears;
> But with righteousness shall he judge the poor,
> And decide with equity for the meek of the land;
> And he shall smite the land with the rod of his
>   mouth,
> And with the breath of his lips shall he slay the
>   wicked.
> And righteousness shall be the girdle of his loins,
> And faithfulness the girdle of his reins. (11:3–5)

The function of the Messiah is not essentially different from that of the Judges in early Israel. What the *shoftim* were doing in the context of contemporary history in Israel, the Messiah is destined to perform on the much more exalted level of universal history. In the same tradition Micah says of himself:

> But I truly am full of power by the *ruah* of Y,
> And of justice, and of might,
> To declare unto Jacob his transgression,
> And to Israel his sin. (3:8)

Here, too, *ruah Y* pours power into the prophet and it is a power that fills Micah with justice and might. Indeed, one whose task it is to declare unto Israel their transgressions, may need all the power with which *ruah Y* alone may provide him.

We may then say that all the cases we have discussed have something in common: the *ruah* that comes upon a man and infuses him with power, be it physical or spiritual, that bestows upon a person authority and leadership, as well as the effectiveness of such wisdom—imbued strength and authority, is referred to as *ruah Y*.

71

Is there a common denominator in those cases in which the spirit that comes over a person is referred to as *ruah Elohim?*

When Balaam lifted up his eyes and saw Israel "dwelling tribe by tribe" and beheld the vision of the goodly tents of Jacob, he was prophesying concerning the future destiny of the Jewish people. At the opening of the vision it is said: "and the *ruah* of *Elohim* came upon him. And he took up his parable."[14] Is it possible that *ruah Elohim,* when it attaches itself to a human being, means prophetic inspiration? So it would seem from this and numerous other passages in the Bible. When Saul, who went on his famous search of his father's asses and found a kingdom, left Samuel and met, as predicted, a "band of prophets," the Bible says of him: "and the *ruah of Elohim* came mightily upon him, and he prophesied among them."[15] Later, when kingship was taken from him, it was *ruah Y* that departed from him; when he too was among the prophets, it was *ruah Elohim* that inspired him. At one occasion, Saul sent his men to capture David, who had escaped to Samuel in Ramah. They were defeated by a company of prophets, who were prophesying at the time. For when the men watched the prophets, they themselves were engulfed by the spirit of the moment, so that the Bible reports: "the *ruah* of *Elohim* came upon the messengers of Saul and they also prophesied." Finally, when Saul himself came to get David, the same thing happened to him too. He too, was overwhelmed by *ruah Elohim* and prophesied, says the text.[16] Quite clearly, *ruah Elohim* stands for prophetic inspiration. When the *ruah* of *Elohim* came upon Azariah the son of Oded or when the *ruah* of *Elohim* clothed Zechariah the son of Jehoiada the priest, they went with their message to king and people as the prophets of God.[17]

There are, however, a number of points still left which require further clarification. In the case of Eldad and Medad, who did not cease to prophesy in the camp, Moses said: "Would that all the people of Y were prophets, that Y would put his *ruah* upon them."[18] One should not see in this an exception that contradicts the rule. Although it is Y who is asked to put his *ruah* upon them so that they may be inspired to prophesy, this *ruah* is not called *ruah Y*. Since Y is *Elohim*, both *ruah Y* and *ruah Elohim* are put upon men by Y. "His *ruah*" in this context may very well mean *ruah Elohim*, which normally is the cause of prophecy. As "His *ruah*" may stand for the specific significance of *ruah Y* and *ruah Elohim*, so, too, "My *ruah*" may mean either *ruah Y* or *ruah Elohim*. Of both these manifestations of divine *ruah* God may say, My *ruah*. We find the phrase carrying both connotation of power and authority or prophetic vocation. Of his servant and elect God says:

> I have put My *ruah* upon him,
> He shall make the right to go forth to the nations.
>
> . . . .
>
> He shall make the right to go forth according to
>   the truth.
> He shall not fail nor be crushed, till he have set
>   the right in the earth;
> And the isles shall wait for his teaching. (Isa. 42:1–4)[19]

All the elements of what we have found to be components of *ruah Y* are present in this text: leadership and judgment, wisdom and might, effectiveness and success of accomplishment. My *ruah* here is *ruah Y*. On the other hand, speaking of the time when Israel will know that God is in their midst and that Y is their *Elohim*, Joel also uses the expression, "My *ruah*," and this is what he has to say about it:

> And it shall come to pass afterward,
> That I will pour out My *ruah* upon all flesh;
> And your sons and your daughters shall prophesy,
> Your old men shall dream dreams,
> Your young men shall see visions. (3:1)

"My *ruah*" in this context is *ruah Elohim*, which bestows prophetic powers on human beings.

There seems to be, however, some exceptions to the rule. In two cases *ruah Elohim* does not mean prophecy. Both refer to the great biblical artist, Bezalel, who was responsible for the workmanship in connection with the setting up of the Tent of Meeting in the wilderness. Of him God said to Moses that he had "filled him with the *ruah* of *Elohim*, in wisdom, and in understanding, and in knowledge, and in all manner of workmanship."[20] While there is no mention here of prophecy, neither is this a case of a man being infused with "counsel and might," with the kind of wisdom and understanding that make for authority and leadership over people. The *ruah Elohim* bestowed upon Bezalel was artistically creative imagination and ability. May this be subsumed under prophetic inspiration? In rabbinical tradition Bezalel was inspired not unlike a prophet.[21] We may also note that whereas in the case of prophecy it is said that the *ruah Elohim* comes upon a person, Bezalel is *filled with ruah Elohim*. Be that as it may, according to our definition the term, *ruah Y,* would certainly be out of place in the case of Bezalel. He was neither a *shofet* nor a leader of men, neither a man of great physical strength and courage or of authority over men. As an inspired artist, he was essentially a man of the spirit. We shall then expand our definition of *ruah Elohim* and say that, when it attaches itself to a human being, it usually means prophetic inspiration but it may also include the divine gift of artistic creativity.[22]

There are, however, a number of passages where *ruah Y* does refer to prophecy. In order to see more clearly their specific nature, we shall list them together. Once again we have to refer to an event in the life of Saul, which we have mentioned before. When Samuel predicted the various signs that Saul would encounter on his way home, after his search for the lost asses of his father, he also said to him:

And the *ruah* of Y will come mightily upon thee, and thou shalt prophesy with them, and shalt be turned into another man.[23]

Here it is the *ruah* of Y that brings about prophecy. One of the great prophecies of Isaiah is introduced with the words:

> The *ruah* of the Lord Y is upon me;
> Because Y hath anointed me
> To bring good tidings unto the humble. (61:1)

Similarly, when Ezekiel tells how he was called upon to prophesy, he reports:

And the *ruah* of Y fell upon me, and He said unto me: Speak.[24]

The false prophet, Zedekiah, who smote Micaiah on the cheek, also refers to the spirit of prophecy as *ruah Y*, when he says:

Which way went the *ruah* of Y from me to speak unto thee?[25]

While these cases seem to be exceptional, it is possible that a careful reading of the sequence of events, as they are told in the story of Saul, may contain a hint for their deeper understanding. When Samuel predicts that Saul will prophesy, he uses the term, *ruah Y;* but when the Bible describes what actually happened, saying: "And it was so," what we are told is that the *ruah* of *Elohim* came mightily upon Saul. Now, if we look again at the four exceptions, we see that in every one of them it is an individual who refers to prophetic inspiration as *ruah Y,* Samuel predicting the future, Isaiah and Ezekiel telling about their personal experiences, Zedekiah mocking Micaiah about his prophetic qualifications. On the other hand, the anonymous author always refers to prophecy as the result of the coming of *ruah Elohim* upon man. We may guess, perhaps, the significance of this usage, if we reflect once more on the difference between *ruah Y* and *ruah Elohim.* The difference between them seems to be consistent with what we have found in the previous chapter in our discussion of the knowledge of God. The manifestation of divine might and power, of judgment and supreme authority, brings the knowledge that He is Y; the revelation of divine providence and care, of God's nearness and concern communicates the knowledge that Y is *Elohim.* It is consistent with this distinction that the divine *ruah,* which bestows power and authority, should be referred to as *ruah Y,* whereas the one that inspires prophecy should

75

be called *ruah Elohim*. The most intimate closeness between God and man is that which exists between God and the prophet. In the moment of prophetic ecstasy, man and God are nearest to each other. It is not divine power and transcendence that are in evidence, but divine love and immanence. It is *ruah Elohim* that makes man a prophet. However, the actual nature of the prophetic communion with God is the great mystery. It is conceivable that the prophet himself is unable to give an adequate account of it after the actual experience. He is left with a certainty; but not necessarily with an intelligent grasping of what happened, so that he might be able to describe it explicitly. In such a situation one is careful with the word and approaches with awe and respect. It is the biblical author alone who can testify that the *ruah Elohim* came upon a person. Human beings, speaking of the event, dare not draw as nigh. They hesitate to designate it with such exactitude. It is not for them to make the clear distinction. It is sufficient unto them to use the term *ruah Y*, which in its comprehensive sense includes the specific meanings of *ruah Elohim* as well as *ruah Y;* for Y, He is *Elohim*.[26]

Concluding Notes

Let it be clearly understood that according to our interpretation, only the expressions *ruah Y* and *ruah Elohim* have the meanings which we outlined. As indicated in our text, such expressions as, "My *ruah*" or "His *ruah*" may have differing meanings, depending on the context in which they occur. It would seem to us that a great deal of misunderstanding in biblical exegesis is due to the fact that Bible scholars have not recognized that *ruah Y* or *ruah Elohim* are termini technici, as it were. Thus they identify every kind of *ruah* which somehow emanates from God with the Spirit of God or the Spirit of the Lord. Characteristic of such misunderstanding is Davidson's quotation (*Theology of the Old Testament*, p. 121) from Job (26:13) as: "By the Spirit of God the heavens are made bright," whereas in the text we have, "by His *ruah*"! "His *ruah*" here has nothing to do either with *ruah Y* or *ruah Elohim*, which are the mark of the charisma of the leader or the prophet. It is equally incorrect to quote Isaiah 30:28, as an example of *ruah Y*, as Snaith does (*The Distinctive Ideas of the Old Testament*, p. 144). "His *ruah*"—we have discussed the passage in our text—is neither *ruah Y* nor *ruah Elohim*, though logically it is God's no less than the earth is His and all the powers of nature are His. Neither is it permissible to identify *ruah hokhmah* with *ruah Y* or *ruah Elohim*. Snaith is altogether wrong trying to describe *ruah-adonai* on the basis of passages in which the term *ruah* occurs, but not the specific formula *ruah Y* or *ruah Elohim* (cf. p. 157). In all such cases one must determine the meaning by the internal evidence of the context.

No less serious are the misunderstandings caused by not distinguishing between *ruah Y* and *ruah Elohim*. Mowinckel, for instance, discussing the Spirit of the Lord (op. cit., p. 16) writes:

Diese Verstellung dient in der alten Zeit und bei der älteren vulgär-profetie eben als Erklärung der extra-ordinären, ekstatischen Phänomen des Nabi'ismus oder bei den "begeisterten" Helden der wilden "Landnahme" Zeit. Nicht so sehr die Worte des Nabi als vielmehr sein "rasendes" Gebähren und die Kampfeswut eines Samson wurden von dem Geiste Y abgeleitet; erst eine viel spätere Zeit hat in dem Geiste Y das inspirierende Medium eines höheren religiösen und sittlichen Lebens gesehen.

It is not proper to treat the inspiration of the hero and the "ravings" of the early prophets as one phenomenon. The "inspiration" of the hero is his acquisition of superhuman strength which is normally brought about by *ruah Y* (for the only apparent exception in the story of Saul, see our comments below); in the language of the anonymous biblical narrator the prophets are always inspired by *ruah Elohim*. See our discussion of this point. Nor is it proper to say that it was

77

more the "ravings" of the prophet which were ascribed to the Spirit of God, rather than what he had to say. The formula is: and the *ruah Elohim* descended upon him and he prophesied. The condition of trance, in which the early prophets were thrown by their experience, seems to be incidental. Nowhere is *ruah Elohim* (or *ruah Y*) directly connected with it.

Davidson (op. cit., p. 125) does catch a glimpse of a possible distinction between *ruah Y* and *ruah Elohim*. He is, however, unable to attach any importance to it, because for him—as we saw in our concluding notes on Chapter 1—Y stands for the God of Israel in a specific sense. As we have pointed out, he reverses the relationship between Y and *Elohim* in those places where Y is declared to be the *Elohim*. But he who does this cannot appreciate the distinction between *ruah Y* and *ruah Elohim*.

Snaith does note the distinction between *ruah Y* and *ruah Elohim* and attempts to explain it. We are, however, unable to agree with him. He maintains that *"Ruach-Adonai* controls the prophet" (op. cit., p. 154). According to our interpretation, *ruah Y* sustains the hero, the man of authority, the leader; *ruah Elohim* inspires the prophets. Let us examine Snaith's proofs. He writes:

Ezekiel II.2 reads, "and the spirit entered into me when he spake unto me, and set me upon my feet," and then we find immediately following, the message which was delivered to the prophet. So also Ezekiel III.24, and especially XI.5, where the spirit which enables the prophet to speak the word of prophecy is called the *ruach-adonai*.

Now as to Ezekiel 2:2 and 3:24, we note first that no mention is made of *ruah Y*. The undetermined *ruah*—a wind, a spirit, a power—occurs. As always in such cases, the meaning has to be elicited from the context. Having described his first momentous vision, Ezekiel continues:

This was the appearance of the likeness of the glory of the Y. And when I saw, I fell upon my face, and I heard a voice of one that spoke. And He said unto me: "Son of man, stand upon thy feet, and I will speak with thee." And *ruah* entered into me when He spoke unto me, and set me upon my feet; and I heard Him that spoke to me. And He said to me. . . .

Quite clearly the Speaker is not to be identified with the *ruah*. The *ruah* here has nothing to do with the spirit of prophecy. Lying on the ground, Ezekiel hears the Speaker. Even before the *ruah* enters him, the prophet is being addressed. This is the beginning of the act of prophecy. Even at the moment of the entry of the *ruah,* the *ruah* is distinguished from the Speaker. The *ruah* has only one function. The words of the Speaker: "Son of man, stand upon thy feet" and the subsequent statement that the spirit that entered Ezekiel set him upon his feet give a full indication of that function. Ezekiel's falling upon his face before the vision was not a completely free act of worshipping prostration. He is physically too overwhelmed by his experience. In a condition of complete bodily exhaustion, he lies there on the ground (cf. Daniel 10:8) before God. He hears a voice that speaks but he is unable to grasp the message. "Stand up and listen" says the voice, but he has no strength left. The *ruah* enters and sets him up on his feet. The *ruah* restores the prophet's bodily energies. The prophet may now receive the message, and the Speaker that was there all the time and spoke to Ezekiel even before the *ruah* approached, continues with his message. The situation is exactly the same in Ezekiel 3:24. In neither of these cases does *ruah* "control the prophet" nor has it anything to do with the spirit of prophecy.

In Ezekiel 11:5, *ruah Y* is mentioned and in connection with the actual act of prophecy. But let us look at the text and compare it with other passages which mention the spirit of prophecy. Of that occasion of prophecy Ezekiel says:

And the Spirit of Y fell upon me, and He said unto me: Speak: Thus saith Y.

This example does seem to deviate from our rule that *ruah Y* is an indication of mightiness and authority and not of the spirit of prophecy. This, however, is not the only departure from the norm. The entire passage is unusual and, indeed, exceptional for two reasons. Nowhere else do we find the expression, "the spirit of Y falling upon the prophet." Usually, *ruah Elohim* is upon, descends on, or clothes the prophet. The expression used here by Ezekiel—especially in its Hebrew connotation—suggests almost an attack by the Spirit. Equally unusual is the phrase: "He said unto me: '*Speak*: Thus saith Y.'" We are familiar with: "Thus says Y"; but the formula: "Speak: Thus says Y" is unique. It gives the impression of talking to a child, making him memorize a message. It is unlike inspiration and more like a technical means of conveying a message by using the prophet as an impersonal instrument of communication. This would explain "the attack" by the Spirit of Y. It would seem to us that this was a lower form of prophecy. It was not the *ruah Elohim,* the spirit of prophecy, which descended upon Ezekiel. The mightiness of *ruah Y* fell upon him, overwhelmed him, and reduced him to an impersonal mouthpiece of the divine message. Be that as it may, the very uniqueness of the passage does not permit us to draw from it general conclusions as to the meaning of *ruah Y.* It certainly does not contradict our analysis of the concept.

The Snaith quotation from Micah 3:8 proves—as we have shown in our text—our position and not Snaith's. The passage does not speak of prophecy, but of mightiness and authority. The Spirit of Y fills Micah with power, judgment, and might to declare unto Jacob his transgressions. To declare Israel his sin requires of a man strength, courage, and authority. This is not the gift of prophecy, but the gift bestowed upon the hero-judges by *ruah Y* in the early history of Israel. It is in the same line of tradition. On the other hand, Nehemiah 9:30 proves nothing. The phrase there is "Thy spirit through Thy prophets." To say that "Thy spirit" is *ruah-adonai,* as Snaith concludes, is begging the question. If, as we have shown, the spirit of prophecy is *ruah Elohim,* then "Thy spirit" in this context is *ruah Elohim* and not *ruah Y.*

The distinction between *ruah Y* and *ruah Elohim* is explained by Snaith in these words (op. cit., pp. 156–57):

At first superhumanness and abnormality is all that is required of the *ruach-adonai*, but gradually the idea ethicized as well as personalized. The ethicizing process can best be seen in the story of the transference of the kingdom from Saul to David. In the first part of the story, that part which deals with the choice of Saul, the two phrases *ruach-adonai* and *ruach-elohim* are used without any difference of interpretation in the variation, I Samuel X, 6, 10, XI, 6. But with the choice of David, a change appears. In I Sam. XVI it says that the *"ruach-adonai* lept upon David from that day forward."* According to the next verse, "the *ruach-adonai* had departed from Saul, and an evil *ruach* from *adonai* terrified him." Henceforward we get the phrases *ruach elohim* and an evil *ruach elohim* used of Saul and his servants, I Sam. XVI, 15, 16, 23, XVIII, 10, XIX, 20, 23. The writers seem to have been guided by two fixed principles. They were determined to retain the phrase *ruach-adonai* for the king whom the Lord had chosen, i.e., for the Messianic King. They wished to avoid saying that the *ruach-adonai* was evil, doubtless intending *elohim* to be understood in the profane sense. On the change-over from Saul to David, they used the phrase "an evil *ruach* from *adonai*." The case of I Sam. XIX, 9 is peculiarly informative as to this editorial process. The Hebrew text reads, "the *ruach-adonai* was evil to Saul. . . ." It is strange that Massoretes let this pass. For whilst they allowed to pass "an evil *ruach* from *adonai*," they have avoided saying that *ruach-adonai* was evil.

Let us consider his points one by one. Is it correct to say that at first all that is required of *ruah Y* is "superhumanness and abnormality"? If superhumanness is "abnormality," which of course it is in a sense, it is correct. But if what he has in mind is the "ravings" of the early prophets, of which—for instance—Mowinckel speaks, it is wrong. *Ruah Y* is never associated with this kind of spiritual abnormalcy. On the other hand, Snaith is right in maintaining that *ruah Y* applies to "the king, whom the Lord had chosen, i.e., for the Messianic King." However, *ruah Y* is reserved for the Messianic King because it stands for "superhumanness," i.e., mightiness, authority, judgment and counsel, leadership. We have shown this in our discussion in our text. The Messianic King is not a prophet, but the ideal Hero-Judge who was also sustained by *ruah Y.* The *ruah Y* which departed from Saul and "lept" upon David is the charisma of royal authority and success, not the spirit of prophecy. This has nothing to do with the "fits" of prophecy which Saul had before and after the event. As we have shown, even after the changeover from Saul to David, *ruah Elohim* retains its meaning of prophecy (cf. II Chronicles 15:1; 24:20, etc.). Nor is it correct to say that *ruah Y* is not used in reference to Saul after the changeover. Snaith is puzzled by I Samuel 19:9. How come the Massoretes let *ruah Y* stand, when—according to the Snaith theory—the "profane" *ruah elohim* was expected? Snaith would have done well to compare I Samuel 19:9 with I Samuel 18:10. Let us take a careful look at both passages.

And an evil *ruah Y* was upon Saul, as he sat in his house with his spear in his hand; and David was playing with his hand. And Saul sought to smite David even to the wall with the spear; but he slipped away out of Saul's presence, and he smote the spear into the wall.

Almost the same situation is described in I Samuel 18:10, but in the following words:

And it came to pass on the morrow that an evil *ruah Elohim* came upon Saul, and he prophesied in the midst of the house; and David played with his hand, as he did day by day; and Saul had his spear in his hand. And Saul cast the spear.

In the first passage *ruah Y* is mentioned; in the second, *ruah Elohim.* Shall we say that the terms are used indiscriminately and without any difference between them? But since this occurs after *ruah Y* has passed on from Saul to David, what becomes of Snaith's theory? There is, however, an explanation. In our second quotation, *ruah Elohim* is followed by the phrase, "and he prophesied in the midst of the house"; not so in our first quotation. Even here we have a strict adherence to the rule that prophecy is connected with *ruah Elohim.* Our first quotation speaks only of Saul's violence. It is in keeping with our findings that *ruah Y*, which normally stands for the communication of might and power, should mean "superhuman" violence even when it is "evil." It is, therefore, not correct to say that after *ruah Y* departed from Saul, only *ruah Elohim* is appropriate for him. When the latter term is applied to him and his servants, it is because some form of prophecy is being described. We see this clearly in the case of his servants and his own in I Samuel 19:20–24. No matter what the value of their propehcy was *ruah Elohim* was responsible for it. At the same time, it should be noted that the manner of association between the human being and *ruah Elohim* in these passages appears to be different from the way it appears in the earlier chapters (13:23; 18:10) where *ruah Elohim* is *ra'ah*, evil. The *ruah Elohim ra'ah* is *el*, to, Saul; but in chapter 19—as everywhere else in the Bible—it is *al*, upon, the person distinguished by prophecy. Since the change in preposition from *al* to *el* occurs only in the cases of the "evil" spirit of God, it must be the clue to the explanation of a prophetic state caused by the "evil" *ruah Elohim*. It would seem—as we have pointed out in our text—that when genuine prophecy is described, the association between man and *ruah Elohim* is indicated by *al; ruah Elohim* is upon the prophet. Where, however, a prophetic condition—and this must be only the outward appearance of the prophetic trance or ecstasy, not its inner contents—is brought on by a *ruah Elohim ra'ah*, the spirit is *to* the man thus affected. (The only exception seems to be I Samuel 16:16. It should, however, be remembered that the words are those of the servants of Saul, to whom the distinction may not have been clear at all.) The appreciation of this distinction may help us to clear up the strange idea of "the evil" *ruah Y* or the evil *ruah Elohim*. We noticed Snaith's puzzlement that the Massoretes allowed, in I Samuel 19:9, the phrase that the *Ruah-Adonai* was evil to Saul. Actually, the Massoretes did not read it that way. They separated *ra'ah* from *ruah Y* by the massoretic sign of the *P'sik*. Accordingly, they read: And there was a *ruah Y;* it was evil to Saul. Even more interesting is their reading of 18:10, where they place the word *ra'ah* between two such signs of separation and must have read: a *ruah Elohim* came—it was evil—to Saul. It would seem to us that in this manner not only did they mean to separate the attribute, evil, from God's spirit, but also wished to interpret the unusual preposition *el* in place of *al*. To refer *el* directly to *ruah* implies certain difficulties. "There was spirit of Y to Saul" or "a spirit of *Elohim* descended to Saul" is awkward. The syntax requires the proposition *al*. But if we separate *ra'ah* from *ruah* and make *el* refer to *ra'ah*, then we get a tolerable sentence. The sentence becomes divided into two parts: And there was a *ruah* of Y; it was evil to Saul. The adjective, evil, no longer describes the spirit, but its effect on Saul. But that the effect of the *ruah* on Saul was evil need have nothing to do with the *ruah;* it might have been due to what was there in the nature of Saul. *Ruah Y,* which normally communicates strength and authority, was turned into violence just as *ruah Elohim,* which is normally the source of prophecy, was turned into "prophetic" ravings, thanks to the manner in which Saul, owing to his own failings, responded to the spirit.

There remain only the passages about the *ruah* which occur before *ruah Y* departed from Saul. Snaith believes that in them, *ruah Y* and *ruah Elohim* occur without any differentiation. We do not think so. It is true that 10:6 has *ruah Y,* where we might have expected *ruah Elohim.* We have discussed this passage together with the other three exceptions in the Bible. We also noted that when Saul's actual experience of prophecy is described (ibid. 10), we have *ruah Elohim.* Chapter 11:6 does have *ruah Elohim* and we might have expected *ruah Y.* But one should read on until verse 10 where we hear the words of Saul and his men addressed to the messengers: "Thus shall ye say unto the men of Jabesh-gilead: To-morrow, by the time the sun is hot, ye shall have deliverance." Such are the accents of prophecy inspired by *ruah Elohim,* and not the style of the Hero-Judge, due to *ruah Y.*

CHAPTER 3

The Name of God

THE NAME AND THE DEED

WHILE the Kabbalists are preoccupied with the mysteries of the divine name, it is no secret that the name of God in the Bible is represented by the tetragrammaton which we have been abbreviating with the letter Y. However, very often in the Bible we come across the expression, *shem Y, Y's name*. As so often, the translation leads one to overlook the strangeness of the expression. When we read in the Bible that "then began men to call upon the name of the Lord" or when we are told of Abraham that he built an altar "and called upon the name of the Lord"; or when in the great song toward the end of Deuteronomy it is declared with solemnity: "for I will proclaim the name of the Lord; ascribe ye greatness unto our God";[1] all this seems well stated. Yet, one ought to realize that the Hebrew makes no mention of "the name of the Lord," but of "the name of Y." Since, however, Y itself is the name of God, the name of Y is the name of the name of God. What does it mean to call upon the name of the name of God, or to proclaim it? A number of other phrases that involve the name of God are equally mysterious. When in the song of Moses it is said that "Y is a man of war, Y is His name,"[2] one cannot help wondering what could be meant by such an apparent platitude. Of course, Y is His name. We have just called him so. Or shall we assume that the second line explains the first one, as if to say: Y is a man of war because Y is His name; and Y means man of war. This would be nonsensical. The entire teaching of the Bible about Y contradicts such a narrow interpretation of the concept expressed by the name, Y. When God declares through Isaiah: "I am Y, that is My name; and My glory will I not give to another,"[3] what is gained by the emphasis that that is his name? As to giving his glory to another, what difference does it make what his name is? Shall we again say that the name, Y, in itself means one who does not give his glory to another? Perhaps, but why so?

In a number of places, "the name of Y" or "Thy name" means simply fame or reputation. When the men of Gibeon came to Joshua to conclude a covenant with the children of Israel, they told him that they came from a far-away country "because of the name of Y thy God; for we have heard the fame of Him, and all that He did in Egypt." The name of Y is here identical with his fame. Similary, in Solomon's prayer concerning the stranger, who will "come out of a far country for Thy name's sake—for they shall hear of Thy great name, and of Thy mighty hand, and of Thine outstretched arm,"[4] God's name is his reputation. Obviously, "Thy great name," of which the gentiles hear is not just the information that his name is Y. This in itself may not impress them very much. God's name will be great in their eyes by hearing of his great deeds, which he performed with his mighty hand and his out-stretched arm. In references to the nations, the prophets speak of the impact that the name of Y makes upon them. According to Isaiah "the isles shall gather . . . unto the name of Y" and, using the same terminology, Jeremiah says: "At that time they shall call Jerusalem the throne of Y; and all the nations shall be gathered unto it, to the name of Y, to Jerusalem."[5] While Israel knows God from immediate experience also, the nations are attracted to him by the name of Y, the fame of his action in the universe. God's deeds create God's name. The idea is stated explicitly in a three-fold repetition within the compass of only a few verses in chapter 63 of Isaiah. When Israel remembers "the days of old," it recalls Him

That caused His glorious arm to go
At the right hand of Moses,
That divided the water before them,
To make himself an everlasting name.
That led them through the deep,
As a horse in the wilderness, without stumbling.
As the cattle that go down into the valley,
The spirit of Y caused them to rest;
So didst Thou lead Thy people,
To make Thyself a glorious name.

.   .   .   .

Thou, O Y, art our Father,
Our Redeemer from everlasting is Thy name [italics added].[6]

God made himself a name by dividing the waters of the Red
Sea; he made himself a glorious name by leading the children
of Israel through the depth of the divided waters. His name is
the Redeemer because he redeems. God's name is what God
does. Thus, if we read in Exodus that "Y—His name is
Jealous—is a jealous God,"[7] the meaning is: his name is
Jealous because he acts with jealousy. His name is the Redeemer and his name is also the Jealous One, because he redeems, when it is time for redemption, and he is jealous, when
jealousy is required.

Since the name is the result of the deed, it often stands for
divine might. In one of God's messages to him, Pharaoh is
informed that, in spite of his recalcitrance, he was made "to
stand, to show thee My power, and that My name may be
declared throughout all the earth."[8] The miracles and the
plagues, performed by God in Egypt, were a showing of divine
power. And the showing of divine power established the divine
"name." The revealing of a divine activity of might established
a form of divine reputation, God the Almighty. Bearing this
in mind, some of the familiar passages in the Bible come to
new life in a new light. When David faces Goliath he says to
him: "Thou comest to me with a sword, and with a spear, and
with a javelin; but I come to thee in the name of Y of hosts,

the God of the armies of Israel, whom thou hast taunted."[9]
We shall yet have to clarify the exact meaning of what has
become the cliché, "in the name of the Lord." It is, however,
obvious in this context that "the name of Y" on David's side is
the parallel to the sword, the spear, and the javelin in the
hands of Goliath; it is David's counter-weapon. The name of
Y means here divine might, the power of Y of hosts, the God
of the armies of Israel. David does not meet Goliath *in* the
name of Y, but as the giant approaches *with* his weapons, so
does David come *with* the "name" of Y, relying on God's
might. We find that God's name stands for God's might in a
number of other passages, especially in the Psalms. When the
Psalmist prays: "O God, save me by thy name and right me
by Thy might,"[10] what does he mean with the first part of his
plea? Quite clearly, Thy name is the parallel to Thy might.
"Thy name" is synonymous with "Thy might"; *shem* here is
the equivalent of *g'vurah*. When God promises David divine
protection against his enemies, it is said: "But My faithfulness
and My mercy shall be with him; and through My name shall
his horn be exalted."[11] One should remember that in biblical
Hebrew the word, *qeren* (horn), symbolizes strength. King
David is promised increase in power, which will reach him
through support by divine might. As man in prayer asks to be
saved by God's "name," so God in promise assures man saving
strength by His "name."

An impressive example of the point we are making, which
includes all the elements of the three passages just quoted, is
a short prayer in Psalm 44.

Thou art my King, O God;
Command the salvation of Jacob.
Through Thee do we push down our adversaries;
Through Thy name do we tread them under that rise up against us.
For I trust not in my bow,
Neither can my sword save me.
But Thou hast saved us from our adversaries,

And hast put them to shame that hate us.
In God have we gloried all the day,
And we will give thanks unto Thy name for ever.[12]

As in the case of David's confrontation with Goliath, here too the "name" of God is opposed to man-made weapons, to bow and sword; as in the other psalms, here too, calling on the "name" of God, one really calls on divine power to help and to save. The gratitude expressed "unto Thy name" at the conclusion of the prayer is thanksgiving for God's actual revelation of his saving might.[13] In Proverbs the "name" of Y is called "a strong tower" in which the righteous find shelter and elevation.[14]

Since Y's name is what he does, we normally find that the mentioning of the name is inseparable from some divine action. As Exodus in the case of Pharaoh, so does Isaiah, too, speak of God making his name known to his adversaries when He does "tremendous things which we looked not for."[15] Because the name represents action, it may even be personified. Announcing the punishment that is to overtake Assyria, Isaiah speaks of "the name of Y that cometh from far," it is burning with anger; it is filled with indignation. Its breath is like an overflowing stream. It sifts the nations with the sieve of destruction.[16] All this may be said about the name, because it stands for divine action in history. It is for this very reason that Isaiah may say in another place that the islands will fear the name of Y, "for distress will come in like a flood, which the wind of Y driveth."[17] It is the coming of distress like a flood, which is God's doing, that brings the name of Y to the islands, thus, Isaiah may also use the previous formula and say of the "name" of Y that it "cometh from far."

While the "name" often means manifestation of divine might, it does not usually mean the mighty execution of divine judgment. We already noted that asking to be saved, the Psalmist pleads with God that it be done by the "name." In fact, what is salvation to the poor may put fear into the haughty. As Isaiah, the Psalmist too speaks of the time when the nations will "fear the name of Y"; not because of the judgment executed over them, but because "Y hath built up Zion," thus appearing in His glory, and because "He hath regarded the prayer of the destitute, and hath not despised their prayer."[18] That God regards the prayer of the destitute and builds Zion, it too is his "name." When he does so, he makes his "name" known in the world. However, the "name" that brings salvation to the destitute, causes fear in the hearts of "the nations and their kings." Thus, Isaiah may well call to the man who walks in darkness and has no light: "Let him trust in the name of Y, and stay upon his God." Let him trust in what God will do for him. The "name" of Y is the enacting of His salvation. Zephamiah, in speaking of the "afflicted and poor people," declares that "they shall take refuge in the name of Y."[19] One is reminded of the verse in Proverbs, in which— as we have heard—the "name" of Y is called a "strong tower." One takes refuge in the "name" of Y by trusting in the coming of His name, in the coming manifestation of His saving providence. Micah says about the Messiah that he shall feed his flock through the strength of Y and by means of the majesty of the name of Y his God.[20]

In innumerable passages the Bible speaks of praising and thanking the name of Y, but practically everywhere the context shows that it, in all these cases, is for the wondrous or saving acts of God that one is grateful or which one praises. We find these passages mainly in the Psalms, but they are found in some of the other books as well. Thus Isaiah declares that he will praise the name of Y. Why does he praise the name of Y and not simply Y? Because the emphasis is on what God did, for He has done "wonderful things."

For Thou hast been a stronghold to the poor,
A stronghold to the needy in his distress,
A refuge from the storm, a shadow from the heat;
For the blast of the terrible ones was a storm against the wall. (25:4)

By what he did, God made his "name"; being praised for what he did, his "name" is praised. The same idea is expressed by Joel in his great prophecy concerning the future of Israel when he says:

Fear not, O land, be glad and rejoice;
For Y hath done great things.

. . . .

And ye shall eat in plenty and be satisfied,
And shall praise the name of Y your God,
That hath dealt wondrously with you;
And My people shall never be ashamed. (2:21–26)

Once again it is the same concept. What God does establishes his "name" for the occasion, thus the praise for God's action is praising the "name" of Y. As already indicated, most of the passages of this category are contained in the Psalms, which—because of the very subject matter of that book of the Bible—was to be expected. We shall list here a number of them. There is, for instance, the beautiful Psalm 113:

Hallelujah.
Praise, O ye servants of Y,
Praise the name of Y.
Blessed be the name of Y
From this time forth and for ever.
From the rising of the sun unto the going down thereof
Y's name is to be praised.

After this introduction follows the praising of Y's name.

Y is high above all nations,
His glory is above the heavens.
Who is like unto Y our God,
That is enthroned on high,
That looketh down low
Upon heaven and upon the earth?
Who raises up the poor out of the dust,
And lifteth up the needy out of the dunghill;
That He may set him with princes,

91

Even with the princes of His people.
Who maketh the barren woman to dwell in her house
As a joyful mother of children.
Hallelujah.

Y is high above all nations and above the heavens. But it is not for that that Y is being praised. He is praised for no one is like unto Him—but not in what He *is,* being enthroned on high, but for what He *does* being so enthroned. He is praised, for although He is enthroned above all nations and above the heavens, yet "He looketh down low." Even though He is so highly exalted in His being, yet in His action He joins the poor and the needy whom He raises up from the dust. Notwithstanding the transcendence of His being, He heals the barren womb that yearns for a child. This is what establishes God's "name." Praise ye the "name" of Y.[21]

In the same spirit, the psalmist also says:

So shall all those that take refuge in Thee rejoice,
They shall ever shout for joy,
And Thou shalt shelter them;
Let them also that love Thy name exult in Thee.
For Thou dost bless the righteous,
O Y, Thou dost encompass him with favor as with a shield. (5:12–13)

At the close of chapter 54 we read:

I will give thanks unto Thy name, O Y, for it is good.
For He hath delivered me out of all trouble;
And mine eye hath gazed upon mine enemies.

Again in Psalm 52 we find:

I will give Thee thanks for ever, because Thou hast done it;
And I will wait for Thy name, for it is good. (vs. 11)

The waiting for God's "name" is the trust in His redeeming action that creates His name among men. The same thought is expressed somewhat differently in Psalm 9.

Y also will be a high tower for the oppressed,
A high tower in times of trouble;

And they that know Thy name will put their trust in Thee.
For Thou, Y, hast not forsaken them that seek Thee. (vss. 10–11)

Those who "know Thy name" are, of course, not those who know that God's name is Y. Even a man without faith may know that his name is Y. One may know this name and yet such knowledge alone may not induce one to put one's trust in God. But if one knows of the manifestations of divine providence in history, which are the name by which God made himself known, then—even in time of trouble, when all hope seems far removed—one may be called upon to put his trust in God, for his name means that he is not one who forsakes them that seek him.

Whereas the Psalmist uses the term, *yod'ei Sh'mo*, those who know His name, the prophet Malachi has, *hoshvei Sh'mo*, those who think upon His name. Who are meant by this term? What does it mean, to think upon His name? The context in which the phrase occurs may enlighten us. This is what the prophet has to say to them:

Your words have been all too strong against Me,
Saith Y.
Yet ye say: Wherein have we spoken against Thee?
Ye have said: It was vain to serve God;
And what profit is it that we have kept His charge,
And that we have walked mournfully
Because of Y of hosts?
And now we call the proud happy;
Yea, they that work wickedness are built up;
Yea, they try God, and are delivered.
Then they that feared Y
Spoke one with another;
And Y hearkened, and heard,
And a book of remembrance was written before Him,
For them that feared Y, and that *thought upon His name*.
And they shall be Mine, saith Y of hosts.
In the day that I do make, even Mine own treasure;
And I will spare them, as a man spareth

93

His own son that serveth him.
Then shall ye again discern between the righteous and the wicked,
Between him that serveth God
And him that serveth Him not [italics added]. (3:13–18)

The text contrasts two different groups of people: the one speaks strongly against God; the other fears God. Those who speak against God do not see the difference between the righteous and the wicked. It does not seem to matter at all whether one serves God or not. On the contrary, the proud are happy and the wicked, "built up" and delivered. It is useless to keep God's charge to man. God himself is indifferent toward the question whether a man walks in His ways or not. According to them, God is unconcerned. He does not act providentially toward man. It is, however, God's providential action toward his creation that establishes God's "name." The people whose words are "all too strong" against God maintain that God is indifferent toward the human condition and does not act in one way or another toward man. According to them, God is but he has no "name." In the language of the psalmist one may say of them that they do not know the name of Y, they do not believe that God does not forsake them that seek him.

The other group, the one designated as "they that feared Y" also speak, but not against God. They speak "one with another." The prophet does not state explicitly what the subject matter of their discussion is. However, a careful reading of the text reveals it. The key word in the Hebrew is *az* at the beginning of the reference to those who fear God. *Then* do they speak to each other. What they have to say continues the discussion started by those who speak against God. Does it profit a person to serve God? Does it matter to God whether a person is righteous or not? Does God act in relation to man? Does he reveal his concern by such action? Does he have a "name"? The first group denies it all; the second group affirms. They put their trust in the "name" of Y. God listens to what they affirm: he hears and remembers them. They are declared

God's own treasure. They are spared, "as a man spareth his own son," so that the difference between the righteous and the wicked becomes clear for all to see. When this happens, God reveals what those who speak against him denied, he makes known his name anew. What now is *hoshvei Sh'mo?* Those who think upon his name? Hardly. Apart from the fact that the expression would be vacuous, it has no place in the context. Both groups which are described think upon God's name: the one negatively, the other positively. However, the Hebrew, *hashav*, does not only mean, to think, but also, to esteem, to value, to respect.[22] The *hoshvei Sh'mo* are not those who think upon His name, as the accepted translation would have it; but those who esteem or respect the name of Y. Those who speak strongly against God, denying that he considers man, really speak against his "name," against the belief that God establishes his name by his providential acts toward man. Whereas those who fear him and, taking up the challenge, "speak to one another" in refutation of such denial, are the ones who esteem his "name"; they respect the manifestations of the divine care for man as they occurred in the past and are willing to put their trust in the continuation of such manifestation in the future. They are exactly what the first group is not, i.e., *hoshvei Sh'mo.*

We may now turn to the interpretation of a rather difficult verse in Proverbs. The author asks God that he give him neither poverty nor riches and says:

> Feed me with my allotted bread;
> Lest I be full, and deny, and say:
> Who is Y?
> Or lest I be poor, and steal,
> And profane the name of my God. (30:8–9)

Such is the rendering of the J.P.S. translation and it seems to make good sense. In fact, the translation is based on some of the classical Jewish commentaries.[23] The only objection one has is that nowhere in the Bible does the verb, *tafas,* mean, to profane. The R.V. is somewhat nearer to the truth when it translates: lest I be poor, and steal, and take the name of my God in vain. Regrettably, while *tafas* may mean, to take, it never means to take in vain. "To take the name of God in vain" is, of course, biblical, but the Hebrew for it cannot— by the widest stretch of imagination—be connected with the verb used here in the Hebrew original. *Tafas* does mean, to take, but, to take by force, to capture, to conquer, to hold someone or something forcefully. But what can it mean: lest I be poor, and steal, and take by force (or capture) the name of my God? On the basis of the parallelism, the verb *tafasti* in the second part of the verse corresponds to *kihashti* (lest I deny) in the first part. As riches may lead a man astray into believing in his independence of God and may cause him to think that he was in no need of Him, poverty too, which might cause him to steal, may lead him to a similar denial. But how? We recall the profuse biblical tradition concerning the relationship between the poor and the name of God. We have heard Zephaniah's call to "the afflicted and the poor" that they should "take refuge in the name of Y." We have heard the same idea expressed by Isaiah and found it repeated in the Psalms. We have seen how, in the same vein, in Proverbs the name of Y is called "a strong tower," a place of refuge. Now, a person who because of poverty steals does not "take refuge in the name of Y," as Isaiah, Zephaniah, the psalmist would want him to do. He does not put his trust in the "name" of God, i.e., in the providential concern of God for the poor, by whose manifestation God's "name" is established. There is a similarity between his action and the attitude of the rich. The man of possession imagines himself independent and in no need of God, thus he denies Him. But the poor who steals does not depend on God either. Instead of relying on the "name" of God that He made for himself as the one who does not forsake those who seek Him, the poor—when he steals—relies on himself. As the rich, he too denies; he denies that the "name" of God is a "strong tower." In a sense, he takes over a divine function. In a situation in which he ought to rely on divine providence, he provides himself for himself, as if there were no God, whose name is Provider, Redeemer, Savior. As if by force, he takes possession of something that does not duly belong to him. He "captures" the "name" of God, the function of providential care, he does it violence. He is a usurper. We therefore translate:

> Or lest I be poor, and steal,
> And usurp the name of my God.

Since God establishes his "name" on every occasion, when he acts, creating, judging, guiding, saving, the psalmist may well exclaim:

> As is Thy name, O God,
> So is Thy praise unto the ends of the earth;
> Thy right hand is full of *sedeq*. (48:11)

Only because God's name is represented by the manifestations of the divine deed in the universe can one praise him according to his name. This is underlined by the conclusion of the verse. Praising God's name, one praises him for what he performs with his "right hand." We leave the word *sedeq* untranslated. For, as we yet plan to show, *sedeq* is much more than righteousness. Indeed, all divine action, directed toward God's creation, may be subsumed under the term of enacting *sedeq*.

NAME AND MEMORIAL

In a goodly number of passages in the Bible we find the words *shem* and *zekher*, name and memorial, related to each other. They are not synonymous, yet there is some connection between them. When at the beginning of his mission, a rather hesitant Moses desires to know what he should say to the children of Israel should they inquire after God's name, the answer is given to him in two versions. At first, God says to

Moses: "Thus shalt thou say unto the children of Israel: I
Am hath sent me unto you." But the Bible continues: "And
God said moreover unto Moses: 'Thus shalt thou say unto
the children of Israel: Y, the God of your fathers, the God of
Abraham, the God of Isaac, and the God of Jacob, hath sent
me unto you; this is My name for ever; and this is My
memorial unto all generations!'"[24] The first form of the answer
to Moses is comparatively easy to explain. The anticipated
question of the children of Israel, what is His name? would
not be a mere matter of curiosity about a name. What difference would it make to them what the name was! What they
would want to know would be: How does this God make himself known? What are his actions like toward man, by which
he may be called and referred to? And indeed, in the answer
not a name is made known to Moses, but an activity. I Am
hath sent me unto you. Let this knowledge be enough for
them. I am the God who sends a messenger to redeem and to
save. It is by this action that I desire to be known by them. I
Am the One who sends thee; that is my "name" for them. But
what is the significance of the more elaborate final answer
which follows? And what is meant by the phrase: This is My
name and this My memorial? What is the name and what the
memorial? The syntax proves that the two are not synonymous.
What is the difference between them? What is the one and
what the other and in which way does the memorial relate to
the name?[25]

We note that *shem* and *zekher*, having once been associated
with each other, often appear together in the Bible. Isaiah, for
instance, says: "To Thy name and to Thy memorial is the
desire of our soul."[26] The intensity of the soul's longing for
the name, which comes through even stronger in the Hebrew
text than in the translation, illustrates significantly our thesis
that God establishes his name from occasion to occasion in
acts of guiding or saving providence. One may associate little
sense with a soul's longing for the name of someone, be it
even the name of God; but one may appreciate the strength of

a deeply religious soul's desire to witness the acts of divine self-revelation which establish God's "name." However, Isaiah's words here, while obviously leaning on Exodus, do not help us in clarifying the distinction between name and memorial. We find an even fuller reflection of the text in Exodus in the words of the psalmist, who says: "O Y, Thy name endureth for ever; Thy memorial, O Y, throughout all generations."[27] This, of course, is no more illuminating than the original phrase in Exodus. We believe that through the analysis of two psalms, which treat our subject, we may be able to cast a light on our present problem. In Psalm 102 we read:

But thou, O Y, sittest enthroned for ever;
And Thy memorial is unto all generations.[28]
Thou wilt arise, and have compassion upon Zion;
For it is time to be gracious unto her, for the appointed time is come.
For Thy servants take pleasure in her stones,
And love her dust.
So the nations will fear the name of Y,
And all the kings of the earth Thy glory;
When Y hath built up Zion.
When He hath appeared in His glory;
When He hath regarded the prayer of the destitute,
And hath not despised their prayer. (vss. 13–18)

What is noteworthy in this text? All the four elements of the text in Exodus, which presented us with our problem, occur here too. In verse 13 we have the word, *l'olam*, for ever, as the phrase, *l'dor va'dor*, from generation to generation, and also the concept of *zekher*, memorial; in verse 16 the name of Y is mentioned. However, in the association of the four terms with each other there is a deviation from Exodus. *Zekher* is connected with *l'dor va'dor* exactly as in Exodus, but *l'olam* is separated from *shem*, unlike in Exodus. *L'olam* is associated with the verb, *tesheb;* the connection between it and *shem* is missing. The concept of *shem* is—one is almost inclined to say—loudly absent in the opening part of our quotation, only to make its appearance in the further elaboration of the theme and, quite clearly, as the consequence of a divine act, that of God's having compassion on Zion. We believe that the specific way in which the four elements of the text in Exodus are used here in deviation from Exodus contains the key to the understanding of the distinction between *shem,* name, and *zekher,* memorial. But before we go any further in the interpretation of the passage before us, it may be useful to introduce another text. In Psalm 74 we read:

They have set Thy sanctuary on fire;
They have profaned the dwelling place of Thy *name* even to the
  ground.[29]
They said in their heart: 'Let us make havoc of them altogether';
They have burned up all the meeting-places of God in the land.
We see not our signs;
There is no more any prophet;
Neither is there among us any that knoweth how long.
How long, O God, shall the adversary reproach?
Shall the enemy blaspheme Thy *name* for ever?
Why withdrawest Thou Thy hand, even Thy right hand?
Draw it out of Thy bosom and consume them.
Yet God is my King of old,
Working salvation in the midst of the earth.
Thou didst break the sea in pieces by Thy strength;
Thou didst shatter the heads of the sea-monsters in the waters.
Thou didst crush the heads of leviathan,
Thou gavest him to be food to the folk inhabiting the wilderness.
Thou didst cleave fountain and brook;
Thou driest up ever-flowing rivers.
Thine is the day, Thine also the night;
Thou hast established luminary and sun.
Thou hast set all the borders of the earth;
Thou hast made summer and winter.
Remember this, O enemy, that hath reproached Y.
A base people have blasphemed Thy *name.*
O deliver not the soul of Thy turtledove unto the wild beast;
Forget not the life of Thy poor for ever.
Look upon the covenant;

For the dark places of the land are full of the habitations of violence.
O let not the oppressed turn back in confusion;
Let the poor and needy praise Thy *name*.
Arise, O God, plead Thine own cause;
Remember Thy reproach all the day at the hand of base man [italics added]. (vss. 7–22)[30]

There are four references to "the name" in these verses. It is repeatedly bemoaned how the enemy blasphemes the name of God. The plaint leads up to the concluding plea that God may bring it about that the poor and needy may praise his name. However, in this psalm we also learn why the adversary is able to blaspheme and on what it depends that the poor and oppressed may be able to praise.

The enemy may profane the name because God has withdrawn his hand, even his right hand. It is the same right hand, of which we have heard the psalmist say at the close of the previous section in this chapter, that it is full of *sedeq*. It is full of *sedeq*, when it acts, when it performs the deeds of divine *sedeq;* thus creating the name, so that the psalmist could exclaim: as is Thy name, so is Thy praise. But when the hand is withdrawn, when God is passive, when he does not act full of *sedeq*, when—as the psalmist also puts it in our text—"we see not our signs" and "there is no more any prophet," when no message from God reaches man and God is silent, then the name fades. It is the hour of the adversary. Then he dare profane the name and blaspheme. Yet, even though the enemy does profane and God is passive and silent, God remains "my King," because he is the "King of old, working salvation in the midst of the earth." Then follow the lines beginning with the words: Thou didst, Thou gavest, Thou hast, which describe the divine deeds of providential order by which God works his salvation in the midst of the earth. But are not these the deeds of divine self-revelation by which, as we have found, God establishes his name! The sequence of thought would then be as follows: because of God's temporary passivity, God may be defied by the adversary and his name be profaned, because indeed God at such an hour has no contemporary "name." God has withdrawn, he is silent; he does not make himself known to the contemporary generation. Yet, he is King, though King of old. For he did establish his name in the past. And with this the psalmist turns to the enemy: "Remember this!" Although at the moment "we see not our signs" and there are no name-creating present-day manifestations of divine providence, there is much to remember. God is still King, for of old he has established his name, which events —though not experienced in the present—ought to be remembered and the resulting name respected. However, a "base enemy" is not impressed by a name that was effective only in the past and exists only if it is recalled by the memory of faith. Thus the psalmist prays for a new revelation of the name, a new manifestation of God's providential guidance and care for his people. Let God give up his passivity; let him draw his right hand "out of his bosom." Let him not forget "the life of his poor for ever." May he act on their behalf, that "the oppressed shall not have to turn back in confusion." "Let the poor and needy praise Thy name," not the name of old, which is to be remembered, but the name newly revealed to them in the act of their contemporary salvation.

The analysis of this psalm leads us to an interesting conclusion. There are two kinds of divine names: those revealed to past generations and that which is made known to a contemporary generation. Those revealed in the past become a tradition, they are remembered; the one of the present becomes known in contemporary experience. Are we not entitled to say that the "names" revealed to past generations, which are preserved by the memory of tradition, are God's memorial, his *zekher;* but a name revealed in a contemporary experience, the name made known to me and not to my ancestors, is God's *shem?*

Let us now turn back to the starting point of our analysis, to our quotation from Psalm 102. We shall bring it once again in a somewhat different and more literal version.

But Thou, O Y, *sittest* for ever;
And Thy memorial is from generation to generation.
Arise, Thou, and have compassion upon Zion;

. . . .

So the nations will fear the name of Y,
And all the kings of the earth Thy glory;
When Y hath built up Zion,
When He hath appeared in His glory;
When He hath regarded the prayer of the destitute [italics added].

We believe that the theme of this psalm is the same as that of 74 and it expresses the same thought. We do not follow the accepted translations of either the first or the second or the third line in our quotation. The verb, *tesheb,* in the Hebrew original does not mean, "sittest enthroned," but simply, "sittest."[31] We fully appreciate the difficulty that such a literal translation raises. That God sittest for ever is a meaningless statement. The difficulty is easily resolved. Undoubtedly, *tesheb* in the first line is the opposite to *taqum* (arise) in the third. One should, however, also realize that *atta taqum* in the third line is not to be translated as, "Thou wilt arise." The phrase is not a prophecy, but a prayer; just as the phrase which follows immediately after it, *t'rahem Zion,* have compassion upon Zion. The meaning is better rendered as, "Arise, Thou, and have compassion upon Zion." The sentence is the exact equivalent of what we have found in verse 22 of Psalm 74: "Arise, O God, plead Thine own cause." But there, as we saw, the plea, arise, and the entire prayer complex connected with it, really meant: give up your passivity, "draw Thy hand out of Thy bosom," and make Thy name known anew. Similarly, in our present text, *atta taqum,* "arise, Thou," is a plea that God act on behalf of Zion. But such a prayer is necessary because, in the psalmist experience, God is passive toward the fate of Zion. It is in this sense that *taqum* and *tesheb* are related to each other as opposites. "But Thou, O Y, sittest for ever" means: Thou, O Y, art passive, showest Thyself unconcerned. In the language of Psalm 74 one might also say: Thou, O Y, hast withdrawn Thy hand, even Thy right hand. And as in Psalm 74, because of God's passivity, there are no signs to be seen, no present-day manifestations of the divine name, so in our psalm too. God "sits," he does not make his name known anew.[32] What is left is the memory of the old manifestations of the name. "Thy memorial from generation to generation." But, of course, the nations and their kings are not much impressed with the remembered manifestations of the name of old. They do not fear "the King of old." Therefore the prayer: Arise, Thou; give up Thy silence and passivity, have compassion on Zion. In the divine act of Zion's salvation, God appears in his glory. Thus he establishes his name anew in a contemporary situation. He will no longer be known only by his "memorial from generation to generation," but also by the revelation of his very present glory. "So the nations will fear the name of Y and all the kings of the earth Thy glory" corresponds to the line in Psalm 74: "Let the poor and needy praise Thy name." What is for the poor and needy cause for praise is cause enough for the haughty and overbearing for fear.

We may now revert to the text in Exodus, which was the starting point of this our discussion. The first answer to the question about the name of God was: "I Am hath sent me unto you." By the sending of Moses to them to save them He who Is establishes His name with the children of Israel. The final answer to the question, however, was: "Y, the *Elohim* of your fathers, the *Elohim* of Abraham, the *Elohim* of Isaac, and the *Elohim* of Jacob, hath sent me unto you; this is My name for ever, and this My memorial from generation to generation." We have left the word, *Elohim* (God) untranslated, in order to recall what we have found in a previous chapter about Y being *Elohim*. We saw that Y becomes *Elohim* for a person or a people through the providential acts by which he relates himself to human beings. Through such acts Y became *Elohim* of each patriarch. But to become *Elohim* for someone in such a manner is the same as establishing Y's name for him through deeds of divine concern. In the very act in which Y makes Himself *Elohim* for a person, He reveals himself to him in such a manner that He can be named; for instance, the Savior, the Redeemer, the Merciful, etc. The *Elohim* of Abraham, of Isaac, of Jacob, each is a name of Y. But they are names of Y only for Abraham, for Isaac, for Jacob. They are not names *for* those who came after them. For them, they are names made known to the patriarchs; names remembered, not experienced in an act of divine concern directed to them. It is this name, "the *Elohim* of your fathers," that the Bible says: "this is My memorial." To what, however, does the phrase refer: "this is My name for ever"? In our opinion it does not relate to Y, with which the longer, second version of God's answer begins. As we pointed out earlier, the question about the name is not to be understood in the literal sense. And indeed, as we also saw, the first, shorter answer to the question was given in terms of divine action. "I Am hath sent me unto you" is the name by which God makes himself known to the children of Israel. But this name is taken up again in the more explicit form of the divine answer. "Y, the *Elohim* of your fathers . . . hath sent me unto you." By sending Moses to them Y makes himself known to them in such a manner they are able to name Him; for instance, He who is leading us out of Egypt. In this manner, Y who in the past was the *Elohim* of Abraham, of Isaac, of Jacob, the *Elohim* "of old," becomes their own *Elohim*. The name is not one that is remembered, but one learned in personal experience. We shall therefore say that "*Elohim* of your fathers," the manifestation of his name-establishing providence, is Y's memorial; He who "hath sent me unto you," or "Your *Elohim*," is Y's name, the one by which He makes himself known to a contemporary generation.

Since the "memorial" is passed on by tradition from generation to generation it is proper that it should be said of it that it is *l'dor dor*. But we do not translate the phrase as "unto all generations." Such rendering makes it synonymous with *l'olam,* that is said of the name. But as distinct as is *shem* from *zekher,* so is also *l'olam* from *l'dor dor.* The memorial is not one unto *all* generations. It is *shem* at least to the generation to which it is revealed, and its impact may be so powerful that it may remain a *shem* even for the immediately proceeding generation. It is for this reason that we translate: this is My memorial from generation to generation. However, what does it mean that the name is *l'olam,* for ever. That God sent Moses to the children of Israel was a single event that happened once in history. By this act God established one of his names with them. But shall we not say that what was name for the generation of the Exodus becomes memorial for future generations? The Exodus, by which God made his name at the time of Moses, has a unique place in the history of the Jewish people. This name is unlike any other name by which God makes himself known to individual Jews or to a specific generation of Jews. Innumerable passages testify to it in the Bible. We shall consider a most revealing passage in Jeremiah which may help us to clarify the point we wish to make. Addressing God in prayer, Jeremiah says, among other things:

Who didst set signs and wonders in the land of Egypt, even unto this day, and in Israel and among other men; and madest Thee a name, as at this day; and didst bring forth Thy people Israel out of the land of Egypt with signs, and with wonders, and with a strong hand . . . ; and gavest them this land, which Thou didst swear to their fathers to give them . . . ; and they came in, and possessed it; but they hearkened not to Thy voice, neither walked in Thy law . . . ; therefore Thou hast caused all this evil to befall them; behold the mounds, they are come unto the city to take it; and the city is given into the hand of the Chaldeans that fight against it. . . .[33]

Three interesting points emerge from this text. Of the signs and wonders which God wrought in Egypt centuries before Jeremiah, the prophet says: "even unto this day." Of the name, which God made himself by bringing them out of the land of Egypt, it is said: "as at this day." The generation that was led out of Egypt and the one that took possession of the promised land, as well as the one that was contemporary with Jeremiah, are all treated as one and the same generation. They were brought forth from Egypt, they were given the land, they came and possessed it, they sinned and were given over into the hands of the Chaldeans. The three points, which we have singled out, have one thing in common: they treat the past as if it were the present. The signs and the wonders, which God did "even unto this day," obviously mean that their impact was lasting, as if they had happened in the days of Jeremiah. The same is affirmed about the name that God made himself by leading Israel out of Egypt through the signs and wonders: "as at this day." This name, He who leads them out of Egypt, never faded. It remained with Israel as if it had been established in Israel as if "at this day." Only because of this may Jeremiah identify the generation of Jews, besieged in Jerusalem in his own days, with the generation of the Exodus. Since the miracles were alive even unto his own days, since the impact of the name was still fresh as in the days on which it was first made known, all past history could be experienced as if it happened unto the contemporary generation, as if they themselves had left Egypt. All the more grievous was their failure.

We see then that the importance of the Exodus in the history of the Jewish people was so decisive that in the days of Jeremiah the name, which God made for himself by the Exodus, was still a name and had not become a memorial yet. And so it was in the days of Daniel and also in the days of Ezra and Nehemiah. In the prayers of their times the events of the Exodus are referred to as the occasion on which God made himself a name "as at this day."[34] And so it remained through all the ages. In the Ten Commandments God calls himself, "Y, thy God, who hath brought thee out of the land of Egypt." This, of course, is addressed to every Jew in every generation. For the Jew the name by which he knows God is: Y, my God, who hath led me out of Egypt. Correspondingly, the historic Jew identifies himself with all Jewish

107

generations of the past. All past for him is one enduring present. This identification of the Jew with all previous generations by way of the name, which God made himself in Egypt "as at this day," is found in numerous places of the Bible. It is most eloquently expressed in the words that were traditionally recited by the man who annually offered the first fruit of his land to God in the Temple of Jerusalem. After the reference to the "wandering Aramean," whom he called, "my father" he continued:

And the Egyptians dealt with us, and afflicted us and laid upon us hard bondage. And we cried unto Y, the God of our fathers, and Y heard our voice, and saw our affliction, and our toil, and our oppression. And Y brought us forth out of Egypt with a mighty hand, and with an outstretched arm, and with great terribleness, and with signs, and with wonders. And He hath brought us into this place, and hath given us this land, a land flowing with milk and honey. And now, behold, I have brought the first fruit of the land, which Thou, O Y, hast given me.[35]

As in the passage we have quoted from Jeremiah, here too the Jew—and this time not a prophet—experiences Jewish history since Egypt as his own life. All generations are one enduring generation. All past is transformed into one lasting present through the name of God, which remains for all generations of Jews, He who has led us out of Egypt.[36]

In whatever manner God reveals himself to an individual or to an entire generation, that becomes His name for that individual or for that generation. As the people pass, what was name for them becomes memorial for those who follow. There is only one exception. The name: Y, thy God, who hath led thee out of the land of Egypt never became a memorial. It has remained His name for the Jew for all times. We are now in a position to understand the full significance of our text from Exodus. The name, *Elohim* of Abraham, *Elohim* of Isaac, *Elohim* of Jacob, was name for each of the patriarchs, but became a memorial for their children after them. But when God made himself known to Israel by sending Moses to them, he revealed a name to them that is everlasting: Y, your God, who leads you out of Egypt. Of it God says: This is my name for ever. *"Elohim* of the fathers" is the memorial from generation to generation; *Elohim* of Israel, the name for ever.

THE NAME CALLED OVER THING OR PERSON

In this section we shall be concerned with the interpretation of the phrase: the name of God is called upon someone or something. Of Israel it is said in the Bible: "the name of Y is called upon thee." Jeremiah says to God: "Thy name was called on me, O Y God of Hosts." Of the Temple of Jerusalem God says through the mouth of Jeremiah: "this house whereupon My name is called."[37] Usually, these expressions are taken to mean that Israel is called Y's people; Jeremiah, Y's prophet; and the Temple, Y's house. This, however, is much too superficial an interpretation. As the phrase is used in connection with Israel, we encounter the same difficulty which we raised at the opening of this chapter. While it is true that Israel is often called in the Bible the people of Y, the expression cannot mean that the name of Y is called upon it. Y itself is the name and the name of Y is the "name" of the name. "The name of Y is called upon thee" means that the "name" of the name is called upon Israel. This, obviously, is not identical with the phrase, the people of Y.

We shall first examine the case of the Temple, upon which God's name is called. We shall do so because of a passage in Jeremiah, in which the expression is practically paralleled by another similar one. In chapter 7 we read:

Is this house, whereupon My name is called, become a den of robbers in your eyes. Behold, I, even I, have seen it, saith Y. For go ye now unto My place which was in Shiloh, where I caused My name to dwell at the first, and see what I did to it for the wickedness of My people Israel. (vss. 11–12)

We learn from these words that "My place" is the places where God causes "his name to dwell." And since it is said that God caused his name to dwell in Shiloh "at the first," it is intimated that now he causes it to dwell in Jerusalem; now the Temple is "My place." But the Temple is described as the house, "whereupon My name is called." Since, however, what Shiloh was "at the first" Jerusalem is now, we may conclude that "whereupon My name is called" is the equivalent of, "where I cause My name to dwell." Only that now we are confronted with a new difficulty. What does it mean that God causes his name to dwell in a certain place? There is a sufficient number of biblical texts available to help us clarify this point.

It is important to note that in the numerous passages in the books of Kings and Chronicles, where the story of the building of the Temple is told, it is consistently stated, and quite clearly for the sake of emphasis, that David and Solomon were planning to build to the name of Y.[38] Most interesting is a passage in I Chronicles. At first we read:

And David said: Solomon my son is young and tender and the house that is to be builded for Y must be exceeding magnificent. . . . I will therefore make preparation for him. . . . Then he called for Solomon his son, and charged him to build a house for Y, the God of Israel.

Upon this follows David's actual charge to Solomon. And now we read:

My son, as for me, it was in my heart to build a house *unto the name of Y* my God. But the word of Y came to me saying: Thou hast shed blood abundantly. . . . Thou shalt not build a house *unto My name*. . . . Behold, a son shall be born to thee, who shall be a man of rest . . . for his name shall be Solomon. . . . He shall build a house *for My name*. . . . Now, my son, Y be with thee . . . and build the house of Y thy God . . . arise therefore, and build ye the sanctuary of Y God, to bring the ark of the covenant of Y, and the holy vessels of God, unto the house that is to be built to *the name of Y* [italics added].[39]

110

The opening phrase of our quotation, "And David said," is, of course, not an introduction for actual words spoken by David. What follows are thoughts of David formulated by the biblical narrator. The narrator uses the expression, "a house for Y," twice. But quite clearly, strongest emphasis is laid on the actual words of David to his son on the idea that "the house of Y" or "the sanctuary of Y," terms used by David himself, are to build to the name of Y. This is brought out in the continuous repetition of the phrase, which is taken up even into the terminology of God's answer to David. The very fact that the narrator uses the phrase, "a house for Y," only to replace it, immediately afterward, with such dramatic emphasis by, a house unto the name of Y, serves the purpose of directing our attention to what is essential in this "house for Y." It is not really a house for Y, but one for the name of Y.

A similar stylistic device is also used in the prayer of Solomon at the dedication of the Temple which David charged him to build. At first we read:

Then spoke Solomon:
Y hath said that He would dwell in the thick darkness.
I have surely built Thee a house of habitation,
A place for Thy dwelling for ever.[40]

As in our quotation above from I Chronicles, the words "And David said," so here the phrase, "Then spoke Solomon," were not actual words spoken to anyone. They might have been thoughts in the mind of Solomon expressed in the language of the narrator, or, if spoken at all, they were addressed to God in the solitude of prayer. As there the narrator speaks of a "house for Y," so here too, in these not really spoken words, a "house of habitation" is built unto God. But here too, as in I Chronicles, as the words are addressed to people, to whom the event is explained, as "the King turned his face about and blessed all the congregation of Israel" and spoke to them, we have the same emphatic

111

repetition that the house was planned "unto the name Y" and was so built "unto the name of Y." Of this house God, too, says that it was to be built that "My name might be there." "A house for Y" or a "house of habitation" for Him was occasionally used as a mere colloquialism. Its meaning was: a house unto the name of Y.

However, what does it mean to build a house "unto the name of Y"? As we have already indicated, what for David and Solomon was built "unto the name of Y," God referred to it as the house where "his name might be there." And indeed, the equivalent of this expression we find in a number of places. In Deuteronomy we read:

Unto the place which Y your God shall choose out of all your tribes to put His name there, even unto His habitation shall ye seek, and thither thou shall come.[41]

"His habitation" is the place where God "puts his name there."[42] But in the same context, the sanctuary is also called, as Jeremiah called it too, the place which God chooses "to cause His name to dwell there."[43] It is the phrase which is most often used in Deuteronomy. We have found then that the house unto the name of Y is the one in which Y's name "is there," into which God "puts his name," or in which "he causes his name to dwell." And once again we are asking ourselves: what is the meaning of all this? We shall turn again to the well-known dedicatory prayer of King Solomon, in which we may find the answer to our quest. Having made reference to the intentions of his father David and to the promise of God, he continues:

Now therefore, O God of Israel, let Thy word, I pray Thee, be verified, which Thou didst speak unto Thy servant David my father.

But will God in very truth dwell on earth? behold, heaven and the heaven of heavens cannot contain Thee; how much less this house that I have builded! Yet have Thou respect unto the prayer of Thy servant, and to this supplication, O Y my God, to hearken unto the cry and to the prayer which Thy servant prayeth before

Thee this day; that Thine eyes may be open toward this house night and day, even toward the place whereof Thou hast said: *My name shall be there,* to hearken unto the prayer which Thy servant shall pray toward this place. And hearken Thou to the supplication of Thy servant, and of Thy people Israel, when they shall pray toward this place; yea, hear Thou in heaven Thy dwelling place; and when Thou hearest, forgive [italics added].[44]

We may now understand why it is emphasized with such intensity that the house of Y is the house built "unto His name." It is to exclude the idea that the place was a dwelling place for God himself. In this prayer Solomon calls the heaven "Thy dwelling place," but even that is only a figure of speech, and it is not to be taken literally. For in the same prayer he also says of God that neither the heaven nor the heaven of heavens can contain God. The emphasis on "the house unto His name" is to exclude the crude concept of an anthropomorphic dwelling of God in space. But Solomon's prayer also reveals a great deal about the meaning of the idea that "My name shall be there." Solomon's plea is that since God promised that his name will be there, he ought to forgive the sins repented there. In the next part of the prayer there follows an elaboration of what he means, by a number of examples. When in a case of litigation a man takes an oath before God's altar in His house, may God take note of it in a visible manner by condemning the wicked "to bring his way upon his own head" and by justifying the righteous "to give him according to his righteousness." When Israel is beaten by an enemy because of their sins, if they then repent and turn in supplication "in this house," may God answer their prayer by help against the enemy. In times of a drought or famine or pestilence, they turn from their sins and "pray toward this place," may God forgive them and grant them rain, satisfy their need, and remove sickness or pestilence from them. And all this is asked for because God said of this house that his name shall be there. But is not such answer to prayer visible manifestation of divine providence? Is not the divine action, which constitutes the answer, the manner in which God makes himself known to people? We have found earlier that exactly by such providential self-manifestations God establishes his "name" among men. We shall, therefore, say that by the manifest efficacy of prayer and repentance submitted in the Temple, God makes himself known to the supplicant. "His name is there" or "He puts His name there" will then mean that through the convincing answer to prayer, God consistently reveals himself in the Temple, he forever makes himself a name there. "He causes his name to dwell there" expresses the constancy of divine self-revelation through acts of divine providence in answer to human plea and repentance. The Temple was built "unto the name of Y," for through the Temple God made himself known, he made himself "a name" in Israel and among the nations. Since, however, Jeremiah, as we have seen, uses the two phrases— "the house where God causes his name to dwell" and "the house whereupon God's name is called"—interchangeably, we may conclude that Jeremiah's "this house whereupon My name is called" means the house through which God makes himself "a name" in the world. It is God's house in the sense that it is the place where God's concern for man is consistently made manifest.

This interpretation is supported by a further passage in Solomon's prayer, which seems to summarize the various points which we have made thus far. It runs as follows:

Moreover concerning the stranger that is not of Thy people Israel, when he shall come out of a far country for Thy name's sake—for they shall hear of Thy great name, and of Thy mighty hand, and of Thine outstretched arm—when he shall come and pray toward this house; hear Thou in heaven Thy dwellingplace, and do according to all that the stranger calleth to Thee for; that all the peoples of the earth may know Thy name, to fear Thee, as doth Thy people Israel, and that they may know that Thy name is called upon this house which I have built.[45]

According to these words the stranger may know of God's name in two different ways. At first, he is attracted to the Temple by God's great name because he has learned of the mighty deeds of the God of Israel. Because of that, he will come and pray in the Temple. When this happens, let God answer his prayer so that "the peoples of all the earth" may know the name. This is a second knowledge. Whereas originally they were attracted by the name that God made for himself by what he did for Israel, let them learn of God's name in a new sense, i.e., by what God does for them, so that they too may fear Thee as "doth Thy people Israel." Let them have the same kind of experience of the divine name. It is, then, here clearly stated that by answering convincingly a prayer, God makes his name known. But since this happens at the Temple chosen by God, by learning of God's name in this manner they will also know that "Thy name is called upon this house." The Temple, in a sense, stands for a name of God; it makes God renowned. In this sense, the name of God is upon it.

As we saw, Jeremiah applies the expression to himself and says of himself that the name of God is called upon him. Now to prophesy, according to biblical terminology, is to speak "in the name of Y."[46] To speak in the name of someone means, of course, to speak with his authority; one may do that if such authority has been communicated to one. But in all such communication something is being revealed to the one who is being authorized by the one who authorizes, a wish, a desire, an intention. The attorney learns to know about his client. But more than that, something of the client, a function, the ability to act in a certain manner, is being invested in the attorney. The prophet knows God because God makes himself known to him in an act of revelation. He can call God by a name appropriate to the divine revelation granted to him. This alone, however, would not enable him to speak in God's name. God also makes Himself known to him by revealing an intention, a will, a desire, a divine word. The prophet knows God

115

also by the meaning of the word that is communicated to him. He can "name" God by this word. But he can speak in the name of God, because the word is not communicated but also entrusted to him. "Thus shalt thou speak!" Authority is invested in him. Something of God is passed on to him. What shall we call it? It is something by which the prophet may call God—a name. Something very similar to what God says of the Temple is also said about the prophet. Of the Temple God said that he "puts his name there"; of the prophet he says: "My name is in him." In another place God says of the prophet: "and I will put My words in his mouth."[47] The words too constitute a divine "name." God is made known by them. God's name is in the prophet because God puts His words in his mouth. Thus, the prophet may speak in the name of God.[48]

There is an interesting passage in Jeremiah which has important bearing on this matter. Of the false prophets it is said there:

That think to cause My people to forget My name
By their dreams which they tell every man to his neighbor,
As their fathers forgot My name for Baal.
The prophet that hath a dream, let him tell a dream;
And he that hath My word, let him speak My word faithfully. (23: 27–28)

Surely, the false prophets did not intend to cause the people to forget that God's proper name was Y. On the contrary, they pretended to bring to them the word of Y. However, the word was not "put in their mouth." What goes by the word of God is not His word. Thus, the name of God is forgotten. Which name? The one created by the word, by which the true prophet knows his God; the name, which—through the word—enters into the prophet and is in him.

The prophet, speaking "in the name of God," represents the name of God in the world. Through his mission God is made known in the world. He stands for a divine act of self-revelation, for a divine name. What was said in this regard of the Temple may well apply to the prophet too, as indeed Jeremiah applied to himself when he said that God's name was called upon him. God is made known through the prophets. The prophet establishes God's reputation.

We turn now to Israel, on whom the name of God is called. Our analysis of some of the passages in psalms 102 and 74 has shown us how closely the dignity of God's name is associated with the destiny of Israel. When the Temple burns and God withdraws himself from Israel, his name is being profaned and blasphemed. When he rebuilds Zion, he reveals his name anew, which is then respected and feared by the nations. Isaiah expresses the same thought, saying:

Now therefore, what do I here, saith Y,
Seeing that My people is taken away for nought?
They that rule over them do howl, saith Y,
And My name continually all the day is blasphemed.
Therefore My people shall know My name;
Therefore! On that day!—for I am the one who speaks;
Behold, here I am. (52:5–6)[49]

The theme is the same as in the psalms we discussed in the previous section of this chapter. The humiliation of Israel causes that God's name is being blasphemed. God made his name through the manifestation of his providential care for Israel, especially by their liberation from Egypt and by leading them to the promised land. But when God withdraws his providence and Israel is taken away into captivity "for nought," God's reputation, his name, is eclipsed. The very howling of the enemy over Israel is blasphemy to God's name. A new act of redemption is needed that not only saves Israel but also re-establishes the divine reputation. "Therefore," promises God, his name will be made known anew to his people.[50] "Therefore" and on the promised day it will happen, for God will say to them: "behold, here I am." By new acts of redemption he reveals to them his presence which was not experienced by them in the days of their humiliation.

The association between Israel and God's name was expressed most succinctly by Joshua. At a moment of crisis, when the men of Israel were beaten back by the men of Ai, he said in his prayer:

Oh, Y, what shall I say, after that Israel hath turned their backs before their enemies! For when the Canaanites and all the inhabitants of the land hear of it, they will compass us round, and cut off our name from the earth; and what wilt Thou do for Thy great name? (7:8–9)

God's "great name," his renown in history, is inseparable from the name of Israel. God's name shares the destinies of God's people.

There are two passages which throw a most surprising light on our subject. The one found in Deuteronomy. We shall first quote it in the R.V.[51]

And Y hath avouched thee this day to be his peculiar people, as he hath promised thee, and *thou* shouldest keep all his commandments; And to make thee high above all nations which he hath made, in praise, and in name, and in honour; and that thou mayest be an holy people unto Y thy God, as he hath spoken. (26:18–19)

We take it that "in praise, and in name, and in honour" refers to "to make thee high above all nations." The meaning would then be that God elevated Israel in praise, in name, and in honor. The praise, name, and honor, would then be distinctions of Israel. Because of such an interpretation, *l'tiferet* was translated as, "in honour." It was apparently felt that the usual meaning of *tiferet* as glory could not properly apply to a people in this context.[52] A more exact rendering of the Hebrew original would be: "for praise, and for a name, and for glory." The literal translation, however, seems to leave us with a somewhat obscure meaning. The difficulty of interpretation induced the translator, as often in such cases, to find a solution in free translation. Thus, the essential biblical meaning was lost.

The theme of these verses from Deuteronomy occurs also in Jeremiah. One must read both passages together in order to illuminate what appears to be obscure in Deuteronomy. The verse we have in mind reads in the R.V. translation[53] as follows:

For as the girdle cleaveth to the loins of a man, so have I caused to cleave unto me the whole house of Israel, and the whole house of Judah, saith Y; that they might be unto me for a people, and for a name, and for a praise, and for a glory; but they would not hear. (13:11)

Undoubtedly, in expressing what Israel might be unto God, Jeremiah uses the same language that we have found in our quotation from Deuteronomy. They are the very words here and there: *l'am,* for a people, there: *l'am s'gullah,* a peculiar people; *ul'shem,* and for a name; *v'lit'hillah,* and for a praise; *ul'tiferet,* and for a glory. Here and there, it is the same text and both passages must be translated alike. The meaning in Jeremiah is unequivocal. God planned to take Israel unto himself for a people, for a name, for praise and glory. Israel is to become God's people. By what God does for Israel's redemption and preservation, he makes himself a name. By hearing of the mighty deeds of God on behalf of Israel, for instance, in Egypt, the nations learn about God. For the sake of the providence so visibly manifested over Israel, God is praised and glorified. What he does for Israel establishes God's renown in history. This is Jeremiah's meaning; and this is also exactly the meaning in Deuteronomy, too. After having stated that God has destined Israel to become "his peculiar people" and that he made it "high above all nations," the text in Deuteronomy states, as the one in Jeremiah, that God did this so that Israel may become "for a praise, and for a name, and for a glory," all this for God. Through his specific relationship to Israel God makes himself a name in the world. Isaiah, combining *shem* and *tiferet,* says of God's providence over Israel in the days of Moses:

119

So didst Thou lead Thy people,
To make Thyself a name of glory. (63:14)

By leading Israel, God made himself a name of glory; he took Israel unto himself "for a name and for a glory." But whereas Jeremiah speaks of God's disappointment with Israel, Isaiah also speaks of the promise of the future, in which God will renew his name through the ultimate redemption of Israel. Of this time Isaiah says;

For ye shall go out with joy,
And be led forth with peace;
The mountains and the hills shall break forth before you into singing,
And all the trees of the field shall clap their hands.

· · · · · · · · · · · · · · · · · ·

And it shall be to Y for a name,[54]
For an everlasting sign that shall not be cut off. (55:12–13)

This act of redemption in the future will be a name for God, an act by which he will be known anew, but this time for ever. For this name will be an "everlasting sign" that will never again turn into a memorial preserved from generation to generation. After that redemption, there will be no more exile, no more hiding of the face, no more profanation of the name, of the praise, and of the glory.

Jeremiah, who—as we saw—spoke of God's disappointment with Israel, who were intended to be for a name for God, speaks even more beautifully than Isaiah of the time when a restored Jerusalem will be "for a name" for God. We shall quote his words more fully.

Behold, I will bring it healing and cure, and I will cure them; and I will reveal unto them the abundance of peace and truth. And I will cause the captivity of Judah and the captivity of Israel to return, and will build them, as at the first. And I will cleanse them from all their inquity, whereby they have sinned against Me; and I will pardon all their iniquities, whereby they have transgressed against Me. And this city shall be to Me for a name of joy, for a praise and for a glory, before all the nations of the earth, which shall hear all the good that I do unto them, and shall fear and tremble for all the good and for all the peace that I procure unto it. (33:6–9)

Once again we hear of the name and the praise and the glory that Jerusalem, symbolizing her people, for which Israel will be to God "before all the nations of the earth." The nations of the earth will learn to know God by the good that he does to the holy city and its inhabitants. The name God will thus gain, will be one of joy for "the good and the peace that he procures," one of praise and glory.

We may sum up our discussion thus far by saying that in the history of the nations Israel represents the divine reputation. God has made Israel unto himself for a name; in a sense, Israel is "a name" of God. This is the deepest significance of the words of Joshua which we have quoted earlier: if they will cut off our name from the earth, what wilt Thou do for Thy great name? It is with reference to "the great name," which God has made himself through Israel, that King David, using the verbalized form of *gadol*, great, prayed:

And let Thy name be magnified for ever, saying: Y of hosts, God of Israel.[55]

This is not a statement that "Y of hosts" *is* the God of Israel. The entire phrase is God's name in its manifestation in the world. God's name is: "Y of hosts, God of Israel." It is magnified whenever "Y of hosts" reveals himself as the God of Israel. As if to explain this last term, the text in I Chronicles adds: *Elohim* to Israel. But we have already learned that Y becomes *Elohim* to someone when he exercises toward him His preserving providence. "Y of hosts" is *that* over his entire creation. His name, *Elohim* of Israel, is his reputation, which he makes himself by performing his providential acts for Israel in a manner visible to all. Of this historically manifest connection between the "name" of God in the world and the destinies of the Jewish people does the Bible say: "And all the peoples of the earth shall see that the name of Y is called upon thee."[56]

121

MAN AND GOD

TO CALL ON THE NAME

"To call upon the name of Y" is a phrase which occurs quite often in the Bible.[57] Usually, it means turning to God in prayer. The exact meaning of the expression may be easily derived from a well-known passage in Exodus. In that mystery-charged confrontation between God and Moses which follows on the drama of the sin of the Golden Calf, Moses made two requests: that God may show him His ways and that He may show him His glory. The second request was denied to Moses. "Thou canst not see My face for man shall not see Me and live" was God's reply. The first request, however, was granted in the words: "I will make all My goodness pass before thee, and will call upon the name of Y before thee."[58] It is rather surprising to hear God say of himself that he would call upon the name of Y.[59] If that meant that God would proclaim before Moses that his name was Y, the sentence would be void of all significance. There was no need at this stage to make any such proclamation to Moses. Nor could that be any answer to Moses' request for being shown the ways of God. The truth, of course, is that God did show his ways to Moses by "calling upon the name of Y." For so we read in the following chapter the evolvement of the divine answer.

And Y descended in the cloud, and stood with him there, and called upon the name of Y:
Y, Y, God, merciful and gracious, long-suffering, and abundant in goodness and truth; keeping mercy unto the thousandth generation, forgiving iniquity and transgression and sin; and that will by no means clear the guilty; visiting the iniquity of the fathers upon the children, unto the third and unto the fourth generation. (34:6–7)

This description represents divine attributes which have rightly been called "attributes of action,"[60] they determine the ways of God, the principles by which he acts toward men. But acting in accordance with these attributes is what establishes God's name in the world. His ways with men create his

122

names among men. In a sense, these attributes, describing how God deals with his creatures, are his "name." Concerning their proclamation before Moses, God says that He will "call upon the name of Y," meaning that he will reveal to Moses His attributes of action toward men which are His ways and constitute His name. When God calls upon the name of Y, He proclaims them; when man calls upon His name, he appeals to God's attributes of mercy; he prays. He calls that God may activate His "name" toward him. It is for this reason that the psalmist calls to God:

O God, help me by Thy name,
And save me by Thy might.
O God, hear my prayer. (54:3–4)

All prayer is a "call upon the name of Y." It is reliance on His ways with men. He who in prayer calls upon the name of Y recalls God's name-creating providential care in the past and puts his trust in it for the future.

However, it is possible for man to "call upon the name of Y" not only in prayerful intercession. Man may do it before God as God did it before Moses—proclaiming it. Of course, when one does it in this manner, the result is a hymn to God or a prayer of thanksgiving. Moses' great song in Deuteronomy is introduced with the words: "For I will proclaim the name of Y; ascribe ye greatness unto our God." What follows is a hymn in praise of God's ways with men from human experience, the same ways which were at first revealed to Moses with divine authority.

The Rock, His work is perfect;
For all His ways are justice;
A God of faithfulness and without iniquity,
Just and right is He. (32:4)

This, too, is "calling upon the name of Y," proclaiming in gratitude His providential concern by which Moses knew Him. It is true that this hymn of Moses is not introduced with the

123

exact wording, "for I will call upon the name of Y." The exact form of the introduction is: "for I will call the name of Y." This, however, is due to the fact that Moses' hymn is not addressed to God. In his farewell song to his people he describes the ways of God for them. He, indeed, proclaims the name of God. One calls "upon the name of Y," when one confronts God. One may do this in a prayer of intercession, putting one's trust in the "name"; but one may also do it in a prayer of thanksgiving, declaring his goodness and mercies, his "name" experienced, to all. One of the most impressive passages of this kind we find in Isaiah. It is the entire contents of chapter 12. Speaking of the day on which God's anger will be turned from Israel and God will become the comforter, the salvation, the strength, and the song of Israel, the prophet says:

And in that day shall ye say:
Give thanks unto Y, call upon His name;
Declare His doings among the peoples,
Make mention that His name is exalted.
Sing unto Y; for He hath done gloriously;
This is made known in all the earth. (vss. 4–5)[61]

In a thanksgiving prayer one "calls upon the name of Y" by praising Him for His glorious doings, which is essentially a grateful proclaiming of the name which He made known to one by revealing Himself as Comforter and Savior.

At least in one psalm we find both forms of calling upon the name of Y exemplified. In the opening verses of that psalm we read:

The cords of death encompassed me,
And the straits of the nether-world got hold upon me;
I found trouble and sorrow.
But *I called upon the name of Y:*
"I beseech Thee, O Y, deliver my soul [italics added]."

The prayer was answered and deliverance came. The psalmist continues:

How can I repay unto Y
All His bountiful dealings toward me?
I will lift up the cup of salvation,
And call upon the name of Y.

. . . .

I will offer to Thee the sacrifice of thanksgiving,
And will call upon the name of Y [italics added]. (116:3–4, 12–
13, 17)

How different is the calling upon the name of Y, which is
mentioned in the first part of the psalm, from those two in
its latter part. The first is a call from the heart of trouble and
sorrow; the last two are exultant expressions of happiness as
part of joyous thanksgiving. Encompassed by "the cords of
death" one calls upon the name of Y, turning to the Deliverer,
asking for deliverance. After salvation, one calls again upon
the name of Y, turning to the Deliverer, thanking for the
deliverance he has granted.

However, it may happen that as a result of suffering or a
sin a man may become so demoralized that he is no longer
able to call upon the name of Y. The prophet Isaiah is describing such a situation when he says:

And we are all become as one that is unclean,
And all our righteousnesses are as a polluted garment;
And we all do fade as a leaf,
And our iniquities, like the wind, take us away.
And there is none that calleth upon Thy name,
That stirreth up himself to take hold of Thee;
For Thou hast hid Thy face from us,
And hast consumed us by means of our iniquities [italics added].
(64:5–6)

We learn from the prophet's words that to call upon God's
name means to stir oneself to take hold of God. Yet, people
cannot do it, when God hides his face from man and lets them
be consumed in their sins. Why not? Because the hiding of the
face is also the hiding of the name. When God removes himself from man, there are no manifestations of his ways toward

man. He is silent; he is indifferent to man's plight. He becomes "unknown." No name is being revealed in the hour of the hiding of the face. It was about exactly such a situation that we heard the psalmist complain that the adversary is free to profane the divine name. Now we hear that at such times, because in the hour of the hiding of the face there is no contemporary manifestation of the name, even Jews may fail to rely on the name of Y and may not call on it. There are times when the name made known in the past, the memorial, is not enough to induce man to call upon the name in the present. The thought may help us to understand a strange expression in a prayer of Nehemiah, at the conclusion of which he said:

O Y, I beseech Thee, let now Thine ear be attentive to the prayer of Thy servant, and to the prayer of Thy servants, who desire to fear Thy name. (1:11)[62]

"To desire to fear Thy name" is a most surprising concept. If they so desire, let them! But if they only desire to fear God's name but do not fear it in reality, how can such desire be mentioned in support of a request that God answer the prayer of his servants, who desire so ineffectively? Apparently, they desire to fear God's name, but there is something beyond themselves which prevents fulfillment of their desire. What could it be? In the light of the word of Isaiah, the answer to the question seems to be simple: the hiding of the face. Together with Nehemiah the majority of the Jews lived in captivity. The remnant in Judah was heavily afflicted. The walls of Jerusalem were broken down and her gates "burned with fire." The servants of God prayed in a dark hour of the hiding of the face. The name of God, his renown established through his guidance of Israel, had become a mere memory. In their prayers they are asking a new manifestation of divine providence for God's people, for a new revelation of God's "name." They desire to fear God's name; they desire to respect, to treat with awe, the contemporary name, for whose revelation they are praying. They cannot satisfy their desire because "the name" is being withheld in that hour of the hiding of the face. Theirs is the desire but it is of a kind that can only be satisfied with the help of God. As if to say: show us "the name" that we may fear it.

At times, the desire to respect the name may be present, yet man may still plead for divine help in order to be able to call upon the name of God. The psalmist says of such a situation in which a man may find himself:

So shall we not turn back from Thee;
Quicken Thou us, and we will call upon Thy name.

There is the determination not to turn from God. But there is also a sensing of some vital weakness, which—notwithstanding the determination not to turn from God—does not let one call upon his name trustingly. One prays for divine help. "Quicken Thou us," enable us to "call upon Thy name." It is a prayer for divine help to enable one to pray. Only after such preliminary prayer does the psalmist continue and prays:

O Y of hosts, restore us;
Cause Thy face to shine, and we shall be saved. (80:19–20)

This is the calling upon the name, for which the psalmist hoped that Israel might be able to undertake with the help of God. The phrase, "cause Thy face to shine," is the indication why it was for them necessary to plead first: "quicken Thou us." There are moments of the hiding of the face, when even those "who desire to fear Thy name" do not have the strength to call upon it without being first "quickened" by God. It is of such travails of the soul that these words of the psalmist, and the verses quoted from Isaiah and Nehemiah, bring us tidings.

Y IS HIS NAME

There is one more phrase incorporating *shem* (name) in relationship to God which we should like to discuss. We came

127

across it at the beginning of this chapter in the quotation from Exodus: "Y is a man of war, Y is His name." We were not sure that we understood the significance of such a statement. What is really conveyed by saying that the name of Y, who is "a man of war," is Y? Jeremiah, too, as well as Amos, use the expression, Y is His name. An interpretation suggests itself in their case which deserves some consideration. Calling upon the house of Israel to seek God and live, Amos says:

Him that maketh the Pleiades and Orion,
And turneth the shadow of death into the morning,[63]
And darkeneth the day into night;
That calleth forth the waters of the sea,
And poureth them out upon the face of the earth;
Y is His name. (5:8)

God is here described as the omnipotent creator and ruler of the universe. Now, in Chapter 1 we have established that whenever reference is made to the manifestation of God's power and authority, we find the statement: "that they may know that I am Y" or the shorter one: "I am Y." We may, then, perhaps say that here, too, since God is represented in his creative and ruling power, the concluding phrase, "Y is His name," is appropriate. It is a reminder that the divine name Y stands for omnipotence and divine transcendence.[64] The phrase may have the same meaning as it is used by Jeremiah too.[65] This interpretation seems to derive further support from another passage in Jeremiah, where the affirmation about Y and His name is varied by the fact that it is made by God, speaking about himself. The words there are:

Therefore, behold, I will cause them to know,
This once I will cause them to know
My hand and My might;
And they shall know that My name is Y. (16:21)

Here the reference to God's supreme might and power is explicit. Such manifestation of sovereign power will bring the nations the knowledge that His name is Y. This is fully in keeping with our findings in Chapter 1. Of such manifestation we heard the Bible say again and again: "and they will know that I am Y." In this case, "And they shall know that My name is Y," would be the equivalent of the knowledge that He is Y. Neither would such an interpretation of the term, which we are discussing here, contradict our previous conclusions about the name of God. Y is of course the divine name in the proper sense of the word. Our deductions in this chapter thus far dealt only with expressions like "the name of Y," which— as we have repeatedly pointed out—could not be Y, and with passages, where the context proved that the name meant a divine manifestation or self-revelation through divine action, essentially of a providential character, revealing God's ways with men. Nevertheless, it is difficult to be satisfied with this interpretation. Following it, we would have to say that Moses wished to affirm that Y, being "a man of war," well knew how to wage war successfully since "Y is His name," i.e., since He is Y, He has the power to do it. It does not ring true. Unlike the rest of Moses' song, it would be a formulation singularly lacking any poetic dignity.

There is also the additional difficulty that not all passages in which the phrase occurs tolerate this interpretation. When God, speaking through the mouth of Isaiah, says:

I am Y, that is My name;
And My glory I will not give to another,
Neither My praise to graven images. (42:8)

Surely he does not mean to say that, since his name is Y, he is all-powerful and will not recognize the claims of the idols. But, perhaps, an analysis of the entire context, and of the place that our quotation has in it may lead us to the solution of our problem. After the opening verses in which God describes the historic function of his servant, whom he "upholds" and upon whom he has "put his spirit," we read:

Thus saith God, Y,
He that created the heavens, and stretched them forth,

129

He that spread forth the earth and that which cometh out of it,
He that giveth breath unto the people upon it,
And spirit to them that walk therein:
I am Y![66] I have called thee in *Sedeq*
And have taken hold of thy hand,
And kept thee, and set thee for a covenant of the people,
For a light of the nations;
To open the blind eyes,
To bring out the prisoners from the dungeon,
And them that sit in darkness out of the prison-house.
I am Y, that is My name;
And My glory will I not give to another,
Neither My praise to graven images. (vss. 5–8)

One wonders what the connection may be between the declaration that God does not intend to give his praise and glory to the idols and the task which he assigned to his servant. Would not the passage be more complete if it had concluded with the line, "I am Y, that is My name"? We are utterly unprepared for a conclusion which seems to introduce a new idea utterly indifferent to the theme of the passage.

The text before us reminds us of the distinction that we were able to make in the first chapter between the phrases: "that they may know that I am Y" and "that they may know that I am Y their *Elohim*," or simply between the two declarations: "I am Y" and "I am Y their *Elohim*." In our text there are two references to God. In the first one he is described as Y, the Creator of heaven and earth and the source of all life. In the second reference it is maintained that Y, who has just been described as the Lord and Creator, is also the one who has called His servant and taken him by the hand and appointed him for a light of the nations to bring about salvation and liberation for man. This function, however, by which God reveals himself as being close to an individual human being and concerned about the plight of man, makes Him known as *Elohim*. We have found it to be fundamental biblical teaching that Y is *Elohim*, that His manifestations in nature or history must not be personified and recognized as deities under Him, to whom He delegated some of His powers and who thus represent Him. In keeping with our findings in the first chapter, the first reference in our text to the omnipotent Creator could very well have concluded with the proclamation: "I am Y!" Whereas the statement that Y is the one who takes His servant by the hand asks for the concluding formula: "I am Y your *Elohim!*", instead of it we have: "I am Y, that is My name."

There is also something else unusual in our text. Instead of the familiar, "Thus saith Y," the opening phrase here is: "Thus saith *ha–El*, God, Y, He that created the heavens." In other words, *Elohim* is being identified here as Y. This is repeated in the opening words, spoken by *ha–El* to his servant: "I am Y, who hath called thee." One, who is known as *ha–El* identified himself as Y. I, *Elohim*, who calls thee, am Y, the very same, who created heaven and earth. Whereas previously we were discussing the affirmation that Y is *Elohim*, we have here the rather unusual one that *Elohim* is Y. It would seem that both affirmations are necessary. When people have formed the idea of a supreme omnipotent Creator, they are inclined to think that, because of His infinite greatness, He could not be concerned with man and his condition. Therefore, they seek for themselves minor deities, to whom they might turn in their need. To counteract such tendencies in the human psyche comes the biblical proclamation: Y, notwithstanding His infinitude and transcendence, is your *Elohim,* the one who is near and concerned about you. But there is also another tendency in human nature which has to be controlled. A man may become too familiar with God, the one whose providence he has actually experienced, the one who has "taken hold of his hand"; he may reduce Him to finite dimensions. The children of Israel were at times subject to such tendencies. The repeated experience of God's mercies toward them, the numerous revelations, the significance of the divine presence in their midst as symbolized by the Holy Temple, brought God rather close to them. He was at hand, as it were. We hear God

131

raise this issue with them through the mouth of his prophet Jeremiah, when He says:

Am I a God near at hand, saith Y,
And not a God far off?
Can any hide himself in secret places
That I shall not see him? saith Y.
Do not I fill heaven and earth?
Saith Y. (23:23–24)

What is the meaning of this seemingly mysterious complaint? They became familiar with God, all too familiar. God had come near and they lost the perspective of His infinitude. His very closeness caused them to reduce the dimensions of the divine. They forgot that their *Elohim*, so near, was yet, Y, the one who transcends the All. Originally, they had to be taught not to look for an *Elohim* beside Y; now that Y had shown himself to be their *Elohim*, they lost sight of Y, the Infinite, and saw only *Elohim*, the one who was near. Having been forbidden to look for an *Elohim* beside Y, they transformed Y into a mere *Elohim* who was near and not also far off. They turned Y into an idol. In such a situation, instead of demonstrating that Y is *Elohim*, one must proclaim that *Elohim* is Y. It is this kind of affirmation that we find in the words from Isaiah which we have been examining. It is *ha–El* who speaks; God, who is known and near to his servant, whom He called; perhaps, all too near. This known God identifies himself as Y. Do not mistake me for a mere *Elohim*. I, who have called you and taken you by the hand, am Y, the very same, who has created heaven and earth. I, who have been so near to you, am also the one who surpasses, and is beyond, all the dimensions of the creation. In essence this means that Y and *Elohim* are one and the same. Yet, what is being said here could not be expressed by the familiar formula, "Y, He is *Elohim!*" one would have to say: the God, with whom you are familiar, He is Y. And indeed, it is exactly what is proclaimed in our text. It is *ha–El*, the God, one known in a definite manner, who speaks and affirms about himself that He is none other than Y. He cannot say about himself: I am Y your *Elohim*. "Your *Elohim*" is the speaker. What he says is: I, your *Elohim,* am Y .

We are now in a position to interpret the phrase: "I am Y, that is My name." It does not mean that Y's name is Y. This would be an empty tautology. "My" refers to the speaker, who is *ha–El.* "My name" means the name of the God. What *ha–El* says is: I am Y and, therefore, know me as Y. The emphasis is necessary. For the acts in which Y reveals himself to men, and by which He becomes *ha–El* to men, may be hypostasized. The danger is that the manifestations of Y in the universe may become personified deities to whom Y has delegated some of His authority. To counter this, the God, who is known to the servant, proclaims that He is Y and He is Y in His "name" too, in all His acts of self-revelation that establish His name. Y is Y and all His manifestations are Y. It is, therefore, proper that the text should read:

I am Y, that is My name;
And My glory will I not give to another,
Neither My praise to graven images.

The last two lines elaborate the theme of the first one. The "name," the manifestations of the divine in the world is self-revelation of Y. Such acts of self-revelation must not be hypostasized as separate deities under Y or with Him. For He does not give His glory to another; He does not delegate either His authority or His love for His creation to anyone. All glory and all praise belong to Him alone.

If our interpretation is correct, the phrase, "Y is His name"—and its appropriate variations—means to warn against the error of mistaking what is a manifestation of Y in the world for a separate deity under Y or beside Him. It would seem to us that most of the relevant passages bear this out. The passage in Jeremiah, to which we had occasion to refer earlier in our present discussion, reads in full:

O Y, my strength, and my stronghold,
And my refuge, in the day of affliction,
Unto Thee shall the nations come
From the ends of the earth, and shall say:
"Our fathers have inherited nought but lies,
Vanity and things wherein there is no profit."

Shall a man make unto himself gods,
And they are no gods?
Therefore, behold, I will cause them to know
My hand and My might;
And they shall know that My name is Y. (16:19–21)

The prophet's words that Y is his stronghold and refuge in times of trouble means that Y is his *Elohim*. It is, however, different with the nations. They have *Elohim*, who is apart from Y; gods who are near and at hand. They will yet discover their mistakes and come to Y and find in Him their strength and refuge; they too will learn that Y, He is *Elohim*. In the second paragraph in our quotation, God refers to these nations who have *Elohim* without Y. The words, which we find most revealing in the exclamatory question of God, are: "And they are no gods." What man makes himself unto gods are referred to as "they"; they may be pointed to. They are. They are not nothing. But they are not gods. What then are they? They are the *shem* of Y, manifestations of the power and the presence of Y made into gods by men. Therefore, when He causes men to know Y, they will also learn that His manifestations, His "name," is Y. The manifestation of the divine in the world is Y's self-revelation.

Various difficult passages may be explained along similar lines. Asking for the punishment of God's enemies, the psalmist says:

Fill their faces with shame;
That they may seek Thy name, O Y.
Let them be ashamed and affrighted for ever;
Yea, let them be ashamed and perish;

THE NAME OF GOD

That they may know that it is Thou alone whose name is Y.
The Most High over all the earth. (Pss. 83:17–19)

We have quoted the J.P.S. translation, in essence not differing here from the R.V., in order to illustrate the difficulty of interpretation. To our mind the idea that they—whoever they may be—have to be shown that Y alone is called Y makes no sense. No one ever rebelled against God because he believed that there was yet another God who too was called Y. Clearly, whatever they should learn about the name of Y continues the subject which was introduced by the psalmist's suggestion that they may seek the name of Y. What does it mean that their faces be filled with shame, so that they may seek the name of Y? In biblical language shame is associated with the worship of idols. When people realize that the gods they worshipped are all foolishness and vanity, they are overcome with a sense of shame. The psalmist asks that the enemies of God may be put to shame by God's act, showing them the futility of their belief in their gods. But how would such an experience lead to their seeking the name of Y? If the gods are indeed not nothing but something, if they are—for instance—the sun and the moon and the stars which have been personified as deities apart from their Creator, then—when one realizes one's mistake concerning them and wishes to understand their nature anew—one is "seeking the name of Y," for the luminaries are indeed manifestation of Y's might and wisdom and goodness which reveal Him to men. The error of the people to whom the psalmist refers, was that they mistook what was a name of Y for a deity beside Him. When, disabused of their illusions, they will ask themselves the question: what then do these forces of nature represent, what do they stand for? they will be seeking Y's name. When they are reduced to utter helplessness[67] and their gods have been proved to be of no avail, they will know. And now let us see what the psalmist really says about the object of their newly gained knowledge. We have pointed out why we disagree with the usual translations.

135

Actually, the Hebrew text does offer some difficulty for the translator. It does not say: that they may know that Thy name alone is Y. The complication arises through the personal pronoun, *atta*, Thou, which is placed before *shimkhah*, thy name. So that we would have to translate: that they may know that Thou, Thy name alone is Y, which of course does not seem to make much sense. The renderings of the J.P.S. and the R.V. translations aim at resolving this difficulty in the syntax. Unfortunately, as we have indicated above, the meaning was lost in the translation. We believe that the unusually placed personal pronoun, *atta*, is the key to the understanding of the passage. We connect, Thou, with *l'badekhah*, alone, and translate:

That they may know that
Thou, whose name is Y, art alone,
The Most High over all the earth.

Now, the continuity of the thought in this concluding sentence becomes clear. Having experienced the futility of their gods and thus compelled to seek the name of Y, they will learn that His name is Y, that He makes Himself manifest in Nature and in History and that His manifestations too are Y, they reveal only Him. All this means that Thou, just because Thy name is Y, art alone, the Most High over all the earth. What was, at first, thought to be god beside Y becomes recognized in its true nature to be but one of the "names" of God.

One of the difficult passages in Isaiah is the verse:

O Y our God, other lords beside Thee have had dominion over us;
But by Thee only do we make mention of Thy name. (26:13)

What is the connection between the first and the second line of this verse? In our opinion, "the other lords" are not kings or princes who at various times subjugated Israel. Speaking of human beings, the prophet could not have called them, "lords beside Thee." The very verb for holding dominion in the Hebrew text is, *ba'al,* which—by association—conjures up the service of Baal. The prophet recalls the fact that in the past Israel often followed idolatrous practices. Nevertheless, as to the present, he affirms that by Thee alone shall we make mention of Thy name. The affirmation is very much to the point. Idol worship in Israel meant the deification of what was, in truth, manifestation of Y. They made mention of Y's name by other gods. The prophet's promise is that, although in the past they transformed the "name" into separate deities beside God, from now on they will relate the name of Y to Y alone. "By Thee only do we make mention of Thy name."

The theme of our present discussion culminates in the famous words of Zechariah:

And Y shall be King over all the earth;
In that day shall Y be One, and His name One. (14:9)

Normally, this is understood to mean that God will be recognized by all as the one God and, therefore, he will be called by all one and the same name.[68] This, however, would be a rather insignificant statement. Once all the people of the earth recognize Y as the One God, what difference does it make whether they call Him all by one name or not. In the language of different peoples He may very well be called by different names. In our opinion, the verse requires an entirely different interpretation. Of course, Y is always One. That is His essential being. He will not be One just on "that day." The difference between now and "that day" is that, while in historic time though God is One, His name is not One, in the fullness of time God will be One and His name, too, will be One. What does it mean? That in the course of history people worship different gods is due to the fact that they are unable to identify Y with His name. They misunderstand the name, Y's manifestations, and self-revelations. They separate it from its source and give it an existence of its own. The innumerable self-manifestations of Y are really all one for they all represent Him. But when they are mistaken to be separate entities, the one name breaks down into a multiplicity of gods. Such is the case in history. But on that day when God becomes known as King over all the earth, the manifestations of Y will be recognized for what they truly are; then not only will God be One but His name, too, will be One. In the numberless acts of His self-revelation which make up His name, all will know Him, who is One. In essence, this is the same thought that we heard God address to his servant through the mouth of Isaiah, when he said: "I am Y, that is My name." This means: I am One, that is My name.

Concluding Notes

Bible scholars do not seem to have noted the distinction between the name of God, which is Y, and the name of Y, which cannot be Y. This has caused a great deal of confusion and misunderstanding in their writings. Thus, for instance, von Rad writes that to call by the name of Y "is originally a cultic term and means to invoke Y by using his name" (op. cit., p. 183). We have found that the name of Y is a manifestation of Y. To call by the name of Y is to appeal to God, trusting in a manifestation of His, in which He revealed His providence. But without grasping the significance of the expression "the name of Y," it is difficult to understand the phrase that God "puts" His name in a place. Again we quote von Rad, who says:

And it is in *Deuteronomy* that we meet with the most striking statements about the name of Y. Y "puts" his name at the one place of Israel's worship, that he might "dwell" there (*Deut.* 12, 5, 12, 21; 14, 24). Y himself is in heaven (*Deut.* 26, 15), but his name "lives" at the place of worship in a well-nigh material way, almost like a being existent in its own right. (op. cit., p. 184)

He senses correctly that "the name" has an almost separate existence from God. But only because it is the divine deed by which he reveals his presence and concern, making himself "known" to man. As we have shown, this name is "put" in the Temple in the sense that the Temple is a place where God's nearness, His self-revelation by the name-creating deed, becomes manifest. Far from existing in "a well-nigh material way," we have found that the continuous emphasis on the house built *to the name* of God has the purpose of eliminating all anthropomorphisms, which would also exclude any such anthropomorphic ideas from the meaning of the name. As usual, H. W. Robinson (*The Religious Ideas of the Old Testament* [New York, 1956], p. 106) is the furthest removed from a true understanding of the Hebrew Bible. When God says of His messenger that His "name is in him," according to Robinson, that means that "Y is present in His messenger." As we have seen, the very opposite is the case. "My name is in him" means that God's mission, His word and message, by which He intends to make Himself known to Israel, is entrusted to the messenger.

Small surprise that one encounters such lack of clarity when attempting to describe the significance of the knowledge of the name of Y. Thus, again, von Rad (op. cit., p. 182) writes: "Thus the name of Y, in which one might almost say, Y had given himself away, was committed in trust to Israel alone. The heathen do not know it (Pss. 79:6)." The truth is that in the Bible God does not "give Himself away" by the mystery of His name. He gives Himself away by the public revelation of His involvement in the history of Israel and the nations. The heathens, of whom the psalmist says that they do not know God and do not call by His name, are not ignorant of "the name." They may well know that His name is Y. They do not acknowledge Y and do not call by His name, i.e., they do not trust the manifestations of His providence by which He makes His name. They have no faith in Him to turn to Him in trusting prayer. Von Rad is much closer to the truth, when in another place—and contradicting himself—he has to declare (op. cit., pp. 184–85):

One of the most important things, however, is that for Israel this name never became a "mystery," to which only the initiated could have access. On the contrary, each and every Israelite was at liberty to avail himself of it, and once she had become fully aware of the distinctiveness of her worship, Israel did not hide this name of God from the Gentiles in fear, but rather felt herself in duty bound to make it known to them.

The full truth is that Israel never hid the name; nor could they have hidden it, even if they had wanted to, because God was revealing it all the time for all to see.

Davidson (op. cit., p. 37) is among the few who show a deeper insight into the meaning of "the name." While the thorough analysis and discussion of the subject is missing, he is putting it aptly as he writes:

So when the Psalmist in Ps. VIII exclaims, "How excellent is Thy name in all the earth!," he means how glorious is God's revelation of Himself. . . . His grace to men is His name here, His revelation of Himself. So when Israel is warned to give heed to the Angel of the Lord that leads them, for His name is in him (Ex. XIII, 21), the sense is that the significance of God is present there. What God is, His majesty and authority, is there embodied. So His name is holy and reverend; He, as being what He is known to be, is *reverendus*.

See, however, in Chapter 4 our interpretation of the term "the holy name."

CHAPTER 4

The Concept of Holiness

═══

THE HOLY ONE AND THE LORD OF HOSTS

WE shall start our investigation by pondering the revelation granted to Isaiah: "Holy, holy, holy, is the Lord of hosts."[1] Since it is necessary to affirm that the Lord of hosts is holy, it would seem logical to assume that whatever is meant by "holy," it needs be explicitly attributed to the Lord of hosts. The idea of the holy is in itself not implied in the idea of the Lord of hosts. We shall, therefore, have to see what these terms convey when they are used independently of each other. How does Isaiah use the concept the Lord of hosts and how that of the holy?

Let us look at a number of passages in which God is referred to as the Lord of hosts [italics added]:

O *Lord of hosts,* the God of Israel, that sittest upon the cherubim; Thou art the God, even Thou alone, of all the kingdoms of the earth; Thou hast made heaven and earth. (37:16)

Thus saith the Lord, the King of Israel and his Redeemer the *Lord of hosts:* I am the first and I am the last, and beside me there is no God. (44:6)

For I am the Lord thy God, who stirreth up the sea, that the waves thereof roar, the Lord of hosts is His name. (51:15)

Therefore saith the Lord, the *Lord of hosts,* the Mighty One of Israel: Ah, I will ease me of mine enemies; and I will turn my hand upon thee, and purge away thy dross with lye. (1:24–25)

For the *Lord of hosts* hath a day upon all that is proud and lofty, and upon all that is lifted up, and it shall be brought low. (2:12)

For, behold, the Lord, the *Lord of hosts,* doth take away from Jerusalem and from Judah stay and staff, every stay of bread, and every stay of water. (3:1)

Hark, a tumult in the mountains, like as of a great people! Hark the uproar of the kingdoms of the nations gathered together! The *Lord of hosts* mustereth the host of the battle. (13:4)

Therefore I will make the heavens to tremble, and the earth shall be shaken out of her place, for the wrath of the *Lord of hosts* and for the day of His fierce anger. (13:13)

One could multiply the quotations almost at will; they would all show the same character and would well find their places in the above grouping.[2] The Lord of hosts alone is God; he is at the beginning of time and at the end of it; he alone and no one besides him. He is the creator of heaven and earth; he is the sovereign power over all nature, as well as over all the kingdom of men. Of this Sovereign Lord it is maintained that he is "the Mighty One" who deals with his enemies, Jew or gentile, as he pleases. He acts, however, as a judge, who "purges away the dross with lye." He brings low the haughty and the proud. He executes punishment, when punishment is required; and, as he does so, like a war lord he mustereth his armies. For Isaiah, the "Lord of hosts" expresses the idea of divine transcendence, of elevation above everything created. This idea of transcendence is connected with divine might and power, which is exercised by the universal sovereign in his capacity as the Supreme Judge and Ruler. Isaiah uses the phrase, the Lord of hosts, consistently in this sense.

No less consistent and definite is he in his handling of the word, holy. In the entire book of Isaiah, the word occurs most frequently in the phrase, "Q'dosh Yisrael," the Holy One of Israel. Again we shall look at some verses in which the term is mentioned [italics added]:

Sing unto the Lord; for He hath done gloriously; this is made known in all the earth. Cry aloud and shout, thou inhabitant of Zion; for great is *the Holy One of Israel* in the midst of thee. (12:5–6)

And thou shalt rejoice in the Lord, thou shalt glory in *the Holy One of Israel*. (41:16)

"When thou passest through the waters, I will be with thee, and through the rivers, they shall not overflow thee; when thou walkest through the fire, thou shalt not be burned, neither shall the flame kindle upon thee. For I am the Lord thy God, *the Holy One of Israel*, thy Savior. (43:2–3)

And it shall come to pass in that day, that the remnant of Israel, and they that are escaped of the house of Jacob, shall no more again stay upon him that smote them; but shall stay upon the Lord, *the Holy One of Israel*, in truth. (10:20)

These passages show that "the Holy One of Israel" occurs in contexts whose message is opposed to those that speak on behalf of the Lord of hosts. The "Holy One of Israel" is the cause of joy and happiness. He is the friend of the poor and the needy; he protects them when they are in trouble. He is the Savior. He is "with thee"; he is in "the midst of thee." He is the One on whom man should rely. The idea is put forward with such conviction that it is recommended by Isaiah as a cornerstone for the foreign policy of the Jewish state of his time. Caught in the power struggle between Assyria and Egypt, the people seek their salvation in a political alliance with Egypt. Thus they reject God on whom alone they ought to rely. It is noteworthy, however, that in the various passages that deal with this theme, God is referred to as the Holy One of Israel. Concerning those who are for the Egyptian alliance, the prophet proclaims that they "trust in chariots, because they are many and in horsemen, because they are exceeding mighty; but they look not unto the Holy One of Israel." The policy suggested by Isaiah is a different one. "For thus said the Lord God," and again he is referred to as, "the Holy One of Israel: In sitting still and rest shall ye be saved, in quietness and in confidence shall be your strength."[3] In times of crisis, one should have trust in the holiness of God. Instead of making alliances with military might, one should ally oneself with the Holy One. Faith in him brings salvation in peace and quietude.

These attributes of the Holy One are rather different from those by which the Lord of hosts makes himself manifest. The Lord of hosts is transcendent, the Holy One is immanent. The Lord of hosts is far removed, he is above man and all creation; the Holy One of Israel is near. The Lord of hosts judges; the Holy One of Israel saves. Quite obviously, the Holy One is not the *mysterium tremendum*. He is close in the midst of Zion; the cause of joy and happiness. The *mysterium tremendum* seems to describe the Lord of hosts more aptly. It is rather significant that, after having heard the threefold "Holy, holy, holy," Isaiah should exclaim: "Woe is me! for I am undone; because I am a man of unclean lips . . . for mine eyes have seen the King, *the Lord of hosts* [italics added]."[4] Not the Holy One, but the beholding of the Lord of hosts is the cause of his terror.

One who reads the Bible in English might, however, point to at least one passage in which the Holy does appear as *orge theory*, the divine wrath. The Revised Version, verse 17, chapter 10, reads:

And the light of Israel shall be for a fire, and his Holy One for a flame; and it shall burn and devour his thorns and his briers in one day.

This surely is an activity that, in the light of so many other passages, we would expect to be performed by the Lord of hosts. Reading the text in the Hebrew original, one realizes easily that the English version is rather misleading. *V'haya or Yisrael l'esh uq'dosho l'lehabah* should be translated as: And the light of Israel shall *become* a fire, and his Holy One, a flame. The Hebrew *haya l'* means to become; it expresses a change of status, condition, or nature.[5] Light is normally something very beneficial. So is, of course, the light of Israel, which is an appellation for the God of Israel here. The prophet, however, warns that the light of Israel will change its nature, as it were. It will cease being light and become a consuming fire. Similarly—and it should be obvious because of the parallelism in the text—the Holy One will *become* a flame. Far from associating any form of destructiveness with the concept of the Holy One, the words imply the opposite. The Holy One will suppress his natural quality. He will change and become a destructive force. He will cease manifesting himself as the holy and will act in another capacity like a flame.

The same distinction, which is made by Isaiah between the two concepts referring to God, we also find in the Psalms. We shall list only a few examples [italics added].

Who is the King of Glory? The Lord strong and mighty, the Lord mighty in battle. . . . Who then is the King of glory? *The Lord of hosts;* He is the King of glory. (24:8, 10)

Nations were in tumult, kingdoms were moved; He uttered His voice, the earth melted. *The Lord of hosts* is with us. . . . Come, behold the works of the Lord, who hath made desolations in the earth. He makes wars to cease unto the end of the earth; He breaketh the bow and cutteth the spear in sunder. . . . I will be exalted among the nations, I will be exalted in the earth. *The Lord of hosts* is with us. (46:7–12)

For, lo, the kings assembled themselves, they came onward together. They saw, straightway they were amazed; they were affrighted, they hasted away. Trembling took hold of them there, pangs, as of a woman in travail. With the east wind thou breakest the ships of Tarshish. As we have heard, so have we seen in the city of *the Lord of hosts.* (48:5–9)

145

In these, and other passages, the psalmists employ the phrase, the Lord of hosts, in the same sense as does Isaiah. It is to be noted that in the last quotation Zion is referred to as the city of the Lord of hosts. The usual appellation for Zion is *ir ha–qodesh*, the city of the holy, or *har ha–qodesh*, the mount of the holy. Here, however, as the psalmist describes the mighty deeds of judgment, performed by God who uses the east wind as the messenger to do his bidding, all this is witnessed in the city of God, who has made himself manifest on this occasion as the Lord of hosts.

The distinction we have established is further strengthened as we compare the psalmist's use of *qadosh* in contrast to "the Lord of hosts." In which context does the idea of the holy occur in the Psalms? We shall look at some of the passages [italics added].

Sing praise unto the Lord, O ye His godly ones, and give thanks to the *name of his holiness*. For His anger is but for a moment, His favour is for a lifetime. (30:5–6)[6]

Our soul hath waited for the Lord; he is our help and our shield. For in Him doth our heart rejoice, because we have trusted in the *name of His holiness*. (33:20–21)

A father of the fatherless, and a judge of the widows, is God in the *habitation of His holiness*. (68:6)

I also will give thanks unto thee with the psaltery. . . . I will sing praise unto thee with the harp, O thou Holy One of Israel. (71:22)

As with Isaiah, the manifestation of divine holiness is the cause for rejoicing and thanksgiving. Far from signifying separateness, the idea of the holy conveys a sense of intimacy and relatedness. We insist on the correct translation, the name of His holiness, in place of the usual, His holy name. The name of His holiness means the manifestation of divine holiness.[7] Such manifestation is a sign that "his anger is but for a moment, His favour is for a life-time." "His holy habitation" might be a point in space. Only the term does not occur in the Bible once. "The habitation of His holiness" is the indwelling of divine holiness, it is divine holiness, the saving force immanent in creation. By means of this, his association with the world, God is "the father of the fatherless and a judge of the widows."

A most striking support for our analysis of the term, holy, one finds in Hosea:

My heart is turned within Me, my compassions are kindled together. I will not execute the fierceness of Mine anger, I will not return to destroy Ephraim; for I am God, and not man, the *Holy One* in the midst of thee, and I will not come in fury [italics added]. (11:8–9)

The familiar traits of the Holy One, as we found them in Isaiah and the Psalms, are stated here almost in the form of a definition. With Hosea too, the Holy One is "in the midst of thee." His signs are neither fury nor anger, but compassion and love.[8]

The same idea is corroborated interestingly by comparing two passages of Amos with each other. In both cases God takes an oath, once "by His holiness" and once, "by Himself." It would, however, be mistaken to assume that both have the same meaning. When God swears "by His holiness" (4:2), it is against the "kine of Bashan," "that oppress the poor, that crush the needy." He swears by His holiness, because it is his concern for the poor and the needy that causes him to resolve what he plans to do in order to save them. But when He swears "to deliver up the city with all that is therein" (6:8), no mention is made of the oppression of the poor. Those that are "at ease in Zion" and "secure in the mountain of Samaria" are punished because of their pride and depraved life. What is resolved this time is not for the sake of the poor and needy, but purely as punishment for the haughty and the degenerate. This time no reference need be made to God's holiness. He swears "by Himself," and the oath is announced in the words: "Saith the Lord, the God of hosts."

147

Jeremiah, too, when he mentions God taking an oath "by Himself" links it to the Lord of hosts and says:

The Lord of hosts hath sworn by Himself: Surely I will fill thee with men, as with the canker-worm, and they shall lift up a shout against thee. (51:14)

In these words judgment is announced in the name of the Lord of hosts. But when according to the psalmist, God promises David that he will sustain him and his dynasty for ever, he swears again "by His holiness":

Once I have sworn by My holiness: Surely I will not be false unto David; his seed shall endure for ever, and his throne as the sun before Me. It shall be established for ever as the moon, and be steadfast as the witness in the sky. (89:36–38)

The sustaining and protecting attribute of divine mercy and love is God's holiness.

Most revealing are those biblical passages which make use of both terms, the Holy One and the Lord of hosts. There is, for instance, God's answer to Hezekiah's prayer. It is couched in the form of an address to Sennacherib, king of Assyria. In its opening words we find the sentences:

Whom hast thou taunted and blasphemed? And against whom hast thou exalted thy voice? Yes, thou hast lifted up thine eyes on high, even against *the Holy One of Israel!* [italics added]

This speech, at the inception of which God is referred to as the Holy One of Israel, concludes with the words: "The zeal of the Lord of hosts shall perform this."[9] Between the beginning and the close of the address Sennacherib is put in his place. In his pride, he imagined that his conquest of nations and countries were his own doings, whereas, in reality God used him as his instrument. But now Sennacherib's time has come.

Because of thy raging against Me, and for that thine uproar is come up into Mine ears, therefore will I put My hook in thy nose, and My bridle in thy lips, and I will turn thee back by the way by which thou comest.

Quite obviously, the judgment to be executed over Senna-cherib is a task for the Lord of hosts. Thus, it is the zeal of the Lord of hosts that shall perform it. On the other hand, the conqueror king of Assur did not taunt and blaspheme the Lord of hosts. He did not know him. Had he known him, he would have thought better of it. What was his message to Hezekiah?

Let not thy God whom thou trustest beguile thee, saying: Jerusalem shall not be given into the hand of the king of Assyria.[10]

Now, of course, the God in whom Hezekiah trusts that he will protect Jerusalem is the God who is "in the midst of thee," the Holy One of Israel. It is the Holy One, on whom Israel relies, that was blasphemed, when Sennacherib declared him not to be relied upon. It is, however, the Lord of hosts that brought low his pride and conceit.

As the Lord of hosts executes judgment on Sennacherib, so he grants power and dominion to another conqueror, Cyrus, to fulfill a divine mission. This mission, however, is related also to the liberation of God's people. Cyrus is chosen "for the sake of Jacob My servant, and Israel Mine elect." Thus, in the description of the events in which Israel and Cyrus are together involved, the Holy One and the Lord of hosts occur alternately. We read:

Thus saith the Lord, *The Holy One of Israel,* and his Maker: Ask Me of the things that are to come; concerning My sons, and concerning the work of My hands, command ye Me. I, even I, have made the earth, and created man upon it; I, even My hands, have stretched out the heavens, and all their hosts have I commanded. I have roused him up in victory, and I make level all his ways; he shall build My city, and he shall let my exiles go free, not for price nor reward, saith *the Lord of hosts* [italics added].[11]

The calling of Cyrus, granting him victory and success, putting it into his heart that he rebuild God's city and let the exiles go are matters which only the divine sovereign can perform. He has the power to do it, because he is the Lord over the universe, the creator of heaven and earth. Therefore, the prophecy concludes, "saith the Lord of hosts." In the beginning of the prophecy, however, these weighty matters are related to the exiles themselves. God speaks "concerning My sons and concerning the work of My hands," meaning Israel. Here he is called the Holy One of Israel.[12]

The most striking passage of this type is found in chapter 5 of Isaiah. It is the familiar verse:

"But the Lord of hosts is exalted through *mishpat,* and God the Holy One is sanctified through *s'daqah.* (5:16)[13]

The distinction between justice and righteousness is parallel to the distinction between "the Lord of hosts" and "the Holy One" and to the distinction between being exalted and being sanctified. This becomes more obvious, if we compare the Hebrew terms *mishpat* and *s'daqah* with each other. *Mishpat* is justice based on adherence to the law; *s'daqah* is doing right with charity or compassion. *Mishpat* is dispensed with authority; *s'daqah* with kindness. He who administers *mishpat* must not consider the person; only because one does consider the person does one practice *s'daqah* toward him. The one who enacts *mishpat* is a judge; he is above you; he who practices *s'daqah* is a friend who is with you. God dispenses justice, *mishpat,* as the Lord of hosts; he practices righteousness, *s'daqah,* as the Holy One. As the one who imposes justice, he is exalted; doing *s'daqah,* he is sanctified. To be exalted indicates remoteness; it is a quality properly ascribed to the Lord of hosts. To be sanctified is befitting the Holy One. We are not yet in a position to define the meaning of being sanctified.[14] However, on the basis of the parallelism between the three pairs of opposite terms in the sentence, we may well venture the guess that as the exaltation of the Lord of hosts through justice implies distance between the judge and the judged, so the sanctification of the Holy One by his acts of *s'daqah* is somehow related to the fact that he is "in the midst of thee." A closer look at the context in which the verse we are discussing occurs, will show clearly why there is reference made to a two-fold manifestation of God's action. Declaring the woes that await the people who indulge in a life of unbridled pleasures and, thus, showing no regard for the work of God, the prophet exclaims:

And down goeth their glory, and their tumult, and their uproar . . . and man is bowed down, and man is humbled, and the eyes of the lofty are humbled; but the Lord of hosts is exalted through *mishpat*, and God the Holy One is sanctified through *s'daqah*. Then shall the lambs feed as in their pastures, and the waste places of the fat ones shall wanderers eat. (5:14–17)

The verse we have analyzed speaks of two functions of God, as the dispenser of justice and as the one who practices *s'daqah*. The context, in which these two functions are mentioned, speaks of two types of people: the lofty and arrogant ones and those who are meek like lambs; the "fat ones" and the "wanderers" who are the homeless poor. God deals with both of them. As to the former, they are silenced and humbled, justice is done to them; as to the latter, they are the meek ones who inherit the land, *s'daqah* is practiced toward them. For "the fat ones," he appears as the Lord of hosts; for the "lambs" and "the wanderers" he is the Holy One. Thus, the Lord of hosts is exalted through justice and God the Holy One is sanctified through *s'daqah*.

Neither is this stylistic idiosyncrasy limited to Isaiah. In Psalm 89 the psalmist addresses himself to God with the words: "O Lord God of hosts" (vs. 9) and praises him for all his transcendent majesty:

Sedeq and *Mishpat* are the foundation of Thy throne; mercy and truth go before Thee. (vs. 15)

However, as we read on, we hear of a people that walks in the light of God's countenance. Of them it is said:

151

In Thy name do they rejoice all the day; and through Thy *s'daqah* are they exalted. For Thou art the glory of their strength and in Thy favor our horn is exalted. For [it is due] to the Lord, our shield, and to the Holy One of Israel, our king.[15]

While the incomparable Sovereign of the Universe is addressed as the Lord of hosts, the one in whom people rejoice because he treats them with *s'daqah,* with kindness and charity, who is the source of their strength, is the Holy One of Israel.

It may be intriguing to compare the use of the word exalted by the psalmist and the place it has in the verse of Isaiah, which we have discussed. Isaiah said that the Lord of hosts was exalted through justice. The psalmist, on the other hand, said of the people that they are exalted through *s'daqah.* Both usages belong to the same world of discourse. Justice exalts God, it elevates him. But the more he is exalted, the further removed he is from man. Through divine *s'daqah* the people are exalted and elevated. And the more they are elevated, the closer they are to God.

The most surprising affirmation of our analysis thus far we find in I Samuel. In the opening chapters we encounter two prayers of Hannah; in the one she addresses the Lord of hosts, in the other she acknowledges the Holy One. Let us compare the two prayers with each other.

O Lord of hosts, if Thou wilt indeed look on the affliction of Thy handmaid, and remember me, and not forget Thy handmaid. (1:11)

In the second prayer, she says:

My heart exulteth in the Lord, my horn is exalted in the Lord, my mouth is enlarged over mine enemies; because I rejoice in Thy salvation. There is none holy as the Lord, for there is none beside Thee; neither is there any rock like our God. (2:1–2)

The two prayers betray two exactly opposite moods. The first may be called a prayer of intercession, the other is one of thanksgiving. The first one, Hannah prayed "in bitterness of soul" and she "wept sore." She was a barren woman. The second prayer she recites in a spirit of elation. Her prayer was answered; God blessed her womb.

In the prayer of intercession, she addresses God as the Lord of hosts. What is her situation? She feels that God has abandoned her. He does not look on her affliction. She is not remembered; she is forgotten, forsaken by God. God is far removed from her; he is inaccessible to her. Thus she calls on the Lord of hosts. It is what God is to her at the moment. But, later, she was remembered after all, she was not forgotten. God turned toward her; he did look on her affliction. And now, she exults in God, rejoices in his salvation. What happened to her is what centuries later Isaiah would declare of "the humble and the neediest among men" who shall "increase their joy in the Lord" and shall exult in "the Holy One of Israel." The surprising thing, of course, is that this woman "from the hill-country of Ephraim" knows how to pray anticipating the ideas and the style of an Isaiah and of the psalmist by centuries. The God of her salvation, the cause of her joy and exultation is the Holy One, he is the rock on whom to rely. Hannah distinguishes between the concepts of God as the Lord of hosts and that of God as the Holy One exactly as was done generations later by Isaiah and the psalmists. Feeling God's remoteness, his anger or judgment, she calls him the Lord of hosts, experiencing his salvation, the "light of his countenance" turned to her, she knows him in his manifestation of the Holy One.

Occasionally we find the expression, Redeemer—the Holy One of Israel. Since God, the Holy One, is "in the midst of thee," since he is the rock on whom one may rely, the salvation of the poor and the needy, it is natural that God acting as the Redeemer should be linked to his manifestation as the Holy One. But the two concepts are not identical. The Redeemer has a function which is not always implicit in that of the Holy One. The Redeemer has to redeem and thus he has to deal with those who prevent redemption, who would hold His

153

people in subjugation. He is the Redeemer because he is the Holy One; but as the Redeemer he cannot remain "in the midst of thee" altogether. He must also direct his attention toward the oppressors and confound their plans and aspirations. Let us consider some of the passages that mention the Redeemer, the Holy One of Israel. They are all found in Isaiah. In chapter 41 we read:

Fear not, thou worm Jacob and ye men of Israel; I help thee, saith the Lord, and thy Redeemer, the Holy One of Israel. Behold, I make thee a new threshing-sledge having sharp teeth; thou shalt thresh the mountains and beat them small, and shalt make the hills as chaff. Thou shalt fan them, and the wind shall carry them away, and the whirlwind shall scatter them; and thou shalt rejoice in the Lord, thou shalt glory in the Holy One of Israel. (vss. 14–16)

We are now familiar with some of the ideas in these verses. After the encouragement and promise of help, we are prepared for the mentioning of the Holy One of Israel. We also expect that those saved should "rejoice and glory" in the Holy One of Israel. However, a new term is introduced and connected with the Holy One; the term—Redeemer. But an activity, too, is described which we do not normally associate with the Holy One of Israel. It is the activity of threshing the mountains and scattering them like chaff in the wind, symbolizing of course the reduction of the enemies or whatever obstacles that may stand in the way of redemption. Help *for* Israel requires action *against* the taskmaster. In other passages, too, where the combined phrase occurs, the two-fold function is unmistakable.[16]

One may, however, easily see how the two-fold function of the Redeemer combines within itself the two manifestations of God, as the Holy One of Israel and as the Lord of hosts. God's activity as the Redeemer moves in two directions; *against* those who oppress and *to* those who are to be redeemed. For the oppressor the Redeemer is the Lord of hosts; for the redeemed, the Holy One. Accordingly, there are some passages which combine the Redeemer, the Lord of hosts, and the Holy One of Israel. In the midst of the prophecy about the approaching downfall of Babylon, Isaiah exclaims:

Our Redeemer, the Lord of hosts is His name, the Holy One of Israel. (47:4)

The reader of the verses immediately preceding this exclamation will find that the heavy blows predicted against Babylon are indeed such as are normally said to emanate from the Lord of hosts.

Thy nakedness shall be uncovered, yes, thy shame shall be seen; I will take vengeance, and will let no man intercede.

On the other hand, immediately following the exclamation and explaining why the "daughter of the Chaldeans" will no longer be called "mistress of kingdoms," it is said:

I was wroth with My people, I profaned Mine inheritance, and gave them into thy hand; thou didst show them no mercy; upon the aged hast thou very heavily laid thy yoke.

The implication is that because of the cruelty with which Babylon treated Israel, God turns from his anger against them. He acknowledges his inheritance and will no longer let it be profaned. He will treat mercifully those to whom no mercy was shown. We are reminded of that other verse in Isaiah about the Lord of hosts who is exalted through justice and God the Holy One who is sanctified through *s'daqah*. It is the Redeemer, the Lord of hosts, dispensing justice for Babylon, the Holy One of Israel, treating with mercy his people.

Unfortunately, often the subtle nuance of meaning gets lost in the translation. For instance, verse 5 in chapter 54 of Isaiah is rendered:

For thy Maker is thy husband, the Lord of hosts is His name; and the Holy One of Israel is thy Redeemer, the God of the whole earth shall He be called.

The dual function of the Redeemer is lost in such a translation. The word, husband, suggests an intimate relationship; to call him the Lord of hosts introduces a jarringly incongruous notion. The Hebrew for husband is, of course, *baal;* the masoretic reading, however, gives us the verbal noun, *boel.* The *baal* is; the *boel* does. The prophet wishes to indicate that Israel's Maker makes Himself her "husband" again. The promise follows immediately after the words: "and the reproach of thy widowhood shalt thou remember no more." Israel will no longer remain husbandless, for her Maker will possess her again. The passage recalls the complaint of Israel, in which the same verb, *boel,* occurs and it should be understood in its light. The complaint was:

O Lord our God, other lords beside Thee have had dominion over us. (26:13)

Only the Hebrew text, using the same terminology in both cases, shows that the promise was meant to counter the complaint. God becoming once again the "husband," takes sole "dominion" over Israel; he replaces the "other lords," who misused Israel. Now, of course, the two-fold function of the Redeemer appears in our text, too. Only by shattering the yoke of the "other lords" can God make himself Israel's Lord. In order to re-possess Israel, the Redeemer must act in history as the Lord of hosts; he has compassion on "the widow" and becomes her "husband" again as the Holy One of Israel.[17]

HOLY AND AWESOME

It would seem that our analysis has to contend with a difficulty that arises from the fact that occasionally *qadosh* is combined with *nora,* holy with awful or awesome. There are two such passages in the Bible; both are found in the Psalms. In view of the numerous passages on which our interpretation is based, two exceptions to the rule would not weigh heavily. Nevertheless, since the term holy, with reference to God, is employed with such uniform and consistent meaning, exceptions that would indicate a meaning contrary to the one found everywhere else do require careful examination.

One of the passages we find in Psalm 99. *Qadosh* and *nora* are placed there in rather uncomfortable neighborliness for our taste. We have in mind the phrase: "Let them praise Thy name—great and awful. Holy is he." It seems to associate the awful with the holy, declaring the awful to be holy.

Beginning with the second verse, we shall quote the Psalm in its main parts:

1. The Lord is great in Zion; and He is high above all the peoples. Let them praise Thy name as great and awful. Holy is He.
2. Thou hast executed *mishpat* and *s'daqah* in Jacob. Exalt ye the Lord our God and prostrate yourselves at His footstool; Holy is He.
3. O Lord our God, Thou didst answer them; a forgiving God wast Thou unto them, though Thou tookest vengeance of their misdeeds. Exalt ye the Lord our God and prostrate yourselves at the hill of His holiness; for the Lord our God is holy.

We number the quotations, in order to indicate the three distinctive parts of the Psalm. Though distinct from each other, they are similar in conceptual structure, as well as in style. This is quite obvious of the second and third sections, but it is true also of the first one. At first, we shall direct our attention to 2 and 3. The sentence, "Exalt ye the Lord . . ." is practically identical in both parts. "His footstool" is the same as the "hill of His holiness"; it is Zion, the symbol of God's presence "in the midst of thee." In both cases, the reason why he should be exalted seems to be given in the immediately preceding sentence. In 2 it is the execution of justice and *s'daqah;* in 3, it is the fact that God answered his people when they called to him and he forgave their sins.[18] However, rather hesitantly it is remembered, almost like an aside, that nevertheless they were punished for their misdeeds. And now it occurs to us that in this point too, there is similarity between 2 and 3. In 2, the execution of justice, *mishpat,* and *s'daqah,* is mentioned. But God's answering of prayers and forgiving of sins is certainly an act of *s'daqah* on his part; and taking "vengeance of their misdeeds" is exercise of *mishpat*. In both cases then the psalmist calls for exalting of God for the same reason. But we have learned already that the doing of *mishpat* alone exalts God and the practice of *s'daqah* sanctifies him. Shall we then say that, Exalt ye the Lord our God and prostrate yourselves at His footstool (or at the hill of His holiness), calls for a two-fold acknowledgment of God's two-fold actions? Exalt ye the Lord for his *mishpat* and prostrate ye yourself before Him as an act of worshipful gratitude for his *s'daqah?*

Let us now glance once again at section 1 of the psalm. As 2 and 3, 1, too, presents us with a two-fold manifestation of God. But whereas in the last two sections God makes himself known "in Jacob" by means of *mishpat* and *s'dagah,* in 1, the two-foldness of his manifestation comes about by the division between Zion and "all the peoples." It should be noted that, as the text puts it, God is great "*in* Zion" and he is "high above all nations." "In Zion" recalls once again the God "in the midst of thee," the Holy One of Israel; whereas God "high above all nations" leads to the association with the Lord of hosts. In a sense, this passage too speaks of God's two-fold function as executing justice and *s'daqah.* It would seem that the phrase following upon: "Let them praise Thy name as great and awful" is now easily explained. "Great" corresponds to "the Lord is great in Zion" and "awful," to "He is high above all the peoples." This is in keeping with what we have found earlier, i.e., that it is his remoteness as the Sovereign and Judge which inspires awe and fear. That "awful" is the manner in which God's name is known among the nations is explicitly stated by Malachi, who lets God say:

For I am a great king, saith the Lord of hosts, and my name is awful [*nora*] among the nations. (1:14)

It was the same prophet who proclaimed that "from the rising of the sun even unto the going down of the same" God's name was great among the nations. Yet, they knew him not as Israel did. They knew him by the awesomeness of his name, as the Lord of hosts; with the intimacy of the Holy One he was not known to them.

Quite clearly, in our psalm, the idea of the holy is not to be associated with that of *nora* (awful). *Nora* describes one specific form of divine self-revelation which is different from that of *qadosh*. In our psalm the idea of the holy occurs at the end of each section. In the first section, it is even by syntax separated from the preceding sentence. "Let them praise Thy name great and awful" is addressed to God. "Holy is He" stands clearly by itself.[19] It is certainly not spoken to God. It is the private meditation of the author. It expresses the idea that God, who is known in a two-fold capacity in Zion and among the nations, is for him holy. He is holy because He is in the midst of Zion. In the second part of the psalm, we understand its place more readily. Mention is made there of God's *mishpat* and *s'daqah*. We have, however, learned from Isaiah that it is in His capacity as the Holy One that God executes *s'daqah*. Whereas in the first section, "Holy is He" stands by itself; in the second it should be read as concluding the thought "prostrate yourselves at His footstool" as an expression of gratitude for *s'daqah* received, "holy is He" as the bestower of *s'daqah*. If we now compare 2 with 3 we find that although both contain the ideas of *mishpat* and *s'daqah,* they do not treat them with the same emphasis. In the second part justice and righteousness are of equal weight, in the third the emphasis is on God's answering and forgiving, on his *s'daqah;* of his *mishpat* we are only reminded by the way, as if it were a second thought. In other words the accent is on God's holiness. May this be the reason why in this section "his footstool" is replaced by "the hill of His holiness" and why instead of the quiet "Holy is He" we have the triumphant affirmation, "for the Lord our God is holy"? It is the crescendo toward which the psalmist has been moving. The other passage, combining *qadosh* and *nora* reads:

159

He hath sent redemption unto His people; He hath commanded His covenant for ever; holy and awful is His name. (Ps. 111:9)

As indicated earlier, "His name" is God's self-manifestation, by which He becomes known. "Holy and awful" would, of course correspond to the combination that we found in the concept of the Redeemer, that of the Lord of hosts and the Holy One of Israel. However, what is the reason here for such a combination? If we read carefully, we notice that as two attributes are associated with God's name, so are also two actions of God mentioned. On the basis of the principle of parallelism we may, perhaps, assume that "He hath sent redemption to His people" corresponds with "holy" and "He hath commanded His covenant for ever" is paralleled by "awful." Now, the sending of redemption to His people may well be considered a manifestation of divine holiness. It would indeed be the function of the Holy One of Israel. This is in keeping with what we found thus far in our investigation. As to the second phrase, independently of our present and immediate interest, it requires elucidation. "He hath commanded His covenant for ever," what exactly does it convey? Fortunately, the idea of the everlasting covenant occurs once more in the same context preceding our text by several verses. The entire passage reads:

He hath given food unto them that fear Him; He will *ever be mindful of His covenant*. He hath declared to His people the power of His works, in giving them the heritage of the nations [italics added].

This time, it is the second part of the passage which offers no difficulty of interpretation. God has shown his power to his people, when he led them into the promised land and gave them the "heritage of the nations." In this connection, we cannot help thinking of the Lord of hosts. The first part of the text, however, is unclear. Is God mindful of his covenant by giving food to those who fear him? One would be inclined to connect the thought of the fulfilment of the convenant with what follows, with "giving them the heritage of the nations."

By doing that, God was mindful of his covenant with Israel and the patriarchs.

Once again, the translation confuses rather than clarifies. The Hebrew rendered here as food is *tereph*. The verb from which the noun derives, *taraph*, means to tear, to rape, to rob. The more adequate word for food is *okhel*. *Tereph* would normally be food of wild animals, who feed by tearing asunder. There is one verse in the Bible in which both terms occur:

The young lions roar after their prey [*tereph*], and seek their food [*okhlam*] from God. (Ps. 104:21)

Tereph has come to mean food in relationship to the wild life that subsist on prey. In a more general sense, anything torn away by force from its owner, anything taken by force, may be called *tereph*. Our text does not speak about food at all. It would be the acme of incongruity to call the food given to "them that fear Him" *tereph*. What God gave them emerges clearly from the context. He gave them "the inheritance of the nations," the land he promised them. It is this that is referred to as *tereph*. And *tereph* indeed it was. It had to be taken by force from the Canaanites and given to the Israelites. Failing a better word, it would be more correct to translate: "He hath given prey unto them that hear Him." And now the succession of the ideas becomes much more coherent. By giving them *tereph*, God was mindful of his covenant. In this manner, he has "declared to His people the power of His works."

We may now revert to the starting point of this discussion. Our difficulty began with the phrase, "He hath commanded His covenant for ever." The meaning is that he maintains his covenant, he orders it to stand for ever; he is loyal to the covenant. From the preceding verses, we have learned that God is ever mindful of his covenant by giving his people "the prey," the "heritage of the nations."

We shall now read our text again.

161

He hath sent redemption unto His people; He hath commanded His
  covenant for ever;
Holy and awful is His name.

We believe that the parallelism becomes now evident. As
the one who sends redemption to his people, his name is holy;
as the one who sustains his covenant by giving them *tereph,*
his name is "awful." In conclusion, it may be worth noting
that the very phrase, holy *and* awful is His name, indicates that
the concept of awful is not included in that of holy.

We might then say that *qadosh v'nora,* holy and awful, expresses two different and opposing attributes of God. In this
sense, the idea is similar to that of the Redeemer, who, in his
relationship to those to be redeemed, acts as the Holy One
and toward those from whose power he redeems, he behaves
as the Lord of hosts. There is, however, another term which
comprehends the two-fold function of the Redeemer most
dramatically. It is the phrase, *z'roa qodsho,* which should not
be translated as His holy arm, but literally as—arm of His
holiness. It is the tool which God uses to bring to fruition the
plans prompted by his quality of holiness. The phrase occurs
in one of the most stirring prophecies of Isaiah, which begins
with the unforgettable words: "How beautiful upon the mountains are the feet of the messenger of good tidings." As we read
on, we come across the passage:

Break forth into joy, sing together, ye waste places of Jerusalem.
For the Lord hath comforted His people, He hath redeemed Jerusalem. The Lord *hath made bare the arm of His holiness* in the eyes
of all the nations; and all the ends of the earth shall see the salvation of our God [italics added]. (52:9–10)

What is described in this great prophecy of redemption is,
of course, God's act in history as the Redeemer. We have
found in numerous other passages that God is the cause of
comfort, joy, and salvation in his capacity as the Holy One.
The Redeemer, however, cannot limit himself to dealing with
his people alone. All the nations are involved in Israel's redemp-

162

tion. It is out of their midst that God's people have to be redeemed. The act of redemption takes place in the sight of all the nations. Because God is the Holy One, he is impelled to redeem; but in order to redeem, his might must become effective in the world. This is symbolized by the baring of the arm of His holiness.

The parallel to this passage, one finds in the opening verses of Psalm 98.

Oh sing unto the Lord a new song. . . . His right hand, the arm of His holiness, hath wrought salvation for Him. The Lord hath made known His salvation: His *s'daqah*[20] hath He revealed in the sight of the nations. . . . All the ends of the earth have seen the salvation of our God.

Salvation is the function of the Holy One, but in history it has to be "wrought"; and that requires an arm. The working of salvation is the revelation of divine *s'daqah* but it has to take place in the sight of the nations. It must be effective. It is performed by "the arm of His holiness."

It will be rewarding to look at another passage, which associates *z'roa,* arm, with redemption, but does not use the expression, *z'roa qodsho.* It occurs in Psalm 77 and reads:

Thou hast with Thine arm redeemed Thy people, the sons of Jacob and Joseph. (vs. 16)

The reference to the other nations is not lacking here either. The verse immediately preceding the one quoted declares:

Thou art the God that doest wonders; Thou hast made known Thy strength among the peoples.

However, the reference to holiness, that is the motivating desire to redeem, is lacking . . . but not altogether. After declaring that he will meditate on all of God's works and doings, the psalmist introduces his meditation with the sentence:

O God, Thy way is in holiness; who is a great god like unto God?

We have now all the material we have been looking for: the "arm," redemption, and the idea of holiness. How do they function in our text, how are they related to each other? Following our method of interpretation, we note that "who is a great god like unto God" says rhetorically the truth that no one is like unto God. It expresses, to speak theologically, God's incomparability, his transcendence, his remoteness. In other words, it expresses what we have identified as the meaning of the idea, "Lord of hosts." This, however, is not holiness. Shall we then assume that this too is one of the "double-function passages" which we have discussed; a *qadosh v'nora* passage? In order to answer the question, we have first to determine what is meant by, Thy way is in holiness. Fortunately, the psalmist explains himself. Toward the end of the psalm, he mentions once again God's way. Of it, he says:

Thy way was in the sea, and Thy path in the great waters, and Thy footsteps were not known. Thou didst lead Thy people like a flock, by the hand of Moses and Aaron.

This conclusion is most revealing. God's way was the path across the waters. But it was not God who went across. It was God's way because he led his people across. His "footsteps were not known," for who indeed could have imagined that there was a path for men there to be led through the waters! This then is "Thy way in holiness." It would indeed be the exact concept on the basis of our understanding of the term, the Holy One, the Savior who dwells in the midst of the poor and needy. It is God's way of holiness, because along with it God exercised his quality of holiness. Thus, we have before us another one of the double-function passages. The psalmist meditates on God's holiness as well as on his wholly-otherness, on his immanence as well as on his transcendence, his nearness as well as his remoteness. Both qualities are needed in order to accomplish what is to be accomplished. We shall now quote the psalmist's meditation in its essential structure. He muses on the miracle of the dividing of the waters of the Sea of Reeds and the salvation of the children of Israel

O God, Thy way is in holiness; who is a great god like unto God? Thou art the God that doest wonders; Thou hast made known Thy strength among the peoples. Thou hast with Thine arm redeemed Thy people, the sons of Jacob and Joseph.

With this introduction, the theme is set. God is holy, but he is also supreme. Because he is supreme and above all other powers, he does wonders; because he is holy, he redeems. Because his way is in holiness, he performs miracles in order to redeem. And now follows the description of how all this was wrought.

The waters saw Thee, O God; the waters saw Thee, they were in pain; the depths also trembled.

The voice of Thy thunder was in the whirlwind; the lightnings lighted up the world; the earth trembled and shook.
Thy way was in the sea, and Thy path in the great waters, and Thy footsteps were not known.
Thou didst lead Thy people like a flock, by the hand of Moses and Aaron.

Performing the saving miracle at the Sea of Reeds, God revealed himself as the Lord of Nature and as the Shepherd of his people, as the awesome, inaccessible power above all powers and as the Redeemer who will lead us as if "by the hand," as the Lord of hosts and as the Holy One of Israel.[21]

The psalm we have just analyzed has certainly been inspired by "the Song," the *shirah,* that Moses and the children of Israel sang after they walked across the Sea of Reeds.[22] There is a great similarity in the ideas and the tone which pervades both texts. At least one phrase has been almost literally borrowed by the psalmist. The words: "Thou didst lead Thy people like a flock" recall the parallel sentence of the song: "Thou in Thy love hast led the people that Thou hast redeemed." The thought is the same in both places and the verb, and its grammatical form, are identical; it is the Hebrew, *nahita.* This similarity induces us to have a closer look at the song from the point of view and interest of our study.

We note that, after introductory verses, the *shirah* may easily be divided into two parts. The first deals exclusively with the destruction of Pharaoh and his armies. There is no mention at all of the children of Israel. The second part still refers to what happened to Pharaoh and describes vividly the fear that befalls the Philistines, the Edomites and Moabites, and all the inhabitants of Canaan, when the tidings of these wondrous events reach them. But quite clearly, the emphasis there is on the acts which God performed in order to save his children and to lead them to his sanctuary. The first part is introduced with the words: "The Lord is a man of war, the Lord is His name." The second part begins with the exclamation: "Who is like unto Thee, O Lord, among the mighty? Who is like unto Thee, mighty in holiness?"[23] We believe that this is as it should be, and it is as we would expect it to be in the light of our discussion. It is appropriate that God should be called "a man of war" in a description of the utter destruction of Pharoah and his chariots. But when the emphasis is on redemption and the acts of war appear as prerequisites of the redeeming purpose, we are again confronted with a two-fold manifestation of divine performance. It is no surprise that this section of the song should open with a reference to God that makes mention of his incomparable elevation above all powers as well as of his being "mighty in holiness." "Mighty in holiness" is the parallel to "Thy way in holiness" in the psalm we have interpreted, just as: "Who is like unto Thee, O Lord among the mighty?" corresponds to: "Who is a great god like unto God?" in the same psalm.

However, what exactly is meant by "mighty in holiness"? We would say that the concept is identical with "*z'roa qodsho*," the arm of His holiness. It is the attribute of the Redeemer, who uses might for the sake of preserving the purpose he envisages because of his holiness. It is worth observing that the first part of the *shirah* contains a phrase which is the exact opposite to "mighty in holiness" and thus its stylistic parallel: it is, "mighty in power." It is an almost perfect correspondence of opposites. *"Ne'dar ba'qodesh,"* in one place: *Ne'dari ba'koah,* in the other. The first paragraph, describing the deeds of the warlord speaks of his "right hand" as "mighty in power"; the second paragraph elaborating on God's doings as the Redeemer, speaks of him as "mighty in holiness."

HIGH AND HOLY

There are, however, several passages that seem to suggest that it is the Holy One who is incomparable, that he dwells inaccessibly in a "high and holy" place. The heavens are often called his holy dwelling. We now propose to investigate those passages in order to see what they convey. A rather significant one we find in chapter 40 of Isaiah, where we read:

To whom then will ye liken Me that I should be equal? Saith the Holy One. (vs. 25)

We have maintained previously that God's incomparability was an indication of his remoteness and transcendence, proper to his quality as Lord of hosts. Here, however, it is the Holy One who speaks of it. As always, we have to consider the context in which the phrase has its place. Having made the statement about God's "unlikeness" to anything imaginable, he continues:

Lift up your eyes on high, and see: who hath created these?
He that bringeth out their host by number, He calleth them all by name: by the greatness of His might, and for that He is strong in power, not one faileth.

Quite clearly, the theme of divine transcendence is further sustained. That God is the creator of the heavens and their hosts is an indication of the fact that he cannot be compared to anything created; the "greatness of His might" and his "strong power" illustrate his elevation above all other powers. Nevertheless, transcendence is not the only theme of this verse. The concluding part of the verse hardly requires further

167

interpretation. God uses his might and power in order to preserve the heavenly hosts so that "no one faileth." In English, the meaning should—probably—be continued as, "no one faileth" in its course or function. The thought of the prophet comes through much clearer in the Hebrew original. The word is *ne'dar,* which is better rendered as missing. God uses his power in order to preserve each one individually, so that not one shall be lost. As to that "He bringeth out their host by number, He calleth them all by name" surely it could not mean that God is an excellent astronomer who knows the exact number of all the stars and planets and is even familiar with their names. To number is mostly a preserving activity. One usually counts that which one wishes to keep, which is of value; normally, what one counts one does not wish to lose. One counts one's money in order to know whether one has lost any. And to call someone by name means to know him, to pay attention to him, to turn to him to have some relationship to him. What Isaiah says is that God, who created "these," continues his interest and care for all these. He numbers them, he knows them individually, he preserves them. God is the Creator, but after the creation he is the Preserver. With his might he created, with his might he sustains and protects.

"To whom then will ye liken Me that I should be equal?" gains now in depth of meaning. We feel that this phrase should be understood differently from those of a similar nature, which we have come across earlier in our study. It is not identical in meaning with the exclamation in Psalm 77: "Who is a great god like unto God?" or with that which we have quoted from the song in Exodus: "Who is like unto Thee, O Lord, among the mighty?" In both these cases the impossibility of the comparison is with the mighty; in both cases the Hebrew word used is the same; in the Psalms, the singular, *el,* in Exodus, the plural, *elim.* In both cases, the subject matter is God's mightiness, which is incomparable. In our present text no reference is made to might. What is said is that no one may be likened to God. The reason emerges from what follows.

God is, indeed, above all creation; yet He uses His might to preserve His creation. By his essential nature, he is far removed from everything created; yet he knows them all "by name." He infinitely transcends them all; yet he cares for them sufficiently so that "not one shall be missing." Not only is he incomparable because he is infinite in essence and power; his true unlikeness to anything else is to be recognized in the fact that, notwithstanding his infinitude, he bends down to his creature caringly and preservingly.

These thoughts of the prophet are aptly followed up with the application of the universal truth to the historic situation of the Jewish people:

Why sayest thou, O Jacob, and speakest, O Israel: My way is hid from the Lord and my right is passed over from my God? Hast thou not known? has thou not heard that the everlasting God, the Lord, the Creator of the ends of the earth, fainteth not, neither is weary? His discernment is past searching out. He giveth power to the faint; and to him that hath no might He increaseth strength. (Isa. 40:27–29)

How can Israel believe that their way is hidden from before God! It is true that God is far removed from man; nevertheless, he is not the God of the deists. As he knows every one of the heavenly hosts "by name," so does he know Israel, their way and their right. He is the Creator; but having created the world, he has not abandoned it; he has not grown weary of it. On the contrary, his power and his might sustain the weak and the powerless. How this may be, why the One who infinitely transcends man should be concerned about him, we may never understand. "His discernment is past searching out." But just because of that, he is even more unequal to anyone to whom he might be compared. "Saith the Holy One" maintains Isaiah. Indeed, only the Holy One can speak like that.

We are now better prepared to understand another passage in Isaiah which contains a similar thought. It is found in chapter 57.

For thus saith the High and Lofty One that inhabiteth eternity, whose name is Holy. (vs. 15)

Once again, the opening phrase is concerning divine transcendence. Of this transcendent God it is said that His name is holy. But how does the prophet continue? "I dwell in the high and holy place, with him also that is of a contrite and humble spirit, to revive the spirit of the humble and to revive the heart of the contrite ones."

The reference to "the high and holy" place seems, of course, to strengthen the impression gained by the opening line that holiness is in transcendence. Yet, practically in the same breath the prophet also informs us that the God who dwells so high also dwells rather low, with him who is of "a contrite and humble spirit." But this is exactly what we found expressed in numerous other passages about the Holy One, who is the salvation of the needy and the poor, the source of strength for the lowly, without any mention of divine transcendence. A more literal translation would be more to the point. The Hebrew original does not have, "the high and holy place," which is rather misleading. We read: "I dwell high and holy, with him also that is of a contrite spirit." "High and holy" does not qualify a place, but the manner in which God "dwells," the way in which He is "present." On the strength of all the passages we have examined, we feel justified in saying that "high and holy" is a paradoxical concept which yet is true of the God of the Bible. "High and holy" is the way God is related to his creation. As the infinite Being, as the Creator, he is inaccessible, he is far removed from everything created; as the Holy One, he is accessible, he is near, he is "in the midst of thee." He is transcendent as well as immanent. The rabbis in the Midrash used to say of him: *rahoq v'qarob*, far and near. "I dwell in the high and holy" means: even though I am so far removed by my absolute nature, yet I am near through my actions. And because of that, as I dwell on high, I also dwell with the one of "a contrite and humble spirit" and revive him.

We know that in the biblical text by the name of God is meant his manifestation, the acts of self-revelation by which he makes himself known. The opening line of the text under discussion, "For thus saith the High and Lofty One that inhabiteth eternity, whose name is Holy," should be understood as saying: It is true, I am the High and Lofty One and I inhabit eternity. Such am I as the Absolute and Infinite, but my manifestation in the world is holy. The Infinite Being does what is beyond all human comprehension, he dwells high and holy.

It is to be noted that whenever God's "holy habitation" is mentioned in the Bible, often identical with the heavens, it is the "place" from which God turns toward man, knowing him and considering him.

In Deuteronomy, we read the prayer:

Look forth from the habitation of Thy holiness, from heaven, and bless Thy people Israel, and the land which Thou hast given us, as Thou didst swear unto our fathers. (26:15)

God's "holy habitation" is not what sets God and man apart; it is the point from which his blessings are expected. God relates himself to his people by blessing them and their land.

Of the prayers of the priests and the Levites at the time of restoration of the Temple service under King Hezekiah, it is said:

And their voice was heard, and their prayer came up to the habitation of His holiness, unto heaven. (II Chron. 30:27)

God's "holy habitation" is not really very far away. It can be reached through prayer.

Isaiah prayed:

Look down from heaven, and see, even from the habitation of Thy holiness and of Thy glory; where is Thy zeal and Thy mighty acts, the yearning of Thy heart and Thy compassions, now restrained toward me? (63:15)

God's zeal and mighty acts are due to the yearning of His heart and to His compassion. Could anyone have known of

God's nearness more intimately than the one who knew of "the yearning" of God's heart for man! It is that intimacy which the prophet is missing and it is for its renewal that he prays. But he directs his plea to the heaven, to God's holy habitation. Even though it is high, yet it is God's "holy place," whence prayers are answered. Needless to say, the place is not a geographic point, but the quality of holiness with which God relates himself to the world and to man.

The psalmist, too, uses the concept of God's "holy habitation" in the same way. In psalm 20 we read:

Now know I that the Lord saveth His anointed; He will answer him from the heaven of His holiness with the mighty acts of His saving right hand. (vs. 7)

The passage is a typical double-function one. He saves and he does so with mighty acts. It is the dual function of the redeemer. Because he dwells on high, he has the power to save; because his habitation is also holy, he has "the yearning and compassion" to save. Thus he answers his anointed from "the heaven of His holiness."

In another place, the psalmist calls on man to "extol Him that rideth upon the skies, whose name is the Lord." And he adds:

A father of the fatherless and a judge of the widows is God in the habitation of His holiness. (68:5)

Though God is exalted above the skies, yet it is from the habitation of His holiness that he acts like a father and protector of orphans and widows.

God turns his attention toward the inhabitants of the earth, "To hear the groaning of the prisoner; to loose those that are appointed to death" (Ps. 102:21); but in order to do so, he looks down "from the height of His holiness, from heaven."

Jeremiah mentions the term *m'on qodsho,* the habitation of His holiness. The passage may, however, require some elucidation in order to be seen in its full significance. It runs as follows:

172

The Lord doth roar from on high and utter His voice from the
habitation of His holiness;
He doth mightily roar because of His sanctuary. (25:30)

The Hebrew, *navehu,* in the text, is God's sanctuary in Zion.
It is the *n've qodsho,* the habitation of His holiness, which
occurs in the Song of Moses and the children of Israel, to
which God was leading his people in his love. The same word,
navehu, is used by King David when, on his flight from Zion
because of Absolom's rebellion, he says to the priest Sadoq: "If
I shall find favour in the eyes of the Lord, He will bring me
back and show me . . . His habitation."[24] Jeremiah juxtaposes,
"m'on qodsho," the habitation of His holiness, to *navehu,* to
his "earthly habitation" in Zion. His "mighty roar because of
His sanctuary" is a symbolical expression of his sorrow over
the destruction of the Temple in Zion, which has become
necessary.[25] God's "holy place" in Zion symbolizes God's nearness to his people; it is a witness to his divine providence; it
is a manifestation that "great is in thy midst the Holy One of
Israel." The destruction of the Temple is the elimination of
that manifestation; it is the withdrawal of the Holy One from
the midst of the people. The divine "yearning and compassion"
have to be curbed; the quality of divine holiness has to be
controlled, its function must be withheld. Thus, it is from the
habitation of His holiness on high that God roars because of
the destruction of the habitation of His holiness below. God's
quality of holiness is tragically involved in the destiny of Zion
and her people.

HOLY, THE LORD OF HOSTS

We are now in a better position to appreciate the entire
significance of the revelation that was granted to Isaiah, with
whose consideration we have started our study. "Holy, holy,
holy is the Lord of hosts; the whole earth is full of His glory."
In the light of our analysis, one might say that the exclamation
declares a coincidence between opposites. It would seem that

the "Holy" and the "Lord of hosts" represent contradictory forces of divine self-revelation. The one stands for love, mercy, and compassion; the other, for might, anger and judgment. The one speaks of God as near, a friend and a protector; the other, as remote, a stern judge, and even as the Wholly Other. But however contradictory both functions may be, they are attributes of the One God. The Lord of hosts is the same as the Holy One of Israel. The Lord of hosts is holy. In God, both attributes are one. This brings the "Lord of hosts" himself closer to the world and to man than he appeared by his own characteristics. If he is holy, then even the divine anger and judgment must somehow be related to God's nearness, to the "yearning and compassion." Only because God remains related to his creation does he act in it; because he considers man does he address himself to him even though with his "anger" and "judgment."

In our opinion that "the whole earth is full of His glory," is a further elaboration of the same theme. Quite obviously it is a statement about divine immanence. If God's glory is present everywhere, then God is not inaccessible. It should be noted that the manifestation of *kabod,* of the divine glory, may be brought about by both, the quality of holiness and that which distinguishes the Lord of hosts. The "high holiness" of God, as we have defined it, is explicitly called by the psalmist the greatness of God's glory, when he says:

All the kings of earth shall give thanks, O Lord. . . .
Yes they shall sing the ways of the Lord; for great is the glory of the Lord. For though the Lord be high, yet regardeth He the lowly, and the haughty He knoweth from afar. Though I walk in the midst of trouble, Thou quickenest me. (138:4–7)

Occasionally, in his prophecies of redemption, Isaiah makes reference to the glory of God, which is being revealed through his comforting acts of salvation.[26]

While these and similar revelations of *kabod* may well be ascribed to the Holy One, others are obviously the function of

174

the Lord of hosts. The psalmist calls the Lord of hosts, *melekh ha–kabod,* king of glory. The glory of God often appears through his power and judgment. According to Isaiah, the glory of God will be feared, "for distress will come in like a flood, which the breath of the Lord driveth." The relationship between glory and judgment is found in Ezekiel, who says:

And I will set my glory among the nations, and all the nations shall see My judgment that I have executed, and My hand that I have laid upon them. (39:21)

This is, however, an activity that we have found always emanating from the Lord of hosts. Both the Lord of hosts and the Holy One reveal the divine glory in the earth. Both express qualities of divine immanence and nearness. Even his judgment is, though beyond human understanding, not apart from his yearning for his creation and for his compassion with it. For holy, holy, holy is the Lord of hosts.

HOLY—THE WORD AND ITS MEANING

Thus far, we have investigated the manner in which the term *qadosh,* holy, is used in the Bible in relationship to God. We have tried to derive the meaning from the work that the word is doing in the numerous passages in which it occurs. However, in order to grasp the application of the concept of holiness to man and to objects, we shall have to attempt to discover the basic meaning of the term, holy, as it appears in the Bible. In our opinion this appears mainly in those passages in which "holy" has no religious significance at all. There are quite a few such passages in the Bible.

We shall list most of these neutral passages together so that the meaning of the word may emerge with accumulative force. We underline the word which is a derivative of the root, *qadosh,* holy.

And they *set apart* Kedesh in Galilee in the hill country of Naphtali, and Shechem . . . and Kiriath-arba . . . these were the appointed

175

cities for all the children of Israel . . . that whosoever killeth any person through error might flee thither. (Josh. 20:7–9)

And Jehu said: "*Designate* a solemn assembly for Baal." And they proclaimed it. (II Kings 10:20)

"I have commanded My *designated* ones, yes, I have called My mighty ones for mine anger. . . . Hark, the uproar of the kingdoms of the nations gathered together! The Lord of hosts mustereth the host of battle. They come from a far country, from the end of heaven, even the Lord, and the weapons of His indignation. (Isa. 13:3–5)

Prepare ye war against her. (Jer. 6:4)

Pull them out like sheep for the slaughter and *prepare* them for the day of slaughter. (Jer. 12:3)

And I will *prepare* destroyers against thee, every one with his weapons. (Jer. 22:7)

Set ye up a standard in the land, blow the horn among the nations, *prepare* the nations against her, call together against her the kingdom of Arrarat, Minni, and Ashkenaz . . . *Prepare* against her the nations, the kings of the Medes. (Jer. 51:27–28)

Prepare ye a fast, call a solemn assembly, gather the elders and all the inhabitants of the land unto the house of the Lord your God. (Joel 1:14)

Blow the horn in Zion, *prepare* a fast, call a solemn assembly; gather the people, *prepare* a congregation, assemble the elders, gather the children. (Joel 2:15–16)

Proclaim ye this among the nations, *prepare* war; stir up the mighty men; let all the men of war draw near, let them come up. (Joel 4:9)

Hold thy peace at the presence of the Lord God, for the day of the Lord is at hand, for the Lord hath prepared a sacrifice, He hath *designated* His guests. (Zeph. 1:7)

As usual, we have adopted the old translation of the Jewish Publication Society of America. However, we deviated from it in the quotation from II Kings, Isaiah, and Zephaniah, as well as in the first two quotations from Joel. As far as possible, we have retained the rendering, prepare.

The passage in Joshua has, of course, no significance whatever of sanctification in the religious sense. The cities of refuge were not sanctified. They were set apart to serve for a specific purpose. The Revised Version has "appointed," which may be even more exact than "set apart." It brings out more strongly the positive idea of being set apart *for* something. The cities were designated to serve as places of refuge. It is in this sense that Jeremiah uses the term. "Prepare them for the day of slaughter," means of course mark them out, give them over for that day. Similarly, "prepare ye war against her," stands for, determine, mark her out for war. The nations and the kings that are to be "prepared" against Babylon, are the powers that have been chosen to wage war against her. In the light of these passages we have translated *m'qudashay* in Isaiah, as "My designated ones," and not "My consecrated ones." As with Jeremiah, God marks out the nations that are to wage war against Babylon, so here too, he causes the warriors, whom he has designated for the task of destruction, to do their work. "My consecrated ones," while not wrong, is misleading because of its religious connotation. The Revised Version has here, "my sanctified ones," which is meaningless. *M'qudashay* are the armies that gather from all the corners of the earth, as "the weapons of His indignation." God calls them *m'qudashay* because they have been given a specific task; they have been designated by the divine plan to perform in a certain manner. Nor should one render the phrase, *hiqdish q'ruav*, in Zephaniah as, "He hath consecrated His guests." He has invited his guests, would be much nearer to the correct sense. We prefer here the Revised Version, which has: he hath bid his guests. To invite implies to mark out from among others and to designate with a definite purpose in view.

As to our deviations in translation in the quotations from II Kings and Joel, they explain each other. *Qad'shu som* in the two passages we have quoted from Joel should certainly not be translated as, sanctify ye a fast. These are the only two occasions in the Bible where the phrase is met. To sanctify a fast sounds suspiciously un-biblical. Moreover, a careful examination of the texts will show that the rendering, sanctify ye, in this connection is a misunderstanding.

In the first passage from Joel, *Qad'shu som* is followed by *Qir'u asara*, call a solemn assembly. Now in the quotation from II Kings, we find the phrase, *Qad'shu asara*. To translate this phrase, as has been done, as: Sanctify a solemn assembly, is quite wrong. For the text continues: "And they proclaimed it"; or in more exact literal conformity with the Hebrew, *vayiqrau*, "and they called it."[27] According to the context, *Qad'shu asara*, means, call ye, or, proclaim ye a solemn assembly. As such the term is in keeping with what we have found to be neutral, not specifically religiously significant. What Jehu said was: set apart a day. That the Bible informs us with the word, *vayiqru*, that they *called* such an assembly as they were asked to, proves that *Qad'shu asara* in II Kings is identical in meaning with *Qir'u asara*, call a solemn assembly, which is used by Joel. One might say that *Qad'shu* in this context equals *Qir'u;* the meaning in both cases is obviously the same: call ye a solemn assembly, designate a day to be observed as such. For this reason we translate in Joel, *Qad'shu som, Qir'u asara*, as: designate (or proclaim) a fast, call a solemn assembly.[28]

Similarly, in our second quotation from Joel, *Qad'shu Qahal*, should not be rendered as, sanctify the congregation. As such the phrase would keep rather strange company. It is immediately preceded by "gather the people" and followed by "assemble the elders, gather the children." The verb, sanctify, flanked by the verbs, gather and assemble, would be poorly placed. It jars on the ear as well as on the mind. Prophets did not write like that. Meant is, preparing a congregation, the bringing together of a congregation for the occasion. It is synonymous with "gather" and "assemble." It is the appointing of the people as a congregation for the observance of the fast proclaimed.

On the basis of the passages we have listed and discussed, we conclude that the word, *qadosh,* does have a meaning without any specifically religious connotation.[29] *Qadosh* is that which is set apart, marked out, assigned, designated. We are employing these many descriptions in order to indicate that no one by itself gives us the full meaning. The *qadosh* is set apart from others but it is also assigned to something; it is marked out, but for a definite purpose and it is thus designated as something to something. To make a something *qadosh* is to remove it from one context and place it into another. The cities of refuge set apart by Joshua at first belonged to one group with all other cities of the land. Later, they were singled out, removed from their group and equipped with a function which related them to a different context of functions and significances. Originally, the day to be proclaimed a fast is like any other day. In order to be designated as a day of fast, it has to be selected, set apart from all other days and associated with a new meaning or purpose.

The primary neutral meaning of the idea of the holy is fully retained in its specifically religious implication. Holy, in the religious sense—and as the word is normally understood—is that which has been removed from its original frame of reference and placed into one in which everything derives its position by reference to God. This is quite obviously so, when we consider the purely ritualistic meaning of the idea. Holy objects, animals, etc., are holy because they have been severed from their "natural" place within the neutral scheme of things and given a function within a realm that is reserved for the service of God. Their character is now determined by the form of their relatedness to the divine, the purely ritualistic meaning of the term is still rather close to what we have found to be its primary non-religious significance. Essentially it means: being set apart from and being assigned to. The assignation, however, is a specific one: assignation to God. Our

179

main interest in this study is, however, not to deal with the purely ritualistic aspect of the holy. Quite obviously, there are various forms and grades of holiness that designate a man in his relatedness to God.

We may distinguish between the ritual and the spiritual aspects of holiness. The holy in relationship to man belongs in the category of the spiritual as does the holiness of God. One might, however, consider the sanctification of the priests as the bridge between the spiritual and the merely ritualistic. Much more than mere ritual is involved in the appointment to priesthood. We adduce this clearly from a passage in Numbers. We have in mind Korah's rebellion against Moses and Aaron. He and his follower sought priesthood. In answer to their request, Moses had occasion to explain how priesthood comes about. He puts it this way:

In the morning the Lord will show who are His; and who is holy, and will cause him to come near unto Him . . . and it shall be that the man whom the Lord doth choose, he shall be holy. (16:5–7)

These are most illuminating words. Holiness, nearness, and being chosen are mentioned and related to each other. The holy one is brought near to God. The chosen one is brought near to God. One is brought near by being chosen. Furthermore, the one whom God chooses is holy. This gives us the definition: to be holy is to be chosen by God by being brought near to him. This is the spiritual factor in the sanctification of man for priesthood. To sanctify may be said to mean, to choose in order to bring near. What in the neutral meaning of the term, holy, meant to be assigned to or, to be designated for, becomes in the spiritual-religious sense nearness, closeness, a personal relation between God and the priest.

We may now better appreciate the nature of the application of the concept of the holy to God, as it revealed itself to us in the previous section of this chapter. While the concept of choosing does imply "singling out" and "separating from," it is not yet sanctification. Sanctification consists of bringing near, establishing the relation, the closeness of association. To single out or separate or to withdraw from is a necessary prerequisite of sanctification. This is, in fact, explicitly so stated in I Chronicles, where it is said of the appointment of Aaron: "and Aaron was separated that he should be sanctified as most holy."[30] Separation is quite clearly not sanctification; it is a pre-condition for sanctification. The holy is separated away, but it is not holy because of its separation. It is holy because it is near, because it is close to God. It can be close because it is withdrawn from association and involvements that would render nearness to God impossible.

How does all this affect the application of the idea of the holy to God? We have found that holiness in the priest and—anticipating what yet has to be shown—in man in general is nearness to God, standing in personal relationship with him. Correspondingly, holiness in God should mean nearness to what alone there is besides God, his creation. As far as man is concerned, it is God turning toward him with love and compassion; it is, indeed, as we have found it, the Holy One "in the midst of thee." As with man the pre-condition for human holiness is separation from that which may prevent nearness to God, so with God, too—as it were—separation and withdrawal are the prerequisite of his holiness. But God is already separate by his essential nature; he is unlike anything created; he is Absolute and Infinite. However, as the Absolute he cannot be near, he cannot dwell in the midst of his people. The Infinite is unrelated to the finite by its essential nature; it is indifferent toward it. Thus God, too, as it were, has to separate himself from his absoluteness in order to turn with care and consideration toward his creation; he has to "withdraw" from the "natural" indifference of his infinitude in order to be "the father of the orphans and the judge of the widows in his holy habitation." He has to "curb" his Wholly Otherness so that he may come near for the sake of his holiness. It is the awe-inspiring greatness of his holiness that he who is infinitely removed draws near and makes himself accessible.

YE SHALL BE HOLY

The spiritual aspect of holiness arises most forcefully from the relationship that, according to the Bible, exists between God and Israel. Only on the basis of that relationship could the children of Israel be commanded:

Ye shall be holy; for I the Lord your God am holy.[31]

With Israel, holiness has a two-fold significance: it is a condition and a goal. They are God's holy people, God has sanctified them; they shall become a kingdom of priests and a holy nation unto God; they have to sanctify themselves.

God has sanctified them in the manner very similar to the designation of the priests, by choosing them and bringing them near. In Deuteronomy, it is said:

For thou art a holy people unto the Lord Thy God: the Lord Thy God hath chosen thee to be His own treasure, out of all the peoples that are upon the face of the earth. (7:6)[32]

Israel was made a holy people by God by his choosing them from among the other nations and taking them unto himself. This is a form of sanctification very similar to the ritualistic one. The people themselves were passive. They were singled out and brought near to God. They had as little share in it as the Aaronites, who were chosen to serve in the sanctuary. Strangely enough, this people that is sanctified by God is commanded to sanctify itself.

Sanctify yourselves therefore, and be ye holy; for I am the Lord your God.
And keep ye My statutes and do them.
I am the Lord who sanctify you. (Lev. 20:7)

These words almost convey the idea that Israel has to sanctify itself because it is already sanctified by God. At least in one other place it is indeed put so, though in somewhat different phrasing. Toward the end of the chapter in Leviticus, from which we have quoted, we read:

182

And ye shall be holy unto Me, for I the Lord am holy, and have set you apart from the peoples that ye should be mine.

We have found that God sanctified Israel by setting them apart and taking them to be his. It is the essence of their being sanctified by God. The children of Israel are thus commanded to be holy because God, who made them holy, is holy. That they shall sanctify themselves and be holy because God is holy is, of course, expressed repeatedly.[33] However, in the above quotation from Leviticus (20:7) the reason that holiness is demanded of them is: "for I am the Lord Thy God." In yet another passage, the command to be holy seems to be related to their redemption from Egypt.

For I am the Lord that brought you up out of the land of Egypt to be your God: ye shall therefore be holy for I am holy. (Lev. 11:45)

Not only Israel's obligation to become holy, but God's own holiness is here related to the Exodus. Our wonder increases as we hear further that God's sanctifying Israel is linked to his bringing them out of Egypt.

I am the Lord who sanctify you, that brought you out of the land of Egypt to be your God. (Lev. 22: 32–33)

We have collected now a rather confusing combination of ideas. Israel shall be holy because God is holy; they shall be holy because God is their God. They shall be holy because God has made them holy. Because God has brought them out of Egypt to be their God, they shall be holy, for he is holy. God, who has brought them out of Egypt in order to be their God, made them holy. The confusion is due to a multitude of concepts, which—at first sight—appeared to be unrelated to each other. Actually, a form of strict logical consistency prevails among them and connects them with each other.

The phrase, "for I am the Lord thy God," which we have found to be used parallel to, "for I am holy," is indeed logically identical with it. What is meant by "I am the Lord thy God" becomes clear if, recalling what has been stated in Chapter 1, we shall render it as: I am Y thy *Elohim*. As we have found in the first chapter of our study, this does not mean: I God, am God, the God whom you acknowledge to be God. Similarly, the two quotations that make mention of the Exodus should read: "I am Y that brought you up from the land of Egypt to become your *Elohim*." God became their *Elohim* by bringing them out of Egypt. "Your *Elohim*" is God who has redeemed them, who has guided them and protected and saved them; the God who is with them, "in the midst of thee." But this is exactly what we have found to be the function of the Holy One of Israel. Thus, "Sanctify yourselves and be holy, for I am holy," is identical with, "sanctify yourselves and be holy, for I am Y thy *Elohim*." But in redeeming the children of Israel from Egypt, God chose them from among the nations and took them to be his. This again we have found to be the meaning of their sanctification by God. Thus, through the Exodus God revealed his own holiness and in doing so, acting because of his holiness as their redeemer, he also sanctified them in choosing them and taking them for his own. Thus the various passages we have quoted say one and the same thing, i.e., sanctify yourselves and be holy for God is holy. He revealed to them his holiness by making himself *their Elohim* through his redeeming acts; in making himself their *Elohim*, he sanctified them by taking them unto himself. We are then left with the one concept which requires interpretation, the command that Israel become holy because God is holy.

What is the connection between Israel's obligation to become holy and God's being holy? God sanctified the priests and Israel by choosing them and bringing them near to himself. This is passive holiness. One is actively holy by bringing about the same relationship to God by one's own effort and endeavor. "Sanctify yourself," therefore, means: seek the nearness of God, choose him, relate yourself to him, cling to him. This is necessary because God is holy; he is your *Elohim*. And he cannot be yours unless you are his. God is not holy because he saves; he saves because he is holy, because he is near, because he is with you, because of his love and compassion, because of his "yearning" for you. His nearness is not a spatial determination, but one of the spirit. His holiness is the bond between himself and his creation. Thus, it requires mutuality. In his mercy, he may help man, even though man does not acknowledge him. But he cannot be near man unless man is near Him. Nearness in the spirit is mutuality of relationship. God sanctified Israel by choosing them and taking them to himself. He brought them near to himself because he is holy. But his holiness must be met with holiness. He took them for his own, but they cannot be his own in the spirit unless they choose him as he chose them, unless they draw near as they were brought near. They cannot be his very own unless they give themselves to him to be his very own. Therefore, "Ye shall be holy, for I Y your *Elohim* am holy."

How does man sanctify himself, how does he choose God and move close to him? In the numerous passages that enjoin on Israel to become holy, the obligation is connected with listening to the voice of God and doing his will.[34] Nor is this limited to any specific aspect of the law, the ritual or the sacrificial. Israel sanctifies itself by striving to fulfill God's will in all matters in which it has been revealed or it may be ascertained. The characteristic passage, supported by all the other related passages, is:

Now therefore, if ye will hearken unto My voice indeed, and keep My covenant, then ye shall be Mine own treasure from among all peoples; for the earth is Mine; and ye shall be unto me a kingdom of priests and a holy nation. (Exod. 19:5–6)

As the various passages show this applies to every branch of the divine commandments, those "between man and God," as well as those "between man and man."

The idea should be understood in its two-fold relevance. Holiness is not the child of faith. One can have faith in a God who is far removed, who is "hiding his face." Faith in itself is not relation to God; it is essentially one-sided. The strength of faith is believing in God, even though he is "hiding his face," even though he seems to be silent and indifferent to man's personal destiny. Faith is not mutuality. Holiness is living with God, near him, in his company. But how can a mere man do that? How can a human being move near God, establishing contact in actuality with the divine? But for the moments of God's self-revelation, when God turns to man in convincing human experience, how can man be with God in reality? And even those rarest of moments are altogether God's doing and not in the least initiated by man. According to biblical teaching, man comes near to God by doing God's will. God revealed to man His will, so that by doing His will man may link himself to God. God is in His voice, in the covenant. By hearkening to His voice and keeping the covenant man holds on to God; it is his very real bond with God. Thus he comes close to God, thus he answers God's holiness by sanctifying himself through his own nearness to Him.

The idea also implies that holiness does not originate in what a man does but in the fact that he does it in fulfilling the divine will or intention; that what is done is done for the sake of God. Holiness is not ethics, for instance. Holiness is a specifically religious category. The highest form of ethics may be unrelated to holiness. It is a noble thing to do the good for its own sake, but it is not holiness. Holiness is being with God by doing God's will. Now, it is the will of God that man should act ethically. But if he acts ethically for the sake of the good, he is an ethical man; if he does so for the sake of God, in order to do God's will, he is striving for holiness.

The connection between sanctification and listening to the voice of God may help us to clarify another concept which has its place within the realm of thought that we are investigating. It is the concept of sanctifying God or of its opposite, that of profaning his name. At least in one place, both are related to the keeping of God's commandments. The passage is found in Leviticus:

And ye shall keep My commandments and do them: I am the Lord. And ye shall not profane the name of My holiness; but I will be hallowed among the children of Israel: I am Y who hallow you, that brought you out of the land of Egypt, to become your *Elohim*. (22:31–33)

We are introduced here to the idea that God, too, has to be hallowed or sanctified. The idea of course occurs in other places as well and we shall yet turn our attention to them. Here, however, it is linked to the keeping of God's commandments. We have found earlier that Israel, who is sanctified by God, has to sanctify herself. Now we hear that God, who is holy, has still to be hallowed. This is indeed surprising. In which sense may it be said that God will be sanctified by human action? How is it to be understood that the sanctification of the divine, or its profanation, are dependent on the keeping of God's commandments or on their rejection?

By doing the will of God man chooses God, he holds on to Him and lives in His company. He sanctifies himself. But man's sanctification is the answer to God's holiness. He is to become holy because God is holy. It is the human end of the mutuality which is required by holiness. The revealed will of God, His voice and His law, is the instrument of man's sanctification. As man does the will of God, he moves to God in response to God's movement toward him; he sanctifies himself responding to God's holiness. Thus by keeping the commandments as a means of human sanctification, man acknowledges God's holiness, which requires that man too be holy. Thus God is being hallowed. On the other hand, the violation of God's commandments is a rejection of the instrument of human sanctification and of the demand, "Be ye holy, for I Y your *Elohim* am holy." It implies a denial of God's holiness. It is tantamount to a profanation of "the name of his holiness."

To put it in simpler language, the violation of God's will is an act of separation between man and God. It is a deed against the manifestation of divine holiness that God is "in the midst of thee." It is an attempt to remove God from the midst of men. It is a rejection of his quality of holiness. But he who does the will of God establishes closeness. He does what needs doing in order to bring God into the midst of men. He acts in harmony with God's holiness, making it manifest in the world through his own way of living. In this way, God is being hallowed through the deeds of man.

SANCTIFYING GOD'S NAME

The profanation and sanctification of God's name forms one of the major themes in Ezekiel. Although with Ezekiel the concept is not directly connected with the keeping of the commandments, in essence the idea is the same as we have analyzed it in the preceding section.

Ezekiel does not mention either the Lord of hosts or the Holy One of Israel. He uses the term *shem qodsho,* name of his holiness, or—as we interpret it—the manifestation of his holiness. A recurring subject in his prophecy is the profanation of this name and what God will do so that it may be sanctified again. A striking passage is, for instance, the one that we find in chapter 36:

And when they came into the nations, whither they came, they profaned the name of My holiness; in that men said of them: These are the people of the Lord, and are gone forth out of His land. (vs. 20)

The strange idea is conveyed here that the exiles profaned the divine name in being exiles, in having moved from their native land. The traditional Jewish interpretation is that, since they are God's people, God should have protected them and their land. To their enemies, the fact that they are in exile proves that their God is unable to protect them. He is lacking in power. This is a lowering of the glory of God.[35] They brought about this degradation of the divine name through their sins, which were the cause of their expulsion from their

188

land. On the basis of our analysis, we would call a suggestion that God was lacking in power a desecration of the name of the Lord of hosts and not of the name of His holiness. However, independently of our own investigation, we find it difficult to accept the traditional interpretation because of the local textual evidence in Ezekiel. The profanation of God's name, which is here attributed to Israel, in another passage is the doing of God himself. Thus God promises: "Neither will I cause the name of My holiness to be profaned any more" (39:7). This has occasioned a great deal of embarrassment for translators. How is it conceivable that God could have actively brought about the profanation of his name. It has been toned down to, "neither will I suffer My holy name to be profaned any more."[36] The fact is that the Hebrew original is *ahel,* which is the active causative. God himself profanes the name of his holiness. Indeed, when the destruction of Jerusalem is prophesied, the prophet says so in a manner which does not permit any circumlocution.

Thus saith the Lord God: Behold I will profane My sanctuary, the pride of your power, the desire of your eyes, and the longing of your soul; and your sons and your daughters whom ye have left behind shall fall by the sword. (24:21)

God himself does the profaning. It is true, no explicit mention is made here of the name of his holiness. So it would seem if one reads only the English translation, but the Hebrew has, *miqdashi,* which means, my holy, my sanctified place. This comes very close to the profanation of his name. When King David spoke of the same sanctuary, he said: "to build Thee a house for the name of Thy holiness."[37] The *miqdash* is holy because it is dedicated to God's name of holiness. In our terminology it is the visible symbol that God dwells in the midst of Israel; it symbolizes the manifestation of God's holiness, the "name" of his holiness. God threatens that he himself will bring about the profanation of the manifestation of his holiness, as he later promises not to do so again. What then is

189

meant by such profanation that can be executed by the people as well as by God?

We may elucidate the meaning of profanation by discovering what is meant by sanctifying the name. This is what is said about it; this is what God promises to do for the sake of the name of his holiness:

> And I will sanctify My great name . . . and the nations shall know that I am the Lord, saith the Lord God, when I shall be sanctified in you before their eyes. For I will take you from among the nations, and gather you out of all the countries, and will bring you into your own land. (36:23)

It is then by taking back Israel unto himself, purifying them and placing his spirit within them, that God sanctifies his name, revealing himself as the Holy One. The thought is repeated several times.

> With your sweet savour will I accept you, when I bring you out from the peoples and gather you out of the countries wherein ye have been scattered; and I will be sanctified in you in the sight of the nations. (20:41)

By redeeming them from among the nations and accepting them again God is being sanctified. This is stated even more clearly in the following verses:

> Therefore thus saith the Lord God: Now will I bring back the captivity of Jacob, and have compassion upon the whole house of Israel; and I will be jealous for the name of My holiness. . . . when I have brought them back from the peoples and have gathered them out of their enemies' lands and am sanctified in them in the sight of many nations. (39:25–27)

God is jealous for the name of his holiness and thus he is motivated to have compassion on Israel and to redeem them from among the nations. But we have found that to redeem them, to have compassion, to accept, to take Israel for his own, are the manifestations of the Holy One of Israel. In exile, God's face is hidden; he seems to be far removed from his people, as if he no longer considered them. God is not revealed as the Holy One of Israel. Thus he is jealous for the name of his holiness. He takes his people back for his own and in this act of reconciliation, God once again becomes known as the Holy One. He sanctifies his name; he makes manifest his attribute of holiness. It is important to note that in all our quotations God is said to be sanctified "in you" or "in them" and "in the sight" or "before the eyes" of the nations. God's sanctification is his self-revelation as being "in the midst of thee." This comes to expression most powerfully in the passage referred to already, in which God promises not to cause again the profanation of the name of his holiness. This is the passage in its entirety:

And I will send a fire on Magog, and on them that dwell safely in the isles; and they shall know that I am the Lord. And the name of My holiness I will make known in the midst of My people Israel; neither will I cause the name of My holiness to be profaned any more; and the nations shall know that I am the Lord, the Holy One in Israel. (39:6–7)

One is reminded of the dual-function passages in Isaiah, of the Redeemer, Lord of hosts, and Holy One of Israel. The Holy One is in Israel, the quality of his holiness will be made known in the midst of his people. But the nations, too, will know that he is Y for the power of Magog will be shattered and the oppressed and persecuted will go free.[38]

We may therefore say that God sanctifies the name of his holiness by acting again as the Holy One; by revealing himself as the one who is with the poor and needy, who may well rely on him. But when God withdraws, when he "hides his face," when he withholds the manifestation of his attribute of holiness, he profanes the name of his holiness. He suppresses his "yearning and compassion," he violates the quality of his relatedness to his creation. But man too can profane God's name of holiness. When man withdraws from God, when he removes himself from association with him, when he severs the relationship, he rejects God's nearness; he denies the manifestation of God's holiness, he profanes it. We believe that it is of such profanation that Ezekiel accuses Israel. A careful reading of one of the key passages seems to indicate it. We already had occasion to quote it in part; we shall now analyze it as a whole.

And when they *came* unto the nations, *whither they came,* they profaned the name of My holiness; in that man said of them: These are the people of the Lord, and *are gone forth* out of His land. But I had pity for the name of My holiness, which the house of Israel had profaned among the nations, *whither they came.* Therefore say unto the house of Israel: Thus saith the Lord God: I do not this for your sake, O house of Israel, but for the name of My holiness, which ye have profaned among the nations, *whither ye came.* (36:20–22)

We have underlined the recurring idea of coming among the nations. The seemingly unnecessary repetition is quite obviously a stylistic method of emphasis. It contains the point the prophet wishes to make. One senses it especially, since it is conceptually connected with the burden of Israel's guilt— they are the people of God and they are gone forth out of God's land. Now, to have been driven out from one's land may be the result of guilt, but it is no guilt in itself. The continuous repetition of the idea that "they came among the nations, whither they came," however, suggests that they came freely, voluntarily. They were, of course, exiles, but their conduct in the land of their exile was such that it gave occasion to the host nations to conclude that they "are gone forth from His land." They had settled down as if they never meant to return, as if they were glad to have left the land. The emphasis here is on "His land." They reject God's land. But the land is God's because it is the place wherein he makes manifest his nearness to Israel. Rejecting God's land, they reject God's nearness to his people, they separate themselves from God, who desires to dwell in their midst. Thus they profane the name of his holiness. That this is the issue at stake, one may gather from the change in the minds of the nations that is brought about as a result of God's being jealous for the name of his holiness. In connection with that it is said:

And the nations shall know that the house of Israel went into captivity for their iniquity, because they broke faith with Me, and I hid My face from them. (39:23)

It is regarding this matter that the nations are originally mistaken. The behavior, the way of life, of the exiles causes them to believe that the people of Israel have rejected God. And so indeed they did. As God, however, takes pity on his name and restores his association with Israel, even though they do not deserve it, the nations learn to understand the true meaning of the exile of God's people. God's name becomes sanctified again, not through Israel but as a result of God's intervention in the course of history.

If, however, man's separation from God and rejection of God's nearness indicates man's profanation of God's holiness, then man's clinging to God and living testimony to his nearness is a form of sanctifying the name of his holiness through human behavior. We believe that Isaiah speaks of such a form of sanctification in a passage which normally causes a great deal of difficulty to commentators. The verses are found in chapter 8. The translation from which we usually quote runs as follows:

Say ye not: A conspiracy, concerning all whereof this people do say: A conspiracy; neither fear ye their fear, nor account it dreadful. The Lord of hosts, Him shall ye sanctify; and let Him be your fear, and let Him be your dread. (vss. 12–13)

This, of course, is an obscure passage. What conspiracy has the prophet in mind? Even more difficult is the parallelism in the text. According to it, to sanctify the Lord of hosts would be the counter balance to the demand not to acknowledge as a conspiracy everything that the people are willing to adjudge as such. What, however, could be the possible connection between these two concepts?

As to our first problem, we prefer the R. V.'s rendering of the Hebrew *Qesher,* as confederacy. The reference in the preceding context to "Rezin and Remaliah's son" shows that the prophet's subject is the policy of alliances of the time. *Qesher* stands here for association, alliance. The people enter into alliances because they are afraid of Assyria. The prophet warns against such alliances. They are not to be relied upon; nor is the power to be feared whom they fear. Instead of relying on alliances, they should rely on God; instead of trembling before Assyria, they should fear God. Now, we have heard Isaiah declare often enough that Israel should rely on the Holy One of Israel. It was the "policy" recommended by him in place of the alliance with Egypt; the same policy is recommended here in a different constellation of power politics. God's people should withdraw from participation in power politics and instead put its trust in God. However, such reliance on God alone is a sanctification of God. It is based on man's conviction that God is to be relied upon, that he is the savior, that he is near, that he looks upon man with love and compassion; in other words, it is the affirmation that God is the Holy One. It is not affirmation by mere words; it is entrusting one's life unto him in the face of an overwhelming enemy, at a moment of supreme crisis. Not to be afraid, because he who fears God need fear no man; not to rely on alliances with any earthly power, because he who is allied to God needs no other alliances; such complete trust that God is near and helps, all appearances to the contrary, is the highest form of sanctifying the name of God's holiness.[39] This is, indeed, how Jews understood the meaning of *qiddush ha–shem,* the Sanctification of the Name, through the ages. To give one's life for the sake of God in loyalty to his command is the act of supreme trust and reliance on him. In the knowledge of His nearness, death itself is being conquered.

In Ezekiel, God is sanctified through divine action, which reveals that God is near his people; in the passage we have just discussed, Isaiah speaks of God's sanctification through

194

human action, which testifies to man's faith in the nearness of God. In our opinion, both these forms of sanctification are encountered in chapter 20 of Numbers in the closest proximity. According to the biblical narrative, Moses and Aaron failed at the waters of *Meribah*. The traditional Jewish interpretation is that their failure consisted in smiting the rock, which eventually yielded water, instead of talking to it, as they were told by God to do. Of their punishment for this transgression the Bible says:

And the Lord said unto Moses and Aaron: 'Because ye believed not in Me, to sanctify Me in the eyes of the children of Israel, therefore ye shall not bring this assembly into the land which I have given them.' These are the waters of Meribah, where the children of Israel strove with the Lord, and He was sanctified in them. (vss. 12–13)

It is surprising to hear that Moses and Aaron were punished for not sanctifying God before the children of Israel, since the passage concludes with the words, "and He was sanctified in them." We believe that the moment of great crisis in which the children of Israel found themselves in a waterless wilderness was an occasion for a two-fold sanctification of God: the one, in Ezekiel's style, God sanctifying Himself and revealing through His saving act His compassion with the people; the other, in the manner of Isaiah, sanctifying God through complete trust and reliance on Him, Who is near to save. The first form of sanctification did take place; water was given to them and they were saved by the grace of God. Concerning this matter it is stated: "and He was sanctified in them." The other form of sanctification was at the moment for the responsibility of Moses and Aaron. Had they quietly spoken to the rock to yield up its water, it would have been a more convincing demonstration of their unqualified reliance on God than was the angry smiting of the rock twice. They missed an opportunity to illustrate to the people the attitude of ultimate reliance on God at a time of crisis. It is of this that the Bible says: "Because ye believed not in Me, to sanctify Me in the eyes of the children of Israel." God was sanctified through His own act of salvation; but did not sanctify Him by complete trust that His salvation was near because He was the Holy One.

THE "HIDING OF THE FACE"

It is hardly possible to pass over the fact that a number of prophets either do not mention the Holy One at all, or refer to Him only incidentally, whereas the term, the Lord of hosts, they use quite frequently. This in itself need not be too surprising. The material that has been preserved in the name of some of those prophets whom we have in mind is not very extensive. That there is no reference to the Holy One in the few chapters of Micah nor in the not much more voluminous books of Haggai and Malachi may be of no specific significance. The scanty references in Jeremiah are, of course, much more unexpected. We raise the point mainly because Jeremiah and Zechariah use the term, Lord of hosts, in a two-fold manner. They use it, as it is done by Isaiah, the Psalms, and in other books of the Bible, to indicate the remote mightiness of God, who executes judgment and punishment; but they also speak in the name of the Lord of hosts in order to announce hope and to promise salvation. We, however, would expect that hope and salvation should be prophesied in the name of the Holy One, a term almost completely absent from the writings of these two prophets.

In numerous places, Jeremiah speaks in the name of the Lord of hosts as Isaiah would;[40] but the prophecy, too, that once again "the voice of joy and the voice of gladness, the voice of the bridegroom and the voice of the bride" will be heard in Jerusalem, is associated with the Lord of hosts.[41] Zechariah is conspicuous for the frequent mentioning of the Lord of hosts. But the great chapter of comfort begins with the words: "Thus saith the Lord of hosts." In it we find, for instance, those precious words, faith in which has sustained Israel through its Exile:

There shall yet old men and old women sit in the broad places of Jerusalem, every man with a staff in his hand for very age. And the broad places of the city shall be full of boys and girls playing in the broad places thereof. (8:4–5)

But this prophecy too, as others of similar quality, is prefaced by the words: "Thus saith the Lord of hosts." While this strange deviation from a pattern that we have found in other books of the Bible has no direct bearing on our analysis of the concept of the holy, we feel that it requires an explanation. The way they employ the term, the Lord of hosts, seems to indicate that with them the Lord of hosts absorbed the function of the Holy One. This is all the more surprising since both Jeremiah and Zechariah, when they do refer to the holy, do it in the manner we would expect.

We have discussed earlier in our study Jeremiah's mention of the term, *m'on qodsho*, habitation of his holiness,[42] which bears out our interpretation. When Babylon's punishment is prophesied, Jeremiah says:

For she hath been arrogant against the Lord, against the Holy One of Israel. (50:29)

The verse recalls a passage in Isaiah, which we had occasion to analyze. Similarly, it was said of the king of Assyria:

Whom hast thou taunted and blasphemed? And against whom hast thou exalted thy voice? Yea, thou hast lifted up thine eyes on high, even against the Holy One of Israel. (Isa. 37:23)

As we saw, Sennacherib "taunted and blasphemed" by declaring that it was foolish for Israel to rely on God for help and salvation. But it is exactly what the Holy One of Israel is to Israel, the One to rely upon. Thus Sennacherib has lifted up his eyes against the Holy One of Israel. Similarly does Jeremiah

197

declare about Babylon that she was arrogant against the Holy One of Israel, believing that Israel was helpless and completely handed over into her grip. There was nothing for them to hope for. This, too, was blaspheming the Holy One of Israel. The Holy One of Israel occurs in one other place in Jeremiah, rather interestingly for our purpose, in closest proximity to the Lord of hosts. The theme is still the fall of Babylon. In that connection it is said:

For Israel is not widowed, nor Judah, of his God, of the Lord of hosts . . . for their land is full of guilt—of the Holy One of Israel. (51:5)[43]

We have departed from the generally accepted translations. The grammatical form of the Hebrew, *miq'dosh Yisrael,* of the Holy One of Israel, is the exact parallel to, *me-YHWH S'baoth,* of the Lord of hosts, and to, *me'Elohav,* of his God.[44] The phrase, "for their land is full of guilt," is an insertion which refers to the reason why Babylon is being punished. This is well borne out by the entire context. The purpose of the insertion is to remind Israel that even though she is not widowed, what is done to Babylon is not done altogether for Israel's sake. She herself may not deserve her deliverance. Nevertheless an important statement is made about the relationship between God and Israel. In spite of all appearances to the contrary, Israel is not forsaken by God, who is the Lord of hosts and the Holy One of Israel. Once again we are reminded of Isaiah. We are first of all reminded of the dual function of the Redeemer. In the case of Jeremiah He is the Lord of hosts who executes judgment over Babylon, "for their land is full of guilt"; and He is the Holy One of Israel and therefore Israel's cause is not forgotten. In addition, the association between Israel's status as a possible widow and the concepts of the Lord of hosts and the Holy One of Israel, recalls that specific passage in Isaiah, which we have discussed earlier,[45] in which Israel is promised that the reproach of her widowhood she will remember no more,

For Thy Maker is thy husband, the Lord of hosts is His name; and the Holy One of Israel is thy Redeemer, the God of the whole earth shall He be called. (Isa. 54:5)

While Jeremiah applies the term, the holy, as expected, Zecharaiah employs it most originally in the two places in which it has been preserved for us. At this stage in our discussion we shall introduce only one of the passages. In that great chapter of comfort, to which we have already alluded once, we read the following:

Thus saith the Lord: I return unto Zion, and will dwell in the midst of Jerusalem; and Jerusalem shall be called The city of Truth; and the mountain of the Lord of hosts the mountain of holiness. (8:3)

According to this prophecy, the name of Zion will undergo a change. When God returns to Zion, the mountain of the Lord of hosts will be called the mountain of holiness. Why this change? The reason for it seems to be well supported by our analysis. Prior to God's return to Zion, Israel experiences divine judgment; as if God had departed, withdrawn from the midst of his people. At such a stage of history Zion is not the visible manifestation of the Holy One of Israel. In her ruin, Zion is a witness to judgment and divine anger. It is the mountain of the Lord of hosts. But when God, through the act of Israel's deliverance, returns to Zion, he reveals himself once again as the Holy One "in the midst of thee." At that time, what was known as the mountain of the Lord of hosts will rightly be called again, the mountain of holiness, the manifestation of God's nearness and indwelling in Israel.

However, this passage in Zechariah may contain the clue for which we have been seeking in order to solve our present problem, i.e., the use of the term, Lord of hosts, as the remote Judge and as the near Redeemer. Jeremiah and Zechariah have something in common; both are witnesses to the judgment executed over Zion and her people. Their prophecies of redemption are made from a situation of either expected or fulfilled doom. The Holy One has severed his association with

Israel. He treats them as the Lord of hosts. It is as such that he deals with them at this stage of their history. We recall how at a time of a similar personal experience Hannah turned in prayer to the Lord of hosts and only after her prayer was granted, did she in her joy address God as the Holy One. There are at least two psalms which affirm the thought that at a time of estrangement and separation from God, one addresses oneself to the Lord of hosts. The one is an intercession on behalf of Israel as a whole. In Psalm 80 we read:

O Lord God of hosts, how long wilt Thou be angry against the prayer of Thy people? Thou hast fed them with the bread of tears, and given them tears to drink in large measure. . . . O God of hosts, restore us; and cause Thy face to shine and we shall be saved.

. . . .

O God of hosts, return, we beseech Thee; look from heaven and behold and be mindful of this vine, and the stock which Thy right hand hath planted, and the branch that Thou madest strong for Thyself. It is burned with fire, it is cut down; they perish at the rebuke of Thy countenance.

. . . .

O Lord God of hosts, restore us; cause Thy face to shine and we shall be saved. (vss. 5, 8, 15–17, 20)

The mood is very similar to the one we find in Hannah's first prayer, only it arises from a national experience of being forsaken by God. God has punished Israel and they plead that the punishment be taken from them; God has left Israel and they pray that he may return. Significantly, the appellation is to the Lord, or God, of hosts. We know, however, that God, when he "returns" and saves is the Holy One. Thus, the deeper meaning of the prayer is that God, who deals with them at the present as the Lord of hosts, may make himself known again as the Holy One. The idea breaks through rather intensely in the refrain that God may cause his face to shine so that they may be saved. The moment is then one of "the hiding of the face"; and the shining of the face is identical with being saved. But we know from Ezekiel that the "profanation" of the name of holiness by God is his withdrawal from Israel; and the hour is that of the "hiding of the face." Correspondingly, God's return in his people, the revelation of his holiness, is the hour in which he causes his face to shine. For in the context of the passage in which we have heard God declare that he will be "jealous" for the name of his holiness, we read:

Neither will I hide My face anymore from them; for I have poured out My spirit Upon the house of Israel, saith the Lord God. (39:29)

When God makes manifest his holiness, his "face shines" on man; but at the time of the "hiding of the face" one can turn only to the Lord of hosts.

The other psalm which we have in mind, begins rather surprisingly:

How lovely are Thy tabernacles, O Lord of hosts. (84:2)

The opening phrase sounds as if it were spoken by a man at ease, who enjoys the nearness of God. However, anyone who might think so is soon disabused, for the psalmist continues:

My soul yearneth, yea, even pineth for the courts of the Lord.

This is an indication that the psalm was composed by someone who was banished or, against his will, separated from "the courts of the Lord." In his yearning love for the sanctuary of God, he was recalling in memory the loveliness of God's tabernacles. The reference to the sparrow that "hath found a house and the swallow a nest for herself" suggests that the individual experience at the root of the psalm is exile and homelessness. Thus the psalmist pleads from the heart of his experience of separation:

O Lord of hosts, hear my prayer; give ear, O God of Jacob. Behold, O God our shield, and look upon the face of Thine anointed. For a day in Thy courts is better than a thousand: I had rather stand at the threshold of the house of my God than to dwell in the tents of wickedness.

Clearly, these are still the words of one whose "soul yearneth" for the threshold of God's house and who is yet condemned to dwell in the tents of wickedness. The phrase, "look upon the face of Thine anointed," reminds one of "cause Thy face to shine and we shall be saved" of Psalm 80. The experience is similar: as if God's face were turned away, as if he did not see, did not consider. Thus, as expected, the intercessions in the psalm are addressed to the Lord of hosts. Nevertheless, the mood of this psalm is rather different from that in the prayer of Hannah or in the plea on behalf of Israel in Psalm 80. The tone of agony, almost despair, is absent here. This psalmist, too, pleads with God in a moment of the hiding of the face; yet, even though it is the Lord of hosts whom he approaches, he does so in a spirit of confidence and reliance on God. The psalm comes to a hopeful conclusion with the words:

O Lord of hosts, happy is the man that trusteth in Thee.

This is, indeed, the authentic strength of faith. It is rather easy to trust in the Holy One of Israel. For this means to trust in God who is near, who makes himself known as the Redeemer, who does cause his face to shine. The test of faith comes in "the hour of the hiding of the face" when God is known as the Lord of hosts, when he comes as a judge to execute justice. When notwithstanding such experiences, a man can turn to Him in quiet confidence and speak: "O Lord of hosts, happy is the man that trusteth in Thee," he has lived by his faith. Even when God treats him as the Lord of hosts, the man of faith trusts in Him, even in the Lord of hosts. For is not holy, holy, holy the Lord of hosts! Even though He may hide His face, He is the same One, who is also the Holy One, no matter what His momentary specific manifestation may be.

From these considerations, we may derive two points. We have seen that in times of "the hiding of the face" one turns to the Lord of hosts. It is the essence of the moment that the closeness to God has been shattered, the contact has been lost. Yet, in spite of it all, it is the Lord of hosts that now becomes the source of hope. For God is God.

This may explain why, beginning with Jeremiah, the term, the Holy One, hardly occurs in the prophetic writings. Most of the prophets of the post-exilic period do not mention the concept of the Holy One at all. With Jeremiah, begins the gloom of "the hiding of the face." More and more God makes himself manifest as the Lord of hosts. Whatever hopes of future redemption are held out to this people, it is done against the background of divine judgment and active wrath. It is the hour of the Lord of hosts; it is to Him that they must turn for their redemption. It is noteworthy that all the prophecies of comfort found either in Jeremiah or Zechariah contain within themselves a very natural reference to the prevailing situation of ruin and desolation. We shall list only a few from among them. There is, for instance, the passage in Jeremiah, where although the Lord of hosts is not mentioned, yet the promise of redemption is made against the present experience of "the hiding of the face."

For thus saith the Lord, the God of Israel, concerning the houses of this city and concerning the houses of the kings of Judah, which are broken down for mounds, and for ramparts; whereon they come to fight with the Chaldeans, even to fill them with the dead bodies of men, whom I have slain in Mine anger and in My fury, and for all whose wickedness I have hid My face from this city:
Behold I will bring it healing and cure, and I will cure them; and I will reveal unto them the abundance of peace and truth. (33:4–6)

Not even the promise of cure and healing and abundance of peace can be made in the name of the Holy One in the sight of the rubble of the houses turned into mounds and ramparts and covered with the bodies of the dead. Similarly, in the same chapter, when the prophecy is made that "this place" will once again become "a habitation of shepherds causing their flocks to lie down," the present condition of "this place" cannot be overlooked, "which is waste, without man and without beast." The prophecy is proclaimed in the name of the Lord of hosts.[46]

The same reference to the present moment of "the hiding of the face" we also find in all the prophecies of salvation by Zechariah. For example:

For thus saith the Lord of hosts, who sent me . . . unto the nations which spoiled you: 'Surely, he that toucheth you toucheth the apple of his eye. For, behold, I will shake my hand over them, and they shall be a spoil to those that served them'; and Ye shall know that the Lord of hosts hath sent me. (2:12)

They are still among the nations and are being spoiled. Even though God will shake his hand over the nations, so that they in turn will become a spoil to their former servants, at the moment they are still serving the nations. Therefore, even the prophecy of hope is introduced with, Thus saith the Lord of hosts, and concluded similarly. The very promise of future redemption implies the present condition of rejection.[47]

Most revealing, however, is the conclusion of chapter 2 in Zechariah. The passage opens with the well-known words:

Sing and rejoice, O daughter of Zion; for, lo, I come, and I will dwell in the midst of thee, saith the Lord.

The verse reminds us of the one in Isaiah: "Cry aloud and shout, thou inhabitant of Zion; for great is the Holy One of Israel in the midst of thee." (12:6). Zechariah, however, does not mention the Holy One of Israel, whereas Isaiah does. In our opinion, the difference between them is that whereas Isaiah can declare, "for great *is* . . . in the midst of thee," Zechariah may only announce, "for, lo, I *come*, and I *will* dwell in the midst of thee." God who *is* in the midst of thee is the Holy One of Israel; but as long as he is on the way to dwell in the midst of thee, he is not yet in the midst of thee, he is not yet revealed as the Holy One. The promise that God *will* dwell in the midst of Zion is repeated in the next verse in

Zechariah, upon which follows the conclusion: "and thou shalt know that the Lord of hosts hath sent me unto thee." The prophet who brings the good tidings is of course sent before the fulfilment of the promise. He is sent by God at a moment when God has not yet returned to Zion; he is sent by the Lord of hosts. But then follows the most illuminating part of the prophecy:

And the Lord shall inherit Judah as His portion in the land of holiness and shall choose Jerusalem again. Be silent, all flesh, before the Lord; for He is aroused out of the habitation of His holiness.

While the Holy One is still not mentioned, the concept of the holy occurs twice. The land in which Judah is once again taken to be God's portion is the land of divine holiness, as the place which makes manifest again God's association with Israel through Israel's redemption. More significant, however, is the phrase: "for He is aroused out of the habitation of His holiness." We have shown above that *m'on qodsho*, habitation of holiness, indicates God responding to man with the quality of His holiness.[48] During Israel's exile God is silent; God does not respond, he is as if removed and apart. Yet, even when his manifestations are those of the Lord of hosts, he is yet holy. His attribute of holiness is not activated, as if it were at rest, "asleep." But when the hour of redemption approaches, one witnesses in silent awe how God is "aroused" out of the habitation of his holiness to come and dwell in the midst of Zion.

THE HOLY AND THE *MYSTERIUM TREMENDUM*

We have shown that the biblical concept of the holy, far from being one with the *mysterium tremendum*, indicates its very opposite, i.e., the attribute by which God relates himself to the world as the source of human salvation, as the one who is near, notwithstanding his Wholly-otherness. God, of course, is the Wholly Other and as such the *mysterium tremendum* is rightly associated with him, but through his attribute of holiness he covers up, as it were, the *mysterium,* in order to be near his creation and to make himself accessible for man. It is through holiness that the remote moves close, that the transcendent becomes immanent. There are, however, a number of passages in the Bible, which do seem to associate the holy with the fear and danger associated with the *mysterium tremendum.* Before we enter into a deeper analysis of these passages, we may state in general that they all have one thing in common: the holiness, which seems to be the source of the trembling and the peril, is not directly associated with God, but with some object or place which is considered holy as being, somehow, related to God. In the first revelation that was granted to Moses at the beginning of his mission, he was told not to approach and to take off his shoes because the ground on which he stood was one of holiness.[49] Nadab and Abihu, who died when they offered strange fire before God, came near the sanctuary, a place sanctified.[50] The danger for the Kehathites emanated from the holy vessels should they touch them or see them without their covers.[51] Uzza was slain because he touched the ark.[52] When King Uzziah, even though not a priest of God, burnt incense in the sanctuary, leprosy broke out on his forehead, because he desecrated the sanctuary.[53] In all these cases, the danger is not due to closeness with God, but to contact with sanctified objects or places. In view of the consistently spiritual meaning of the term of the holy as a divine attribute, it is difficult to accept the theory that in these passages we have remnants of the primitive concept of holiness as *avanda,* the almost demonic divine mightiness which spells danger for everyone who comes near it.[54] Nor is it likely that, if such primitive ideas should indeed have been retained, that they should uniformly be applied to holy objects and places, but never to God himself.

There is one important distinction between the primitive *avanda* or *mana* and the peril that threatens in the Bible from the holy. *Avanda* works automatically, blindly, with the power of a natural force. Some authors refer to it as divine electricity. The danger in the Bible is due to some improper action. It is not the approach that is dangerous, but the wrong approach. Moses does stand on holy ground; he is ordered to take off his shoes. The sons of Aaron are obviously punished for offering "a strange fire" which they were not commanded to do. Uzzah did not die *of* touching the ark, as if he had been in contact with a high-power wire. He was killed *because* he touched the ark, which he was not permitted to do. "God smote him for his error." Neither was the leprosy of Uzziah caused by some automatically effective *mana*. It was punishment for transgression.

This may explain why the Bible associates the peril only with holy things. Holy objects or places are holy either because they are dedicated to God or because God uses them for the manifestation of his holiness. In either case they are set apart for God; they do symbolize God's nearness, his indwelling. Through their sanctification, they become indeed what they symbolize. Because of that they have to be treated with awe and respect. There are, therefore, ritualistic rules regulating the reverent approach to them. He who violates these rules, acts with disrespect, or even abuse, toward the One whose nearness they symbolize. It is in this way that the passage in Numbers, too, which we have quoted, must be understood. In the light of the other passages, which we have discussed, it should be understood that not to touch the holy vessels and not to look at them without their being covered is the law of approach for the Kehathites. As with Uzzah, it is not the touching or the seeing that spells disaster, but the breaking of an explicit law, which in this case is equal to sacrilege. So it happened to the men of *Beth Shemesh,* who gazed upon the ark of God. They did not die of gazing at the ark; but *because* they gazed, as they were not permitted to do as a sign of reverence, they were punished by God.[55]

The connection between God's nearness and the peril of the improper approach to his holy places is dramatically illustrated by what is said by Moses to Aaron concerning the death of Nadab and Abihu. Explaining the significance of the event to Aaron, Moses says:

This is it that the Lord spoke, saying: Through them that are nigh unto Me I will be sanctified, and before all the people I will be glorified.[56]

God is sanctified, whenever his quality of holiness is made manifest. This may be done by God Himself, who—as we saw in Ezekiel—may sanctify the name of His holiness by accepting Israel again and redeeming them from among the nations. It may be done by man, as Israel was enjoined by Isaiah "to sanctify Him" by relying on God unquestioningly, because He is near. And now we hear of a third form of sanctification: punishment for improper approach to the sanctuary. It is sanctification because this, too, reveals that God dwells in the midst of his people. The holy place is the visible and tangible symbol of the nearness of God. Because God is indeed near, the symbols are true and testify to God's indwelling, to his holiness. Only because they are such true symbols, does one have to treat them with awe and can one offend against God by approaching them contrary to the prescribed form of service. When then men are punished for improper approach, God's holiness is affirmed; He is sanctified. Most significant, however, is the phrase; "Through them that are nigh unto Me I will be sanctified." It relates sanctification to nearness. The further removed God is, the less the likelihood that man may approach Him without due respect. The Infinite cannot be approached at all. Only because He is near, can one violate the boundaries set by awe and respect. The nearer one is to Him, the greater the risk of trespassing the set boundaries. Only a priest, who is engaged in the temple service, will make the mistake of offering "a strange fire." The nearer the person, the greater the risk that he may become too "familiar" with the tangible accoutrements that symbolize divine holiness. Thus it is through those who are nearest to Him that God will be sanctified.[57]

We are now in a better position to appreciate those last words Joshua addressed to the people before his death:

Ye cannot serve the Lord, for He is a holy God; He is a jealous God; He will not forgive your transgressions nor your sins. If ye forsake the Lord, and serve strange gods, then He will turn and do you evil, and consume you, after that He hath done you good. (24:19)

Is this an indication that God's holiness excites fear and trembling? We do not think so. Human transgressions are to be feared, the forsaking of God by man. There is of course a connection between God's holiness and human transgressions. Only God, who is close to man and considers man, can be forsaken by man. Were He not holy, He could not be forsaken. Only because He is holy and considers man does He consider human transgressions too. Only because He is holy and turns toward man with His providential care does it matter to him how man lives. Only because He is a holy God is He also a jealous God. The Infinite, the transcendental Wholly Other, cannot be approached by man either rightly or wrongly; it can neither be forsaken by man nor can it be jealous for man. Only the Holy One knows man; only because God knows man is man a responsible being, a being responsible to God. Because God is holy, man is graced by responsibility. In responsibility lies man's risk as well as his chance. For He is a holy God and, being a holy God, He is a jealous God.

The ritualistic rules regarding the treatment of sanctified places and objects also have their spiritual counterpart. We find it in Psalm 24.

Who shall ascend into the mountain of the Lord: And who shall stand in the place of His holiness? He that hath clean hands and a pure heart. Who hath not taken My name in vain and hath not sworn deceitfully. (24:3–4)

Because God is near, man may ascend to the place of His holiness. Because he may ascend, he should ascend. Since he should ascend, let him know how to ascend. Let him accept

His nearness by drawing nigh. Let him sanctify Him, who by revealing His will and His law for man, sanctified man.

HOLY AS ADJECTIVE AND AS NOUN

In this study, we have been rather insistent on translating such terms as *z'ro'a qodsho* or *shem qodsho* not as they normally are rendered as "his holy arm" or "his holy name" respectively, but as "the arm of his holiness" or as "the name of his holiness." The adjective, holy, is *qadosh;* in these and similar terms, however, we have the noun, *qodesh* in a construct with a possessive suffix, meaning "his holiness." It is not for the sake of pedantry that we prefer our rather cumbersome English to the simpler rendering of the word as an adjective. The adjectival form is confusing and often misleading; it very often obscures and distorts the Hebrew concept. For example, "his holy arm" was interpreted as being holy because it is God's. This, and similar terms, give rise to the idea that holy meant either belonging to God or being of God. And since no one gives an arm to God, and one cannot speak of ritual sanctification of the divine arm, the conclusion was drawn that to be holy meant to be of God, to be God. It was only a very short step from here to the misleading thought that holy was an "otiose epithet," identical with the nature of God. The exact Hebrew rendering could never have given rise to such misinterpretations.

We believe that one has to distinguish carefully between holy as adjective and holy as noun, as it occurs often in the construct. Holy is that which has been sanctified either ritually or spiritually. For instance, a holy place (Exod. 29:31), a holy people (Deut. 7:6), a holy camp (ibid. 23:15), a holy man (II Kings 4:9), Aaron, God's holy one (Pss. 106:16), a holy congregation (Num. 16:3), etc. These things or persons are holy, because they have been made holy in one way or another. However, the *makom qadosh,* the holy place, where the "ram of consecration" was prepared is not to be confused with the *Admat qodesh,* on which Moses stood, when God appeared to him in Midian. The first one is a holy place, dedicated as such to the divine service of the tabernacle. The ground on which Moses stood was not dedicated or consecrated in this sense at all. Nor does the text refer to it as *adama q'dosha,* holy ground. It was ground like any other ground. It possessed only the momentary distinction that God made his presence known to Moses there. God revealed him His nearness, His concern for Israel. At that spot, he revealed himself as the Holy One. This is what the Bible calls not holy ground, but ground of holiness, i.e., ground associated with God's revelation of his holiness. Its distinction lasts as long as the revelation lasts. Similarly, "his holy arm" should be *z'ro'o ha–q'dosha,* which is meaningless. The Hebrew has *z'ro'a qodsho,* which must be rendered as, "the arm of his holiness"; referring to the power that God employs in order to execute the plans prompted by his attribute of holiness. "His holy name" would be a name reserved for God alone. But the name of God, as we have shown stands in the Bible for the actions by which God makes himself known in the world. "His holy name" would mean, "his holy manifestation," and we are back again to the spurious interpretation, according to which everything that appertains to God is holy, because holiness is identical with divine nature. But the Bible does not speak of "his holy name," but of "the name of his holiness," which is a specific type of divine manifestation, i.e., that of his holiness. Neither is *sh'me qodsho* (Pss. 20:7), his "holy heavens," but "the heaven of his holiness," whence—as we saw—he reveals his holiness by answering the prayers of those who call him. *Kise qodsho* (ibid. 47:9) is not his holy Throne, but "The Throne of his holiness," implying that God who rules and judges like a king, yet dispenses *s'daqah* because of his quality of holiness. Zion is called, *har ha–qodesh,* (Joel 4:17; Zech. 8:3) "the mountain of holiness," the mountain on which God, through his sanctuary, reveals that he is the Holy One who dwells in the midst of Zion. In the same sense does Isaiah

211

speak of "cities of Thy holiness," emphasizing the aspect of their distinction due to God's manifesting his holiness in them or through them. In Deuteronomy (7:6), where the emphasis is that God has chosen Israel to be a nation unto him, they are called, *am qadosh,* "a holy nation"; holy because God sanctified them. But when Isaiah proclaims the approach of God's salvation, the time when Zion will be "sought out" and "not forsaken," he says of the people in Zion that they will be called, *am ha–qodesh;* which does not mean, "a holy nation," but, "a nation of holiness." What Isaiah declares is not the sanctification of Israel through God, but the redeeming acts of God on behalf of Israel. God reveals his holiness by what he does as the Redeemer of Israel. That road, on which God's redeemed ones will return with singing to Zion is not a *derekh ha–qadosh,* a holy road, but *derekh ha–qodesh,* a road of holiness. It is the road of return, of salvation and help, along which God makes potent his quality of holiness.

Nor do we find anywhere in the Bible the expression *ruah ha–q'dosha,* "holy spirit"; but either *ruah qodsho,* spirit of his holiness, or *ruah qodsh'kha,* spirit of Thy holiness. It will be interesting to take a good look at the three passages in the Bible where the term occurs. Two of them are found in the same context in chapter 63 of Isaiah. We read there:

In His love and in His pity He redeemed them; and He bore them and carried them all the days of old. But they rebelled and grieved *the spirit of His holiness;* Therefore He was turned to be their enemy, Himself fought against them. (vss. 9–10)

It is said most appropriately that it was the spirit of God's holiness that was grieved by their rebellion, for it is the continuation of the thought that God redeemed them in His love and in His pity and cared for them "all the days of old." We have found in numerous places that God's redeeming love and caring pity is the activity of his holiness. When they rebelled they offended the spirit of divine holiness that redeemed them and protected them. And Isaiah continues:

Then His people remembered the days of old, the days of Moses: Where is He that brought them up out of the sea with the shepherd of His flock? Where is He that put *the spirit of His holiness* in the midst of them? That caused the arm of His glory to go at the right hand of Moses? That divided the water before them . . . that led them through the deep . . . *the spirit of the Lord* caused them to rest; so didst Thou lead Thy people.

The entire context shows that the spirit of His holiness is the power with which God led them across the waters of the Sea of Reeds, guiding them and saving them. This is, as we know, the work of the Holy One. "He put the spirit of His holiness in the midst of them" means that God as the Holy One was helping them. The passage reminds one very much of the verses in Psalm 77, which we analyzed above.[58] There too, the psalmist describes the miracle of the crossing of the sea, as God "led His people like a flock by the hand of Moses and Aaron." The striking similarity of construction we see in the following. The psalmist begins his meditation by mentioning God's way in holiness. What is meant by it becomes clarified in the development of the theme, but especially at the point where the term "Thy way" is taken up again in the sentence:

Thy way was in the sea, and Thy path in the great waters, and Thy footsteps were not known. Thou didst lead Thy people like a flock.

We have found that reintroducing the idea of God's way, the concept of God's way in holiness is defined. Isaiah, too, describing the same event in Israel's history in very similar terms, mentions first "the spirit of His holiness in the midst of them" and, after elaborating the idea further, reintroduces the spirit of God in the words: "The spirit of the Lord caused them to rest; so didst Thou lead Thy people." This, then, is "the spirit of His holiness in the midst of them"—the spirit of God that leads them and brings them to rest and lets them find peace. It is the power of love and compassion through whose activity God reveals his holiness.

213

Exactly the same is also the meaning of *ruah ha-qodesh,* spirit of holiness, in the third passage, where it occurs in the Bible. Its place is in psalm 51. We find there:

Cast me not away from Thy presence; and take not the spirit of Thy holiness from me. Restore unto me the joy of Thy salvation; and let a willing spirit uphold me. (vss. 13–14)

To be cast away from the presence of God is to be separated from him. It is the dissolution of the bonds with the Holy One. The restoration of the joy of God's salvation is a plea that God may act as the Holy One. It is most fitting in this context to pray that the spirit of God's holiness be not taken from man, that the power of divine holiness may sustain man, that he may stay in the presence and be upheld by God's salvation.

Concluding Notes

A Bible scholar of my acquaintance has insisted that *shem qodsho* is "his holy name" (and similarly in the other cases in which I limit the suffix to the second noun in the construct). His reference to Gesenius-Kautzsch, 135n., is certainly very much to the point. However, we do not mean that, "his holy name" is incorrect, but inexact and therefore confusing. While, normally, it is sufficient to render in translation the pronominal suffix of the second noun of the construct as referring to the entire phrase, Gesenius-Kautzsch fails to prove their point that that is indeed the exact meaning of the Hebrew usage. The example, *elile khaspo,* may well mean, the gods of his silver, i.e., gods made out of his silver. As such it would contain the sarcastic allusion, not unfamiliar in the Bible, to the fact that man makes himself gods from what he owns and controls. For all practical purposes, *khle milhamto* may well be rendered, his weapons of war. May it nevertheless not be the case that the Bible preferred to speak of the weapons of his war, since the ownership of the weapons as such is irrelevant? Similarly in Ezekiel 9:1, *khle mashhito,* the ownership of the instrument of destruction is irrelevant; the men were charged with the task of destruction, each to his destroying task. Again no harm is done if one translates *beth t'fillati* as "my house of prayer"; the emphasis in Hebrew, however, is on "my prayer." *Beth t'fillati* is the house where prayers are offered to God; it is God's house because of "my prayer." The literal rendering as "the house of my prayer" may reflect the spirit of the Hebrew concept more exactly. The distinction in meaning between the rendering in translation and the exact Hebrew construction is well illustrated by *sa'ade ono.* Gesenius misses here the point by translating "his strong strides." Even an average person may walk with strong strides. The "strides of his strength" conveys a rather different picture from the rather colorless "his strong strides." Again, the rendering of *alize ga'avathi,* following Gesenius, as "my proudly exulting ones" is a considerable weakening of the forcefulness of the Hebrew original. The term *ga'avathi* is paralleled by *m'qudashai* and *gibborai.* Those called by God are not the proudly exulting ones. But the exulting ones that are called are God's pride, representing His might as do His *gibborim.* In the case of all the other examples to which Gesenius-Kautzsch make reference, it is possible to show that by limiting the pronominal suffix to the second noun of the construct, the meaning of the concept becomes enriched, whereas its application to the entire phrase impoverishes both style and meaning.

Be that as it may, it is certainly permissible to refer the pronominal suffix only to the second noun, especially where to do so makes good sense. In fact, there are sufficient examples in the Bible to show that in certain cases no other reference is possible, Cf., for example, Isaiah 41:11; Psalms 41:10, etc.

Christian Bible scholars seem to agree among themselves that the original meaning of the term, holy, is hardly recoverable now. On the whole they are inclined to follow von Baudissin's interpretation that the word, *qadosh*, probably signifies separation and withdrawal. (W. E. H. E. von Baudissin, *Der Begriff der Heiligkeit im Neuen Testament*, in *Studien zur Semitischen Religionsgeschichte* [Leipzig, 1878], II, 20). However, notwithstanding the etymological difficulty of establishing the original meaning of the word, certain concepts are associated with the meaning of the idea of the holy. It would appear that A. B. Davidson in his Ezekiel commentary (*Ezekiel, The Cambridge Bible for Schools and Colleges* [Cambridge, 1893]) has succeeded in interpreting the idea in a manner that was accepted by many scholars after him. According to him, "holy" does not express any definite attribute of the deity. It is a rather general notion of what is meant by the godhead. The holy God is the same as God. He is holy because he is God. Holy is a mere "otiose epithet" for God. Because of that the word may be used rather elastically, depending on what we mean by God. Whatever our idea of the godhead may be, it is the contents of God's holiness. If one's idea of the deity is that of some mysterious power before whom one must tremble, then the holy God means the fearsome and frightening super-human being. If, on the other hand, one's concept of God comprises His righteousness and love, then the idea of the holy will be identical with divine righteousness and love (op. cit., Introduction, pp. xxxix–xl and p. 279).

This interpretation has been taken over completely by W. Robertson Smith (*The Prophets of Israel* [London, 1902]).

Its force [of the word, holy] lay in its very vagueness, for it included every distinctive character of godhead, and every advance in the true knowledge of God made its significance more profound; thus the doctrine of YHVH's holiness is simply the doctrine of his true godhead. (pp. 225–26)

According to Robertson Smith's insight, in the Hebrew Bible God alone is holy, because He alone is the true God. Robinson follows in the same tradition, as he reaches the conclusion that the essential fact to be remembered about man's approach to God is the gradual transformation of man's ideas about God. In his opinion, only with the eighth-century prophets of Israel does holiness become associated with morality, because only then were the moral ideas of God's righteousness and love fully comprehended. At this stage, holiness stands for the transcendent majesty of God. The original, primitive concept of holiness as separation and inaccessibility of the godhead because of the mysterious dangers connected with the approach becomes now the transcendent holiness of God which becomes manifest in divine righteousness and grace (*The Religious Ideas of the Old Testament*, pp. 69–70, 153–54).

The idea of transcendence as the meaning of holiness is, of course, closely connected with the concept of the Wholly Other that is the subject of Rudolph Otto's famous investigation (*Das Heilige* [München, 1947]). For him the holy is the numinous, the mysterious, the unknown power to which man responds with fear and trembling. There are of course levels of development in the religious experience of the human race. Abraham's reaction is the classical biblical example of the numinous experience. Standing before God, Abraham sees himself as the creature in his "absolute profanity," as "dust and ashes." Sensing God as the Wholly Other, one becomes aware of the unbridgeable gulf between creature and creator. In one's creaturely worthlessness one experiences God as "absolutely inaccessible," the *mysterium tremendum*. However, the holy has an ambivalent quality. While as the *mysterium tremendum* it is inaccessible, it is also the *fascinans* that fascinates and attracts. One desires the inaccessible and unapproachable (*Das Heilige*, pp. 21, 62–65). Otto maintains that in the Hebrew Bible the divine "anger," "wrath," "zeal," "the consuming fire," are terms related to that of holiness (ibid., p. 91). It is quite understandable that on the basis of his interpretation, he should declare that the holy in itself is indifferent toward the ethical and that it may be considered independently of it. In the history of religious development the holy

217

has to be "moralized." In its essential nature, it represents the irrational element in religion. Through its moralization, the holy incorporates the rationality of ethical principles and ideals (ibid., pp. 9, 158). Eventually, the holy does become accessible. This, however, is not to be taken for granted. On the contrary, it is altogether due to the incomprehensible grace of God (ibid., p. 68).

These various aspects of the holy are neatly united into one pattern by a more recent author. Snaith, in *The Distinctive Ideas of the Old Testament,* follows in the footsteps of all his predecessors. He accepts Otto's interpretation that the holy is identical with the concept of the Wholly Other, the *mysterium tremendum.* He also agrees with Davidson that the holy is a mere "otiose epithet" of the deity. "Whatever that Other was realized to be that was Holiness. 'Qodesh' never meant anything else among the Hebrews. It meant precisely that which at any period was recognized to be the inner Nature of the Deity" (ibid., pp. 51–53). He accepts the idea of the "moralizing" of the concept. As with Robinson, with him too, it was brought about by the eighth-century prophets. Since their conception of the Deity "was without parallel," the idea of the holy became associated with righteousness. For Snaith, too, this association with righteousness gives us the concept of "transcendent Holiness." Since holiness for him is identical with divine nature, we assume that by transcendent holiness he means the transcendent quality of divine righteousness. It is still holiness as the "otiose epithet," the meaning being: God is God and not man; and God, who is God, is righteous.

Theologians normally understand by the holiness of God his absolute transcendence in the metaphysical sense of the word. Thus Paul Tillich, for instance, declares: "The unapproachable character of God, or the impossibility of having a relation with him in the proper sense of the word, is expressed in the word 'holiness.' God is essentially holy, and every relation with him involves the consciousness that it is paradoxical to be related to that which is holy" (*Systematic Theology,*

[Chicago, 1961], I, 271–72). According to Tillich, the idea of the holy expresses the ontological discrepancy between the finite and the infinite, between the absolute and the contingent. The holy is a quality that belongs only to God, the ground of all being.

In the light of the preceding interpretations of the term, we might say that to theological-historical research "holy" means the nature of the godhead as that nature is understood at each phase in the history of religion. For the psychological investigator, "holy" expresses the impact made on the human mind by the Wholly Other in its mysterious inaccessibility and otherness. For the theologic-philosophical understanding, the concept of the holy is identical with that of absolute divine transcendence.

In Jewish tradition, the word *Qadosh* is taken to mean separateness. The idea is adopted by the classical commentators of the Bible. The interpretation seems to have its source in a midrashic explanation of the biblical injunction, "Ye shall be holy; for I the Lord your God am holy" (Lev. 19:2). The observation is made: "As I am holy, so shall ye be holy; as I am separate, so shall ye be separate" (Torat Kohanim, ch. 11, par. 168 and 170; see also ch. 20, par. 128. Arabic commentators of the Koran also seem to understand the term, holy, as being separate.) In the sense of separateness, *Qadosh* applies to both, to God and to man. With God it is transcendence beyond everything created. This is how the term is understood, for example, by Nachmanides (*Nachmanides Commentary on Leviticus*, 19, 2). Applied to man, it is the demand for self-control, separating oneself from certain forms of conduct which are contrary to—or not in keeping with—the will of God. Y'huda Hallevi, explaining the significance of the word, holy, in relationship to God, writes:

Holy expresses the notion that He is high above any attribute of created beings. . . . For this reason Isaiah heard an endless: 'Holy, Holy, Holy,' which meant that God is too high, too exalted, too holy, and too pure for any impurity of the people in whose midst His light dwells to touch Him. For the same reason Isaiah saw him sitting upon a throne, high and lifted up. Holy is, further, a description of the spiritual which never assumes a corporeal form, and which nothing concrete can possibly resemble. (*Kuzari*, Part IV, 3., trans. Hartwig Hirschfeld)

Holy, according to Hallevi, apparently means the same as, unlike anything created, transcendent, divine. It is the essence of the separateness of God.

Surveying the various types of interpretation, we remain unconvinced. The idea that "holy" is identical with the nature of the godhead, in whichever way that may be understood, is the least convincing. Quite obviously the word *Qadosh* in the Bible is not an "otiose epithet." "Holy, holy, holy, is the Lord of Hosts" does not mean, Godly, Godly, Godly is God. The only proof Davidson offers for his contention—a proof which is repeated by Snaith—are two verses in Amos (4:2 and 6:8). In the one, God swears by His holiness; in the other, by Himself. Davidson remarks that He does so in both cases "without difference of meaning" (op. cit., Introduction, p. xxxix). This is a dictum, but no proof. He is begging the question. If "holy" means what he says it does, then there is no difference of meaning between the two passages. On the other hand, if "holy" should have a specific meaning of its own, there may well be a difference in meaning between the two passages in Amos. That God swears in each case need not mean that that by which he swears is the same in each case.

As to the theory of Otto that the holy is the *mysterium tremendum*, one should note that, as far as the Hebrew Bible is concerned, he does not quote a single passage to sustain his interpretation. He quotes the expression, "Eymat YHVH," the terror of God, from Exodus (23:27) and from Job (9:34; 13:11). However, neither in these passages is mention made of God's holiness. Needless to say that we know of the concepts of God's terror, wrath, and anger from the Hebrew Bible;

and Otto is justified in saying that they are the character of the numinous. However, in none of the passages he quotes, are those terms associated with the attribute of holiness. When Jacob awakes from his sleep at Beth El, he is afraid and does exclaim: "How full of awe is this place! this is none other than the house of God, and this is the gate of heaven" (Gen. 28:17). The passage might justify the association of fear and awe with the numinous, but Otto should not use it—as he does—to connect the holy with fear and awe. The term, holy, does not occur in that context. There is one more passage which he quotes to prove his point. It is God's address to Moses from the burning bush: "Draw not nigh hither; put off thy shoes from off thy feet, for the place whereon thou standest is holy ground" (Exod. 3:5). The word, holy, is mentioned in this sentence. Strangely enough, it is not said here that God is holy, but the ground on which Moses stands. There are many biblical verses in which holiness is attributed to God himself. The most significant aspect of Otto's study of the idea of the holy is his complete neglect of all the numerous passages which mention the holiness of God. In view of the rich biblical material on divine holiness, one cannot hope to define the idea either by relying on a few passages that speak of the *mysterium tremendum* but not of holiness or by the one solitary passage quoted which does mention holiness but not in relationship to God.

A remarkable failing in Otto's study is that it does not at all define divine holiness, but presents us with the description of human reaction to the Wholly Other. The numinous, the *mysterium tremendum,* do not exist objectively. They result from a certain form of human reaction to a certain type of human experience. The holy emerges from Otto's study as a subjective quality of a state of mind which is characteristic of man when he is confronted with the non-human or super-human. Otto's distinction between the *fascinans* and the *augustum*—see op. cit., pp. 64–65—cannot overcome this criticism. The *augustum* too is the outcome of a purely subjective

221

evaluation of the Unknown. Tillich, in his *Systematic Theology* (I, 216), insists that Otto's analysis is phenomenological and not psychological. If so, it is the phenomenological analysis of a certain state of mind, but not that of the holiness of God. The theological view of the holy as the absolutely transcendent is not very convincing either. The classical passage in Isaiah runs: "Holy, holy, holy, is the Lord of hosts; the whole earth is full of his glory." Surely, rather than speaking of divine transcendence, the words seem to suggest God's immanence in the world by means of his "glory." The phrase, the Holy One of Israel, so often found in Isaiah, as well as in other books of the Bible, does not indicate inaccessibility either. On the contrary, it would seem to suggest an extremely close relationship between the Holy One and Israel. The greatest difficulty that renders the transcendence theory hardly acceptable we find in the fact that the term holy does not apply to God alone. It is useless to maintain in this connection, as some scholars have done, that it applies also to people and objects in a secondary sense, as that which belongs to the holy, which is the Godhead alone (cf. Davidson, op. cit., Introduction; repeated also by Snaith, op. cit., pp. 43–44). We are not thinking here of the merely ritualistic usage of the word. Holiness is an obligation upon all Israel to be a holy people. Surely, the injunction: "Ye shall be holy; for I the Lord your God am holy," does not speak of ritualistic belonging to the sphere of the holy, but of holiness as a form of human existence. If holiness is a concept which can be ascribed to the deity alone, if it stands for divine transcendence and inaccessibility, to enjoin man to be holy "for I the Lord your God am holy" does not seem to make good sense.

The difficulty is not quite as pronounced, if we follow the traditional Jewish interpretation that "holy" means separate. One can perhaps ask man to separate himself from certain practices, for he should imitate God, who too is separate. Perhaps! We find it difficult to accept. God's separateness is his transcendence. To say to man, transcend yourself for I the Lord your God am transcendent, carries very little convincing logic within itself. It would be almost more logical to say to a mere human being: don't even attempt to be holy, for holiness applies to God alone.

In our own analysis, interest was concentrated on the meaning of the term as it is applied to God and man, but we have not lost sight of its purely ritualistic significance either. We have found that the word, holy, does not stand for divine nature in whatever way that nature is understood, it is not a mere "otiose epithet" of God; but it is a specific attribute of the deity and it is consistently used all through the Bible in that specific sense. Rather than indicating transcendence, it seems to be inseparable from the idea of immanence. Far from meaning inaccessibility, it reveals closeness and association. It is not the *mysterium tremendum;* if anything, it is its very opposite.

CHAPTER 5

The Biblical Meaning of Justice

LAW, JUDGMENT, AND THE PLIGHT OF THE POOR

IN order to understand what is meant in the Bible by justice, we have to examine the various uses to which the noun *mishpat* and the verb *shafat* are put. *Mishpatim* are rules, laws, ordinances, which are often mentioned together with *huqqim*, statutes, which God gave to the children of Israel that they do them and live by them. They cover a wide area of civil, criminal, and ritual law. Often *mishpat* is the case before the court, the entire process of administering the law. When the Bible says, "Ye shall not respect persons in *mishpat;* ye shall hear the small and the great alike; ye shall not be afraid of the face of any man,"[1] the term is not used in the narrower sense of judgment. The injunction refers to the entire conduct of the case in court. *Mishpat* is the suit before the judge. When the daughters of Zelophehad made their claim to the possession which was due to their father, the Bible says: "And Moses brought their *mishpat* before the Lord."[2] Moses brought their case before God, as well as the question whether their claim was justified or not. We do not think that King Solomon asked God for an understanding heart to discern judgment or justice.[3] He asked for understanding *lishmo'a mishpat,* to hear wisely, with the proper insight, the suits brought into his court. *Mishpat* may also mean the specific verdict delivered in a certain case, the judgment delivered by a judge. *Mishpat* is, for instance, used in this sense in the case of King Solomon who judged the case of the two women before him.[4] We believe that, at least, in one place *mishpat* stands for the place where justice is administered. We translate:

Therefore the wicked shall not stand in the house of justice,
Nor the sinners in the congregation of the righteous. (Pss. 1:5)

Our translation is suggested by the parallelism, which the verse seems to demand. *Mishpat* may also mean the Law in the abstract sense. This is how it is used, for instance, in the verse:

Ye shall have one manner of *mishpat,* as well for the stranger, as for the home-born. (Lev. 24:22)

This injunction employs the concept of *mishpat* as the general idea of a law equally binding on all people. However, *mishpat* may also mean simply, justice. When Abraham exclaims before God: "shall not the Judge of all the earth do *mishpat?*" what he means is: shall not God Himself act justly, shall He not enact justice?

Obviously, all these various meanings derive from the basic idea of what is meant by *mishpat* or *shafat.* It is normally understood that basically these words mean law and justice or judging in accordance with the law and administering justice. What is the meaning that the Bible itself expresses by these terms?

Often, the meaning seems indeed to be, justice, judgment in accordance with strict principles of justice, the full application of the law in all its consequence. So that the psalmist has reason to say:

My flesh shuddereth for fear of Thee;
And I am afraid of Thy judgments. (Pss. 119:120)

There is reason to fear the *mishpat* of God, even though in the same context the psalmist has occasion to affirm that:

Righteous art Thou, O Lord,
And upright are Thy judgments. (vs. 137)

225

To judge may even mean to execute judgment, so that *mishpat*—or its verbal form—becomes the equivalent of punishment. The psalmist speaks of this kind of *mishpat* done, when he prays:

I know, O Lord, that Thy judgments are righteous,
And that in faithfulness Thou hast afflicted me. (vs. 75)

God's *mishpatim* in this case were judgments actually executed which were the psalmist's affliction. Quite often is this the significance of *mishpat*. It is the punishment following the judgment and in accordance with it. We shall quote a few important examples of this usage. Isaiah once expresses God's indignation over the nations in the words:

For My sword hath drunk its full in heaven;
Behold, it shall come down upon Edom,
And upon the people of My ban,
To *mishpat*. (Isa. 34:5)

Needless to say that the sword does not come down in order to judge Edom, but in order to execute the judgment already passed over Edom, i.e., to punish. In the same sense Ezekiel speaks of the doing of *mishpat* by God.[5] When Jeremiah announces the downfall of Moab, he introduces the terrible description of its collapse with the words: "And *mishpat* is come upon the country of the Plain." He repeats the same phrase at the close of his prophecy of doom saying: "Thus far is the *mishpat* of Moab."[6] Of the fallen Babylon it is said:

We would have healed Babylon, but she is not healed;
Forsake her, and let us go everyone into his own country;
For her *mishpat* reacheth unto heaven,
And is lifted up even to the skies. (Jer. 51:9)

If Babylon cannot be healed, she must already be afflicted. The *mishpat* that reacheth unto heaven is the measure of her punishment. Because of the vastness of the punishment, Babylon cannot be healed. In the prophecy concerning the future of the house of Eli, which was intimated to the young Samuel, God did not say—as the translations would have it—that He would judge his house for ever. A judgment is pronounced once; there is no such thing as a continuous judging for a crime once committed. What God said was that the punishment would not depart from Eli's house. As it is also stated explicitly "that the iniquity of Eli's house shall not be expiated . . . for ever."[7] The prophet Zephaniah calls upon the daughter of Zion to sing and to be glad and rejoice for

The Lord hath taken away thy *mishpatim*,
He hath cast out thine enemy;
The King of Israel, even the Lord is in the midst of thee;
Thou shalt not fear evil any more. (3:15)

Again, quite clearly, *mishpatim* are not only judgments, but judgments already executed which afflict the daughter of Zion. This comes to expression more dramatically in the Hebrew original which should better be rendered: the Lord hath *removed* thy *mishpatim*. Something to which they have already been subject is taken from them. The enemy already entered Zion. But now that the *mishpat*, that this punishment has been removed from them and, instead of the enemy, God dwells in their midst, there is nothing to be feared.

In all the cases which we have quoted, and in numerous others, *mishpat* stands for the strictness of the law and its implementation. And God is the Judge who executes such justice and law. It is in view of this aspect of divine activity that it is said of God in Deuteronomy that:

the Lord your God, He is God of gods, and Lord of lords, the great God, the mighty, and the awful, who regardeth no persons, nor taketh reward. (10:17)

It is the description of the mighty and powerful Judge who is impartial and who cannot be deflected from his course of executing judgment. It is, however, important to note that immediately after these words the text continues:

He doth execute justice for the fatherless and widow, and loveth the stranger, in giving him food and raiment. (vs. 18)

This very stern judge, who "regardeth no persons," does regard the fatherless and widow. He exacts justice for their sake. His insistence on justice is motivated by his concern for the weak and the oppressed. He executes justice just as he loves the stranger. Because of his love for the oppressed, he judges the oppressor. He may be "awful" as he judges, but he judges because he is "a father of the fatherless and a judge of the widows."[8] As terrifying as he may appear to those whom he judges, as comforting is he to those for whose sake he executes judgment. God's insistence on justice is dictated by his concern for those to whom justice is denied. It is for this reason that the biblical command to do justice is so often connected with the injunction to protect the right of the weak and helpless. Typical of this attitude is the commandment in Exodus:

Thou shalt not wrest the judgment of thy poor in his cause. Keep thee far from a false matter; and the innocent and the righteous slay thou not; for I will not justify the wicked. (23:6–7)

Any justification of the wicked is not only an offense against an abstract ideal of justice, but the actual betrayal of the poor and the innocent. Every perversion of justice is also the imposition of suffering on someone who is unable to defend himself against it. It is with the one, who is so imposed upon, that the biblical demand for justice is concerned. As it is also written:

Thou shalt not pervert the justice due to the stranger, or to the fatherless; nor take the widow's raiment to pledge. But thou shalt remember that thou wast a bondman in Egypt, and the Lord thy God redeemed thee thence; therefore I command thee to do this thing. (Deut. 24:17)

It is the continually recurring accusation of the prophets that they do not espouse the cause of the poor and the

228

oppressed, that their denial of justice to the fatherless and needy is what brings on the anger of God. Jeremiah, for instance, expressed it in indelible words, saying:

They are waxen fat, they are become sleek;
Yea, they overpass in deeds of wickedness;
They plead not the cause, the cause of the fatherless,
That they might make it to prosper;
And the right of the needy do they not judge.
Shall I not punish for these things?
Saith the Lord;
Shall not My soul be avenged
On such a nation as this? (5:28–29)

It is the denial of justice that causes God to exact justice. His anger has its source in the compassion for those, who by the denial of the justice which is due to them, are made to carry the yoke of human wickedness. When God calls upon the people to repent and to purify themselves, he says to them through the mouth of his prophet Isaiah:

Wash you, make you clean,
Put away the evil of your doings
From before Mine eyes,
Cease to do evil;
Learn to do well;
Seek justice, relieve the oppressed,
Judge the fatherless, plead for the widow. (1:16–17)

To seek justice is to relieve the oppressed. But how else is the oppressed to be relieved if not by judging the oppressor and the crushing of his ability to oppress. History is not a Sunday school where the question is to forgive or not to forgive. The toleration of injustice is the toleration of human suffering. Since the proud and the mighty, who inflict the suffering, do not as a rule yield to moral persuasion, responsibility for the sufferer demands that justice be done so that oppression be ended. When the psalmist calls on God, "to whom vengeance belongeth," to render to the proud their recompense, his concern is not with the principle of justice that has been violated, nor with the letter of the law that must be fulfilled. What does concern him, he states clearly when he follows up his call to "the Judge of the earth" with the words:

Lord, how long shall the wicked,
How long shall the wicked exult?
They gush out, they speak arrogancy;
All the workers of iniquity bear themselves loftily.
They crush Thy people, O Lord,
And afflict Thy heritage.
They slay the widow and the stranger,
And murder the fatherless.
And they say: The Lord will not see,
Neither will the God of Jacob give heed. (Pss. 94:3–7)

The psalmist's concern is with the reality of an intolerable human situation. God's people are being afflicted and crushed. Who are the people of God? They are represented by the widow, the stranger, and the fatherless. They are the weak, the helpless, the oppressed, and the persecuted. Compassion for them, love for them, demands that an end be put to the arrogance and power of the proud and the wicked. God must see and give heed. Love for man is at the root of the demand for justice. All injustice is human suffering. Once more we shall quote the words of the psalmist to illustrate the intrinsic connection which exists between the two in the biblical interpretation of the reality of human existence. Of God, who made heaven and earth and "who keeps the truth for ever," the psalmist also says:

Who executeth justice for the oppressed;
Who giveth bread to the hungry.
The Lord looseth the prisoners;
The Lord openeth the eyes of the blind;
The Lord raiseth up them that are bowed down;
The Lord loveth the righteous;
The Lord preserveth the strangers;

He upholdeth the fatherless and the widow;
But the way of the wicked He maketh crooked. (Pss. 146:7–9)

Justice alone will not feed the hungry nor raise up those who are bowed down, but without justice neither of these acts of kindness and compassion can be performed. The love for the righteous and the concern for the stranger will be mere sentimentalism if injustice is permitted to be rampant. One cannot uphold the fatherless and the widow without at the same time protecting them against the overbearing arrogance of the mighty. One must make the way of the wicked "crooked." One must not let it lead to its goal, if the way of the innocent is to be straight before them. There is no other alternative in history.

TO JUDGE AND TO SAVE

The purpose of judgment is to save the innocent from injustice. The idea is so deeply anchored in biblical thought that to judge becomes the equivalent of, to save. Of the terrible anger of God the psalmist says:

Thou didst cause sentence to be heard from heaven;
The earth feared, and was still,
When God arose *to judgment*,
To save all the humble of the earth [italics added]. (Pss. 76:9–10)

God judges in order to save. Ezekiel expressed the same idea in the following manner:

Because ye thrust with side and with shoulder, and push all the weak with your horns, till ye have scattered them abroad; therefore will I *save* my flock, and they shall be no more a prey; and I will *judge* between cattle and cattle [italics added]. (34:21–22)

He who wants to save the flock must judge between cattle and cattle. Isaiah says it in his own majestic style:

My favor is near,
My salvation is gone forth,
And Mine arms shall judge the peoples;

231

The isles shall wait for Me,
And on Mine arm shall they trust. (51:5)

If salvation is to go forth, judgment is to be instituted. And indeed from numerous passages in the Bible emerges the idea that the function of the judge is to save. In the case of unintentional homicide, the Bible decrees:

Then the congregation shall *judge* between the smiter and the avenger of blood according to these ordinances; and the congregation shall *deliver* the manslayer out of the hand of the avenger of blood, and the congregation shall restore him to his city of refuge [italics added]. (Num. 35:24–25)

The commandment to judge is the responsibility to deliver. According to Jeremiah God speaks to the house of David, saying:

Execute justice in the morning,
And *deliver* the spoiled out of the hand of the oppressor,
Lest My fury go forth like fire,
And burn that none can quench it,
Because of the evil of your doings [italics added]. (21:12; see also 22:3)

The association between judgment and deliverance is so intimate that they are, at times, interchangeable. Isaiah, for instance, could say:

We look for *mishpat*, but there is none;
For salvation [*y'shu'ah*], but it is far off from us. (59:11)

The justice or judgment they were looking for would have been their salvation. In two places in Samuel, the verb *shafat* (to judge) actually means to save. David, fleeing and hiding from Saul, on one occasion confronts his enemy with the words:

The Lord therefore be judge, and give sentence between me and thee, and see and plead my cause, and deliver me out of thy hand. (I Sam. 24:16)

The English translation, as so often, hides what is the most characteristic feature of the Hebrew original. In our case it is the phrase which is here rendered as: "and deliver me out of thy hand." The Hebrew says: *v'yishp'tenee miyadekha* which, translated literally, gives: "and judge me out of thy hand." Of course, one cannot say it this way in English, because in English to judge does not mean to deliver. But it is essential for the understanding of the biblical concept of justice to know that the Bible does say it so. Needless to say that to judge one out of the hand of someone else does mean to deliver him. The Hebrew phraseology underlines the connection between judging and saving; the English translation hides it. How dangerous such inattention to the implied meaning of the Hebrew idiom is, one may realize by examining carefully two passages in II Samuel. The tragic story of Absalom's rebellion against his father ended with Absalom's death. The question arose, who should bring the news to the king. At first, Ahimaaz volunteered. He said:

Let me now run, and bear the king tidings, how that the Lord hath avenged him of his enemies. (II Sam. 18:19)

Joab, however, did not allow Ahimaaz to go. Instead, the Cushite was sent. When the Cushite stood before the king, he communicated the news of the death of Absalom in terms very similar to those proposed by Ahimaaz. He said to David:

Tidings for my lord the king; for the Lord hath avenged thee this day of all of them that rose up against thee. (vs. 31)

Nothing could be more misleading than such a translation.[9] There is nothing in the Bible about God having avenged David of his enemies. The Hebrew idiom in both these passages is identical with the one used by David himself, when he confronted Saul and asked that God be judge between them. It is *shafat . . . miyad*. For some mysterious reason both the R.V. and the J.P.S. editions translate the phrase when spoken by David as to deliver from the hand of, but when spoken to

233

David as to avenge someone of. When one writes English
there may be justification for such literary freedom. But
when one translates, the disregard for the Hebrew idiom is a
form of re-writing the biblical text in a manner that is
actually a misrepresentation of biblical thought. As in the case
of David, so also in that of Ahimaaz and the Cushite,
shafat . . . miyad, means the same thing: to deliver one from
the hand of someone else. Only in Hebrew, because to judge
in Hebrew is also to save, we say: to judge someone out of the
hand of someone else. What Ahimaaz and the Cushite actually
said was rather different from what the translations maintain
that they said. They did not speak of vengeance, but of
deliverance. Ahimaaz' words were:

Let me now run, and bear the king tidings, how that the Lord hath
delivered [judged] him out of the hand of his enemies.

The Cushite, too, expressed himself similarly, using the
same idiomatic phrase and saying:

Tidings to my lord the king; for the Lord hath delivered [judged]
thee this day out of the hand of all those that rose up against thee.

We are now in a position to understand a rather unusual
title that the leaders of the Jewish people had at a certain
time in history. After Joshua, and up to the election of Saul
to kingship, the leaders of Israel were called Judges. But why
Judges? They were of course judges, too, but that was not their
chief function. They were the heads of the people, fulfilling
the function that later on was that of the kings. It is rather
strange that they should have been called Judges. However, it
is strange only if for us the meaning of the word is its meaning
in the English language. The title, however, is quite proper if
we attempt to think in biblical terms. What does the Bible say
about the Judges?

And the Lord raised up *judges,* who *saved* them out of the hand of
those that spoiled them. . . . And when the Lord raised them up
judges, then the Lord was with the judge, and *saved* them out of

the hand of their enemies all the days of the judge [italics added]. (Judg. 2:16, 18)

This makes, of course, very poor sense in English. Since when is it the task of judges to save their people out of the hand of their enemies? This sounds altogether different in Hebrew, especially as one recalls that instead of, "who saved them out of the hand of those that spoiled them," one could almost say, who judged them out of their hands; or as one remembers that, as we saw, Isaiah uses *mishpat* (judgment) and *y'shu'ah* (salvation, deliverance) as parallels. Since to judge in Hebrew may well mean to save, the judge may well be the savior or the one through whom God sends deliverance to His people. How inseparable is the function of the judge from that of the savior comes to magnificent expression in the words of Isaiah:

For the Lord is our Judge,
The Lord is our Lawgiver,
The Lord is our King;
He will save us. (33:22)

THE SYNDROME OF *MISHPAT, HESED, RAHAMIM,* AND *S'DAQAH*

We have not yet achieved an adequate insight into the positive meaning of the biblical concept of justice. We have learned that to judge means the passionate rejection and combatting of injustice, the protection of the innocent and the poor and weak. In this way, the term seems to achieve its significance as an act of saving deliverance. But as yet, we have not discovered the contents of the idea of *mishpat* itself. What is the biblical concept of justice? Of what does biblical justice consist? It is probably the most surprising aspect of the idea of *mishpat* that it is able to keep comfortable company in the Bible with such other biblical ideas as, *hesed* (love or lovingkindness), *rahamim* (compassion or mercy), and *s'daqah* (any good deed not obligatory upon the doer or, simply, charity).[10] In Jeremiah, for instance, God is called, "the Lord who exercises lovingkindness (*hesed*), justice (*mishpat*), and charity[11] (*s'daqah*)."[12] Even a single passage like this one ought to suffice to show that the biblical *mishpat* is not to be confused with the idea of justice as it is understood in the context of Western civilization. It is extremely doubtful that in the vast realm of Western thought a single text might be found to parallel this one in Jeremiah, in which justice is placed between lovingkindness and charity. Within the sphere of Western culture and religion the three concepts cannot be co-ordinated. Justice there is opposed to lovingkindness as well as to charity. For the Western mind, he who exercises lovingkindness and practices charity foregoes the implementation of justice. *Hesed* and *mishpat*, *s'daqah* and *mishpat* are opposites within the frame of reference of practically all cultures and their religions. A judge is either just or merciful. One exercises either *hesed* or *mishpat*. But no judge may exercise lovingkindness, justice, and charity, and certainly not in that order. One either loves or judges. And God, too, is either a God of love or a God of justice. Not so in the Bible. The meaning of *mishpat* must be different in its essence from that of justice, as the word is understood in most languages, if it is possible to say of God that he exercises lovingkindness, justice, and charity in the earth, for "in these things he delights." Most surprising of all is the placing of *mishpat* between *hesed* and *s'daqah,* as if it were the required order, whereas in all Western literature the very sequence would be utterly illogical. The logic of the Western mind may be able to move on from justice to love and charity or to charity and love, but never from love to justice and from justice to charity.

That we are confronted here with a uniquely biblical—and because of the inevitably misleading translations hardly ever understood—concept is proven by the fact that the close association between *mishpat* and *hesed, rahamim,* and *s'daqah* is a continually recurring theme of the Bible. What is it that God requires of man according to Micah? To do what, according to Jeremiah, God himself does: to do *mishpat* and to love *hesed*, to exercise justice and to love practicing lovingkindness. No European knows how one may be called upon to practice both to do justice and to exercise lovingkindness. Like Micah, Hosea, too, associates *mishpat* and *hesed*, when he says:

Therefore turn thou to thy God;
Keep *hesed* and *mishpat*,
And wait for thy God continually. (12:7)

Even more impressive are the words in Zechariah:

"Execute true *mishpat* [judgment, justice], and exercise *hesed* [lovingkindness] and *rahamim* [compassion] every man to his brother. (7:9)

Whereas Hosea called upon Israel to keep *hesed* and *mishpat*, Isaiah's admonition is to keep *mishpat* and to do *s'daqah*.[13] *Mishpat*, justice, seems to be a member of the same group of values to which *hesed*, love, *rahamim*, compassion, and *s'daqah*, charity, too, belong. The association between *mishpat* and the other members of the group seems to be even closer than the passages quoted thus far suggest. Isaiah speaks mysteriously about God when he says of Him:

And therefore will the Lord wait, that He may be gracious unto you,
And therefore will He be exalted, That He may have compassion
    upon you:
For the Lord is a God of justice [*mishpat*],
Happy are all they that wait for Him. (30:18)

The difficulty of interpretation cannot be overlooked. It is a moving thought that God himself waits impatiently for the right moment to be gracious to Israel and to exercise compassion (*rahamim*) toward them. And as God waits for that moment, so let Israel too wait for God. However, the reason given for God's anxious desire to show grace and compassion for Israel requires explanation. How can one say that God is waiting to be gracious and compassionate because he is a God

237

of justice? Is God *rahamim* and *hanun,* merciful and gracious, because he is just? The usual translation of *mishpat* as justice, law, judgment, breaks completely down when we hear the psalmist pray:

Hear my voice according unto Thy lovingkindness [*hesed*];
Quicken me, O Lord, according to Thy *mishpat.*

. . . .

Great are Thy compassions [*rahamim*], O Lord;
Quicken me according to Thy *mishpatim.* (Pss. 119:149, 156)

The words of the psalmist belong to the same world of discourse as those of Isaiah. There is some intrinsic, almost causative, connection between *hesed* and *rahamim* on the one hand and *mishpat* on the other. All this compels us to conclude that the biblical concept of *mishpat* has little in common with what the idea of justice connotes in Western thought. What, then, is meant by *mishpat?* What is justice in the Bible?

MISHPAT, GOD'S WAY AND LAW—
THE COSMIC PRINCIPLE OF PRESERVATION

It would seem that the original meaning of *mishpat* is to be sought on a more primary level of human interest than that of justice or law. When Joseph interpreted the dream of Pharaoh's butler and told him that he would be restored to his office, he said to him: "and thou shalt give Pharaoh's cup into his hand, after the former manner when thou wast his butler."[14] Now, the Hebrew version for "after the former manner" is: according to the former *mishpat.* Obviously, *mishpat* here is neither justice nor law. It is more habit, the way a thing was customarily done. There are many examples in the Bible which show this, or a related, usage of the word *mishpat.* For six days the children of Israel went around the walls of Jericho in a certain order. On the seventh day, says the Bible, they rose early at dawn "and compassed the city after the same manner seven times."[15] On the seventh day they surrounded the city following the same order which they had adopted on the previous days. Again, the Hebrew for "after the same manner" reads: according to the same *mishpat*. On the seventh day they were really following a routine which they had devised on the previous six days. *Mishpat* might well be rendered here as routine. Of the spies from the tribe of Dan the Bible tells us that they came to the city of Laish "and saw the people that were therein, how they dwelt in security, after the manner of the Zidonians, quiet and secure."[16] For "after the manner of the Zidonians" we have in the Hebrew, according to the *mishpat* of the Zidonians. *Mishpat* here would be a certain manner of living, a certain style or conduct. *Mishpat* may even mean the character, the appearance, the nature of someone and something. Ahaziah, king of Israel, sent messengers to Ekron to inquire of the god whether he would recover from his sickness. The prophet Elijah met the messengers on the way and sent them back to the king with the message that he would die. When they came before the king, he asked them: "What manner of man was he that came up to meet you, and told you these words?" Their answer was: "He was a hairy man, and girt with a girdle of leather about his loins."[17] For "what manner of man" we have in the original: what was the *mishpat* of the man? meaning: what were his characteristic marks? what was typical of him? Of the heathen population which was transplanted from Babylon to Samaria, the Bible tells: "They feared the Lord, and served their own gods, after the manner of the nations from among whom they had been carried away."[18] Here, too, "after the manner" corresponds to "according to the *mishpat*," the meaning being, according to the customs.

The word *mishpat* is used in a most interesting context in I Samuel. The people asked for a king. God tells Samuel to listen to their request and says: "howbeit thou shalt earnestly forewarn them, and shalt declare unto them the manner of the king that shall reign over them."[19] "The manner of the king" is *mishpat ha–melekh*, which is described as the way he would rule over them, making the people his servants, exacting tribute for his personal aggrandizement, taking from them the fruit of their labor. *Mishpat* is here the custom of the king, the manner in which he usually exercises his authority, the way he acts toward his people. One can, of course, easily see how customs of a king, and of a people as well, may one day be regarded as laws, yet we have to bear in mind that the original meaning of *mishpat ha–melekh* is the manner in which the king customarily exercises his authority, it is the characteristic mark or nature of kingship, the way in which kings behave. What can be said of kings may also be said of God. When the king of Assyria first settled people from the provinces of his empire in Samaria, they were plagued by wild animals as a punishment from God, Whom they refused to acknowledge. The explanation given to the king was that this visitation came over the new settlers because they "know not the manner of the God of the land."[20] Here, too, the manner is the *mishpat* of God. According to the understanding of the Syrians, the God of the land, like the gods of other lands, had his customary way of behavior; he ruled over the land in a certain manner and was wont to make certain demands on the inhabitants of the land. To know his ways was to know his *mishpat*. And he who wished to live securely in the land of God had to adjust himself to the *mishpat* of God. Such was the understanding of the Assyrians of the matter. Yet, it was not too far from the truth. None other than the prophet Jeremiah spoke in similar language of the *mishpat* of God. Desperate over the stubbornness of his people who refused to return to God, the prophet said:

Surely these are poor,
They are foolish, for they know not the way of the Lord,
The *mishpat* of their God;
I will get me unto the great men,
And will speak to them;
For they know the way of the Lord,
The *mishpat* of their God?

But these had altogether broken the yoke,
And burst the bands.

· · · · · · · · · · · · · · · · · ·

Their transgressions are many,
Their backslidings are increased. (5:4-6)

We maintain that careful attention to the Hebrew syntax shows that *mishpat* in our text is synonymous with *derekh*, way.[21] The *mishpat* of their God is not another object of their ignorance, but an explanatory parallelism to "the way of the Lord." This causes no difficulty of interpretation if we recall that *mishpat* means manner of action or customary behavior. As the Assyrians spoke of "the *mishpat* of the land," so did Jeremiah, too, use the phrase of "the *mishpat* of their God." Taken in this sense, the *mishpat* of God is indeed synonymous with the way of the Lord. It is in this sense that the psalmist uses the term *mishpat* in the surprising passage which we quoted at the close of the previous section:

Hear my voice according unto thy lovingkindness [*hesed*];
Quicken me, O Lord, according to thy *mishpat*.

· · · · · · · · · · · · · · · · · ·

Great are Thy compassions [rahamim], O Lord;
Quicken me, O Lord, according to thy *mishpat*.

It is God's *mishpat*, his way, his manner of acting toward his creation, to grant life and strength to those whose strength is failing. He does this according to his lovingkindness (*hesed*) and his compassion (*rahamim*). In this sense, both *hesed* and *rahamim* might be considered God's *mishpat*, God's customary way of exercising providence.[22]

Needless to say that Jeremiah's understanding of "the manner of their God" was rather different from what the Assyrians meant by "the manner of the God of the land." For them the *mishpat* of God was probably quite similar to the *mishpat* of the king, as it was presented to the people by Samuel. All lands had their gods and all gods had their own ways. For

Jeremiah the *mishpat* of God, the way He acted, the manner in which he ruled the universe, the way he treated man and was concerned about his creation, was the right way; the way one ought to act. God's way with his creation is God's law for his creation. God's law for man emanates from God's way with man. All law is God's way, appropriately reflected onto the realm of human existence. All biblical law, in a sense, is *imitatio dei*. To practice *hesed* and *rahamim*, which is way for God, thus itself is God's law for man. This is in keeping with the numerous passages in the Bible to which we have referred earlier in our presentation and which require of man that he keep or do lovingkindness, compassion, and charity. But of course, *mishpat* is also used in a specific sense, in which—as we saw—it is co-ordinated to *hesed, rahamim,* and *s'daqah.* It must be one specific aspect of God's way with the world which may become, in its application to human conduct, *mishpat* in the specific sense of justice and right. What is the material contents of such *mishpat?* Can we define it?

There are a few passages in the Bible which may help us in our effort to define it. At first we shall examine a well-known passage in Isaiah. In chapter 40 we read:

Who hath measured the waters in the hollow of his hand,
And meted out heaven with the span,
And comprehended the dust of the earth in a measure,
And weighed the mountains in scales,
And the hills in a balance?
Who hath meted out the spirit of the Lord?
Or who was His counsellor that he might instruct Him,
With whom took He counsel, and who instructed Him,
And taught Him in the path of *mishpat,*
And taught Him knowledge,
And made Him to know the way of discernment? (vss. 12–14)

What could be the meaning of *mishpat* in this context? It does not seem to be an ethical or legal concept. The text emphasizes God's omnipotent mastery over the universe and not his dealings with men and nations. In our text *mishpat* is co-ordinated to counsel, knowledge, and discernment. It must be something upon which understanding and wisdom have some bearing. Now, we may well see how counsel, knowledge, and understanding relate to the first verse in our quotation. The measuring of the waters and of the dust of the earth, the meting out of the boundaries of the heavens, the weighing of the mountains and the hills is not just a poetic description of the Almighty's play with his toy, the universe. This measuring and weighing is the establishment of the principle of balance between the various parts of the universe, it is the introduction of the right proportion between the contending forces without which God's creation could not last but would tumble back into *Tohu vaBohu* again. To have meted out to each its share and to have placed them into a balanced-proportion to each other that they may stand together was the establishment of God's creation as a universe. Such a deed, among men, normally requires counsel, knowledge, understanding. But who was there to be God's counsellor and teacher, and who taught him in the path of *mishpat*, exclaims the prophet. There is only one thing left in the text with which we may identify *mishpat*: it is the measuring and the weighing, the establishing of the balance by which alone the universe is able to stand, the bringing together of the various universal forces in harmony so that in mutuality they may constitute the cosmos. This is the way God made the universe, and his way of doing it is the law of the universe. We would then say that *mishpat* here is the cosmic principle of balance and harmony that is required for the preservation of God's creation.

This *mishpat*, because it is the sustaining law of the universe, embraces the whole of existence, all created reality. Whatever exists is due to its functioning and man encounters it continually. If man desires to live, he must take cognizance of the ramifications of cosmic *mishpat* in his own sphere of existence and co-operate with them. In a rather surprising passage the prophet Isaiah describes the implications of *mishpat* in the labors of the plowman.

243

Give ye ear, and hear my voice;
Attend, and hear my speech.
Is the plowman never done with plowing to sow,
With the opening and harrowing of his ground?
When he hath made plain the face thereof,
Doth he not cast abroad the black cummin, and scatter the cummin,
And put in the wheat in rows and the barley in the appointed place
And the spelt in the border thereof?
For He doth instruct him to *mishpat;*
His God doth teach him.
For the black cummin is not threshed with a threshing-sledge,
Neither is a cart-wheel turned about upon the cummin;
But the black cummin is beaten out with a staff,
And the cummin with a rod.
Is bread corn crushed?
Nay, he will not ever be threshing it;
And though the roller of his wagon and its sharp edges move noisily,
He doth not crush it.
This also cometh forth from the Lord of hosts:
Wonderful is His counsel, and great His wisdom. (28:23–29)

The *mishpat,* which God teaches the plowman is not essentially different from the one by which, measuring and weighing the various parts of his creation, he establishes their relationship to each other and makes the universe an enduring and functioning entity. It is the same *mishpat* of relatedness and balance, applied to the corner of the world in which the plowman performs his task. How the earth is to be plowed, how the various seeds are to be sown in relationship to each other, how each of the seeds is to be treated after having yielded the hoped–for harvest, all has to be done according to a *mishpat* which is from God and which, like the original comprehensive, universal *mishpat,* reveals God's wonderful counsel and wisdom. But why was it so important for the prophet to draw the attention of the people to the *mishpat* that the plowman has to obey? Surely, he was not lecturing to them on the art of agriculture. The point he was making was that *mishpat* is a universal principle. It prevails everywhere, in the realm of the spirit no less than in the realm of nature. As there is an orderliness, an appropriateness, and a balanced relatedness of all things in nature without which life is not possible, so is there also the same kind of *mishpat* in all matters of the spirit. Not to take cognizance of them leads to disaster. The idea is expressed with somewhat greater clarity by Jeremiah. Complaining about the backslidings of Israel, God, speaking through the mouth of the prophet, says:

Yea, the stork in the heaven
Knoweth her appointed times;
And the turtle and the swallow and the crane
Observe the time of their coming;
But My people know not
The *mishpat* of the Lord. (8:7)

If we understand *mishpat* to mean ordinance, law, commandment, the comparison between Israel and the seasonal birds who follow their instincts, is difficult to interpret. If, however, the *mishpat* of the Lord is a cosmic principle of measured, balanced relatedness which applies to the whole of life, to the realm of the spirit no less than to the realm of nature, then the meaning of these words of Jeremiah becomes clear. These seasonal birds know their appointed times, they sense the orderliness and interrelatedness in nature, thus they know when to come and when to go, but Israel does not acknowledge the same *mishpat* as it prevails in the spiritual life of the world. How shall we formulate this cosmic principle of *mishpat*, when projected onto the scene in which human beings find themselves in contact with each other? Is it not also a weighing and a measuring of claims, drives, and desires, of balancing and harmonizing of the whole with a view to its preservation and its God-intended functioning? Justice and law are like God's *mishpat* in the act of creation; an appropriateness, determined not by abstract consideration, but by the reality of man's condition and subserving the meaningful preservation of human life. Because it is not mere adherence to an abstract principle or ideal, but a principle of order that has its place within the cosmic balance of the coordinated interrelatedness of all life, it is a justice that is exacting. Its implementation may be frightening, especially when it is done by God himself, who intervenes in the course of history in order to restore the disturbed balance which threatens life itself. Justice is done not that justice prevail, but that life prevails; it is done out of concern with a concrete situation, in which life is endangered and calls for its salvation. Thus, while *mishpat* may be grim, it is always also an act of saving and deliverance. *Hesed,* loving concern for life itself, may well be the source of such *mishpat.*

That *mishpat* means such a principle of measure and appropriateness, whose very purpose is to sustain life, comes to beautiful expression in two passages in Jeremiah. In one place the prophet lets Israel pray:

O Lord, correct me, but in *mishpat;*
Not in Thine anger, lest Thou diminish me. (10:24)

The meaning of *mishpat* here, far from being an exception, reveals its true meaning. It is a principle of preservation; the restoration of a disturbed balance which is needed because life has become disbalanced. As if in answer to this prayer of Israel, Jeremiah also lets God speak to Israel and say:

For I am with thee, saith the Lord, to save thee;
For I will make a full end of all the nations whither I have scattered thee,
But I will not make a full end of thee;
For I will correct thee in *mishpat.*
And will not utterly destroy thee. (30:11)

God is with Israel to save it, yet God is also judging Israel to correct it. To save and to judge are not exclusive of each other. The *mishpat,* which is imposed, may itself have its origin in God's nearness and concern. It is difficult to state exactly where in such *mishpat hesed* ends and objective justice

246

begins. A justice that never loses sight of the actual human situation with which it is benevolently concerned is never wholly objective. Its main concern is not with what is due to a person, but what may hurt a person. It is not a formal legal concept, but a material moral one. Of his servant, upon whom He put His spirit, God says in the words of Isaiah that he shall make *mishpat* go forth to the nations. And of his *mishpat* it is said that:

A bruised reed shall he not break,
And the dimly burning wick shall he not quench;
He shall make *mishpat* to go forth according to the truth. (42:3)

Mishpat according to the truth is the non-abstract, the non-objective justice. A justice that does not respect persons in judgment, but does consider their need. It is a justice that does not break, but delivers; and if it breaks, it is in order to deliver. Such justice may easily be coordinated with *hesed* and *rahamim* and it may unashamedly call for the practice of *s'daqah,* as we saw it to be the case in numerous passages in the Bible. At times, it even merges with *hesed.* Because He is a God of *mishpat,* we heard Isaiah say, He waits for the moment when judgment has passed and He may again be gracious and compassionate toward Israel. When Moses said of God:

The Rock, His work is perfect;
For all his ways are *mishpat.* (Deut. 32:4)

he could not have meant that all God's ways were justice. That would not be true. According to the entire testimony of the Bible, God is not only just, he is also merciful and longsuffering, and compassionate, and loving. But he could well have meant the *mishpat* which we have found to be the cosmic principle of the measured balance and harmonized coordination which is the God-implanted appropriateness of the universal order. It is because of that *mishpat* that His work is perfect. Therefore all His ways, along which His work grows,

247

are ways of *mishpat*. But since this *mishpat* is the order of all life and its preservation, one might also say that what God does as *mishpat* is altogether *hesed* from the viewpoint of his creation. As indeed the psalmist put it:

All the paths of the Lord are *hesed* and *emeth*[23]
Unto such as keep His covenant and His testimonies. (25:10)

JOB'S PROBLEM AND ITS SOLUTION

The problem that often occupies man's mind is, however, not that God is a judge who is too exacting, executing justice without mercy and charity, but rather that he seems to be so often indifferent toward the evil perpetrated by man and the suffering of the innocent. It is not the task of this study to discuss the age-old theological problem of theodicy. However, one classical version of theodicy has a direct bearing on our immediate subject. It is the version which is found in Job. The story is well-known. Job queries the justice of God. One ought to appreciate the seriousness of Job's inner struggle. Not his undeserved suffering is his chief preoccupation, nor the self-righteous affirmation of his innocence. His concern is with the nature of God. How can God be unjust? It is the most serious problem that may perturb a believing soul. It is for this reason that he must reject all the arguments of his friends. The issue is a fundamental issue of religious faith. It must not be blurred over with pious words. How can God be unjust?! And we who read the book and know from the introduction what was hidden from the eyes of Job, also know that what was done to Job was not justice. Demanding justice of God, Job is the great hero of faith who struggles for the honor of his God. He will not rest until he is given answer, until he understands. For it cannot be, it must not be, that God should not act justly; and yet, he has experienced injustice at the hand of God. The issue must be faced for the sake of God.

The more one senses the believing fervor with which Job struggles to understand the God in whom he puts his trust, the more is one puzzled by God's answer. For what was God's answer? The Bible says:

Then the Lord answered Job out of the whirlwind, and said:
Gird up thy loins now like a man;
I will demand of thee, and declare thou unto Me.
Wilt thou even make void My judgment [*mishpat*]?
Wilt thou condemn Me, that thou mayest be justified?
Or hast thou an arm like God?
And canst thou thunder with a voice like Him?
Deck thyself now with majesty and excellency,
And array thyself with glory and beauty.
Cast abroad the rage of thy wrath;
And look upon everyone that is proud, and abase him.
Look upon everyone that is proud, and bring him low;
And tread down the wicked in their place.
Hide them in the dust together;
Bind their faces in the hidden place.
Then will I also confess unto thee
That thine own right hand can save thee. (40:6–12)

Upon this reference of God to his own overwhelming power, follows the great poetic description of the majestic might of some of his creatures, like *behemoth* and *leviathan*. Can Job compete with that? And God continues:

Who then is able to stand before Me?
Who hath given Me anything beforehand, that I should repay him?
Whatsoever is under the whole heaven is Mine. (41:2–3)

The more we read on, the more our amazement deepens. The answer seems to sidestep the issue. God owes no one anything—except justice. No one doubted God's omnipotence, but to take a stand on it does not seem to meet Job's quest for divine justice. If one is puzzled by God's answer, one is even more mystified by Job's reaction to it.

Then Job answered the Lord, and said:
I know that Thou canst do everything,
And that no purpose can be withholden from Thee.

Who is this that hideth counsel without knowledge?
Therefore have I uttered that which I understood not,
Things too wonderful for me, which I knew not.

. . . .

I had heard of Thee by the hearing of the ear;
But now mine eye seeth Thee;
Wherefore I abhor my words, and repent,
Seeing I am dust and ashes. (42:1–6)

Job is duly impressed by God's omnipotence and omniscience. But what has become of the heroic struggler with the problem of divine justice? Has he been answered or only silenced? One may well understand that God's self-revelation would overwhelm a mere man who would then be willing to abhor and repent the words which he had uttered, but then, after having posed the question mightily, we are left without an answer. Yet, Job's conduct after God had revealed Himself to him suggests that somewhere along the line he was given an answer which brought peace to his anguished soul.

A great deal has been written on the mystery of the conclusion of the book. It would seem to us, however, that a great deal depends on the proper understanding of the word *mishpat* in the key line in God's answer: "Wilt thou even make void My *mishpat?*" If we translate the word in this context as justice, or as judgment, then indeed what follows becomes rather questionable. It would seem to us that such an interpretation is excluded by the very words spoken by God to Eliphaz after the denouement. When all was said, God turned to him with the words:

My wrath is kindled against thee, and against thy two friends; for ye have not spoken of Me the thing that is right, as My servant Job hath. (42:7)

One may wonder. If the answer to Job was that one should not dare question the justice of an omnipotent God, in which way did Job speak rightly about God, whereas his friends did not? Were not the arguments of his friends rather similar to the ultimate answer which he was given, i.e., that one must not question God's justice? Having done just that, having demanded justice even of God, in which way did Job speak of God "the thing that is right"? Therefore we maintain that "Wilt thou even make void My *mishpat?*" does not mean: dare you question My justice (or judgment, in the sense of executing justice)? Job did say the right thing about God. What was done to him was not justice. He did ask the right question: how can God be unjust? All that was well spoken about God, unlike his friends who tried to defend what was not justice as God's just judgment. They were distorting justice in order to defend God. That was speaking wrongly about God. God does not stand for the bending of justice for the greater glory of his name. He is a just God. But he is God and not man. Apart from justice, he has also other considerations in the management of his universe, like—for instance— the terrifying testing of the faith of the righteous, as was the case with Job. Such a thing cannot be justified on the basis of justice. But it may have its place within God's *mishpat,* if we understand the term in the sense of the cosmic principle of universal appropriateness, as we found it used in chapter 40 of Isaiah. "Wilt thou even make void My *mishpat?*" means: wilt thou invalidate the way in which I run the universe? So understood, the mocking challenge to Job, whether he had an arm like God? whether he could thunder like a God? was justified. God was not reproaching Job for having doubted the justness of what befell him. But God taught him that in the plan of a universal creator there are other considerations, too, apart from that of justice alone, whose validity may only be understood from the viewpoint of the Creator alone. In order to understand, not God's justice, but God's *mishpat,* the principle of cosmic appropriateness by which he sustains his creation, one would have to be God oneself.

If we have said earlier that the ways of God with men become the laws of God for men, it applies only to the extent to which those ways may be projected to the human scene.

Insofar, however, God's way is God's *mishpat* as the cosmic order of God envisaged appropriateness, no *imitatio dei* is possible. Thus, in history, a chasm may open between the way of God that is just and the one that, though not justice, yet is *mishpat*. And the heart of faith which alone may bridge the chasm, plays with the thought that in the end, when all is known, even God's inscrutable *mishpat* may turn out to be one of those paths of God, of which it has been said that they all are *hesed* and *emeth*, lovingkindness and faithfulness.

CHAPTER 6

Emeth, the Concept of Truth

THE SYNDROME OF *EMETH, SHALOM,* AND *HESED*

AMONG the various theories of truth which occupy epistemological inquiry, the one closest to common sense is the theory of correspondence. According to it, a judgment is true if it corresponds to the fact to which it refers. We certainly do find that truth, *emeth,* in the Bible does have the common sense meaning of correspondence to a fact. In the case of certain inquiries which had to be made, the Bible says: "if it be *emeth,* truth, and the thing certain." The queen of Sheba tells Solomon that the report she heard in her land about the king's wisdom was *emeth,* true. The king of Israel enjoins on Micaiah, the prophet, to speak to him in the name of God nothing but *emeth,* the truth. Isaiah and Jeremiah use the word in the same sense. According to Proverbs, a witness of *emeth,* truth, saves lives. It is easy to find numerous other examples showing that truth in the Bible is correspondence between judgment and the object of which the judgment is predicated.[1] But neither is it difficult to appreciate that the correspondence theory of truth is far from exhausting the meaning of the biblical concept of *emeth.* It is hard to believe that God's promise to his people was that he will be their God "in truth [*b'emeth*] and in righteousness."[2] What could it mean, to be their God in truth? To understand it as meaning that the promise will correspond to the fact, that God will really be their God, verges on the banal. It is even more difficult to believe that the psalmist prayed to God that He may answer him "with the truth of Thy salvation."[3] It is hardly possible to associate any significance with the concept of the truth of God's salvation. God either answers a prayer with his salvation or he does not. The suggestion however that there is a truth aspect to God's salvation, as if his salvation could also be untrue, is preposterous. The concept of *emeth* seems to have an important place in the life of King Hezekiah. It is said of him that "he wrought that which was good and right and *emeth* before the Lord his God." Obviously, *emeth* here is not the intellectual idea of truth, but something in the nature of an ethical deed. Immediately after this passage, the invasion of Judah and the siege of Jerusalem by Sennacherib is introduced with the words: "After these things and this *emeth* . . . ."[4] Undoubtedly, *emeth* here is not the abstract idea of truth, but an event that occurred or a deed which was performed, to which one may refer with the adverb of time, after. When Isaiah predicted to him the downfall of his dynasty after his death, Hezekiah's words were: "If but there shall be peace and *emeth* in my days."[5] It would be hardly meaningful to say that Hezekiah was looking forward to peace and truth in his lifetime. Only if *emeth* has a social and ethical significance similar to that of *shalom* may the two be associated with each other in the manner in which it was done by Hezekiah. The association between *shalom* and *emeth* is, of course, found in other places of the Bible as well. Zechariah, for instance, calls on the people: therefore love ye *emeth* and *shalom*.[6] The juxtaposition of truth and peace offers a fine excuse for a preacher to prove his homiletical skill. The truth, however, is that *emeth* here is a virtue which belongs in an ethico-social category as much as peace itself.

That *emeth* means something quite different from the abstract and intellectual concept of truth becomes quite clear as one compares the numerous biblical passages in which *emeth* is associated with *hesed,* love (or lovingkindness). It is most unlikely that what Abraham's servant said to Rebekah's family about the God of his master was that He did not forsake "His mercy (*hesed*) and His truth (*emeth*) toward my master." What indeed could that truth be and what bearing may it have on guiding the servant to the place for which he set out? Similarly, when the servant requested the decision of the family in his suit on behalf of his master's son, he could not have said to them: "And now if ye will deal kindly and truly with my master."[7] What on earth could dealing *truly* with someone mean? And especially, what could it mean in the situation in which the expression was used by Abraham's servant? What the servant really said was: "And now if you are [willing] to do *hesed* and *emeth* with my master." Had Jacob really prayed: "I am not worthy of all the mercies, and of all the truth, which Thou hast shown unto Thy servant," we would not know what he could have meant. What was "all the truth" which God had shown to Jacob, of which Jacob was not worthy? What Jacob said was: "I am not worthy of all the *hasadim* [acts of love] and the *emeth,* which Thou hast *done* unto Thy servant."[8] As in the previous example, *emeth* is here action, something that is done to someone just as *hesed.* As in its association with *shalom,* so in its connection with *hesed, emeth* is an ethical virtue that is to be practiced toward others. *Hesed* and *emeth* are also associated with each other as divine attributes. Of God it is said that he is long-suffering and abundant in *hesed* and *emeth.*[9] There is a rich biblical tradition for which the association between *hesed* (love, lovingkindness) and *emeth* is most natural. As the other examples which we have discussed earlier, this association leads us to the conclusion that the biblical concept of *emeth* is not to be found in the realm of abstract ideas of pure rationality, but in that of values of practical reason. The biblical *emeth* is not an epistemological idea, but an ideal of ethics.

THE MEANING OF *NE'EMAN*

In order to analyze the meaning of the idea of *emeth*, we may do well to examine at first the adjective, *ne'eman*, and the noun, *emunah*, which have the same root as *emeth*. The adjective *ne'eman* is often applied to objects. Of Eliakim, the son of Hilkiah, the prophet says that God will establish his rule firmly. The idea is, however, expressed symbolically in the words: "And I will fasten him as a peg in a sure place." The sure place is the *maqom ne'eman*. The peg is set in a ground that holds it firmly. Yet, according to the prophet, the day will come on which even "the peg that was fastened in a place *ne'eman* gives way."[10] The giving-way of the place which is sure is the unexpected. *Ne'eman* is then that which does not give way, which holds firm; it is something that endures, lasts. In this sense, the term is often applied to the Davidic dynasty. Abigail, for instance, is convinced that God will make for David a *bayith ne'eman*, which is "a sure house" in the same sense in which Isaiah spoke of the peg in "a sure place," i.e., a house that does not give way, a lasting dynasty. In God's explicit promise to David, the idea of *ne'eman* is applied to the dynasty in its verbal form. God's words are: "And thy house and thy kingdom shall be made *ne'eman* for ever before thee; and thy throne shall be established for ever."[11] *Ne'eman* was here quite obviously the meaning of enduring, lasting. But whereas in the example from Isaiah, *ne'eman* means firmness in space, in its application to the house of David it stands for endurance in time. There are other passages, too, which show a usage which comprehends both significances. In one of those moving passages in which Jeremiah calls out in his loneliness for God's help against his persecutors, he turns to God with these words of bitterness: "Wilt Thou indeed be unto me as a deceitful brook as waters un-sure."[12] Un-sure waters are waters which are not *ne'emanim;* they are the parallel to the deceitful brook. They are not reliable. At times, they are found; at others, they disappear. The meaning of the prophet's simile is self-explanatory. Will God's help be forthcoming for the prophet in the same unsteady fashion in which waters, which are not *ne'emanim,* disappoint a thirsty wanderer? In a country in which water is always a problem, the concept of *mayim ne'emanim,* sure, reliable water, presents itself readily to the mind. It seems to have been a familiar idea. Isaiah uses it, too, when he describes the lot of the person who walks righteously and speaks uprightly. Among other things, he says of him: "His bread shall be given, his waters shall be *ne'emanim* [sure]."[13] Reading these words in the light of Jeremiah's complaint, what Isaiah asserts concerning the righteous is that his water resources will not be deceiving; they will be steadily available. In this sense of steady availability, *ne'eman* encompasses both meanings, that of firmness in space and endurance in time.

Ne'eman, in its application to the world of objects, means then, enduring, lasting, steady; it is something on whose presence one may count.[14] It is not difficult to see how the idea is broadened when applied to human beings and to qualities of human character. Steady availability in man is an ethical concept. It is reliability. A witness, who is *ne'eman,* is one who is reliable.[15] However, when in Proverbs it is said of a messenger that he is *ne'eman,* the idea encompasses even more than reliability. It is said of such a messenger that he is "as the cold of snow in the time of harvest, for he refresheth the soul of his master."[16] *Ne'eman* here expresses the quality of the relation between two people. The messenger is *ne'eman* to the one who sent him. This is more than objective reliability; it is trustworthiness, faithfulness. Reliability of a witness in court is objective trustworthiness; reliability as a quality of relation between two people is subjective loyalty and faithfulness. It is in this sense that in Nehemiah it is said of Abraham that God found his heart *ne'eman* before Him.[17] In the relation between God and Abraham, Abraham was unquestioningly reliable; he was faithful to God. Occasionally, *ne'eman* expresses the mutuality in the relation. The one who is trustworthy is trusted. Thus God says of Moses that he is *ne'eman* in all God's house. The context shows that there exists a certain intimacy between God and Moses. God entrusts Moses with certain mysteries of "His house" with which others could not be entrusted. In one of the prophecies sent to Eli the priest, God says: "And I will raise Me up a priest who is *ne'eman,* that shall do according to that which is in My heart and in My mind; and I will build him a house that is *ne'eman.*"[18] For the purposes of our discussion, this is a most interesting passage. It uses the concept of *ne'eman* twice; once, applied to an object, a house, and once, as a bond between God and the priest God is to raise unto himself. As in all other similar examples, here, too, in its application to an object, *ne'eman* means, enduring, lasting. God promises to raise up a priest whose house, or dynasty, will be an enduring one. But the priest, too, will be *ne'eman,* he will be "enduring" in the relation with God. He will be reliable; he will do as required of him by God. Since he will be trustworthy, he will also be trusted by God. As a sign of God's trust in him, his house will be established enduringly. Of Samuel it is said that, when it became clear that God was with him and all Samuel's words were fulfilled as prophesied by him, all Israel knew that Samuel was *ne'eman* to be a prophet of God.[19] Prophecy is a relation between the prophet and God. The prophet is God's *ne'eman* in a two-fold sense. He is faithful to God and because he is faithful, he is trusted by God.

Ne'eman may also qualify an abstract idea. Of the guidance that the fathers are to give the children it is said: "that they might put their confidence in God . . . and might not be as their fathers . . . a generation that set not their heart aright, and whose spirit was not *ne'emanah* with God."[20] In keeping with what we have found thus far, the meaning may well be that their relation to God was one of unreliability; their loyalty was unsteady, lacking in consistency. Since, however, *ne'eman* also expresses the mutuality in a relation, that of being trustworthy and trusting, what the psalmist says here of the stubborn generation of the fathers is that their spirit was not trusting in God; they were not relying on him wholeheartedly. This seems to be supported by the distinction that is made between the two generations. Let the children be so taught that they may put their confidence in God, not forget the works of God, and thus be led to the keeping of God's commandments. The memory of God's works on behalf of Israel inspires reliance on God and trust in him. It is what the generation of the fathers were lacking. They were rebellious because they forgot God's work. Having forgotten what God had done for them, they did not put their confidence in him. Their spirit was not trusting; it was not *ne'emeneth* with God. One may also be *ne'eman* or not in a covenant. It is said of Israel that they were not *ne'eman* "in His covenant." As the context shows, they proved to be not *ne'eman* in that "they beguiled Him with their mouth, and lied unto Him with their tongue."[21] They were not trustworthy, they did not keep the covenant in loyalty to the Partner in the covenant, to God. God keeps his covenant rather differently. His promise to King David is: "For ever will I keep for him My *hesed* [love], and My covenant will be *ne'eman* to him."[22] Here, *ne'eman* seems to possess all the riches of meaning that we have found in it. The covenant will be lasting and enduring. As such, the phrase is the parallel to God's love, which God will keep for him for ever. It is for this that the psalmist continues: "His seed also will I make to endure for ever, and his throne as the days of heaven." It is a reliable covenant, one which God will keep faithfully. Undoubtedly, Isaiah was bearing in mind this passage when he let God exclaim:

Incline your ear, and come to Me;
Hear, and your soul shall live;
And I will make an everlasting covenant with you,
Even the sure *ne'emanim* [acts of] *hesed* of David. (55:3)

The psalmist spoke of God's everlasting love for David and of His covenant, which was *ne'eman* to David. The prophet varies the application of the attributes and calls the covenant everlasting and the *hesed, ne'eman*. This is an indication that *ne'eman*, qualifying *hesed*, is enduring love. *Hasde David ha–ne'emanim* are lasting acts of divine lovingkindness assured to David. It is *hesed* of the kind on which one may rely, which will never let one down.

We know that a city, too, may be called *ne'emanah*. This is what Isaiah calls Jerusalem in a famous passage. First there is the plaint:

How is the faithful [*ne'emanah*] city
Become a harlot!
She that was full of justice,
Righteousness lodged in her,
But now murderers. (1:21)

One does not expect faithfulness from a harlot. She is not *ne'emanah*. But Jerusalem used to be *ne'emanah;* her inhabitants kept faith with each other. She was *ne'emanah*, because her government could be relied upon to practice *mishpat* and *sedeq*. There is, however, also the promise that this is not to be the lasting condition of the holy city. God will yet restore the judges and the counsellors of the city "as at the beginning":

Afterward thou shalt be called The city of righteousness [*sedeq*],
The faithful [*ne'emanah*] city (Isa. 1:26)

A city is *ne'eman* if its inhabitants may trust to live in it without fear, relying on the faithful observance of its laws and the loyal preservation of its social ideals.[23]

THE ETHICAL SIGNIFICANCE OF *EMUNAH*

We shall now consider the noun *emunah*, which is formed from the same root as the adjective *ne'eman*, and the noun *emeth*. As *ne'eman*, it too may apply to the world of objects. On one occasion in the Bible it describes the hands of Moses. When in the battle of the Israelites against Amalek, Moses' uplifted hands tired and were held up by Aaron and Hur, the Bible says: "and his hands were *emunah* until the going down of the sun."[24] As all other nouns of the same grammatical form, *emunah*, too, is an abstract noun. Thus it causes some problems of interpretation. One would expect here the adjective, *ne'eman*, meaning that the hands of Moses, once supported, held firm, they endured in their position. A literal translation of "his hands were *emunah*" would be: his hands were steadfastness, reliability. In the English language, steadfastness and reliability are qualities of human character. In biblical Hebrew, it would seem, one may say for the sake of emphasis that a thing is all steadiness and durability. In this sense, it could be said of the hands of Moses that they were *emunah* rather than *ne'eman*. They were so firmly held up that they were not just steady but steadiness itself. A most interesting use is made of *emunah* in this connotation by Isaiah, who employs it in a construct with time, when he says: "And wisdom and knowledge shall be the *emunah* of thy times, [and] strength of salvation; the fear of the Lord [is] his [i.e., man's] treasure."[25] *Emunah* of the times as firmness and reliability of the days of man on earth is security, the very opposite of such uncertain conditions when in the morning a man wishes for the night and at the night he longs for the morning because of the fear that fills his heart.[26] Such security of the times is synonymous with the strength and stability of man's salvation. According to the prophet, it can only be had as the result of wisdom and knowledge and the fear of God. The comparison of the fear of God to a treasure further underlines the idea of security. Usually a man puts his trust in his treasures. But it is not material treasures which constitute the *emunah*, the reliability and security of man's time on earth, but the fear of God together with wisdom and knowledge.

In its application to man's character and behavior, *emunah* seems to have the same significance as a noun as we found the adjective *ne'eman* to have. During the rule of King Jehoash, funds were raised for the repair of the temple. No accounting was demanded of the officials whose task it was to pay the workman, for—as the Bible puts it—they were acting in *emunah*.[27] In other words, the temple officials were trusted with the funds. In our opinion, nothing is said here about the actual manner in which these officials carried out their responsibilities, whether they were in fact honest or not. *Emunah* was the basis of the understanding between the officials and the king or the temple government. The officials were trustworthy people and were trusted. *Emunah* here is indicative of the relation that prevailed between the officials and society; it was one of mutual reliability and faithfulness. The term "in *emunah*" means that the officials were acting in a condition of mutual trust. *Emunah* may, therefore, be rendered as reliability, faithfulness, trust. A most interesting use of the word is found in I Chronicles. In the genealogies of the families of Israel, it is said of those who were chosen to be "porters in the gates," that "they were reckoned by genealogy in their villages, whom David and Samuel the seer did establish in their *emunah*."[28] The context suggests that *emunah* here is an established office. Now the aspect of lasting and enduring was, of course, present, since the office was hereditary; it was passed on from generation to generation. This alone, however, would hardly justify calling an office *emunah*. But an office to which one is chosen is also a matter of trust. These men were entrusted with their offices. *Emunah,* in this context, signifies an enduring trust.[29]

Most significantly, however, *emunah* is a character trait or a form of human behavior. Confronting Saul, David said: "And the Lord will render to every man his *s'daqah* and his *emunah;* forasmuch as the Lord delivered thee into my hand to-day, and I would not put forth my hand against the Lord's anointed."[30] David believes that God will recompense him for the act of *emunah* which he rendered to Saul. Even though Saul was in his power, he did not put his hand on him. He was faithful to God's anointed; he acted faithfully and reliably toward him. *Emunah* is loyalty to someone, which determines one's behavior toward him; it is the quality of reliability in human relations. Jehoshapat, setting up judges in the land, enjoined them saying: "Thus shall ye do in the fear of the Lord, in *emunah,* and with a whole heart."³¹ The judges should be reliable, faithful to their charge, execute their duties in *emunah,* in loyalty. Here, too, *emunah* is an inner attitude of reliability which determines human action in the area between man and God and man and man. The other passages in the Bible which connect the dispensation of justice with *emunah* should be read in the light of Jehoshapat's injunction to the judges. Isaiah's plaint is not that "none sueth in truth," but that "none is judged in *emunah.*"³² The judges, in pronouncing judgment, do not act in faithfulness. Similarly, Jeremiah has the judges in mind when he lets God say:

Run ye to and fro through the streets of Jerusalem,
And see now, and know,
And seek in the broad places thereof,
If ye can find a man,
If there be any that enacts justice,
That seeketh *emunah;*
And I will pardon her.
And though they say: As the Lord liveth,
Surely they swear falsely [literally, lyingly].
O Lord, are not Thine eyes upon *emunah?*
Thou hast stricken them, but they were not affected;
Thou hast consumed them, but they have refused to receive correction. (5:1–3)

The *emunah* that the judges do not seek is reliability and faithfulness; they do not seek to establish it in the arguments of the parties or in the testimony of the witnesses. As in the passage we quoted from Isaiah, the statement that none is judged in *emunah* is followed by the explanatory remark: "They trust in vanity, and speak lies," so here, too, the complaint that they seek no *emunah* is elaborated by the observation that they swear *la'sheqer,* to a lie. The judge, who does not seek *emunah,* trusts lies; he who does not judge in *emunah* relies on vanity. The theme is appropriately continued by Jeremiah in the exclamation: "O Lord, are not Thine eyes upon *emunah?*" Unlike the judges who do not, God does seek *emunah.* He watches man to see whether he acts reliably and in faithfulness. As He is willing to pardon man for the sake of *emunah,* so is He ready to punish him because of man's betrayal of *emunah.*

In the last example, *emunah* and *sheqer* (lie) appeared as opposites. As *emunah* is not just truth in the sense of objective conformity with a fact, but reliability and loyalty, so is its opposite *sheqer* not just objective disagreement with a fact, but unreliability in the ethical sense. The passage we have quoted from Isaiah is preceded by the words: "Your lips have spoken lies, your tongue muttereth wickedness." The lie is a manifestation of moral corruption; as wickedness toward a fellow man it is unreliability and disloyalty. The contrast between *sheqer* in this sense and *emunah* comes to clear expression in the following words of Jeremiah:

And they bend their tongue, their bow—*sheqer* [falsehood];
And they are grown mighty in the land, but not for *emunah;*
For they proceed from evil to evil,
And Me they know not,
Saith the Lord. (9:2)

They are mighty, but they do not use their might for the sake of *emunah,* to establish a society based on loyalty and faithfulness. Their weapon is *sheqer* and their purpose is "to proceed from evil to evil." *Sheqer* is the rejection of *emunah* in the service of evil. Because of the nature of the contrast between *sheqer* and *emunah* do we read in Proverbs:

Lips of *sheqer* are an abomination to the Lord;
But they that practise *emunah* are His delight. (12:22)

The practicing of *emunah* is acting in a reliable manner, keeping trust with others. To speak *sheqer* is the opposite; it is the betrayal of a trust.

THE THEOLOGICAL SIGNIFICANCE OF *EMUNAH*

The ideas of *ne'eman* and *emunah* receive their theological significance through their application to God. God Himself is *ne'eman*, He is loyal to man; He is a God of *emunah*, one Who keeps faith with man and His creation. Thus it is said of him in Deuteronomy: "Know therefore that Y thy *Elohim*, He is the *Elohim*, the El [God] who is *ne'eman*, who keepeth covenant and love [*hesed*] with them that love Him and keep His commandments to a thousand generations."[33] As a man who keeps a covenant preserves love for another human being is *ne'eman*, faithful, so is God, too, *ne'eman*, reliable and loyal, for he, too, keeps a covenant and preserves his love for a thousand generations. In this passage we also meet the association between the concept of *ne'eman* and the idea of *hesed* in one of its clearest formulations. God is loyal because He keeps His love for many generations. To be *ne'eman* to someone is in itself a form of *hesed*. But whereas love as such may be momentary, it may even be fickle, of short duration and, therefore, not altogether reliable, the love of one who is *ne'eman* is enduring, it may be relied upon. In this sense, God is *ne'eman* in the keeping of covenant and the practicing of *hesed*. The thought is underlined by the qualification that he does it for "a thousand generations." Isaiah makes use of the same thought, when— prophesying about *Ebed* Y, the servant of God—he promises his elevation in the name of the "Redeemer of Israel, his holy One."

Kings shall see and arise,
Princes, and they shall prostrate themselves;
Because of the Lord that is *ne'eman*,
Even the Holy One of Israel, who hath chosen thee. (49:7)

Notwithstanding Israel's humiliation and degradation by the nations, God keeps his covenant with, and his love for, his people. He will yet make himself known as Israel's Redeemer, for he is *ne'eman*, everlastingly reliable and loyal.

265

God is also himself a God of *emunah,* of loyalty and faithfulness. In the great song of Moses, He is called "a God of *emunah* and without iniquity."[34] Iniquity is, as we saw, the work of *sheqer,* which is the opposite of *emunah,* trustworthiness and reliability. According to Hosea, God betroths Israel unto himself in *emunah,* which, of course, means that God will keep faith with Israel. A most revealing passage is the one in Psalm 33, which reads as follows:

For the word of the Lord is upright;
And all His work is done in *emunah,*
He loves *s'daqah* and *mishpat* [justice];
The earth is full of the lovingkindness [*hesed*] of the Lord.
(vss. 4–6)

The passage is of great interest to us because it further illustrates the validity of our findings in our discussion of the biblical concept of justice.[35] Not only is *mishpat* here associated with *s'daqah,* which—as we shall yet see—is a good deed rendered freely to another person, and *hesed,* but God's love for it elaborates the earlier statement that all His works are done in faithfulness. As we saw, the love of justice is not adherence to an abstract principle, but must be understood as a form of divine concern for man. We found it to be that which was appropriate in a given situation. We learn now that God's love for justice, just as his love for *s'daqah,* is a manifestation of his *emunah.* Because he keeps faith with man, he loves justice and *s'daqah.* As the psalmist puts it in another place, God judges the peoples in *emunah.*[36] Even God's judgment is an act of faithfulness toward man. The thought is most clearly expressed in the words of the psalmist when he says:

I know, O Lord, that Thy judgments are righteous,
And that in *emunah* Thou hast afflicted me. (Pss. 119:75)

Even when afflicting a person with His judgment, God acts in faithfulness; even then, He is to be relied upon. One is reminded of the verse in Proverbs, which says that wounds of a friend are *ne'emanim,* faithful, whereas the kisses of an enemy are importunate.[37] A friend, even when he hurts us, may have our interest in mind; so God, too, even when he executes judgment, he acts in faithfulness.

It is extremely interesting to note that just as we have found *mishpat* to be a cosmic principle, by which God sustains the harmonious balance in the universe, so is *emunah,* too, a cosmic principle. God maintains the entire creation in *emunah.* God's faithfulness to his creation seems to be the guarantee of its stability. In fact, at least in one passage both terms are used in their cosmic significance. We find them so used in the words of the psalmist, who says:

For ever, O Lord,
Thy word standeth fast in heaven.
Thy faithfulness [*emunah*] is unto all generations;
Thou hast established the earth, and it standeth;
They stand this day according to Thine ordinances [*mishpatim*];
For all things are Thy servants. (Pss. 119:89–91)

The theme of these words is the idea of firmness, of standing lastingly, of being established enduringly. However, the thought is elaborated not in its limited application to the world of man alone, but in its comprehensive meaningfulness in heaven and earth and in relationship to "all things." "All generations," which are mentioned, are not the generations of men, but the generations of all creation. The word of God, which "standeth fast in heaven," is the word of creation which sustains the heaven. The universe is reliably established because of God's faithfulness to "all generations." They stand, of course, by the laws of nature which are God's "ordinances," his "*mishpat,*" for the creation. The world is not *Tohu vaBohu* because its existence is based on *mishpat,* on the principle of harmonious balance between its manifold powers and parts; the world endures in such *mishpat* because God so maintains it in *emunah,* in faithfulness to its needs. Without

God's *emunah* by his creation, there would be no reliance even on the laws of nature. Without God's *emunah*, without divine loyalty toward the universe, God's cosmic *mishpat*, the orderliness of the universe itself might come to an end at any moment and all may return into some aboriginal chaos. The passage is a further illustration of what is meant by the statement that all God's work is done in *emunah*.

We have already observed the connection between *hesed* and *emunah*. We shall take a closer look at it now. The two concepts are coordinated in numerous passages. According to the psalmist, when God redeems Israel, he remembers "His *hesed* [love] and His *emunah*" toward them.[38] As we noted earlier, in a passage like this, *emunah* reinforces *hesed* through its aspect of consistency. The meaning of the psalmist may adequately be rendered by saying that God saves Israel by means of the consistency, the faithfulness of his love toward them. Calling it "a good thing" to praise God and to give thanks to Him, the psalmist continues saying: "to declare Thy *hesed* in the morning and Thy *emunah* in the night season."[39] The explanation suggests itself that the change in the times of the day is guided by the difference between *hesed* and *emunah*. In the morning, during the day, people are awake; night is the time of sleep. An act of lovingkindness one experiences in a state of consciousness. On the other hand, when one is asleep, one must be able to trust someone, some order, society, neighbors, that one will not be harmed in one's state of unconsciousness. So it is with God's *hesed* and His *emunah* toward man. His acts of lovingkindness we experience consciously, thus we declare his *hesed* in the morning. At night, however, we entrust our lives to God's faithfulness; we rely on him because he is reliable, for he is a God of *emunah*.[40] It is of the very essence of loyalty that one may count on it, even when its visible manifestations are absent. As we heard earlier in our discussion, even in affliction, if it comes from a friend, one may discern the marks of faithfulness toward one.

The relationship between *hesed* and *emunah* comes to most emphatic expression in Psalm 89. It is the psalm from which we have quoted the qualification of covenant by the adjective *ne'eman*. God's covenant with David is an enduring (*ne'emeneth*) one; it will be reliably kept with David's descendants to the furthermost generation. The theme, however, is introduced with the words: "But my *emunah* and my *hesed* shall be with him." It is the direct consequence of God's love and faithfulness for David that the covenant concluded with him is an enduringly reliable one. A covenant concluded in *emunah* is one which is *ne'emeneth;* it is lasting for ever. The full import of the idea is expressed in the following statement:

If his children forsake My law,
And walk not in Mine ordinances;
If they profane My statutes,
And keep not My commandments;
Then will I visit their transgression with the rod,
And their iniquity with strokes.
But My *hesed* will I not break off from him,
Nor will I be false to My *emunah*.
My covenant will I not profane,
Nor alter that which is gone out of My lips.
Once have I sworn by My holiness:
Surely I will not be false unto David;
His seed shall endure for ever,
And his throne as the sun before Me.
It shall be established for ever as the moon;
And be *ne'eman* as the witness in the sky. (Pss. 89:31–38)

Notwithstanding the sinfulness of David's progeny, they will endure for ever. God's *emunah* guarantees God's everlasting love for David's seed. Withdrawing this love, God would betray his own *emunah;* it would be an act of disloyalty. Because of his *hesed* and *emunah*, God will not dissolve his covenant, because of his faithful love, he will not alter his word. God's love may be relied upon. It is the essence of the combination of *hesed* and *emunah* as divine attributes. Be-

269

cause of it, God will never be false to David. David's throne will be established for ever. Through God's *emunah,* David's throne, too, will be *ne'eman;* it will be as enduring as the sun and the moon in the sky. *Hesed* and *emunah* together, thus, become practically the one attribute of enduring, faithful love. But whatever is lasting with God is eternal. God's *emunah* is forever to be relied upon. It is for this reason that, in the same psalm, the psalmist may well complain: "How long, O Lord, wilt Thou hide Thyself for ever?" God cannot for ever hide his faith from his anointed and from his people, his servants. For what would become of His former *hasadim* which He swore unto David in His *emunah?* God's promise of lovingkindness to David may never be withdrawn, for they were made in *emunah,* in everlasting divine loyalty to David. A careful reading of Psalm 89 will show that its theme is altogether based on the combination of the two concepts of *hesed* and *emunah.* The opening words, given in the second verse, should be read as a title to the entire psalm:

I will sing of the *hasadim* of God for ever;
To all generations will I make known Thy *emunah* with my mouth.

One may sing of God's *hasadim* for ever because they are everlasting. They are everlasting because God is a God of *emunah.* Because His faithfulness endures for ever, can it be made known to all generations. This enduring love of God does the psalmist identify with His goodness, saying:

For the Lord is good;
His *hesed* endureth for ever;
And His *emunah* unto all generations. (Pss. 100:5)

God's *hesed* combines with his faithfulness to become everlasting.

Since God is a God of *emunah,* his Torah, the testimonies and commandments, share in his faithfulness and are, therefore, *ne'eman.*[41] The word, in this context, is usually translated as sure. While *ne'eman,* as we saw, does have that meaning, to say that God's commandments are sure does not impress us as too significant a statement. It would seem to us that "reliable" and even "faithful" would be a more appropriate rendering of the Hebrew original. God's testimonies and commandments have a purpose and one may rely on them as serving that divine purpose. They are meant for man and are given to him in his own best interest. In this sense they keep faith with man, they do not let him down. They are faithful. It would seem to us that this meaning of *emunah* in its application to God's law comes to expression in a passage in Psalm 119. "All Thy commandments are *emunah;* they persecute me for nought; help Thou me"; by itself this verse does not seem to make much sense. What connection is there between God's commandments which are "faithfulness" and the fact that the psalmist is being persecuted without a cause? In order to understand it, one must read the verse in its fuller context. Read in this manner, it runs as follows:

The proud have digged pits for me,
Which is not according to Thy law.
All Thy commandments are *emunah;*
They persecute me for nought;
Help Thou me.
They had almost consumed me upon earth;
But as for me, I forsook not Thy precepts. (Pss. 119:85–87)

We believe that the key phrase for the understanding of the human situation in which the psalmist found himself is: "not according to Thy law." It suggests that those who were persecuting him were really judging him in the name of the law, but not in the name of God's law. Or perhaps, he was condemned in the name of God's law, which, however, was distorted for the special purpose of digging a pit for the man. That is the reason why the psalmist exclaims that he is being persecuted in the name of the law, which, however, cannot be God's law since all "Thy commandments" are *emunah*. It is a sign of the passion in the exclamation that not the adjective

271

ne'emanim is used here, but the noun *emunah*. As if to say, surely God's commandments must not be used for such nefarious purposes, since they are all a manifestation of God's *emunah*, of his faithfulness to man and man's vital interests. Now, a person who is mistreated unlawfully might easily fall upon the idea that he was justified in defending himself by any means available, in his turn disregarding the law, too, completely. But the psalmist seeks God's help against his persecutors; in God alone does he wish to find his salvation. For even though they have almost "consumed" him, he himself would not forsake God's precepts in dealing with them.

One may also add that God's *emunah*, which determines the quality of God's commandments, is also the reason why a man turns to Him for help when he is persecuted "not according to His law." For the sake of man, God gives man His law in His faithfulness. When His law is misused or misapplied, the persecuted turn to God for help for He is a God of faithfulness. As He gave the law, so may He also be appealed to for succor; both God's law for man and His salvation are due to His faithfulness. It is thus natural that God's *emunah* and His salvation should also be associated with each other. Thus the psalmist maintains: "I have declared Thy faithfulness [*emunah*] and Thy salvation."[42] God's salvation is a manifestation of His faithfulness. One may rely on Him.

The concept of *emunah* also determines the biblical idea of belief. To believe, *he'emin*, means to put one's trust in someone or something, to rely on him or on it. This may be verified by numerous examples. It is interesting to note that the grammatical form of the verb, to believe, is the causative (*hiph'il*). To believe means to make someone or something trusted. By relying on a neighbor we make him a *ne'eman*, a trusted one. Our chief concern is to see how the idea of belief is used in the Bible when it is used as an expression of religious faith in God. One might say that belief or faith in the Bible is not a theological concept but a religious one. It is, for instance, never used as belief that God exists or as faith that his essential nature or substance is to be imagined in accordance with certain metaphysical ideas like infinity, omnipotence, absoluteness, etc. In the Bible, faith and belief are purely religious concepts describing a relationship of trust between God and man. When God promised Abraham that his descendants will be like the stars in the sky, the Bible says of Abraham that he believed in God.[43] Even though he was childless and his wife was a barren woman, he relied on God's promise. He trusted in God's *emunah*, in God's faithfulness. After the crossing of the Red Sea, the children of Israel "believed in the Lord, and in His servant Moses."[44] After experiencing the supernatural event of their deliverance under the leadership of Moses, they became convinced that God was with them and that Moses was his messenger to them. Now, they had confidence in God and trusted his servant. When the Bible says that the people of Nineveh believed in God,[45] the meaning is not that under the impact of the prophet's message they became frightened and now believed that God existed and could do with them as he pleased. "They believed in God" means: they put their trust in him. They turned to him in confidence, knowing that—even though the destruction of their city had already been decreed by God—they could still return to him, penitently relying on him. They remembered what Jonah knew all the time, i.e., that "Thou art a gracious God, and compassionate, longsuffering, and abundant in lovingkindness, and repentest Thee of the evil."[46] They remembered it and were now willing to put all their trust in it. They had faith.

On the other hand, not to believe in God does not mean not to believe in his existence, but not to rely on him, not to trust his *emunah*, his faithfulness. When the spies, sent out by Moses, returned with evil tidings from the promised land, despair overtook the children of Israel. Joshua and Caleb, who spoke confidently of God, who would bring them into the land, were stoned by the people. At this moment God said to Moses: "How long will this people despise Me? and how long will

273

they not believe in Me, for all the signs which I have brought among them?[47] This was a moment of crisis of trust in God. He had promised them the land. Can He keep his promise? It was unbelievable that it was so in view of the might of the inhabitants of the land. Yet, God had shown them His signs and miracles which should have been enough to convince them that He had both the intention and the power to fulfill His promise to them. But in spite of it all, they did not believe Him, they did not rely on Him.[48] Of the people of Samaria, who were carried away into captivity, it is said that "they would not hear, but hardened their neck, like the neck of their fathers, who believed not in the Lord their God; and they rejected His statutes, and His covenant that He made with their fathers, and His testimonies . . . and they went after things of nought, and became nought."[49] This passage is of special interest to us, because it makes mention of the statutes, the covenant, and the testimonies. We found earlier in our discussion that God's commandments, his covenant, and testimonies were all called *ne'emanim*, trustworthy, and to be relied upon. Those, however, who do not believe in God, who do not rely on him, will of necessity not rely either on the covenant which was concluded with him, or on his commandments and statutes, which—as we saw—were in themselves given to Israel as an act of God's faithfulness toward them.

There seems to be only one passage left which may require further elucidation. It is found in Isaiah:

Ye are My witnesses, saith the Lord,
And My servant whom I have chosen;
That ye may know and believe Me, and understand
That I am He;
Before Me there was no God [*El*] formed,
Neither shall any be after Me. (43:10)

It would be a mistake to think that to believe is used here in the theological sense, i.e., as faith in the existence of God and his eternity perhaps. The entire passage speaks of the glorious salvation that God promises Israel. God calls to Israel not to be afraid for God has redeemed them; Israel is God's. When they pass through water or fire, God is always with them. For He is Y, their *Elohim*, the Holy One of Israel, their Savior. We refer here to what we have said in earlier chapters on Y's making Himself known as *Elohim* as well as on the concept of the Holy One of Israel.[50] Both concepts yield the idea of God as the Savior. Y makes the promises of His salvation because He is their *Elohim*, the Holy One of Israel. One may easily see the connection between these thoughts and the idea that God is a God of *emunah*. His manifestation as *Elohim*, or as *Qadosh*, as the One who is near and exercises providence, is identical with the practice of his *emunah*, of his faithfulness. Israel is a witness because it can witness to God's faithfulness as their *Elohim*, the Holy One of Israel. They witness to his reliability as the Savior. They may so bear witness because God grants them the actual historic experience of his salvation. Thus they learn to know and they learn to believe. They learn to know Him as the One on whom to rely. In this manner the somewhat mysterious phrase, "that I am He," becomes meaningful. "I" is the remote, transcendent Y. But Y reveals Himself as the familiar "He," the one to whom man may point and say, He, because He is near through His acts of providential care. "I am He" means that the unknown, hidden, and mysterious Y is identical with Him, the familiar *Elohim*. This is now properly followed up with the words: "Before Me there was no *El* formed, neither shall any be after Me." Purposefully, God is referred to here as *El*. What is said here is not that before God there was no God, which—theologically speaking—would be vacuous. It is Y who is speaking. What he says is that apart from Y there is no *El* or *Elohim*. To believe in Y means to place one's full reliance on Him, for He is *Elohim*, the God of *emunah*, the God who is near and faithful.

If, however, *emunah* is reliability, loyalty, enduring faithfulness, how are we to understand the well-known words of

275

the Habakkuk: "But the righteous shall live by his *emunah*"?[51] Normally, the phrase is taken to mean that the righteous lives by his faith. But we have not found anywhere *emunah* to have the meaning of faith. Even when it is said of the Messiah that *"emunah* shall be the girdle of his veins"[52] the meaning of *emunah* is not faith but faithfulness. Even here, as in all other cases, *emunah* means personal loyalty. As is required of the judge, so will the Messiah, too, in his capacity as a judge, act with faithfulness toward the people. What, then, is the *emunah* by which the righteous lives? It is what it always is— faithfulness. The righteous lives by the faithfulness that he practices toward men as well as toward God. To be reliable in one's dealings with one's fellow men implies not hurting them, respecting their rights, to be concerned about their welfare and their interest. All this, of course, does not apply to man's relation with God. One cannot hurt God and one need not be concerned about God's rights or his well-being. To be loyal to God means to have faith in God's faithfulness, to rely on his word, to know that his laws and his testimonies are *ne'emanim* (reliable), to put one's trust in him, being convinced that all his works are done in *emunah*. To have such faith in God is being faithful to him. The only thing man can give God is his trust in God. It is the essence of his loyalty to God.

THE MEANING OF *EMETH*

If we now turn our attention to the examination of the concept with which we opened our discussion in this chapter, we find that *emeth* seems to be used in all the various contexts in which the concepts of *ne'eman* and *emunah* were employed. It is difficult to agree that the angel who spoke to Daniel said that he would reveal to him "that which is inscribed in the writing of Truth."[53] An affirmation by the angel that the mysterious script, whose contents he was revealing to Daniel, was true, would seem to us completely superfluous. Nor does such a translation correspond to the Hebrew original. The Hebrew makes no mention of "the writing of truth," which describes the contents of the writing as truth. A more exact rendering would be: "inscribed in true writing," which does not refer to the contents of the inscription but to the manner in which the script was executed. The technique, in which the inscription was done, was that of "true writing." But what could "true writing" be? Recalling that *ne'eman*, qualifying an object, usually means sure, lasting, enduring, we may well translate here: inscribed in sure writing. *Emeth* is indeed used here as the adjective *ne'eman*. The inscription was sure in the sense of its being indelible, hard to erase, symbolizing that the meaning of its contents was meant to be lasting. The false prophets, who in the days of Jeremiah, misleading the people, prophesied that God would give them *sh'lom emeth,* did not speak of a peace of truth, but a sure peace and a lasting one; a peace that was *ne'eman,* on which one could count.[54]

Occasionally *emeth* has the same meaning as *emunah.* Translating the words of Hezekiah, upon receiving God's message through Isaiah, as: "If but there shall be peace and truth in my days,"[55] leaves one wondering as to the meaning of the juxtaposition of peace and truth. What could the king have meant by looking forward to truth in his days? We, however, recall another passage of Isaiah which we have discussed earlier in this chapter, in which *emunah* in reference to the lifetime of a man meant stability, security. Surely, it is exactly what Hezekiah must have meant with *shalom* and *emeth* in his days. He was hoping for peace and stability, at least, in his own lifetime. It is exactly in the same sense that Jeremiah, too, relates *shalom* and *emeth.* He did not say: "And I will reveal unto them the abundance of peace and truth." *Emeth,* understood as truth in this context, would be without any meaning. We shall quote the entire passage with our translation of the concept of *emeth:*

Behold, I will bring it healing and cure, and I will cure them;
and I will reveal unto them the abundance of peace [*shalom*] and
stability [*emeth*].
And I will cause the captivity of Judah and the captivity of Israel to
return, and I will build them, as at the first. (33:6–7)

Clearly, *emeth* in the sense of truth is completely out of
place here. What is meant by it are conditions of stability and
security which are the accompaniments of peace.

It would also seem to us most unlikely that the letters of
Mordecai and Esther were sent to the Jews "with words of
peace and truth [*emeth*]."[56] Here, too, *emeth* is used as we
have found *emunah* so often employed, as steadfastness or
faithfulness. The letters were sent with words of greeting,
greetings of peace and encouragement or greetings of peace
and expressions of loyalty.

In numerous places, just as *emunah,* so *emeth,* too, stands
for reliability or faithfulness. The *oth emeth*, the true token[57]
for which Rahab asked the two spies, was really a sure token,
on which she and her family could rely; a token that could be
trusted. This meaning of *emeth* finds one of its most moving
expressions in the divine plaint over Israel:

Yet I had planted thee a noble vine,
Wholly a seed of *emeth*;
How then art thou turned into the degenerate plant
Of a strange vine unto Me? (Jer. 2:21)

God called Israel into being as a sure seed, one that could
be relied upon to grow and become the expected plant. But
they let God down; they did not act toward him in *emeth.*
God's expectations were disappointed. They proved unreliable.
Of the remnant of Israel Isaiah says that they "shall no more
again stay upon him that smote them; but shall stay upon
the Lord, the Holy One of Israel, in *emeth*."[58] Since it is not
possible to lean on God "in lie," it is meaningless to say that
anyone will lean on him "in truth." The meaning of "in
emeth" is indicated by the phrase, "they shall no more again."

The key word here is the little word, *od,* again. In the past, Israel was at times leaning on God; at others, relying on political alliances which proved futile and, often, treacherous. They were wavering between relying on God and relying on men. But, says the prophet, it will no more happen that they will *again* put their trust in allies, who ultimately betray them. They will lean on God *b'emeth,* with steadfastness, with unwavering loyalty. Abimelech was not quite sure that the men of Shechem acted in *emeth* when they appointed him king over themselves.[59] He was not sure whether he could rely on them, whether they dealt with him faithfully. According to various biblical passages, one should serve God in *emeth,*[60] one should walk before him in *emeth.* It is much more meaningful to interpret such expressions as a call to serve God with steadfastness, to walk before him with constancy, rather than to render *b'emeth* with the hackneyed, "in truth," or "truly." Only because *emeth* means loyalty could it be coordinated with *tob* and *yashar* and, thus, it was said about Hezekiah that "he wrought that which was good and right and faithful (*emeth*) before the Lord his God."[61] And so the story of that king could be continued with the words: "After these things and after these acts of *emeth.*" *Emeth* is the comprehensive term. Acts of goodness and uprightness are themselves manifestations of reliability and loyalty. According to the Psalms, God is near to all who call upon him in *emeth.*[62] Here, too, *emeth* loses much of its riches of meanings if it is translated as truth. What the psalmist meant was that God is near to all who call on him in trust, in a spirit of unquestioning reliance, which—as we have found—is the essence of man's faithfulness toward God. The expression *mishpat emeth* reminds us of the injunction to the judges that they should dispense justice with *emunah.* *Mishpat emeth* is judgment arrived at in *emunah,* in loyalty to both parties. [63]

We shall now consider the application of the concept of *emeth* to God. At least in two places in the Bible, *emeth,* as a description for God, means, simply, true. Jeremiah says that

"Y is *Elohim emeth,* He is the living *Elohim,* and the everlasting King."[64] The statement, as the context shows, distinguishes Y from other forces and powers which are so foolishly worshipped as *Elohim.* Y alone is the true *Elohim.* He alone is the living God. Only about Y is it true to say that He is *Elohim.* It is in the same sense that in II Chronicles it is said that "for long seasons Israel was without the *Elohim* of *emeth.*" The meaning is that they worshipped powers that they believed to be *Elohim,* who, however, were not *Elohim.* In these passages the idea of *emeth* is understood as correspondence with the facts. Y is the true *Elohim* because that as a fact is so; the idols, on the other hand, are false gods, gods of *sheqer* because—as a matter of fact—they are not *Elohim.* However, at least on one occasion the expression, God of *emeth,* is used much in the same sense as God of *emunah.* Because of its importance for our discussion, we shall quote the passage in its entirety. It reads as follows:

For Thou art my rock and my fortress;
Therefore for Thy name's sake lead me and guide me.
Bring me forth out of the net that they have hidden for me;
For Thou art my stronghold.
Into Thy hand I commit my spirit;
Thou hast redeemed me, O Lord,
Thou God of *emeth.*
I hate them that regard lying vanities;
But I trust in the Lord. (Pss. 31:4–7)

Needless to say that *emeth* as truth, in its purely logical and intellectual sense, could hardly find a comfortable place in this context. The God of *emeth* is one's rock and fortress, He is the One to whom one commits one's spirit, Who redeems, in Whom one trusts. Quite obviously, He is the God of *emunah,* the God on whom one may fully rely, a God of faithfulness.

While God is the God of *emeth,* quite often the Bible also makes mention of God's *emeth.* What is the *emeth* of God? Once again, we shall quote a key passage in full, one which is very similar in emotional and thought contents to the one which we have just discussed. The psalmist exclaims:

I will say of the Lord, who is my refuge and my fortress,
My God, in whom I trust,
That He will deliver thee from the snare of the fowler,
And from the noisome pestilence.
He will cover thee with His pinions,
And under His wings shalt thou take refuge;
His *emeth* is a shield and a buckler. (Pss. 91:2–4)

His *emeth* is his faithfulness, his protection. God's truth is the sureness and the stability which he introduces into the world, that he delivers, that under his wings one may find refuge. Thus his *emeth* is a shield and a buckler to man. When on another occasion the psalmist declares that he will give thanks unto God for His *emeth,* he does not have in mind the truth of divine teachings or the theological truth of revelation. This emerges quite convincingly as one reads the phrase in the context in which it occurs.

Thou, who hast made me to see many and sore troubles,
Wilt quicken me again, and bring me up again from the depths of
the earth.
Thou wilt increase my greatness,
And turn and comfort me.
I also will give thanks unto Thee with the psaltery,
Even unto Thy *emeth,* O my God;
I will sing praises unto Thee with the harp,
O Thou Holy One of Israel.
My lips shall greatly rejoice when I sing praises unto Thee;
And my soul, which Thou hast redeemed. (Pss. 71:20–23)

The *emeth,* for which God is thanked, is not a true idea but an act of providence and divine faithfulness. He quickened the man who saw "many and sore troubles," He comforted him, He redeemed his soul. He acted with *emeth,* with loyalty toward him. God's truth is God being true to someone. God's *emeth,* thus, at times is practically synonymous with his help and salvation. This is its meaning in Hezekiah's thanksgiving prayer after his recovery from sickness, saying:

But Thou hast in love to my soul delivered it
From the pit of corruption;
For Thou hast cast all my sins behind Thy back.
For the nether-world cannot thank Thee,
Death cannot praise Thee;
They that go down into the pit cannot hope for Thy *emeth*.
The living, the living, he shall thank Thee,
As I do this day;
The father to the children shall make known Thy *emeth*.
The Lord is ready to save me. (Isa. 38:17–20)

Emeth for which one hopes must be a saving truth. As long as a man is alive, one hopes for God's *emeth*; one is grateful for it, if it is granted one; one praises God for it. Hezekiah may do all this because God delivered him from the pit. He may thank God for God's *emeth* which was revealed to the king in God's deliverance; he may tell about it to his children. He may continue hoping for God's *emeth*, believing that God is ready to save him. In very similar words the psalmist expresses the same thought, when in his supplication, pleading for life, he says:

What profit is there in my blood, when I go down to the pit?
Shall the dust thank Thee? shall it declare Thy *emeth?*

The question is immediately followed by the words:

Hear, O Lord, and be gracious unto me;
Lord, be Thou my helper. (Pss. 30:10–11)

The psalmist asks for God's help that he may be able to declare God's *emeth*. If he were dead, God's *emeth* would be of no use to him. Requesting that God deal graciously with him and be his helper, he pleads that God's *emeth* be made known to him in God's gracious salvation. The psalmist deals with the same subject in another passage, but there he uses the phrase that God's *emunah* would not be declared "in de-

282

struction." [65] It is the same thought. The use of *emunah* instead of *emeth* shows that the two are interchangeable. The *emeth*, for which only the living may hope, and for which they alone can be grateful, is God's act of saving loyalty to man.

God's *emeth* is often associated with a way or guidance along a path. It would, however, again be a mistake to interpret it to mean the abstract idea of some divine truth by which a person may be guided along his way in life. The Bible does not speak in such non-committal abstract homilies. A passage which might easily lend itself to such misunderstanding is the one in Psalm 25. David is praying:

Show me Thy ways, O Lord;
Teach me Thy paths.
Guide me in Thy *emeth,* and teach me;
For Thou art the God of my salvation;
For Thee do I wait all the day. (vss. 4–5)

One could, perhaps, think that "guide me in Thy *emeth*" is a request for some form of illumination by some divine truth, by which to guide the psalmist. Such an interpretation would hardly fit into the context of the prayer. The psalm begins as a plea for help against David's enemies. He expresses his trust in God and asks that he be not put to shame by the triumph of his enemies. Immediately upon it follows the request that God teach him His ways and guide him in His *emeth,* as we have quoted it. The thought of our quotation is brought to a conclusion with the words:

Remember, O Lord, Thy compassions and Thy [acts of] loving-kindness;
For they have been from of old.
Remember not the sins of my youth, nor my transgressions;
According to Thy love [*hesed*] remember Thou me,
For Thy goodness sake, O Lord. (vss. 6–7)

Unquestionably, this is a prayer for help, for God's mercies and love. There is no place here for the sophisticated prayer for divine guidance by divine truth. In a concrete situation of danger, David is asking for very real practical help against his enemies. But what are the ways of God and his paths which David desires to be taught? In the same chapter, only a few verses below, their nature is described explicitly. Pursuing his strain of thought further, David muses:

He guideth the humble in justice [*mishpat*];
And He teacheth the humble His way.
All the paths of the Lord are love [*hesed*] and *emeth*
Unto such as keep His covenant and His testimonies. (vss. 9–10)

Why should God guide only the humble in justice? Once again we have to recall what we have said earlier about the biblical concept of justice. We have found it to be an idea which could very well associate with *hesed*. God guides the humble in justice by securing for him his right, by protecting him against those who attempt to wrong him. That is the way of God; along it the humble, the poor are safeguarded. God's way is the way of God's help. For all His paths are *hesed* and *emeth*. *Hesed* and *emeth* are coordinated in our text. Once again *emeth* has the meaning of *emunah*. God's path is the path of *emeth* and *emunah*; along it people are guided by God's love and his faithfulness. It is for this way and this path that David prayed. He never said: "guide me in Thy truth," but "guide me by Thy faithfulness and teach me [i.e., Thy path]." The reason that he gives for his request becomes now much more meaningful: "For Thou art the God of my help; for Thee do I wait all the day." It is natural for one to ask for help and protection from the God of one's help. To wait for God all the day is hoping for his saving support.[66]

We are now in a better position to interpret the passage in Genesis which caused us some difficulty in the opening section of this chapter in our discussion. Speaking to the family of Rebekah, Abraham's servant describes the way, along which God has led him, as a way of *emeth*.[67] To render it as, a true way, would be rather empty; the translation, a right way, is an attempt to hide a difficulty of exegesis by a plausible version. We, however, recall that of the same way the servant said earlier: "Blessed be the Lord, the God of my master Abraham, who hath not forsaken His *hesed* [love] and his *emeth* toward my master; I am on the way the Lord hath led me to the house of my master's brethren." God has shown His love and His faithfulness toward Abraham by leading the servant along the way whither his master wanted him to go. This same way, which testifies to God's love and faithfulness, is then called by the servant the way of *emeth*, along which God led him. This is not just the right way, in the sense of leading to the intended goal. It is the way of faithfulness; a way along which God, keeping faith with Abraham, led his servant.

The examples which we have just discussed lead us to a more thorough examination of the term, "*hesed* and *emeth*." The combination between "*hesed*" and *emeth* is an indication of similarity between the two. It corresponds to the association between *hesed* and *emunah*, which we have discussed earlier. Indeed, "*hesed* and *emeth*" seems to have the same meaning as "*hesed* and *emunah*." As we saw already, *emeth*, too, has the quality of sureness, of stability and enduring effectiveness. A striking example of such usage of *emeth* is what the psalmist says of God's oath to David.[68] It is near blasphemy to say that "the Lord swore unto David in truth." What is more, such rendering is grammatically not justified. "In truth" occurs quite often in the Bible but always in the correct grammatical version, *b'emeth*. Of God's oath to David the psalmist says: "The Lord swore unto David . . . *emeth*; He will not turn back from it." The meaning of such an oath is then summed up in the promise that David's descendants will "for ever sit upon thy throne." God's oath to David was an irrevocable commitment that, if his children will keep God's commandment, his dynasty will be preserved through all generations. It is a somewhat different version of the idea with which we have met earlier in this chapter as we discussed the meaning of the term *ne'eman*. The "oath" is another way of describing what we have heard Isaiah sum up in the phrase of *hasde David ha–ne'emanim*, God's enduring acts of love toward David. The oath was *emeth*, not true or truth, but an enduring commitment. It was not an oath with a validity limited to a certain time. The obligation undertaken by it was to last for ever. There was no turning back from it. If David's children fulfilled the condition under which God made his promise, God's commitment to them could not be terminated. "God swore unto David—*emeth*" means that God obligated himself irrevocably.

Emeth, like *emunah*, meaning sureness, steadfastness, reliability, faithfulness, also carries the connotation of enduring in time, continuously valid or effective. On many occasions *emeth* suggests lasting validity. Thus, the psalmist says:

The works of His hands are faithfulness [*emeth*] and justice [*mishpat*]:
All his precepts are sure [*ne'emanim*].[69]
They are established for ever and ever,
They are done in faithfulness [*emeth*] and uprightness.

(Pss. 111:7–8)

Since God's works are executed in faithfulness, they are established for ever and ever. A loyalty which is not lasting is a contradiction in terms. What is the meaning of *emeth* when it qualifies the word or the law of God? Let us see. According to the psalmist:

The beginning of Thy word is *emeth*;[70]
And all Thy order of righteousness endureth for ever. (Pss. 119:160)

Now to compliment God that his word is true seems to us rather unconvincing. *Emeth*, however, is here paralleled by "endureth for ever," and that is indeed its meaning. The word of God is *emeth*, it is valid for ever. A similar parallelism between God's righteousness and his Torah we find in the same psalm. The psalmist exclaims:

Thy righteousness is an everlasting righteousness,
And Thy law is *emeth*. (vs. 142)

That God's law is true needs no affirmation. What is proclaimed here is that God's law is valid for ever, just as his
righteousness is everlasting. God's commandments, too, are
called *emeth*. The expression is found in this context:

Thou art nigh, O Lord;
And all Thy commandments are *emeth*.
Of old have I known from Thy testimonies
That Thou hast founded them for ever. (vss. 151–2)

Once again, the parallelism between "commandments" and
"testimonies" and between *emeth* and "founded . . . for ever"
proves our point. Needless to say that God's commandments
are true, but it is not self-evident that they were meant to be
valid for ever. That does require explicit affirmation.

We are now enabled to appreciate the significance of a
phrase which we were compelled to leave unexplained in the
introductory part of our discussion of the concept of *emeth*
at the beginning of this chapter. The phrase was found in the
verse:

But as for me, let my prayer be unto Thee, O Lord, in an accept-
able time;
O God in the abundance of Thy love,
Answer me with the *emeth* of Thy salvation. (Pss. 69:14)

We found it difficult to understand what the truth of God's
salvation might signify. *B'emeth* qualifies *yish'ekha* (Thy
salvation) as *b'rab* (in the abundance) qualifies *hasdekha*,
Thy love. We assume it therefore to have a meaning similar to
abundance. But how can *emeth* bear such a connotation? It
may very well if it qualifies God's salvation as spread over a
long period of time. That, too, would be "an abundance" of
salvation. We interpret the psalmist's prayer as: Answer me
with continuous, lasting salvation.

Our last example is, at the same time, a good illustration

for the meaning of the concept of "*hesed* and *emeth*." *Hesed* is love or lovingkindness; *emeth* is sureness, steadfastness, reliability, enduring strength, lasting faithfulness. *Hesed ve'emeth* would then be lovingkindness that is sure, that is reliable, that endures and may be even irrevocable. When Jacob made Joseph swear that he would not bury him in Egypt, he asked his son to do with him *hesed* and *emeth*.[71] Jacob could be fairly sure of the love of Joseph. However, his request involved a vital question of policy. How would returning the old father's body for burial in the old homeland affect the position and political condition of the entire family in Egypt? Would it not be interpreted by the Egyptians as a proof that the children of Israel were strangers and were themselves looking for the time when they would leave the country? Considerations of political expediency might induce Joseph to feel justified in breaking the promise made to his father. It is, perhaps, for this reason that Jacob asked for an act of love and enduring faithfulness, for *hesed ve'emeth*, for lovingkindness in the form of an irrevocable commitment. The *hesed ve'emeth* that the spies promised to Rahab[72] was such a promise of unqualified commitment. It was to be an act of *hesed* that was sure and could not be changed under any conditions.

The translation of *emeth* as truth in its association with *hesed* is most misleading in the famous passage in Exodus, where it appears as one of the divine attributes. "The Lord, the Lord, God merciful and gracious, long-suffering, and abundant in love [*hesed*] and *emeth;* keeping mercy unto the thousandth generation, forgiving iniquity and transgression and sin."[73] What place could *emeth*, in the sense of truth, have in the midst of all these attributes of divine mercy and graciousness. The meaning of the relevant phrase, however, is: abundant in love and faithfulness. His lovingkindness is enduring, it is always sure. And indeed, God's *hesed ve'emeth* are always represented as qualities of divine mercy. The very attributes, as they appear in Exodus, are also quoted by the psalmist, up to the one which describes God as "abundant in *hesed* and *emeth*," and leads to the supplication:

O turn unto me, and be gracious unto me;
Give Thy strength unto Thy servant,
And save the son of Thy handmaid. (Pss. 86:16)

Now, one does not turn to God with such prayers because He is abundant in truth, but because He is plenteous in loving-kindness and faithfulness. So in all places. God's *hesed ve'emeth* are attributes of mercy that preserve a man.[74]

We direct now our attention to a verse in Isaiah which, requiring interpretation, further illustrates the point that we are making. We shall quote it first in the usual translation:

And a throne is established through mercy [*hesed*],
And there sitteth thereon in truth [*be'emeth*] in the tent of David,
One that judgeth, and seeketh justice, and is ready in righteousness.
(16:5)

We cannot help wondering as to the meaning of such words. How is a throne established through mercy? Is it the mercy that the king practices? If so, is it correct to say that a throne is established by mercy? What of all the other requirements that are needed for establishing a throne? And again, what could be meant by sitting on a throne "in truth"? It could, perhaps, mean that the king exercises his function, pursuing the truth. However, because of the close succession in which *hesed* and *emeth* occur in our quotation, we are inclined to apply to the exegesis of this verse the idea which we have found to be expressed by the concept of *hesed ve'emeth*. Once again, we have to recall the theme of *hasde David ha–ne'emanim*, which we had occasion to discuss so often. God's relation to David was one of *hesed ve'emeth*, of love whose faithfulness endured through all the generations. We have heard God say of him in the words of the psalms: "For ever will I keep for him My *hesed* [love]."[75] Now, *hesed*, which is kept for ever, is love sustained by lasting

289

faithfulness. It is exactly what is meant by God's *hesed ve'emeth*. The throne, of which Isaiah says that it is established in *hesed*, is the throne of David established by God's *hesed*, love, for David. The king who sits on the throne is an offspring of David. He sits on the throne of his ancestor because God's covenant with David was an everlasting one, a *brith ne'emeneth*; or as the psalmist also put it, because of God's oath, which was meant to be *emeth*, enduring without any possibility of its being annulled. Thus the king, who sits on David's throne, sits there *be'emeth*, by God's sure faithfulness toward David. We would render the verse from Isaiah as follows:

And a throne is established by [God's] love [*hesed*],
And there sitteth thereon through [God's] faithfulness [*emeth*] in
 the tent of David,
One that judgeth, and seeketh justice.

At least one verse in the Psalms suggests that an act of *hesed* promised becomes an act of *emeth* in its state of fulfillment. We refer to the verse:

Let Thy [acts of] lovingkindness come unto me, O Lord,
Even Thy salvation, according to Thy word;
That I may have an answer for him that taunteth me;
For I trust in Thy word.
And take not the word of *emeth* utterly out of my mouth;
For I hope for Thy ordinances. (119:41–43)

It is hardly conceivable that the psalmist prayed that the word of truth should not be taken away from him. Why would God do that and what danger was there that it might happen? Nor would it seem to make much sense. He prays for God's lovingkindness and salvation, so that he might answer his enemies. What connection could there be between such a plea and the request that the word of truth should not be taken from his mouth? We recall, however, various passages which have a bearing on the elucidation of the thought in this verse.

The most helpful is probably the following words of the psalmist:

I have not hid Thy righteousness within my heart;
I have declared Thy faithfulness [*emunah*] and Thy salvation;
I have not concealed Thy lovingkindness [*hesed*] and Thy *emeth*
   from the great congregation. (Pss. 40:11)

As the following verse shows, God's *hesed* and *emeth* are what continually preserve David, the author of the psalm. God's *hesed* and *emeth* are God's enduring and steady acts of lovingkindness. Of it the psalmist says that he did not conceal it, but declared it in the midst of the multitude. Accordingly, we are justified in saying that the declaration of God's faithfulness may well be called the word of *emeth*. It is in this sense that the phrase "Take not the word of *emeth* utterly out of my mouth" is to be understood. If God's promise of *hesed* and salvation come true, then indeed man may declare God's *emeth*; but if he is not granted help and redemption, if the promise of *hesed* is not realized, then man is unable to proclaim God's faithfulness. In this case, the word of *emeth,* the word praising God's *emeth* has been taken "out of his mouth." That this may not happen is the prayer of the psalmist.

We may, therefore, say in conclusion that while *emeth* may well mean truth in the epistemological sense of correspondence to a fact, its foremost biblical meaning is ethico-religious. Very much like *emunah, emeth* is an attitude or an action whose meaning is steadfastness, reliability, enduring loyalty, saving and preserving faithfulness.

CHAPTER 7

Sedeq and *S'daqah*

―――――

S'daqah

THE PRACTICE OF *S'DAQAH*—"CHARITY"

READERS of the Bible are, of course, fully aware of the close-ness of meaning between the two concepts we plan to discuss in this chapter. In fact, at times it would appear as if *sedeq* and *s'daqah* were identical and, therefore, interchangeable. Both terms are often translated as righteousness. The dis-tinction between the two ideas seems to be altogether a differ-ence in emphasis; *sedeq* being closer to the legal concept of justice, whereas *s'daqah* apparently stands for righteousness in a more general, less legalistic sense. Having, however, found that the biblical idea of justice (*mishpat*) itself is not to be understood in a strictly legalistic manner, that it keeps comfortable company with lovingkindness, mercy, and salva-tion, we are open to surprises in our investigation of the con-cepts of *sedeq* and *s'daqah*.

We shall first analyze *s'daqah* mainly because we believe that its meaning is more easily ascertained than that of *sedeq*.

In numerous places *s'daqah* occurs as the opposite to *resha* or *rish'ah*, evil, wickedness. The children of Israel, for instance, were warned not to imagine that God brought them into the promised land because they deserved it on account of their *s'daqah*. Rather, it was because of their wickedness that the original inhabitants were driven out from before Israel.[1] "Wickedness," of course, is used here in its widest sense. It has no legal connotation of any kind. It is ethical and moral corruption. It includes any act of conduct which is objectionable on moral or religious grounds. This is borne out by the numerous other references in the Bible to the guilt of the original inhabitants of Canaan. This makes it somewhat difficult to define *s'daqah,* which is here opposed to "wickedness." Would *s'daqah* have to be the complete opposite to everything that is here comprehended by "wickedness" or should we be justified in calling *s'daqah* any act or attitude that is contrary to any part of the evil, which is comprehended by the wider term, wickedness? As might be expected, Proverbs is quite rich in passages in which "evil" and "wickedness" are contrasted to *s'daqah,* but there, too, the terms are used in too general a sense to allow us to draw more exact conclusions from them. There is, for instance, the saying: "The establishing of *s'daqah* tendeth to life; but he that pursueth evil pursueth it to his own death."[2] "The pursuit of evil" seems to include any kind of evil, in which case "the establishing of *s'daqah*" may mean any act of goodness which is the opposite to any kind of evil. Reading again in Proverbs that "the doing of evil is an abomination to kings, for the throne is established by *s'daqah,*"[3] it is easy to misunderstand "the doing of evil" as acting against the law safeguarded by the king, and to interpret *s'daqah,* accordingly, as righteousness in the sense of justice or the monarchic order. We know however, from other passages that the establishing of a throne is not only a question of law and justice, but also of *hesed* and *emeth,* of lovingkindness and faithfulness.[4] (This, of course, is so because in the Bible, as we have shown, lovingkindness and faithfulness belong in the same category of values as "law" and "justice.") Neither the evil, which is a king's concern, nor *s'daqah,* which establishes his throne, should be taken to have a juridical significance. As everywhere else in the Bible, here, too, their implication is ethico-moral and religious.

Fortunately, there are also various passages in the Bible in which the term *s'daqah* is applied to specific deeds whose nature is clearly understood. When it once chanced that David could have rid himself of Saul, who was pursuing him, he did not put a hand on the king. Of this action he said:

And the Lord will render to every man his *s'daqah* and his faithfulness; forasmuch as the Lord delivered thee into my hand to-day, and I would not put forth my hand against the Lord's anointed. And, behold, as thy life was much set by this day in mine eyes, so let my life be much set by in the eyes of the Lord, and let him deliver me out of all tribulation.[5]

The fact that David did not harm the king, that he valued his life when he could have justifiably killed him in self-defense, is considered an act of *s'daqah* and faithfulness. It would seem that the sparing of the life of an enemy was *s'daqah*, that the enemy was the king and God's anointed, to whom normally people owe loyalty, was a deed of *emunah*, of faithfulness. What is here meant by *s'daqah* becomes even more clear by David's wish. He hopes that God will return to him his *s'daqah*; he expresses the desire that God may extend to him the same consideration with which he treated Saul. May God set as much value by his life as he set by the life of Saul and may he, thus, deliver him "out of all tribulation." *S'daqah*, here, is then valuing the life of another person and, on account of it, helping or protecting him in a situation of danger or trouble. It is very much in this sense that Samuel, too, uses the word *s'daqah*. Before giving Israel a king, for whom they have clamored, Samuel addresses the people saying:

It is the Lord that made Moses and Aaron, and that brought your fathers up out of the land of Egypt. Now therefore stand still, that I may plead with you before the Lord concerning all the acts of *s'daqah*, which he did to you and to your fathers.[6]

Now, the acts of *s'daqah*, which Samuel enumerates, are the sending of Moses and Aaron to them in order to lead them out of Egypt, as well as the sending of the Judges in order to save them from their enemies each time the children of Israel called to God from their tribulations. It is hardly proper to call such deeds acts of righteousness; they are more like acts of lovingkindness and saving mercy. The prophet Micah uses the same phrase, the Lord's acts of *s'daqah*, and he uses it in exactly the same manner as it was used centuries before him by Samuel. His words are:

O my people, remember now what Balak king of Moab devised and what Balaam the son of Beor answered him; from Shittim unto Gilgal—that ye may know the acts of *s'daqah* of the Lord.[7]

God's undoing of the plans of Balak and Balaam, his continuous guidance for the children of Israel all along the way from Shittim to Gilgal, were God's acts of *s'daqah*. They showed that God valued Israel and extended his protective care to them. This interpretation is strongly supported by a passage in Joel, where we read:

Be glad then, ye children of Zion, and rejoice
In the Lord your God;
For He giveth you the former rain for *s'daqah*,

. . . .

And the floors shall be full of corn,
And the vats shall overflow with wine and oil. (2:23–24)

The word *s'daqah* in this context has posed quite a problem for commentators and translators. The rendering of the phrase *lis'daqah* as "moderately" or as "in just measure,"[8] are more an illustration of the difficulty than a solution of the problem. In our opinion, *s'daqah* means here what we have found it thus far to mean, i.e., an act of help or of deliverance. The badly–needed rain would be given by God to the children of Zion for a deliverance from famine and poverty.

In the light of these examples we may say that *s'daqah*, like *mishpat* and *emeth* and *emunah*, represents a bond between the two that motivates the one to act toward the other with kindness and charity because one sets value by the other. *S'daqah* seems to be the action itself which is indicative of the bond that motivates the act. *S'daqah* may be enacted by a person toward another or by God toward man. It is, however, not to be expected that man could practice *s'daqah* toward God. Yet, there seems to be at least one such example in the Bible of a man doing *s'daqah* to God. When God promised Abraham that his seed would be as numerous as the stars in the heaven, the Bible says: "And he believed in the Lord; and He counted it to him for *s'daqah*."[9] To say that what is meant here is that God counted Abraham's faith in Him for righteousness does not seem to make much sense. Not only is it difficult to accept the suggestion that to put faith in God's promise could be adequately designated an act of righteousness. If such an act of faith could indeed be called righteousness, even greater would be the exegetic difficulty presented by the phrase, "and He counted it to him" as such. That God counted it to him for *s'daqah* implies that what Abraham did was not really *s'daqah* but, nevertheless, he was credited for it, as if he had performed an act of *s'daqah*. We suggest that here too, *s'daqah* means what we have found it to mean in the other examples, i.e., an act of kindness, of help, based on respect and acknowledgement of another person. Only, in this case, the other person was God. God's promise was indeed incredible. Abraham and Sarah were both already advanced in years and they were childless. Nevertheless, contrary to all natural expectation, Abraham believed in God. This was, indeed, an act of "kindness" and "charity" toward God. We have put these words between quotation marks in order to indicate that they are not to be taken literally. No mere man can be kind or charitable toward God. One may render *s'daqah* only "to a son of man."[10] Yet, to put one's faith in God's promise, when every phase of the given situation contends against it, is an act that comes closest to *s'daqah*, which one may extend to a man. To believe in God's word against all reason and all nature is like an act of helping kindness toward God. It is like it; it is not it, for God is never in any need. It is for this reason that the Bible says of Abraham's faith that God "counted it to him for *s'daqah*." While no man can act with *s'daqah* toward God, Abraham's act of faith was counted to him as if he had performed an act of *s'daqah* toward God.

S'DAQAH RECEIVED—REWARD OR DELIVERANCE

There are, however, other passages which seem to indicate that *s'daqah* requires an entirely different interpretation as well. Having agreed with Laban that the speckled and spotted among the flock shall be his in recompense for his labor, Jacob says to Laban:

So shall my *s'daqah* witness against me hereafter, when thou shalt come to look over my hire that is before thee; every one that is not speckled and spotted among the goats, and dark among the sheep, that is found with me shall be counted stolen.[11]

What could be the meaning of *s'daqah* in this context? Surely Jacob could not have meant that his righteousness (as the word is usually translated) should witness against him. It would make no sense at all. What he is saying is that should Laban wish to come and check on what Jacob took for his hire, any one sheep or goat in Jacob's flock that would not have the color agreed upon will be a witness against Jacob's honesty. How can one say that in such a case Jacob's righteousness would be witness against him? In such a case Jacob's righteousness would be in question and the stolen animal would be a witness against it. There is little doubt that *s'daqah* is here the actual reward given to Jacob by Laban for his work. The sheep and the goats which they agreed upon that should be Jacob's share, would witness against or for Jacob. *S'daqah* would then mean something received in return for something else. But do we find the word to have this meaning in any other context? We are also curious to know whether it is possible to establish any connection between this meaning and the former one which we have established. There are indeed a number of passages, all of the same kind, which require an interpretation very similar to the one which we have just given. In the case of a pledge that one takes from a poor man, the Bible says that one should restore it to him for the night "that he may sleep in his garment, and bless thee; and it shall be *s'daqah* unto thee before the Lord thy God."[12] We submit that to render *s'daqah* here as righteousness, as it is usually done, is meaningless. The statement would amount to nothing more than the empty tautology that the act of righteousness of returning the pledge would be regarded by God, too, as such an act of *s'daqah*. The same phrase that occurs here in relationship to one specific commandment is also applied to the fulfillment of all God's commandments in general. Thus we read in Deuteronomy:

And it shall be *s'daqah* unto us, if we observe to do all this commandment before the Lord our God, as He hath commanded us.[13]

It is not at all convincing that to say that righteousness consists of doing all God's commandments is a significant statement. Even less can one make peace with the phrase, "it shall be *s'daqah* unto us," or, as in the previous quotation, "it shall be *s'daqah* unto thee." Having observed such commandments, one will have practiced *s'daqah*. But we doubt that anyone is able to associate any good meaning with the statement that such a practice of doing God's commandments will be *s'daqah* unto the one who pursues it.

We believe that the meaning of these two passages is well illuminated by some verses in Isaiah. The words are addressed to Israel in the name of God.

Oh that thou wouldest hearken to My commandments!
Then would thy peace be as a river,
And thy *s'daqah* as the waves of the sea;
Thy seed also would be as the sand,
And the offspring of thy body like the grains thereof;
His name would not be cut off
Nor destroyed from before Me. (Isa. 48:18–19)

Undoubtedly, *s'daqah* in this context cannot mean righteousness. It belongs in one category together with the promise of peace and of the multitude of offspring. The idea of righteousness would be an ugly interruption in the unity of thought which is so poetically sustained by the metaphors of the river, the waves of the sea, and the sand. Quite clearly, *s'daqah* is here, like *shalom* and the blessing of children, the reward for hearkening to God's commandments. *S'daqah* would then be what we found it originally to mean, an act of lovingkindness, of help and deliverance, as an expression of appreciation for the one to whom it is extended. If they observe God's commandments they will be granted peace, help in trouble, and numerous descendants. It is in the same sense that the psalmist, too, uses *s'daqah* when he says:

But the lovingkindness [*hesed*] of the Lord is from everlasting to everlasting upon them that fear Him, and His *s'daqah* unto children's children; to such as keep His covenant and to those that remember His precepts to do them.[14]

The juxtaposition of *hesed* and *s'daqah* is in itself sufficient to indicate that *s'daqah* is not to be rendered as righteousness. The psalmists' idea is the same as that of Isaiah. God's acts of lovingkindness and of his help and deliverance (i.e., *s'daqah*) are the lot of those who hear Him and live in accordance with his precepts. In Proverbs, Wisdom describes the rewards of those who follow her. Elaborating on what one may find with her, she says also:

Riches and honor are with me;
Yea, enduring riches and *s'daqah*. (8:18)

Here, too, it is quite impossible to render *s'daqah* as righteousness. As in Isaiah it is part of the reward, just like riches and honor in the same context. *S'daqah* will be granted to the one who follows *hokhma*; he will find honor, riches, and deliverance.

We may now return to a new consideration of the two passages in Deuteronomy with which we have opened this part of our discussion. The expression, *l'kha tih'yeh s'daqah*, in the case of a person who returns a pledge, should not be rendered as "it shall be *s'daqah* unto thee," but as "thou shalt have *s'daqah*." As is well known, the grammatical form of the phrase is the possessive. The translators had to disregard it because for them *s'daqah* meant righteousness. It made no sense to say that a person who returns a pledge would, as a result, acquire righteousness in the future. The meaning, however, is the same as in our quotations from Isaiah and the Psalms. The reward for fulfilling God's commandment will be *s'daqah*, God's help and protection. *L'kha tih'yeh s'daqah*, before the Lord your God, means thou shalt have, possess *s'daqah*, that God will grant you. This is also the meaning of the phrase, *s'daqah tih'yeh lanu*, in our second example from Deuteronomy. We shall have, we shall acquire *s'daqah*, help and deliverance, if we observe all God's commandments. This passage is the exact parallel to the ones we have quoted from Isaiah and the Psalms.

We have found that *s'daqah* has a two-fold significance: it is the deed and it is also the fruit of the deed. The one who acts as David acted toward Saul, or as God has acted toward Israel, does *s'daqah*; whereas the one who receives the fruits of such a deed, as Saul did or as has been promised to the one who observes God's commandments, has *s'daqah*. He has received and is in possession of what is the result of the act of *s'daqah*. One's *s'daqah* may thus mean either the *s'daqah* that one does to others or the *s'daqah* that one receives from another. God's *s'daqah*, of which we heard the psalmist say that it lasts unto children's children, is the *s'daqah* that He practices. But when the psalmist speaks of the *s'daqah* of the man that fears God, he means the reward that is his. The phrase occurs twice in the same psalm. At first it is said of the man "that feareth the Lord, that delighteth greatly in His commandments" that:

the generation of the upright shall be blessed.
Wealth and riches are in his house;
And his *s'daqah* endureth for ever. (112:2–3)

A little further on in the same psalm it is also said of the same man:

He hath scattered abroad, he hath given to the needy;
His *s'daqah* endureth for ever;
His horn shall be exalted in honour.
The wicked shall see, and be vexed. (vss. 9–10)

In the first place *s'daqah* is used exactly as we found it in our quotation from Proverbs. Together with riches it was the reward of the pursuit of wisdom. Here it is part of the blessing of "the generation of the upright." Here, too, it is the parallel to riches. The *s'daqah* given by God to the God-fearing man is an enduring blessing. But in the second part of our quotation, too, *s'daqah* has the same meaning. It is the act of providence granted to the man as a reward for his generosity, for his own act of *s'daqah* toward the needy. This interpretation is borne out by a careful reading of the text. It could hardly be stated that a man's righteousness "endureth for ever"; nor is there anything to support such a statement in the fact that a person gave generously of his means to the poor. But one may very well say of God's blessing, of the fruits of God's *s'daqah* received by a man, that its substance will be enduring for a long time. It is exactly what the psalmist was indicating when he said of God's *s'daqah* that it was "unto children's children." In fact, the very phrase that is used in this psalm about a man's *s'daqah* is also applied, in the previous one, to God himself. There we read:

His work is glory and majesty;
And His *s'daqah* endureth for ever. (111:3)

While one may well say of God's practice of *s'daqah* that it endures for ever, surely one cannot make the same statement about man's doing of *s'daqah*. It is, however, properly held that when the fruits of God's *s'daqah* have been bestowed upon a man, the substance of the *s'daqah* granted to him will endure for a long time, just because its origin is in God's doing. One should also pay attention to the context.

Immediately upon "His *s'daqah* endureth for ever" follow the words: "His horn shall be exalted in honor." Now, this is, of course, the reward for the deeds of charity which were mentioned earlier. And so is also "his *s'daqah*"; it is the God-fearing man's reward and it is an enduring one. *S'daqah* received is a reward or a grant given to a person. Thus, Jacob could well say to Laban: "So shall my *s'daqah* witness against me hereafter." His *s'daqah* was the part of the flock which he was given for his labor. It is true that what Jacob was granted was his due as payment for his work. It would, however, appear from the discussion that preceded the agreement between the two that it was a rather unusual form of paying wages. Laban says to Jacob: "Appoint me thy wages, and I will give it." But he is not answered directly. Instead, Jacob tells about his devoted service and about the blessing he brought for his father-in-law. "And now when shall I provide for mine own house also?" Laban understands. It is not ordinary wages that Jacob wants, but a house of his own. Laban repeats the question, but now he asks: "What shall I give thee?" No mention is made of wages any more. But Jacob's answer is: "Thou shalt not give me aught; if thou wilt do this thing for me." The arrangement between them was a most unusual one. This thing that Laban does for Jacob is not the norm between a flock owner and his shepherd. Laban does something for Jacob. What Jacob receives is not wages but a reward. It is his *s'daqah*.

With the help of the idea of *s'daqah* received, a number of other rather obscure passages become clear. When Sanballat and his group were attempting to interfere with the rebuilding of the walls around Jerusalem, Nehemiah said to them:

The God of heaven, He will prosper us; therefore we His servants will arise and build; but ye have no portion, nor *s'daqah*, nor memorial, in Jerusalem.[15]

For our translations *s'daqah* suddenly becomes "right." But how can right be placed stylistically between "portion" and

"memorial"? In our opinion, *s'daqah* here is an actual possession as are "portion" and "memorial." It is *s'daqah* received,
a grant or a reward. What Nehemiah said to these men was
that they had no share of any kind in Jerusalem. They had
neither a portion in it, which would have belonged to them as
of right; nor do they have a privilege which was given to them
as *s'daqah*; nor do they even have as much as a memorial in
the city. The usage here is very similar to what we find in
II Samuel. Mephibosheth's words to King David are:

For all my father's house were deserving of death at the hand of
my lord the king; yet didst thou set thy servant among them that
did eat at thine own table. What more *s'daqah* do I have and to cry
more unto the king?[16]

We translated literally in order to present the difficulty of
exegesis. The J.P.S. translation has here: "What right therefore have I yet? or why should I cry any more unto the king?"
We cannot accept it. Having stated that his entire father's
house deserved to be put to death, but yet the king made him
sit at his table, it would be worse than tactless for Mephibosheth to continue exclaiming, what more right do I still have
left. What he has already received was not of right but charity
and kindness. Furthermore, the concluding phrase, or why
should I cry any more unto the king? standing there by
itself does not seem to make any sense. Why indeed should he?
What is he talking about? We believe that from the point of
view of syntax, the Revised Version is much closer to the
Hebrew when it reads: "What right therefore have I yet to
cry any more unto the king?" "What have I *s'daqah* and to
cry" is clearly an idiomatic phrase and are not to be separated
from each other. They are one phrase and express one idea.
Thus far, we agree with the interpretation of the R.V. But
the actual rendering of the Hebrew is unacceptable to us.
Once again we are guided by the context. The Bible reports
the king's reply to the words of Mephibosheth. He said to
him:

Why speakest thou any more of thy matters? I say: Thou and Ziba divide the land. And Mephibosheth said unto the king: yea, let him take all, forasmuch as my lord the king is come in peace unto his own house.

From the king's answer we learn that Mephibosheth was not saying that he had no more rights or that he had no right to cry any more to the king. Mephibosheth was speaking about "his matters." He was actually asking something of the king regarding his land. The king, believing the calumnies of Ziba about his master, had earlier given all Mephibosheth's property to Ziba.[17] In his meeting with the king, Mephibosheth does mention that he was slandered by his servant. But he must have also raised this matter of his possessions which were given to Ziba. We have to find this, then, in the words which he addressed to the king. The Hebrew, *za'aq el,* is not the vague crying to somebody. It has the very definite meaning of asking something of someone. In our opinion, the sentence: what more *s'daqah* do I have and to ask more of the king? should be rendered as: what more *s'daqah* shall I ask of the king? The king preserved him in life and made him to sit among the king's servants at the king's table. What more could he ask for. Yet, he does ask, but in the typically ambiguous language of diplomacy. This is what caused the difficulty of translation. On the surface he seems to say that he has already received more than he deserved, yet there is also a hint in his words of a petition for more; a hint only, because he does not dare to express his request explicitly. The idiomatic phrase is awkward and need not be taken idiomatically. If one listens carefully to the halting manner in which Mephibosheth pushes from himself the idea of asking for any more, he does seem to ask: "What more *s'daqah* do I have?" By itself this means: what other privileges do I have? what else has been awarded to me? This is a complaint about the lands which have been taken away from him. It is a complaint which hardly uttered is immediately taken back by the words: "and to ask more of the king." Now, linking up with the first

304

part of the sentence, we get the idiomatic whole: what more *s'daqah* shall I ask of the king. Yet, there is something left of the suggestion of a petition, which is so close to the literal meaning: what other *s'daqah* do I own . . . and to ask more of the king . . . that is what I am here for. It is a masterpiece of ambiguity, a combination of obsequiousness and boldness. The king understood and with an obvious sign of annoyance he answered: "Why speakest thou any more of thy matters? I say: Thou and Ziba divide the land."

In our quotation from Nehemiah we found *s'daqah* associated with *heleq,* portion. In a significant passage in Isaiah it is preceded by *nahalah,* heritage. God's promise to Israel is:

No weapon that is formed against thee shall prosper;
And every tongue that shall rise against thee in judgment thou shalt condemn.
This is the heritage of the servants of the Lord,
And their *s'daqah* from Me, saith the Lord. (54:17)

In the expression of "their *s'daqah* from Me" both aspects of *s'daqah* are combined: *s'daqah* practiced and *s'daqah* received. The act of the promise is God's *s'daqah* toward Israel; the substance of the *s'daqah,* given to Israel, becomes their possession, their *s'daqah.*

GOD'S *S'DAQAH* OR SALVATION; AND THE SYNDROME OF *S'DAQAH, HESED,* AND *Y'SHU'AH*

Practically in the entire Bible, God's *s'daqah* belongs in the same category of divine attributes as his *hesed,* his goodness, charity, and salvation. The psalmist says, for instance:

They shall utter the fame of Thy great goodness,
And shall sing of Thy *s'daqah.*
The Lord is gracious, and full of compassion;
Slow to anger, and of great mercy. (Pss. 145:7–8)

God's grace, compassion, and mercy are manifest in God's deeds toward his creation. They constitute the *fame* of his goodness. Singing of God's *s'daqah,* one praises him for his

305

help and saving kindness. Occasionally, *s'daqah* appears as the parallel to *hesed*. We have already heard the psalmist declare:

But the *hesed* of the Lord is from everlasting to everlasting upon them that fear Him,
And His *s'daqah* unto children's children. (Pss. 103:17)

S'daqah is, not unlike *hesed,* an act of love and kindness. It is therefore natural in asking for God's help to appeal to his *s'daqah*. Psalm 143 opens with the words:

O Lord, hear my prayer, give ear to my supplications;
In Thy faithfulness answer me, and in [or with] Thy *s'daqah*.

We do not believe that a person in trouble, pleading with God that He may lend an ear to one's prayer and entreaty, beseeching God that He answer one in accordance with His faithfulness, could conclude such a plea with the cold and impersonal: "and in Thy righteousness." In our opinion, *s'daqah* is here what we have found it to be, an act of kindness and protective providence. The psalmist asks for God's answer of faithfulness and saving help. He asks for an answer not in *s'daqah* but with *s'daqah*. The meaning becomes even clearer toward the close of the same psalm where we read:

For Thy name's sake, O Lord, quicken me;
With Thy *s'daqah* bring my soul out of trouble.
And with Thy *hesed* cut off mine enemies,
And destroy all them that harass my soul.

Once again we have the parallelism of *hesed* and *s'daqah*. Again we maintain that no one ever turned to God that He may bring one's soul out of trouble "in His righteousness." One entreats God that He may do it with His *s'daqah*.[18]

The connection between *s'daqah* and God's lovingkindness and mercy comes to appropriate expression in a prayer of Daniel as well. In that prayer occurs the plea:

O Lord, according to all Thy *s'daqoth*, let Thine anger and Thy fury, I pray Thee, be turned away from Thy city of Jerusalem. . . . O

306

my God, incline Thine ear, and hear; open Thine eyes, and behold our desolations, and the city upon which Thy name is called; for we do not present our supplications before Thee because of our *s'daqoth,* but because of Thy great compassion. O Lord, hear; O Lord, forgive; O Lord, attend and do, defer not.[19]

In both cases we left the plural form of *s'daqah* stand. All God's *s'daqoth* are, of course, not God's righteousness; they are God's acts of *s'daqah.* Israel's *s'daqah* is confronted with God's. We do not rely, says Daniel, on our good deeds, but on God's; we turn to God in prayer, "because of Thy great compassion." This latter phrase is a variation on the subject of God's *s'daqah.* God acts with *s'daqah* because of his compassion. Appealing to God's *s'daqah* comprehends the manyfold request that he "hear, forgive, attend and do, and defer not."[20]

It is natural for the psalmist to appeal to God's *s'daqah* when he prays for salvation. Such a prayer in which the idea of God's *s'daqah* is referred to most often, is Psalm 71. It opens with the moving words:

In thee, O Lord, have I taken refuge;
Let me never be ashamed.
Deliver me by Thy *s'daqah,* and rescue me;
Incline Thine ear unto me, and save me.

"Deliver me in Thy righteousness" would be a jarring note here, much too intellectual and therefore destructive of the emotional longing and intimacy with which the psalmist turns to God. God's *s'daqah* occurs repeatedly in the psalm, but usually in connection with his "mighty acts," his "wondrous works," and "the great things which he has done." The works and acts are mighty deeds of rescue and salvation. The thought comes to complete expression in the verse:

My mouth shall tell of Thy *s'daqah,*
And of Thy salvation all the day;
For I know not the numbers thereof. (vs. 15)

It is for God's *s'daqah* and salvation, which were granted to him, that the psalmist gives thanks and sings God's praises toward the end of the psalm which reaches its conclusion in the words:

My lips shall greatly rejoice when I sing praises unto Thee;
And my soul, which Thou hast redeemed.
My tongue also shall tell of Thy *s'daqah* all the day;
For they are ashamed, for they are abashed, that seek my hurt.

There is little doubt that in this entire psalm *s'daqah* is synonymous with salvation; it is God's act that brings redemption about. Thanksgiving and praise are offered for God's *s'daqah* which was bestowed upon the psalmist. Indeed, the prophets occasionally use *s'daqah* in the form of the parallelism with *y'shu'ah,* help, salvation, or as having the same meaning. We find this quite often in Isaiah. God, apparently addressing himself to the enemies of Zion who are far removed from the practice of *s'daqah,* exclaims:

Hearken unto Me, ye stout-hearted,
That are far from *s'daqah*;
I bring near My *s'daqah,* it shall not be far off,
And My salvation shall not tarry;
And I will place salvation in Zion
For Israel My glory. (Isa. 46:12–13)

What God proclaims that he will "bring near" and that is "not far off" is tangible, material, actual help; it is the parallel to the salvation which will not tarry in its coming. In another place we read:

But My *s'daqah* shall be for ever,
And My salvation unto all generations. (Isa. 51:8)

This couplet recalls the lines in the Psalms which we have encountered already twice in our discussion, according to which God's *hesed* is everlasting and his *s'daqah* unto children's children. The terms *hesed, y'shu'ah, s'daqah* become practically interchangeable.

308

One of the most significant passages which illustrates our point is also found in Isaiah. In chapter 61 we read:

I will greatly rejoice in the Lord,
My soul shall be joyful in My God;
For He hath clothed me with the garments of salvation,
He hath covered me with the robe of *s'daqah*,
As a bridegroom putteth on a priestly diadem,
And as a bride adorneth herself with her jewels.
For as the earth bringeth forth her growth,
And as the garden causeth the things that are sown in it to spring forth;
So the Lord will cause *s'daqah* and glory
To spring [literally, grow] forth before all the nations. (vss. 10–11)

Needless to say that it would be utterly meaningless to render here *s'daqah* as "righteousness." To cover someone with the robe of righteousness does not seem to make much good sense. Nor may one attach much significance to God's causing righteousness and glory to grow before all the nations. What is more, in both places in our quotation, *s'daqah* has the same meaning. If *s'daqah* cannot mean righteousness in the first place, neither will it have that meaning in connection with "glory" in the end. But neither is there any need for the far-fetched translation of *s'daqah* as "victory."[21] That *s'daqah* here has no other meaning than anywhere else one might guess by the verb *samah*, to grow, which is used in order to say that God will cause *s'daqah* "to spring forth." Now this is a familiar expression in connection with *s'daqah*, but in the other places the growth of *s'daqah* never means "victory."[22] Our quotation will best be understood if we compare it with a passage in the Psalms. We refer to the first verses of Psalm 98:

O sing unto the Lord a new song;
For He hath done marvelous things;
His right hand and the arm of his holiness, hath wrought salvation for Him.
The Lord hath made known His salvation;

His *s'daqah* hath He revealed in the sight of the nations.
He hath remembered His *hesed* and His faithfulness toward the
house of Israel;
All the ends of the earth have seen the salvation of our God.

The theme is the same as in the text from Isaiah; the
terminology, too, is identical. *S'daqah* is given a place by the
psalmist amidst *y'shu'ah* (salvation), *hesed* (love), *emunah*
(faithfulness). There is no room here for "victory." One
cannot say that God reveals his victory in the sight of the
nations. One reveals something that is present all the time but
has remained hidden. The phrase cannot be applied to victory. Victory over Israel's enemies would be an entirely new
event which was nonexistent before. *S'daqah* here, as so often,
is synonymous with the other terms with which it is associated. One may well say that in Israel's salvation God
reveals his *s'daqah* toward them. As everywhere else *s'daqah*
is help, protection, an act of redemption. And indeed, according to the psalmist, when God reveals his *s'daqah* in the sight
of the nations, then "all the ends of the earth have seen the
salvation of our God."

Let us now have another glance at our quotation from
Isaiah. "The robe of *s'daqah*" is the parallel to "the garments
of salvation." And, indeed, *s'daqah* brings about salvation.
"The robe of *s'daqah*" is the robe of help or redemption.
Similarly, the *s'daqah* which God will cause to grow forth
"before all the nations" is Israel's redemption of which the
psalmist says that God will reveal it as His *s'daqah* toward
Israel "in the sight of the nations." Jeremiah uses the concept
of *s'daqah* in the same sense when he declares:

The Lord hath brought forth our *s'daqah*;
Come, and let us declare in Zion
The work of the Lord our God. (51:10)

Here, too, the theme is the same as in our texts from
Isaiah and the Psalms. In fact, the verb *hozee,* brought forth,
is the same as the one used by Isaiah in the simile of the

earth "that bringeth forth her growth" as God causes *s'daqah* to grow "before all the nations." Jeremiah's "brought forth" is identical with Isaiah's "will cause to grow." Jeremiah, too, speaks of God's salvation and redemption that His work has brought about.

We are already familiar with the prophecy of Joel that God will give the children of Zion "the former rain for *s'daqah.*" It means, of course, he will give them rain for a salvation. Malachi, too, used *s'daqah* with the same significations when he let God speak in these terms:

But unto you that fear My name
Shall the sun of *s'daqah* arise, and with healing in its wings;
And ye shall go forth, and gambol
As calves of the stall. (Mal. 3:20)

We submit that "a sun of righteousness" does not make much sense in this context; the sun of redemption does. The prophet uses the sun as a symbol of healing; he speaks of the day that will bring help and healing to those who fear God's name. Finally, there are the well-known words in the Psalms which are the answer to the question: "Who shall ascend into the mountain of the Lord? And who shall stand in His holy place?"

He that hath clean hands, and a pure heart;
Who hath not taken My name in vain,
And hath not sworn deceitfully.
He shall receive a blessing from the Lord
And *s'daqah* from the God of his salvation. (24:4–5)

When these words are fully translated, we usually get: "And righteousness from the God of his salvation." If only we knew why the God of one's salvation should be concerned about granting one righteousness. Not to mention the fact that we have not the slightest idea how a man of clean hands and pure heart, as he is described in the Psalms, may receive righteousness from God. He seems to possess it already in fullest measure. In fact, we cannot see how anyone may receive righteousness as if it were a gift. The truth is that there is no mention made here of righteousness. *S'daqah* here is the parallel to *b'rakha*, blessing. Just as God's blessing is a reward to the man of clean hands and a pure heart, so is also *s'daqah*. Its meaning is help and redemption, which is— indeed—granted by the God of one's salvation.

SEDEQ AND *MISHPAT*

We shall now turn our attention to the examination of the concept of *sedeq*. Its meaning seems to be rather close to that of *s'daqah*. In fact, some commentators and translators often treat the two as if they were interchangeable. We shall see whether this interpretation is correct.

On numerous occasions, *sedeq* appears as an attribute of *mishpat,* of the administration of justice. According to biblical injunction, one must not respect the person of the poor or favor the mighty in judgment; "but in *sedeq* shalt thou judge thy neighbor." Of the judges, who had to be set up "in all thy gates," it is said: "and they shall judge the people *mishpat sedeq.*" In the first example *sedeq* means "justice," in the second "just." Similarly, it is also said: "and judge *sedeq* between a man and his brother, and the stranger that is with him."[23] God is called a *shofet sedeq,* a just judge.[24] Isaiah prophecies concerning the Messiah that he will judge the poor with *sedeq.*[25] *Sedeq* is also required of a man's trading. The scales, the weights, the measures, they all must be *sedeq,* just.[26] And who is not familiar with the biblical admonishment: "Thou shalt not wrest judgment; thou shalt not respect persons; neither shalt thou take a gift; for a gift doth blind the eyes of the wise, and pervert the words of the righteous. *Sedeq, sedeq* shalt thou pursue, that thou mayest live, and inherit the land which the Lord thy God giveth thee."[27] Here, too, *sedeq* means justice. Looked at superficially it would seem to be rather removed from what we have found *s'daqah* to indicate. However, we should recall what has been said on the biblical concept of *mishpat* (justice) and immediately the gap between *sedeq,* in the sense of just or justice, and *s'daqah* will narrow considerably. The full significance of the idea of a judgment which is *sedeq* comes to clearest expression in the exultation of the psalmist over such a judgment.

Let the heavens be glad, and let the earth rejoice;
Let the sea roar, and the fulness thereof;
Let the field exult, and all that is therein;
Then shall all the trees of the wood sing for joy;
Before the Lord, for He is come;
For He is come to judge the earth;
He will judge the world with *sedeq,*
And the peoples in His faithfulness. (Pss. 96:11–13)

When God comes to judge the world with *sedeq,* it is an occasion for universal joy. As we have found his *mishpat* to be, so is his *sedeq,* a protecting and saving act. According to the psalmist, God's judgment with *sedeq* is the parallel to His judging "the peoples in His faithfulness." *Sedeq* is a form of justice that is the manifestation of faithfulness toward the people to whom justice is denied. Such justice is rather close to salvation. The joyous abandon, to which the psalmist calls all God's creation, testifies to a sense of liberation as the outcome of God's judgment with *sedeq.* Indeed, in one of the psalms, the psalmist links the theme of redemption with God's judging the earth with *sedeq.* We have already quoted and analyzed the first part of this psalm in our discussion of *s'daqah* and we shall quote it, assuming the meaning we gave it in our analysis.

O sing unto the Lord a new song;
For He hath done marvellous things;
His right hand, and the arm of His holiness, hath wrought salvation
    for Him.
The Lord hath made known His salvation;
His *s'daqah* hath He revealed in the sight of the nations.

313

He hath remembered His *hesed* [love] and His faithfulness toward
   the house of Israel;
All the ends of the earth have seen the salvation of our God.
Shout unto the Lord, all the earth;
Break forth and sing for joy. yea, sing praises.
Sing praises unto the Lord with the harp;
With the harp and the voice of melody.

. . . .

Let the sea roar, and the fulness thereof;
The world, and they that dwell therein;
Let the floods clap their hands;
Let the mountains sing for joy together;
Before the Lord, for He is come to judge the earth;
He judges[28] the world with *sedeq,*
And the peoples with equity. (Pss. 98)

It would seem to us that the psalm has one theme. The
"new song" is a song of salvation, a song over *s'daqah,* redemption granted and *hesed,* love remembered in faithfulness.
It is the same song to which "all the ends of the earth" are
also called, for God has judged with *sedeq.* Judging with
sedeq, he wrought salvation and revealed *s'daqah* and *hesed.*
It is worth noting that, whereas in the previous psalm God's
faithfulness was the parallel to his *sedeq,* in our last quotation he remembers his love and his faithfulness. It is God's
faithfulness that causes him to judge with *sedeq,* the same
faithfulness that induces him to work salvation and redemption.

While *sedeq* is used as an attribute of *mishpat,* when
mishpat stands for judgment, *sedeq* is different from *mishpat,*
when the latter means "justice." Perhaps the best known
example is the verse in Hosea:

Yea, I will betroth thee unto Me in *sedeq,* and in *mishpat,*
And in lovingkindness [*hesed*], and in compassion [*rahamim*]. (2:21)

The quotation shows that *sedeq* and *mishpat* are not identical. Similarly, it is said of God's throne that *sedeq* and

mishpat are its foundations.[29] Proverbs is introduced as having the purpose, among other things, to communicate "*sedeq* and *mishpat* and equity." In another place we read that through wisdom one understands "*sedeq* and *mishpat*, and equity, yea, every good path."[30] In our discussion of *emeth* we had occasion to quote the words of Isaiah:

And a throne is established through *hesed*,
And there sitteth thereon enduringly [safely, i.e., in *emeth*], in the
    tent of David,
One that judgeth, and seeketh *mishpat*, and is ready in *sedeq*. (16:5)

A number of other passages, too, show that *mishpat* in the sense of justice is not identical with *sedeq*.[31] The question arises, how is *sedeq* to be understood, if it is distinct from justice and yet it is required of judgment that it be *sedeq*.

SEDEQ RECEIVED—REDEMPTION

As if to complicate matters further, *sedeq*, very much like *s'daqah*, is often identical with *y'shu'ah*, salvation or redemption. One finds this meaning in a famous passage in Isaiah, where we read:

For Zion's sake I will not hold My peace,
And for Jerusalem's sake I will not rest,
Until her *sedeq* go forth as brightness,
And her *y'shu'ah* [salvation] as a torch that burneth.
And the nations shall see thy *sedeq*.
And all kings thy glory. (62:1–2)

Needless to say, in our present quotation, *sedeq* cannot have the meaning of either justice or righteousness. The passage reminds us of the two texts from Isaiah and the Psalms, which we have discussed earlier in this chapter, in which it was said of *s'daqah* that God reveals it before the nations. As *s'daqah* in those examples, so *sedeq* here seems to be synonymous with *y'shu'ah*. The theme is the same—God granting salvation and redemption to Israel in the sight of all mankind. Once this is seen clearly, a number of otherwise obscure passages in the Bible become illuminated. The psalmist, for instance, prays:

Answer me when I call, O God of my *sedeq*,
Thou who didst set me free when I was in distress;
Be gracious unto me, and hear my prayer. (Pss. 4:2)

We maintain that the rendering "God of my righteousness" is meaningless. The concept itself does not seem to have much sense. No intelligent notion may be associated with the "God of one's righteousness." What, indeed, could that be? Furthermore, there is certainly no room for such an idea in the context of our quotation. The psalmist turns in prayer to the God who "set him free when he was in distress." It is the God who saved him in the past. He appeals to God's graciousness and pleads for an answer to his call. In keeping with the subject and the mood of the plea, "God of my *sedeq*" should be rendered as, God of my redemption. "God of my salvation" is, of course, a familiar biblical concept.

Psalm 118 is the great psalm of thanksgiving. With exuberance the psalmist praises and thanks God for his deliverance. He was in dire straits, God chastened him sorely; but God became his refuge and salvation. In this mood of elation over his deliverance, the psalmist exclaims:

Open to me the gates of *sedeq;*
I will enter into them, I will give thanks unto the Lord.
This is the gate of the Lord;
The *sadiqim* shall enter into it.
I will give thanks unto Thee, for Thou hast answered me,
And art become my salvation. (vss. 19–21)

We have left the word *sadiqim* untranslated. As long as we do not comprehend the meaning of *sedeq*, it is hardly possible to know exactly what a *sadiq* might be. One thing, however, seems plausible. It is unlikely that the psalmist calls for the opening of the gates of righteousness. Why should he refer to the gates of righteousness when he wishes to enter through them in order to thank God for deliverance and salvation. It is more likely that, as in our previous example, here, too, *sedeq* means help and redemption. The psalmist calls God the God of his redemption (*sedeq*); by the same reasoning, the gates of God's temple are the gates of redemption (*sedeq*). It is natural to enter such gates in order to offer thanks.

In Psalm 23 occurs the phrase, paths of *sedeq*. Standing by itself, it would not be difficult to interpret it as, paths of righteousness. Unfortunately, the context does not allow such an interpretation. Let us consider the words of the psalmist.

The Lord is my shepherd; I shall not want.
He maketh me to lie down in green pastures;
He leadeth me beside the still waters.
He restoreth my soul;
He guideth me in paths of *sedeq* for His name's sake.
Yea, though I walk through the valley of the shadow of death,
I will fear no evil,
For Thou art with me. (vss. 1–4)

Surely, the renderings "paths of righteousness" or "straight paths"[32] are no translations but rather destructive interruptions of the singular beauty in the sequence of the psalmist's thought. The paths of *sedeq* are paths of redemption or deliverance, as the gates of *sedeq* are gates of divine salvation.

We are now in a position to clear up another, usually misunderstood, biblical passage. It is found in Isaiah. God's Anointed, who is sent "to bring good tidings unto the humble" and "to proclaim liberty unto the captives," also has the task

To comfort all that mourn;
To appoint unto them that mourn in Zion,
To give unto them a garland in place of ashes,
The oil of joy in place of mourning,
The mantle of praise in place of the spirit of heaviness;
That they might be called the terebinths of *sedeq*,
The planting of the Lord, wherein He might glory. (61:3)

Surely, the text does not tolerate the translation, "tere-

317

binths of righteousness." In this great prophecy the mourners in Zion are promised divine consolation. The ashes on their heads will be replaced by a garland; their mourning will give room to joy, "the spirit of heaviness" will be taken from them. But why should God's comfort and consolation cause them to be called "terebinth of righteousness"? Obviously, the theme of terebinth of *sedeq* is further elaborated by the phrase which follows immediately after it, the planting of the Lord. The terebinths of *sedeq* are God's planting; God has planted them with *sedeq*. But we know from the context that God grants them new strength and a new life, plants them anew that they may grow like mighty terebinth, by binding up the broken–hearted and liberating the captives, by comforting them over their past, and bringing them joy for a new day. Because he does all this to them, they are called God's planting and terebinth of God's *sedeq*. *Sedeq* is then what God does for them, as he "plants" them anew. They are, therefore, properly called, terebinth of redemption, the planting of God's acts of deliverance.

It is quite in keeping with our analysis thus far that we hear Jeremiah use the phrase, habitation of *sedeq*. It occurs in the following passage:

Thus saith the Lord of hosts, the God of Israel:
Yet again shall they use this speech
In the land of Judah and in the cities thereof,
When I shall turn their captivity:
The Lord bless thee, O habitation of *sedeq*,
O mountain of holiness.
And Judah and all the cities thereof
Shall dwell therein together:
The husbandmen, and they that go forth with flocks.
For I have satiated the weary soul,
And I every pining soul I have replenished. (Jer. 31:23)

The theme of the passage is Israel's redemption. There is no reason at all why in this connection one should refer to Jerusalem as the habitation of righteousness. But we recall

Isaiah's prophecy that "thou shalt call thy walls Salvation and thy gates Praise."[33] In the same sense does also Jeremiah speak of Jerusalem as the habitation of *sedeq*, by which he means that Jerusalem has become the city of redemption. Recalling what has been said in our analysis of the concept of holiness, we may well see why "the city of redemption" is followed by the phrase, O mountain of holiness. As Jerusalem becomes the city of salvation, so is God's closeness to Israel revealed anew which is symbolized by the Temple of Jerusalem. Jeremiah uses the expression "habitation of *sedeq*" in one other place. It occurs in the following context:

All that found them have devoured them;
And their adversaries said: We are not guilty;
Because they have sinned against the Lord, the habitation of *sedeq*,
Even the Lord, the hope of their fathers. (50:7)

The parallelism between *sedeq* and *mikveh* (hope) indicates that *sedeq* is unlikely to stand here for "justice." The habitation of *sedeq* is the hope of their fathers. We, therefore, maintain that here, too, *sedeq* is to be understood as redemption. Surprising and most original, is the application of the term to God. God, who was the hope of the ancestors of Israel, is the dwelling of their salvation. The enemies of Israel believe that they are free of guilt for the cruelties they inflict upon them, because Israel has sinned against God who is their only hope and the only source of their redemption. We are already familiar with the psalmist's appellation for God as *sidqi*, my salvation. It is in the same spirit that Jeremiah calls God, habitation of *sedeq*. Of course, Jeremiah himself also uses *sedeq*, directly refering to God, very much like the psalmist. It is found in a famous passage which occurs twice in Jeremiah Of "the shoot" that God will raise unto David it is said:

And he shall reign as king and prosper,
And shall do *mishpat* [justice] and *s'daqah* in the land.
In his days Judah shall be saved,

And Israel shall dwell safely;
And this is his name whereby he shall be called,
The Lord—our *sedeq*. (23:5–6; see also 33:16)

We have already indicated in our discussion that the phrase, the God of our righteousness, is unintelligible. So is also the expression now before us: the Lord (is) our righteousness. As to the context, quite clearly there is no occasion here for mentioning either justice or righteousness. Raising the Messiah, who practices *mishpat* and *s'daqah*, and in whose days Judah is saved and Israel dwells safely, is neither justice nor righteousness. It is an act of salvation. The Messiah will be known by what God does through him for Israel. Through him God will be revealed as the Lord—our *sedeq*, our redemption. We may now revert once again to Isaiah's formulation which we have discussed earlier, terebinth of *sedeq*. According to Isaiah, Israel—comforted and saved by God—will be called: the terebinths of *sedeq*, the plantings of the Lord. Bearing in mind that *sedeq* is occasionally an appellation for God, we may very well say that here *sedeq* is synonymous with "the Lord," in the phrase which follows the parallelism would then be complete. The inhabitants of Zion will be known as the terebinths of Redemption, i.e., as God's terebinths, the work of his planting.

We have found that like *s'daqah*, *sedeq*, too, is used in the two-fold meaning of *sedeq* done and *sedeq* received. Since *sedeq* received is synonymous with redemption or deliverance, we have a fair idea of what is meant by the practice of *sedeq*. May we conclude from this that *sedeq* and *s'daqah* are identical? There are a number of passages in the Bible which exclude the possibility of such identification. Isaiah, for instance, says:

Drop down [i.e., cause to rain], ye heavens, from above,
And let the skies pour down *sedeq;*
Let the earth open that they may bring forth salvation,
And let her cause *s'daqah* to spring up together;
I the Lord have created it. (45:8)

A careful reading of the text will show that *sedeq* and *s'daqah* here have different meanings. *Sedeq* comes from on high; it is compared to the rain. Salvation and *s'daqah* grow from the earth which has been rendered fruitful through *sedeq*. They are the earth's response to the blessing from the heavens. It is as little possible to identify *sedeq* with *s'daqah* as it is to identify the rain with the flowers of the field or the fruits of the trees. According to this text *sedeq* is instrumental in bringing forth *y'shu'ah* (salvation) and *s'daqah*. We have already had occasion to refer to the allegory of growth from the earth which is applied to *s'daqah*. It is used by Jeremiah as well as by Isaiah.[34] It is, however, interesting to note that the relationship between *sedeq* and *s'daqah* which we have just established in the style of Isaiah exists also for Hosea. The relevant verse is:

Sow to yourselves for *s'daqah*
Reap according to *hesed* [love].
Break up your fallow ground;
For it is time to seek the Lord,
Till He come and cause *sedeq* to rain upon you. (10:12)

The first line in our quotation is rather difficult to interpret. We do not follow the Revised Version because *li-s'daqah* does not mean *in* righteousness, just as *l'phee hesed* should not be rendered as *in* mercy. The J.P.S. translation of the latter phrase as, according to mercy, is more correct; yet we cannot follow it when in the first line it reads *according to righteousness*. While it does make good sense to say that one reaps according to the love that was spent on the act of sowing, it is difficult to see how one sows *to oneself* according to righteousness. "Sow according to righteousness" may be acceptable, but not, sow to yourselves according to it. However, in our discussion of the concept of *s'daqah* we have analyzed the meaning of such expressions as, *l'kha tih'yeh s'daqah* or *s'daqah tih'yeh lanu* (thou shalt have *s'daqah* or we shall have *s'daqah*). We have found that they meant that acting in

321

accordance with God's commandments would yield *s'daqah*, reward, help from God. In this sense does Hosea say: sow to yourselves for *s'daqah*. Live so that God may grant you his *s'daqah*. The actions of man are the seeds that will yield *s'daqah* for him in the end. However, in the allegory of Hosea, man's work is like that of the tillers of the soil. One breaks up the fallow ground, one plants the seed. But for the seed to grow, rain is needed. God's *sedeq* from on high turns man's sowing into *s'daqah* for man. The relationship between *sedeq* and *s'daqah* is the same as in Isaiah. *S'daqah* is the fruit which has been made to grow by God's *sedeq* from above. We shall yet return to a further consideration of this connection between the two concepts. For the time being suffice it to show that *sedeq* and *s'daqah* are not identical. This is also indicated in the following words of the psalmist:

I have made known *sedeq* in the great congregation,
Lo, I did not refrain my lips;
O Lord, Thou knowest.
I have not hid Thy *s'daqah* within my heart. (Pss. 40:10–11)

Again we are unable to follow the R.V. and the J.P.S. edition which read the first line as *I have preached righteousness*. The Hebrew *bisser* does not mean to preach, but to tell, to make known, to announce some news. It is the exact parallel to the phrases that follow, i.e., "I have not hid," "I have declared," "I have not concealed." Verses 10–12 form one theme. However, if one does not distinguish between *sedeq* and *s'daqah*, the line with *s'daqah* becomes redundant. Since, however, *bisser* does mean to make known and not to preach, the conclusion we have to draw from this psalm is that *sedeq* and *s'daqah* are not identical.

SEDEQ AND GOD'S LAWS AND COMMANDMENTS

It appears that we have still not exhausted all the connotations that *sedeq* has. According to Isaiah those who pursue *sedeq* are seekers of God and those who know *sedeq* are the ones who have God's law in their heart.[35] In keeping with these ideas, the doing of *sedeq* is equated by the psalmist with the fulfilling of God's commandments. When the psalmist prays that he be rewarded according to his *sedeq* and the cleanness of his hands, he elaborates his meaning by saying:

For I have kept the ways of the Lord,
And have not wickedly departed from my God.
For all his ordinances were before me,
And I put not away His statutes from me.
And I was single-hearted with Him,
And I kept myself from mine iniquity.
Therefore hath the Lord recompensed me according to my *sedeq*,
According to the cleanness of my hands in His eyes. (Pss. 18:22–25)

This psalm gives us practically a definition of *sedeq*. It is something akin to the cleanness of one's hands in the sight of God. It is accomplished by keeping the laws and ways of God and being "single-hearted with Him." In this sense one might well say that he who pursues *sedeq* is a God-seeker and he who knows *sedeq* has God's law in his heart.

Isaiah, too, seems to associate such a comprehensive meaning with *sedeq*. We find it in one of his most famous passages.

Is not this the fast that I have chosen?
To loose the fetters of wickedness,
To undo the bands of the yoke,
And to let the oppressed go free,
And that ye break every yoke?
Is it not to deal thy bread to the hungry,
And that thou bring the poor that are cast out to thy house?
When thou seest the naked, that thou cover him,
And that thou hide not thyself from thine own flesh?
Then shall thy light break forth as the morning,
And thy healing shall spring forth speedily;
And thy *sedeq* shall go before thee,
The glory of the Lord shall be thy rearward. (58:6–8)

It would seem that the observance of "the fast," as described by the prophet, would constitute one's *sedeq*. *Sedeq* would then be all that "the fast" requires: the crushing of the power of evil, the liberation of the captives, the shattering of all yokes that oppress men, the feeding of the hungry, the clothing of the naked, and the housing of the poor. All this would be one's *sedeq* which would walk ahead of a man like a protective shield. It would be identical with the psalmist's definition of *sedeq* as the keeping of the ways of God. However, the position of *sedeq* in our quotation is somewhat ambiguous. It is preceded by the light and the healing that will break forth for the benefit of the one who observes "the fast" as it should be observed. But the light and the healing are the results of this kind of observance. It would then follow that *sedeq* in the same context is not what one does, but the outcome of one's doing. Parallel to light and healing, *sedeq* would then have the meaning that we have found it to have quite often, i.e., salvation. The symbolism of God's salvation walking ahead and his glory following behind as a rearguard would be most appropriate. There are, however, other passages, too, which seem to give us the comprehensive view of *sedeq*. Of the Messiah, for instance, God says through his prophet:

I the Lord have called thee in *sedeq*,
And have taken hold of thy hand,
And kept thee, and set thee for a covenant of the people,
For a light of the nations;
To open the blind eyes,
To bring out the prisoners from the dungeon,
And them that sit in darkness out of the prison-house. (Isa. 42:6–7)

The theme here is very similar to the one in our previous quotation. We assume that God's calling the Messiah in *sedeq* is a reference to the purpose for the sake of which the Messiah is called. His function is to implement *sedeq*. He fulfills his task by being a light for the people, making the blind see, and by liberating the prisoners from their dungeons. Doing this would then be the doing of *sedeq*. We may now

324

take up the discussion of a passage in Psalms, a part of which we already had occasion to refer to, when we showed that *sedeq* and *s'daqah* are not identical. It reads in full as follows:

I have made known *sedeq* in the great congregation,
Lo, I did not refrain my lips;
O Lord, Thou knowest.
I have not hid Thy *s'daqah* within my heart;
I have declared Thy *emunah* [faithfulness] and Thy salvation;
I have not concealed Thy *hesed* and Thy *emeth* [enduring loving-kindness] from the great congregation. (40:10–11)

We are by now familiar with the concepts of *s'daqah, emunah,* and *hesed—and—emeth.* But what position does *sedeq* have in our quotation? We believe that the entire passage has one common theme. This is indicated by the parallelism of "I have made known," "I have not hid," "I have declared," and "I have not concealed." The unity of the theme is further underlined by the repetition of the phrase, *qahal rab,* great congregation. We understand the relationship between *s'daqah, emunah,* and *hesed—and—emeth.* The deed of *s'daqah* toward the psalmist God enacted in faithfulness to him; the deed itself, God's salvation, was a manifestation of God's enduring lovingkindness toward him. These terms are closely knit into one interrelated complex of ideas. How does *sedeq* refer to this complex? We note that *sedeq* appears in a grammatical form which is different from that which the other constituents of the one theme have in common. They all have the suffix, which corresponds to the possessive pronoun, thy. *Sedeq* alone does not have that suffix. It is a stylistic indication that *sedeq* is outside the complex of ideas formed by *s'daqah, emunah, y'shu'ah* (salvation), and *hesed—and—emeth.* Yet, it is part of the one theme. We believe that verse 10 of our text is the thesis and verse 11 is its elaboration. The psalmist declares that he made known *sedeq* in the great congregation; he did not refrain his lips from announcing it. And now follows the explanation.

325

How did he do it? By not hiding God's *s'daqah* in his heart, by declaring His faithfulness and His salvation, by not concealing His enduring lovingkindness from the great congregation. The declaration of *sedeq* is the theme. One declares *sedeq* by revealing God's *s'daqah, emunah, y'shu'ah, hesed—and—emeth*. These latter would then add up to *sedeq*. The psalmist speaks here about *sedeq* received from God. But such comprehensive definition of *sedeq* received would correspond to the comprehensive idea of *sedeq* which is to be practiced and which consists in following the ways of God. Being a light unto others, feeding the hungry, clothing the naked, freeing the captives, and breaking the yoke of iniquity, as the doing of *sedeq,* imply the enacting of *s'daqah, emunah, y'shu'ah,* and *hesed—and—emeth*.

Thus far, we have found that *sedeq* is consistent with a number of meanings. It may apply to *mishpat* in the sense of just or justice. It may stand for redemption or salvation performed or received. It may also have the meaning of what is right in the widest sense of the word, as following the ways of God and fulfilling his law. Such *sedeq* again may have the meaning of *sedeq* practiced and *sedeq* received. We noted that *sedeq* may qualify *mishpat,* it is not identical with it. Similarly, we have established that, while there exists some relationship between *sedeq* and *s'daqah, s'daqah* seems to be subordinated to *sedeq*. What, then, is *sedeq?*

Before attempting to answer the question, we shall survey the uses that the term *sadiq* has in the Bible.

THE *SADIQ*

The *sadiq* is, of course, the opposite to the *rasha,* the wicked. The examples are too numerous to require proofs from the sources. We are concerned with the special qualities that characterize a *sadiq*. In connection with *mishpat, sadiq* seems to have a purely negative significance. In the courts, a *sadiq* is he who is free from guilt or has the right on his side. It is in this sense that *sadiq* is used in Exodus: "Thou shalt not wrest the judgment of thy poor in his cause. Keep thee far from a false matter; and the innocent and the *sadiq* slay thou not for I will not justify the wicked."[36] *Sadiq* here does not stand for a positive characteristic of the person. It is the one who is not guilty in the case before the judges. Similarly, Abimeleh pleads with God: "Lord, wilt Thou slay even a nation that is *sadiq*. . . . In the simplicity of my heart and the innocency of my hands have I done this."[37] Here, too, *sadiq* is not a positive trait of personality. It is absence of guilt and innocence. Since the purpose of *mishpat* is to protect the poor whose right is denied, the *sadiq*, the innocent, the man who has the right on his side, is often found among the ranks of the weak and the humble. Thus, Amos castigates Israel for selling the *sadiq* for silver and the needy for a pair of shoes. Among their many sins weighs heavily that they "afflict the *sadiq*, take a ransom and turn aside the needy in the gate."[38] The needy, who cannot defend himself when justice is denied him, is also the *sadiq* in such a situation. It is for this reason that in the same context, in which the psalmist speaks of God's executing judgment for the oppressed, he also has reason to mention that "the Lord raiseth up them that are bowed down; the Lord loveth the *sadiq*."[39]

However, not only the innocent in court is considered a *sadiq*; the judge, too, who judges justly, is a *sadiq*. Ezekiel announces that Oholah and Oholibah will be judged by men who are *sadiqim*.[40] According to Proverbs, the *sadiq* knows the cause of the poor.[41] In this case, of course, the term *sadiq* is not a mere indication of innocence but it becomes a positive expression of character. *Sadiq* is a person who is just, who enacts *sedeq*, in the sense in which *sedeq* applies to the dispensation of justice. But the idea of the *sadiq* has to be broadened further. Jeremiah, for instance, who describes "the shoot" that God will raise unto David as a *sadiq*, says of him that he will execute *mishpat* and *s'daqah* in the land.[42] Shall we then say that the practice of *mishpat* and *s'daqah* makes one a *sadiq?* At the same time we also find that being a *sadiq* is associated with being merciful and charitable. According to the Psalms, whereas the wicked borrows and does not pay back, the *sadiq* is merciful and gives.[43] Of the *sadiq* it is said that he regards even the life of his beast, but the tender mercies of the wicked are cruel.[44] Since the compassionate consideration of the life of a beast or charity shown to others are acts of *s'daqah,* it would seem that he who practices *s'daqah* may be called a *sadiq.* The most comprehensive view of the *sadiq* is that he is a servant of God. In the words of Malachi, on the day on which God will spare Israel like a man spares his son who serves him, they shall know how to discern "between the *sadiq* and the *rasha,* between him that serveth God and him that serveth Him not."[45] This, too, corresponds to a definition of *sedeq.* It is the one that we have found to comprehend the search for God, having his law in one's heart, and following his ways. All that constitute *sedeq* and he who acquires and practices it serves God, he is a *sadiq.* This most comprehensive idea of the *sadiq* is spelled out in full detail by Ezekiel in the following great passage.

But if a man be a *sadiq* and do *mishpat* and *s'daqah,* and hath not eaten upon the mountains, neither hath he lifted up his eyes to the idols of the house of Israel, neither hath he defiled his neighbor's wife, neither hath he come near to a woman in her impurity; and hath not wronged any, but hath restored his pledge for a debt, hath taken nought by robbery, hath given his bread to the hungry, and hath covered the naked with a garment; he that hath not given forth upon interest, neither hath taken any increase, that hath withdrawn his hand from iniquity, hath executed enduring [reliable] justice between man and man, hath walked in My statutes, and hath kept Mine ordinances, to deal faithfully; he is a *sadiq,* he shall surely live, saith the Lord.[46]

This, of course, is a tall order. Yet, it describes the *sadiq* of Malachi, who serves God. Ezekiel's definition of what might be called the *sadiq* in the total sense contains all the elements of *sedeq* in its most comprehensive connotations.

It would seem that the concept of the *sadiq* retains its various connotations appropriately, when it is used as an attribute of, or an appellation for, God. God is *Sadiq* as a party to a suit in which He might be engaged by man for the treatment that God may mete out to him. In such a confrontation with God's punishment Pharaoh concedes that he has sinned and God is the *Sadiq*. Faced with God's punishment, who delivered them into the hands of Shishak, King Rehoboam and the people of Israel exclaim: "The Lord is *sadiq*."[47] In a famous passage, speaking for Zion, Jeremiah laments: "The Lord is *sadiq;* for I have rebelled against His word."[48] It is true, of course, that in our examples there is also present the idea that God is the just judge. His punishment is his judgment. However, the reference to God the *Sadiq*, who dispenses *mishpat*, occurs also explicitly. The prophet Zephaniah calls God *Sadiq*, who brings his *mishpat* to light every morning. The psalmist exclaims: "Thou art *Sadiq*, O Lord, and upright are Thy judgments [*mishpatim*]."[49] But God is *Sadiq* not only because he is just; God who is *Sadiq* loves acts of *s'daqah*. The psalmist, praying to God for the deliverance of his soul, affirms: "Gracious is the Lord and *sadiq;* yea, our God is compassionate." God is appealed to as *sadiq*, who practices *sedeq* in the sense in which it is closest to *s'daqah*, i.e., as mercy and deliverance.[50] Because, as we saw, *sedeq* does have the meaning of deliverance or redemption and is, thus, synonymous with *y'shu'ah*, salvation, God could say of himself through his prophet Isaiah that he was a God who was a *Sadiq* and a Savior.[51] The reference there is not to God's justice, but to his redeeming acts. The call to man in the same context is: "Look unto Me, and be ye saved, all the ends of the earth." He who practices *sedeq* in its significance as redemption is indeed the Savior *Sadiq*. Since *sedeq* has the connotation of deliverance and since God is called *Sadiq* in his capacity as Savior, Isaiah does not say, at the conclusion of the same passage, as his words are usually rendered, that Israel will be *justified* in the Lord. The subject of that passage is not justification but salvation. What he says should be rendered as follows: "In the Lord shall all the seed of Israel be redeemed and shall glory."[52] Bearing this significance of the term of *sadiq* in mind, we are in a position to interpret an otherwise difficult use of it by Ezra. At the conclusion of one of his prayers, Ezra said: "O Lord, the God of Israel, Thou art *sadiq;* for we are left a remnant that is escaped."[53] It is difficult to interpret *sadiq* here as "just" or "righteous," for in the same prayer Ezra also maintained that God punished Israel less than they deserved and left them a remnant. The escape of a remnant was, therefore, the result not of God's justice or righteousness, but of his mercy. What Ezra meant by calling God a *Sadiq* was the same that Isaiah had in mind when he referred to God as *El Sadiq u-Moshia,* a God Deliverer and Savior. That is what God was to Israel in the days of Ezra, for they were "left a remnant that escaped."

Corresponding to the most comprehensive meaning of *sedeq,* as far as it is applicable to God, God is referred to as *Sadiq* in the most comprehensive sense in Deuteronomy. It is in the well-known verse:

The Rock, His work is perfect;
For all his ways are *mishpat;*
A God of *emunah* and without iniquity,
Sadiq and upright is He. (32:4)

We recall what we have said in the interpretation of the second line of our quotation in our discussion of the subject of *mishpat.* Only if one does not narrow the meaning of the term to "justice," only if we understand *mishpat* as the cosmic principle of preservation and providence by the balancing of all contending tendencies in the universe, can we say that *all* God's ways are *mishpat.* As we saw, it is a *mishpat* that often requires acting with *hesed* and *rahamim,* with lovingkindness and mercy. God does this with *emunah,* in loyalty and enduring faithfulness toward his creation. Thus, there is no iniquity with him and all his work is perfect. This indeed is the

Absolute *Sadiq* who is the divine counterpart to the one described by Ezekiel whom we called the *sadiq* in the total sense.

TOTAL *SEDEQ*—THE GOOD

It would seem that *sedeq* is the most comprehensive concept
for that which is right. It is the idea of the Good. It subsumes
mishpat, s'daqah, emunah or *emeth,* and *y'shu'ah.* All these
are aspects of *sedeq.* Thus, *sedeq* qualifies *mishpat. Mishpat*
is a manifestation of *sedeq,* therefore it should be appropriate
to it. This has to be emphasized in the case of the administration of justice because it is possible to distort *mishpat.* Often
mishpat is not *sedeq.* There is no need to urge that the other
aspects of *sedeq* should be adhered to in *sedeq,* because it is
not possible to practice *s'daqah, emunah,* or to work for
y'shu'ah, without *sedeq.*[54] *Sedeq* is not a legal concept, but the
highest moral good. It is for this reason that *mishpat* could
not be defined in purely legal terms. As an expression of *sedeq*
it continually tends to merge with *hesed, rahamim, s'daqah,*
and *y'shu'ah.*

As to the significance of *sedeq* as *y'shu'ah,* it follows logically from its meaning. Only we have to bear in mind that, as
s'daqah, sedeq, too, at times means *sedeq* done, at others
sedeq received. Because *sedeq* is the good in its comprehensive
sense, when it is done to someone, the recipient of it has
received his salvation or deliverance. In this sense, *sedeq* and
s'daqah have the same connotation. Yet, there is a difference.
Often *s'daqah,* as help or reward, may indicate something
specific and concrete, as the reward given to Jacob by Laban
or David's action toward Saul or Mephibosheth's request for
the award of the land. *Sedeq,* on the other hand, never seems
to have this concrete significance. It always has the meaning of
redemption in the abstract and is the result of varied activ-
ities that together bring salvation. This distinction would agree
with our understanding that *s'daqah* is one specific and limited
aspect of *sedeq.*

331

In order of values we would place *sedeq* first, to be followed by *mishpat* and *s'daqah*. *Mishpat* is the practice of *sedeq* in balancing the claims of two parties against each other. *S'daqah* is the doing of *sedeq* in one specific manner without paying attention to the balancing of one's own claim as against the claim of the other party. The Bible seems to consider *mishpat* of greater importance than *s'daqah*. Almost always in the Bible *sedeq* preceeds *mishpat,* just as *mishpat* preceeds *s'daqah*. For instance:

Then shalt thou understand *sedeq* and *mishpat,*
And equity, yea, every good path. (Prov. 2:9)

Yea, I will betroth thee unto Me in *sedeq,* and in *mishpat,*
And in *hesed* and in *rahamim* [compassion]. (Hos. 2:21)

Thus for *sedeq* and *mishpat,* but in the case of *mishpat* and *s'daqah* we have:

And David executed *mishpat* and *s'daqah* unto all his people.
(II Sam. 8:15)

Then *mishpat* will dwell in the wilderness,
And *s'daqah* shall abide in the fruitful field. (Isa. 32:16)

The Lord is exalted, for He dwelleth on high;
He hath filled Zion with *mishpat* and *s'daqah*. (Isa. 33:5)[55]

Of interest is a passage in Jeremiah where both associations occur in the same context.

Woe unto him that buildeth his house without *sedeq;*
And his chambers without *mishpat;*
That useth his neighbour's service without wages,
And giveth him not his hire.

. . . .

Did not thy father eat and drink, and do *mishpat* and *s'daqah?*
Then it was well with him. (22:13–15)

There are a few exceptions which can be explained.[56] The rule, however, is that *mishpat* follows *sedeq* and *s'daqah, mishpat*. It suggests the order of values as: *sedeq, mishpat, s'daqah.*

SEDEQ, THE COSMIC PRINCIPLE OF CREATION

There is, however, one other rather important connotation of *sedeq* which requires careful consideration. It is mainly associated with God's *sedeq*. On numerous occasions the subject of *sedeq* is introduced by reference to God's creative power and activity. God's address to the Messiah, who is called in *sedeq*, is introduced with the words:

Thus saith God the Lord,
He that created the heavens, and stretched them forth,
He that spread forth the earth and that which cometh out of it,
He that giveth breath unto the people upon it,
And spirit to them that walk therein: (Isa. 42:5)

Upon this introduction follow the words: "I the Lord have called thee in *sedeq*." Similarly in the case of Cyrus, the introductory statement reads as follows:

Thus saith the Lord,
The Holy One of Israel, and his Maker:

. . . .

I, even I, have made the earth,
And created man upon it;
I, even My hands, have stretched out the heavens,
And all their host have I commanded. (Isa. 45:11–12)

Only after such introduction do we hear the words: "I have roused him up in *sedeq*." In both examples the introductory statement describes God's work of creation. One cannot help wondering what connection there may be between God's creative activity and His calling or arousing His respective Anointed? Even more puzzling, at first sight, is the following passage which is found in the same chapter in Isaiah from which our previous quotation stems:

For thus saith the Lord that created the heavens,
He is God;

333

That formed the earth and made it,
He established it,
He created it not *tohu* [a waste],
He formed it to be inhabited:
I am the Lord, and there is none else.
I have not spoken in secret,

. . . .

I said not unto the seed of Jacob:
"Seek ye Me *tohu*";
I the Lord speak *sedeq*,
I declare things that are right. (vss. 18–19)

Once again, the theme of creation introduces the subject of *sedeq*. But one may well be mystified attempting to establish a logical connection between the first part of our quotation which appears unlike its concluding idea. We have left the word *tohu* untranslated because it is the link between the subject of creation and that of *sedeq*, the vital bridge which is lost completely in the translation. *Tohu* is the formless and worthless, that which is without purpose and without meaning. God created the world not that it be *tohu*. The act of creation was not a mere manifestation of might and power. It was a purposeful act; he formed it to be inhabited. Creative might was purposefully directed. And when God asked to be acknowledged by Israel, he did not demand it for the sake of *tohu*, as the worthless worshipping of divine might, as one may pay homage to a tyrant. God did not ask of them *tohu*; he spoke to them *sedeq* and declared to them that which is right. The word of God to Israel, His law to them, was a continuation of God's act of creation. Both had the same goal. The goal is the rejection of *tohu*. The plan of creation that "the earth be inhabited" was continued when God spoke to Israel *sedeq* and revealed to them that which is right. *Sedeq* is the opposite to *tohu*. The concept of *tohu* molds the two parts of our text into one theme. The act of creation was not an act of *tohu* but an act of divinely planned purpose; just as the word of God is not the word of *tohu* but the word of *sedeq*. This gives us an equation which tells us that the act of creation was an act of *sedeq*.

There is at least one more passage in Isaiah which shows *sedeq* and *tohu* as opposites. It is expressed in the following words:

None sueth in *sedeq*,
And none pleadeth in *emunah*,
They trust in *tohu*, and speak lies. (59:4)

The rejection of *sedeq* is reliance on *tohu*, just as affirmation of *sedeq* is rejection of *tohu*. However, these words also add another feature to our understanding of both ideas of *sedeq* and of *tohu*. "They trust in *tohu*" implies that one should not trust in *tohu*, but in *sedeq*. *Tohu* is not only the unformed, that which is without meaning and value; it is also not to be relied upon. It has no future. The valueless is also without strength, without staying power.

It is in keeping with the entire complex of these ideas that Hosea says, in continuation of a subject which we have discussed in our analysis of *s'daqah*:

For it is time to seek the Lord,
Till He come and cause *sedeq* to rain upon you. (10:12)

The verse recalls Isaiah's statement that God did not ask to be sought in *tohu*, but offered *sedeq*. It is for this reason that the seeking of God leads to "*sedeq* to rain upon you." We also recall that Isaiah, as we have heard, refers to those who pursue *sedeq* as *seekers* of God. It is, however, noteworthy that Hosea, after calling upon Israel to seek God and to wait for His *sedeq*, continues as follows:

Ye have plowed wickedness, ye have reaped iniquity,
Ye have eaten the fruit of lies;
For thou didst trust in thy way,
In the multitude of thy mighty men.

They did not seek God, they did not pursue *sedeq*, but trusted in their own way, in their own might. It corresponds

335

to what Isaiah calls trusting in *tohu*. Once again we have an identification between *tohu* and the futility of might without *sedeq*. *Sedeq* is not only the good but also power. Thus the psalmist may exclaim:

> With wondrous works dost Thou answer us with *sedeq*,
> O God of our salvation;
> Thou the confidence of all the ends of the earth,
> And of the far distant seas;
> Who by Thy strength settest fast the mountains,
> Who art girded about with might;
> Who stillest the roaring of the seas, the roaring of their waves,
> And the tumult of the peoples. (Pss. 65:6–7)

Whereas in the passages quoted earlier from Isaiah, the description of God's work of creation is the introduction to the theme of God's *sedeq*, the psalmist praying for God's *sedeq* and salvation, supports his plea by referring to God's might and power over all creation. The God of *sedeq* is the Lord of the universe and "the trust of all the ends of the earth." His is indeed might which is not *tohu*. Within God, mightiness and *sedeq* are one. The act of creation was manifestation of might and right in one. In God alone might is right and right is mighty. That God's *sedeq* is mighty in saving comes to expression in some passages in Isaiah and the Psalms. God addresses these words to Israel, his servant, and Jacob, whom he has chosen:

> Fear thou not, for I am with thee,
> Be not dismayed, for I am thy God;
> I strengthen thee, yea, I help thee,
> Yea, I uphold thee with my right hand of *sedeq*. (41:10)

The psalmist, too, speaks in much the same vein of God's right hand when he declares:

> As is Thy name, O God,
> So is Thy praise unto the ends of the earth;
> Thy right hand is full of *sedeq*. (Pss. 48:11)

As is well-known, God's right hand is the symbol of divine might. When, according to Isaiah, God encourages Israel not to fear, promising them strength and help, He assures them *sedeq* which is the *sedeq* of His might. Similarly, the psalmist praises God because His might is might of *sedeq*. God's right hand of *sedeq* is the might with which he created the earth not for *tohu,* but so "that it be inhabited."

We may now be in a better position to appreciate the full significance of two phrases to which we have referred earlier in our discussion. God calls the Messiah "in *sedeq*." The description of God's creative activity, which forms the introduction, is the statement that God created the world with *sedeq,* with might that serves the Good which is comprehended in the idea of *sedeq.* With this very same *sedeq* God calls the Messiah, giving him the strength that he needs to fulfill his redeeming function in history. It is for this reason that, after announcing to the Messiah that he is called "in *sedeq*," the text continues:

And have taken hold of thy hand,
And kept thee, and set thee for a covenant of the people,
For a light of the nations. (Isa. 42:6)

He who is called in *sedeq* is granted strength and is destined to become a light to the nations. It is in this two-fold sense that Cyrus, too, was "roused in *sedeq*." His ways were made level for him, who was to build God's city.[57] The *sedeq* in which the Messiah is called is the strength that is right and the right become mighty. Thus it is possible for Isaiah to say of him that "*sedeq* shall be the girdle of his loins." The girdle of one's loins is what gives support, that which strengthens a man in battle. The Messiah will need no such support. With him *sedeq* will turn into might. Thus, he will be able to "smite the land with the rod of his mouth, and with the breath of his lips shall he slay the wicked."[58] He will rule by the mightiness of the spirit.

This insight may help us to understand more fully a passage

in Jeremiah. It occurs twice in the book with but little variation. It is a passage with which we are already partly
familiar. It reads as follows:

Behold, the days come, saith the Lord,
That I will raise unto David a shoot of a *sadiq,*
And he shall reign as king and prosper,
And shall execute *mishpat* and *s'daqah* in the land. (23:5)

Now, the same passage occurs in chapter 33 in the following version:

In those days, and at that time,
Will I cause a shoot of *s'daqah* to grow up unto David;
And he shall execute *mishpat* and *s'daqah* in the land. (vs. 15)

"A shoot of *s'daqah*" may mean a shoot that is granted to
Israel as an act of God's *s'daqah* toward them. Or it may
simply be rendered as a root of redemption. The significant
divergence between the two versions is to be seen in the fact
that the first version "the shoot of a *sadiq*" is followed by
a reference to his kingship. The second version, however, that
has "a shoot of *s'daqah*" omits the reference entirely. It would
seem to us that the *sadiq* in our text is the Messiah, is the
man of *sedeq,* the one who is called in *sedeq,* the girdle of
whose loins is *sedeq.* He is the man in whom, through God's
call, *sedeq* is history-working mightiness. Because of that the
sadiq has power, the authority of kingship; this *sadiq* is a
ruler.[59] It is properly said of him that "he shall reign as king
and prosper." *S'daqah,* however, does not carry the connotation of mightiness. Thus, "the shoot of *s'daqah*" is not followed by reference to kingship.

There is but one more point left in our discussion of *sedeq.*
We have found earlier that occasionally *sedeq* appears as a
heavenly power that exercises its influence upon the earth
like the rain from on high. As the rain causes the earth to
yield its fruit, so does *sedeq* from above cause salvation and
s'daqah to grow in the earth. We shall repeat one of the most
characteristic passages which expresses this symbolism:

338

Drop down, ye heavens, from above,
And let the skies pour down *sedeq;*
Let the earth open, that they may bring forth salvation,
And let her cause *s'daqah* to spring up together,
I the Lord have created it. (Isa. 45:8)

This was one of the passages which showed us that *sedeq* and *s'daqah* were not identical. But now we are better able to appreciate the reference to the work of creation with which the verse concludes. What is its significance? The great problem of human history is the suffering of the weak, the exploitation and the persecution of the poor. Salvation tarries for ever and *s'daqah* does not have much of a chance. Those who trust to *tohu* do seem to prosper. Nevertheless, the vision of salvation will not be confounded for ever, the day of *s'daqah* is sure to dawn. Because God created *sedeq;* because creation itself is an act of *sedeq.* The universe incorporates the principle of *sedeq* which is one with the principle of creation. Because God's *sedeq* is the cosmic principle alive in the world, in the final reckoning it will bring forth the triumph of salvation and *s'daqah* on earth. The *sadiq,* who will reign as king and prosper, who will execute *mishpat* and *s'daqah,* in whose days Judah shall be saved and Israel shall dwell safely, may tarry; yet come he will. God, our *Sedeq,* is the guarantor.

Summing up our findings in the last three chapters, it would seem that the three concepts, *sedeq, mishpat, emunah,* all apply to God and in this their application they represent cosmic principles by which God relates himself to the universe. *Sedeq* is the very principle of creation. It is the principle of potency in fullest identity with the Good. *Mishpat* is the principle of the appropriate balancing and "measuring" of the universe which is responsible for the law and orderliness intended by God's plan. *Emunah* is God's faithfulness in maintaining His creation; it is the principle of universal continuity sustained by God's loyalty toward His handiwork. They are principles of being, foundations of cosmic reality. As God's

339

ways with the world, they are archetypes of values. Because the world came into being in *sedeq*, because it is ordered by *mishpat*, because it is sustained in *emunah*, man, too, in imitation of God, should strive in *sedeq*, order his life in *mishpat*, and act toward all life with *emunah*.

Concluding Notes

It is doubtful that among the many ideas of the Hebrew Bible any have suffered more from misunderstanding, and often biased misrepresentation, than the concepts of *sedeq*, *mishpat*, and *s'daqah*. The guilt of numerous Bible scholars can hardly be exaggerated. Speaking of the biblical concept of *sedeq*, Robinson, for instance, unburdens himself in the following manner:

The idea of "righteousness" is not to be confused with that of "morality" or that of "holiness." Morality is properly actual "rightness" of conduct, judged by the customs of the society. . . . But the primary conception in the idea of righteousness is not actual rightness, nor Godlikeness; it is forensic, a product of the primitive court of justice. . . . In the realm of religion therefore, the righteous man is not the man morally perfect, but he who is acquitted at the bar of God. (*The Religious Ideas of the Old Testament*, p. 168)

For generations the interpretation of the biblical ideas of justice and righteousness as purely forensic and juridical has been the treasured contribution of Christian scholars to biblical scholarship. How such ideas could be maintained in face of the rich biblical material to the contrary (which we have quoted and analyzed) is a mystery to us. N. H. Snaith makes the observation that the Hebrew *mishpat* means much more than a legal term in the courts. The full meaning of the idea "has been largely lost because the Old Testament came to us first in a language other than the original Hebrew" (*The Distinctive Ideas of the Old Testament*, p. 74). We wonder whether the insufficient knowledge of Hebrew provides an adequate explanation for such a long history of misunderstandings, which in actual fact meant a misrepresentation of basic biblical teaching. Thus, von Rad is correct in stating that the German rendering of *s'daqah* as *Gerechtigheit* (justice, righteousness) "is unfortunately not only a very inadequate rendering of the Hebrew *s'daqah*, but is often virtually misleading" (*Old Testament Theology*, p. 374). The remark applies not only to the German, but also the English rendering; and not only to the rendering of *s'daqah*, but also to that of *sedeq* and *mishpat*. Our discussion has shown that all translations of these concepts are mostly misleading.

Von Rad is very close to the meaning of the Hebrew text when he declares:

It cannot be held that this Old Testament concept of righteousness is specifically forensic, for it embraces the whole of Israelite life, whenever men found themselves in mutual relationships. And in particular, conduct loyal to a relationship includes far more than mere correctness or legality, that is, righteousness in our sense of the word. Such dependence upon one another demanded the showing of kindness, faithfulness, and, as circumstances arose, helpful compassion to the poor or the suffering. (op. cit., pp. 373–74)

All this is borne out in detail in our discussion of the subject. Both Davidson (*The Theology of the Old Testament*, p. 144, 271) and Snaith (op. cit., pp. 69–70, 77) show an understanding and insight which would let them underwrite von Rad's opinion.

While our own position touches occasionally upon ideas set forth by Davidson, Snaith, and von Rad, we regret that, notwithstanding their deeper insight into the spirit of the Hebrew Bible, they—like most Bible scholars—do not distinguish between *sedeq* and *s'daqah*, nor do they give us an adequate analysis or definition of the concept of *mishpat*. Snaith, for instance, writes explicitly: "The Hebrew words for 'righteousness' are *sedeq* (masculine form), *s'daqah* (feminine). There is no difference in meaning. The choice . . . is a matter of style or caprice" (op. cit., p. 72). Other writers use the term

341

interchangeably. The classical Jewish commentators disagreed on this point. Some maintained that *sedeq* and *s'daqah* were identical; others insisted that they differed in meaning from each other. We have shown the distinction between the two ideas. In fact, *s'daqah* never has any forensic or legal connotation and should therefore never be rendered as righteousness. Because Davidson does not see this clearly, he interprets the rain, which God, according to Joel (2:23) promises to grant Israel *li–s'daqah* as "a token of righteousness, right standing with God" (op. cit., p. 139). As we have shown in our discussion, as everywhere else, here, too, *s'daqah* is an act of kindness and preserving and saving faithfulness. It has nothing whatever to do with righteousness. God promises them rain for their salvation.

While the connection between *sedeq* or *s'daqah* and salvation and redemption is often recognized (see, for instance, Sellin, *Die Theologie des Alten Testaments,* pp. 29–30; Snaith, op. cit., p. 69), the distinction between *s'daqah* (or *sedeq*) practiced and *s'daqah* (or *sedeq*) received is not adequately appreciated. Thus, for instance, von Rad (op. cit., p. 380) struggles with the difficulty of interpreting Job 33:26 which he paraphrases as follows: "If [then] he prays to God, then God is gracious to him, he can see God's face with joy, and God gives him back his righteousness." To this rendering von Rad attaches the comment: "This too obviously alludes to a ritual, according to which a prayer of penitence was followed by a declaration of righteousness by Y." In our opinion the ritual, of which he speaks, exists only in the imagination of the author. The expression "to return to someone his *s'daqah*" (not his righteousness) is an idiomatic phrase in Hebrew. The meaning of the idiom may be seen clearly in I Samuel 26:23–24. a passage which we interpreted. "To return to someone his *s'daqah*" means to reward someone for his deed of *s'daqah*. As to Job 33:26, the idiom is not used merely in reference to penitential prayer, as von Rad understands it, but in connection with the theme of the entire context. This theme is indicated in verses 23–24; "If there be for him an angel, an intercessor, one among a thousand, to vouch for man's uprightness; then He is gracious unto him and saith: 'Deliver him from going down to the pit, I have found ransom.' " Man's uprightness is constituted by the *s'daqah* he does. This his *s'daqah* is "returned" to him when God delivers him from going down to the pit. The meaning in Job is exactly the same as in I Samuel 26:23–24.

As to *mishpat,* even an author like Snaith, who sees clearly how misleading the familiar translations often are, is not quite certain about the exact significance of the idea. He rightly observes that *mishpat* is quite removed from the strictly legalistic concept which is suggested by the Septuagints rendering of the term as *dikaioma* or the Vulgate's *judicium* (op. cit., p. 76). We wholeheartedly agree with his statement that

there is to the Hebrew no *Ananke* (Necessity) and no *Dike* (Justice) to which both gods and men must conform. God is His own necessity. Justice is what God wills because such is His nature. If His thoughts were as our thoughts, then He would insist upon justice first, which usually means retribution, as *dike* tended to do among the Greeks. If His ways were our ways, then He would seek first to establish a Kingdom of Justice. (op. cit., p. 77)

He is among the very few Bible scholars who have realized that in the Bible there is no room for "Justice, blindfoldedly holding the scales in just equality" (ibid., p. 72). This is also the conclusion that we have reached. Yet, in another place, he reveals his uncertainty by saying that justice represents only "in part" the "will of God, because God's will is wider than justice. He has a particular regard for the helpless ones of earth to rescue them from the clutches of those that are stronger than they" (op. cit., p. 70). It is, of course, true that God's will is wider than justice. For Snaith this wider will of God is *sedeq*. What, however, he calls *sedeq* is still not more than *mishpat*. As we have seen, it is God's particular regard

343

for the helpless ones that motivates him to execute *mishpat*.
It would have been more to the point had Snaith insisted that
justice in the Western sense was only "in part" God's will,
since *mishpat* is wider than mere justice, for in instituting
mishpat God has "particular regard for the helpless ones of
the earth, etc."

On the whole, however, Snaith and von Rad come nearest
to our analysis. Von Rad is, probably, somewhat more definite
in his grasp of the idea of *mishpat*. We are in full agreement
with him, when he writes:

If we start from a preconceived idea of "justice," we can certainly
say that the characteristic permeating quality of Israel's religion
prevented her from achieving an objective justice. . . . Here it is no
neutral law, but Y himself in person, that is addressing men. Thus
law was for Israel something much more personal: it was God's will
for order, which in the end could never become really stabilized
and objective. (op. cit., pp. 94–95)

The objective, neutral, stabilized justice or law is the *dikaioma*
or *judicium* of the West, impersonal, absolute. As we saw, it
is not what the Bible means by *mishpat*.

If we overlook the mistaken equation of *sedeq* and *s'daqah*
and the lack of a distinct order of values as between the two
and *mishpat,* the most penetrating comment on the entire
complex of our present discussion comes again from von Rad.
This is a key passage in his discussion of the subject:

Theology has for long now ingenuously explained the concept [of
s'daqah] in the light of her own presuppositions, that is, in the
presupposition of the West. Its content seemed to be given by the
translation in the Vulgate (iustitia), and by the German word
Gerechtigkeit, namely a man's proper conduct over against an absolute ethical norm, a legality which derives its norm from the absolute idea of justice. From this absolute norm, it was supposed, issued
absolute demands and absolute claims. In social respects justice so
understood watches with complete impartiality over these claims and
takes care that each man gets his own (iustitia distributiva). Thus,
the only remaining question was, what is the norm that the Old

Testament presupposes? But, oddly enough, no matter how urgently it was sought, no satisfactory answer to this question of an absolute norm could be found in the Old Testament. The reason was that the question itself was a wrong one, and in consequence the statements in the Old Testament simply could not be brought into harmony with this way of thinking. . . . As we now see it, the mistake lay in seeking and presupposing an absolute ideal ethical norm, since ancient Israel did not in fact measure a line of conduct or an act by an ideal norm, but by the specific relationship in which the partner had at the time to prove himself true.

Von Rad is able to clarify his position further with a quote from H. Cremer's *Biblisch-Theologisches Wörterbuch* (7th ed. Gotha, 1893). As Cremer puts it:

Every relationship brings with it certain claims upon conduct, and the satisfaction of these claims, which issue from the relationship and in which alone the relationship can persist, is described by our term, *sedeq*. The way in which it is used shows that *sedeq* is out and out a term denoting relationship, and that it does this in the sense of referring to a real relationship between two parties . . . and not to the relationship of an object under consideration of an idea. (cf. von Rad, op. cit., pp. 370–71)

This is admirably expressed. We would only add that it applies not only to *sedeq*, but also to *s'daqah* and *mishpat*. So that in addition to such penetrating insight, one must still attempt to define the three ideas each one by itself.

Since we found that the wider meaning of *sedeq* was not the forensic righteousness but the comprehensive ethical idea of the good and the right, we did not interpret the term, *sadiq*, doer of *sedeq*, in the comprehensive sense, as *righteous*. Since *sedeq* is much more than righteousness, so must also be the *sadiq*, in the appropriate context. We found, therefore the phrase in Isaiah (45:22) of an El *Sadiq u'Moshia*, a God who is a *Sadiq* and a Savior, a most natural one. To save is the vital function in the doing of *sedeq*. The misleading and distorting translation is, of course, "a righteous God and a

Savior." We are in full sympathy with Davidson's comment on this expression. He writes: "The antithesis which in dogmatics we are familiar with is a righteous or just God and yet a Saviour. The Old Testament puts it differently—a righteous God, and therefore a Saviour. It is His own righteousness that causes Him to bring in righteousness" (op. cit., p. 144). Of course, he is right in stating that in the Hebrew Bible there is no antithesis between the *sadiq* and the *moshia*. The relationship between the two is one of casual nexus. *Because* God is *Sadiq*, He is Savior. But is Davidson right in saying: a righteous God, and therefore a Saviour? He would have to put righteous in quotation marks, indicating that the Hebrew equivalent is different from the English, righteous. Without such qualification, he ought to reverse his concluding remark. Instead of: "All His redemptive operations are performed in the sphere of His righteousness," he should have said: All His righteousness and justice are performed in the sphere of His redemptive attribute. Indeed, the *sedeq* practiced by God is much nearer to redemption than to righteousness. But perhaps that is what Davidson had in mind. For in another place he speaks of God's nature being "the standard of His action. What might be called the tone or disposition of His being is a redemptive disposition toward men." (ibid., p. 211). Now, if His disposition is a redemptive one, then both *mishpat* and *s'daqah*, which He enacts, must themselves be manifestations of His redemptive disposition. This redemptive disposition is the all-embracing *sedeq*, within which *mishpat* and *s'daqah* find—as we have established—their subordinate place.

The most penetrating interpretation of the idea of *sedeq* we find in Davidson's work. Having said that *sedeq* meant a standard of behavior, Davidson continues:

But there are other passages which seem to go further, and to show that Y's actions, which are *b'zedeq*, were some of them anterior to His relation to Israel, and that His forming this relation illustrated His *zedeq*—in other words, they rise to the elevation of making the salvation of Israel, and through Israel that of the world, to be the thing which is conformable to the Being of Y, and expresses it. F. i. Y says to Israel: "I have called Thee in *zedeq*." (Is. 42, 6). And in a remarkable passage (Is. 45, 8): "Thus saith the Lord that created the heavens; He is God, that formed the earth; He made it to be inhabited. I have sworn by Myself that to Me every knee shall bow etc. . . ." Here the salvation of the world and the original creation are brought together, and the first seems anterior to the second. (op. cit., p. 271)

Sedeq is indeed anterior to all standard. To see this is of the utmost importance for the understanding of the theology implied in the Hebrew Bible. Our only criticism of this admirable statement of Davidson is that it does not draw all the conclusions from the texts. In the concluding section of our chapter on *sedeq* and *s'daqah* we have analyzed and interpreted the same texts on which Davidson bases his comments. We have shown that *sedeq* is ultimately the cosmic principle of the creation of a world that God established not as *Tohu* but in order that it be "inhabited." *Sedeq*, therefore, represents a combination of creative might serving the purpose of the Good. In its ultimate significance *sedeq* is the divine attribute of the Creator. This corresponds to what Davidson says on the subject in his own style, commenting:

What might be called the tone or disposition of His being is a redemptive disposition towards men, for in creation He contemplated an orderly moral world, purposing the earth to be inhabited, and not subject to the devastations caused by evil in men or due to the cruelties of idolatry. (op. cit., pp. 271–72)

However, if *sedeq* is a divine disposition to create with the purpose of the Good in view, then we are led to the conclusion that *sedeq*, ontologically speaking, is the principle of identity between Being and Value and its efficacious mightiness. We have shown how this identity between Being and Value comes to expression in Isaiah 45:18–19. The understanding of the identity of Being and the Good and the *Tohu* quality of evil is essential for the appreciation of the biblical idea of redemption and, indeed, of the Messianism of the Hebrew Bible. We may best illustrate our point by discussing a comment of Snaith. This is what he has to say about *sedeq* as salvation:

God is going to establish His will and vindicate His right. He is going to do this with particular reference to the righteous poor . . . the godly humble remnant of Israel. . . . Further, if this norm is to be established, then where is God going to establish it? It must be either on this earth, or not on this earth. If a people has no belief in any life beyond the grave worthy of the name, then of necessity this *zedeq* (vindication of right) must show itself in this life, on this earth, and in the things of this life. It follows therefore that the *zedeq* which God establishes must involve the blessing of honour from men and of general prosperity. (op. cit., pp. 88–89)

This is most ingenious, yet it misses the point completely. In this matter Snaith lacks Davidson's penetrating insight. For Snaith, *sedeq* is the norm, the standard. He does not see that *sedeq* as principle of creation is anterior to all standard or norm. Since it represents the ontological identity of being and value, it cannot find its triumph in a kingdom which is not of this world. If the vindication of right were deferred to a life beyond the grave, then the earth was created *tohu* and not "to be inhabited" and God's creative purpose irrevocably defeated. History represents a scandalous separation between being and value; it is an ever-present challenge to the proposition that God created the world not *tohu*, but "to be inhabited." The challenge cannot be met in a world to come, leaving this world as the realm of unredeemed *tohu*. Not a norm is to be vindicated, but created being itself as an act of God's *sedeq*. It cannot find its vindication outside itself. This world, planned by God's *sedeq* as creation to be inhabited must be ultimately inhabited as God intended it. In history alone can God's original creative act of *sedeq* be vindicated in the actual everyday realization of the identity of being and value, in the form of this worldly manifestation of the efficacious mightiness of the Spirit. This is the core of the biblical idea of salvation and of the messianism of the Hebrew Bible.

Notes

CHAPTER 1

1. We leave the tetragrammaton untranslated in this chapter. The reason for it will emerge clearly from our discussion.

2. The many parallel passages, especially in Ezek., show that through the act of divine judgment it becomes known that He is YHVH. Both the King James translation ("and they shall know that I the Lord have spoken it in my zeal") and the J.P.S. translation ("and they shall know that I the Lord have spoken in my zeal") are incorrect and misleading.

3. As to the rendering of this passage in the Revised Version as well as in the J.P.S. translation, see previous note.

4. Here, too, we are deviating from both the Revised Version and the J.P.S. translation. *V'yad'u ki ani YHVH eloheykhem* in verse 30 is the parallel to *V'yad'u ki ani YHVH* of verse 27. Furthermore, *V'hema ami beyt Yisrael* in verse 30 corresponds to *V'yad'u ki ani YHVH eloheykhem* at the beginning of the verse. "I am their God and they are My people" is a well-known biblical conjunction.

5. Although in the passage in Ezek. 39:21–22, which we discussed earlier, the manifestation of divine judgment over the nations is, from the point of view of Israel, seen as an indication of providential care which calls for the recognition that YHVH is Israel's *Elohim,* such a passage does not exclude the possibility that where the emphasis is being shifted from divine transcendence to immanence, the formulation, too, should change from "that He is YHVH" to "that He is YHVH their God." It should also be noted that in our present passage it is stated clearly that they shall know that He is YHVH, *when* he reveals his mightiness in breaking the bars of their yoke. Whereas in Ezek. 39 it is not stated that they will know that He is YHVH their God, *when* he judges the nation. Having mentioned God's judgment over the nation, the prophet continues saying: And the house of Israel shall know that I am YHVH their God, from that day and forward. Whereas in our present passage the knowledge of God and the manifestation of His might are causally connected, God's judgment and Israel's knowledge of Him are associated only in time. In our passage the knowledge is the *result* of the divine deed, in

349

Ezek. 39 it follows upon it. There the judgment is the prelude to God's association with Israel that will teach them that He is YHVH their God. The Revised Version, retained by the J.P.S. translation, which renders Ezek. 39:22, "So that the house of Israel shall know . . ." is incorrect and misleading. It associates the judgment with the knowledge of God that accrues from it for Israel causally. The Hebrew original contains no causal nexus, but only a temporal sequence.

6. We have found only two passages which seem to be exceptions to the rule. They are Ezek. 29:21 and 36:38. In both cases the words used are: and they will know that I am Y. However, in neither of them is it clear who the subject is. In 29, the main theme is the manifestation of divine might over the nations. In verse 17 of the same chapter, in the same phrase, "and they will know" refers to the nations. If in verse 21, too, the reference is to the nations, there is no exception to the rule. We have already discussed the theme at the conclusion of chapter 36. Witnessing the exercise of divine providence over Israel, the nations learn that He is Y. In verse 36 there the subject is explicitly stated, *ha–goyim,* the nations. If, as it is not unreasonable, we assume that the subject remains the same in verse 38, there is no exception to the rule either. As to Isa. 49:23, 26 and 60:16, see our following discussion in note 22. Another deviation from our rule seems to be Ezek. 36:11. However, that prophecy is addressed to the mountains of Israel which will be redeemed from their desolation. That the trees will yield their fruits, that the field will be tilled and sown once again, that the mountains of Israel will be inhabited again, will reveal to the mountains that He is Y, but not that He is Y their God. The providential relationship that makes Y one's God can only exist on the personal level of existence. It is God's mightiness and sovereignty that is revealed in nature.

7. For this unusual rendering see the discussion that follows.

8. Exod. 32:4–5. The J.P.S. translation, "this is thy god, O Israel," is more true to the Hebrew than the Revised Version's, "these be thy gods, O Israel." Nevertheless, neither the plural nor the singular brings out the meaning that is contained in the Hebrew *Elohim* in this, and in all related, contexts.

9. Ibid. 32:1.

10. I Kings 12:28.

11. Ibid. 18:24. We translate the first *ha–Elohim.* It refers to both Y and Baal and obviously does not have the specific meaning of the second, at the end of the verse.

12. Both the Revised Version and the J.P.S. translation have here, "hear me." However, the condition of the test was that God answer. "*Aneynee*" is not, hear me, but, answer me.

13. The English rendering: The Lord, He is God; the Lord He is God, is a meaningless tautological statement that completely misses the significance of the event. There never was a question whether Y was a God or not, only whether He was an answering God.

14. Deut. 4:35–39.

15. In all passages we read, Y He is the *Elohim,* with the definite article in front of *Elohim;* the only exception being Pss. 100:3. The verse there runs: "Know ye that Y He is *Elohim;* it is He that hath made us and we are His, His people, and the flock of His pasture." The passage conforms exactly to our analysis. That "He hath made us" means that He is the Creator, He is Y; that "we are His, His people . . ." proves that He is *Elohim.* Therefore, "know ye that Y He is *Elohim.*" A careful reading of the various passages will show that wherever the definite article precedes *Elohim,* the affirmation is made to counter other claims. Y is *the Elohim* and none else. In the verse from Pss. just quoted, no such emphasis is required; no reference is made to any counter claims.

16. Exod. 20:2–3; Deut. 5:6–7.

17. Cf. also Isa. 45:21 and our discussion of it below.

18. Judg. 11:14–27.

19. Deut. 6:4.

20. I Kings 8:59–60.

21. Ibid., vss. 41–43.

22. There are two passages in Isa. where, instead of "Thou shalt know that I am Y," we should expect: "Thou shalt know that I am Y thy *Elohim.*" They are Isa. 49:23, and 60:16. However, in both cases the phrase is completed by words which are the equivalent of "thy *Elohim.*" In Isa. 49 we have: "And thou shalt know that I am Y whose waiters [those who wait for him] shall not be ashamed." The Revised Version and the J.P.S. translation have: "And thou shalt know that I am the Lord, for they shall not be ashamed that wait for Me." This is felicitous English but an all-too-free translation that distorts the meaning. According to it, Israel will know that He is Y because those who wait for him shall not be put to shame. However, whenever those who wait for him are not disappointed or let down, they know that He is Y their God. But in truth the Hebrew, *asher lo yeboshu qovai,* is not the reason given for how they shall know that he is Y. The words qualify Y. They will know that he is Y who does not let down those who wait for him. The meaning is identical with the phrase: they shall know that I am Y their God, exactly what is expected. In Isa. 60, too, "that I am Y" is completed in a manner that renders it in meaning equal to: that I am Y thy *Elohim.* The complete phrase runs: that thou shalt know that I am Y thy Saviour and thy Redeemer, the Mighty One of Jacob.

23. Isa. 45:4–7.

24. In our rendering we depart from both the Revised Version and the J.P.S. translation. Both versions disregard the poetic rhythm of the Hebrew original and obscure the meaning completely. Our rendering agrees with the Masoretic cantillation.

25. Cf. Gen. 16:7; Exod. 6:3; Ibid. 6:29.

26. Exod. 12:12.

27. Ezek. 5:15–17. Cf. also Ibid. 21:22; 24:13–14; 30:12; 17:21, 24; 22:14; 21:37; 26:14. See also Ibid. 23:34; 26:5; 28:10; 39:5. It would be mistaken to believe that Ezek. 34:24 was an exception to the rule. It is true that in the context mention is made of the fact that God will save "His flock" that "they shall no more be a prey," that he will appoint His servant David to be a shepherd over them and He will be their *Elohim,* nevertheless the passage concludes: I am Y, I have spoken. However, a careful reading will show that the words are not addressed to God's flock, but to "the fat cattle" (cf. ibid., vs. 20), who are not satisfied with feeding on the good pasture but tread down with their feet what they leave, so that the weak ones that follow after them should not be able to enjoy it; they are the ones that drink from "the settled waters" but "befoul the residue"; the ones who "thrust with side and with shoulder" and "push all the weak with their horns"—it is to them that God's words are addressed. God is going to judge "between the fat cattle and the lean cattle." The very saving of "the lean cattle" is brought about through the judgment that will descend on the "fat cattle." Since the words are directed to the latter, the passage concludes, as to be expected, with the phrase: I am Y, I have spoken. This is similar to what we have already had occasion to point out in connection with Ezek. 36:35–36. The restoration of the people of Israel will bring it about that the *nations* will know that He is Y. What for Israel is the revelation of divine love and providence, for the nations around about them it is a manifestation of divine might. Seen from the point of view of the nations, that passage, too, concludes appropriately: I am Y, I have spoken it, and I will do it. The salvation of the weak, that are God's flock, is judgment over the mighty.

28. Levi. 26:44.

29. Ibid 25:55.

30. Isa. 41:9–13, 17.

31. Zech. 10:6.

32. For the reason for our rendering the Hebrew in this manner, see the discussion below on this point.

33. Lev. 26:45.

34. Exod. 6:6–8.

35. Isa. 60:20–22.

36. In the three passages which we have analyzed in which overriding promises are made, it may very well be that "I am Y" at the conclusion may have the meaning: I may be relied upon to keep my promise; I have the power to do it; for I am Y. This is, indeed, how the rabbis in Talmud and Midrash often interpret the phrase: I am Y, to be relied upon to punish the transgressor and to reward those who do my will. It may be interesting to compare Num. 16:41 with Lev. 22:33. In both cases reference is made to God's bringing Israel out from Egypt that he may be *Elohim* unto them; in Numbers the verse concludes with, "I am Y your *Elohim,*" whereas in Lev. we have, "I am Y." A careful attention to the Hebrew shows that in Num. the reference to the Exodus is in the past, whereas the declaration, "I am Y your

NOTES

Elohim," refers to the present. There is no promise in that text. The meaning is that God, who took them out of Egypt to be their *Elohim,* is even now Y their *Elohim.* In Lev., however, for whatever reason, God's function as the redeemer from Egypt is mentioned in the present tense. "I am Y, who sanctifies you, who brings you out of the land of Egypt to be unto You for an *Elohim*" are the words in Lev. As indicated in our discussion, such a statement may be concluded only with, I am Y, and not with, I am Y your *Elohim.*

37. Cf. Lev. 19:37; 18:4; 22, 31.

38. Ibid. 18:2–4.

39. Ibid. 24–30.

40. Ibid. 20:22–24.

41. Num. 15:39

42. Lev. 11:43–45; 20:7–8.

43. Lev. 20:26 is no exception. That he set Israel apart that they should be his, means, of course, that he is their *Elohim.* Therefore, "for I Y am holy, and have set you apart . . ." equals: for I Y, your *Elohim,* is holy.

44. Ibid. 19:33–36.

45. Lev. 26:1. Cf. also Ibid. 19:4; Ezek. 20:7, 18–19.

46. Lev. 20:31 also belongs in the same category. "Ghosts and familiar spirits" are like idols, meant to stand between the Supreme Power and man. But since Y is your *Elohim,* there is no room for them in the system of Judaism. As to Lev. 19:21, "I am Y" is sufficient since it is directly preceded by, "and thou shalt not profane the name of your *Elohim.*"

47. Ezek. 20:20.

48. Exod. 31:13.

49. Cf. also Ezek. 20:12 which shows that Ezekiel uses the formula of Exod. very much in the manner in which he uses the one discussed in our text.

50. Cf. *Torat Kohanim, K'doshim,* 5; *Talmud Babli Y'bamoth,* 5/B. The principle is then expanded to include all God's commandments.

51. *Torat Kohanim, K'doshim,* 68.

52. Deut. 29:11–12; Jer. 31:32; 32:38.

53. Lev. 11:45; cf. also, ibid. 22:33; 25:38; 26:45; Num. 16:41.

54. Cf. also Lev. 26:12.

55. Jer. 32:37–40; cf. also ibid. 30:22; 31:32.

56. Ezek. 37:21–23; cf. also ibid., 26–28.

57. Cf. also Lev. 26:12 where that Israel will become a people unto God is introduced with the words: "If ye walk in My statutes, and keep My commandments, and do them." Quite clearly in Deut. 29:12 the entering into covenant with God and into his oath, by means of which God establishes Israel as a people unto himself and becomes *Elohim* for them, implies that Israel walk in the way of God. Even more explicitly, ibid. 26:17–18.

58. Ezek. 11:20; 36:28.

NOTES

59. I Sam. 2:12.
60. Ibid. 3:7.
61. See, for instance, Gen. 4:1.
62. Isa. 59:2.
63. Ibid. 19:21–25.

CHAPTER 2

1. II Kings 2:16. Cf. also the J.P.S. translation.
2. I Kings 18:12; cf. the Revised Version and the J.P.S. translation.
3. The J.P.S. translation has: and the Lord carried me out in a spirit. This is ingenuous. It separates Y from *ruah* and connects it with the verb *vayisoenee* which seems to be without a subject. However, there is no need for such distortion of the syntax. As so often in the Bible, the subject is assumed and quite clearly it is Y of *Yad Y*, immediately preceding the verb. *B'ruah* is not "in a spirit." The prefix, *beth,* is instrumental. Ezekiel was carried out by a wind from God.
4. Hos. 13:16.
5. Isa. 40:7. Cf. the Revised Version and the J.P.S. translation.
6. Vs. 19. See the J.P.S. translation; cf. also the forced and unconvincing translation in the R.V.
7. Judg. 14:6. See also Ibid. vs. 19.
8. Ibid. 15:14.
9. Ibid. 6:34.
10. Ibid. 11:29.
11. Ibid. 3:10.
12. Ibid. 13:25.
13. I Sam. 16:13–14.
14. Num. 24:2.
15. I Sam. 10:10.
16. Ibid. 19:20 and 23.
17. II Chron. 15:1; 24:20.
18. Num. 11:29.
19. Cf. also Zech. 4:6 where "My *ruah*" stands for *ruah Y,* signifying effective mightiness of the spirit.
20. Exod. 31:3 and 35:31.
21. Cf. *Onkelos,* ibid. 35:31.
22. Naturally, the *ruah Elohim ra'ah* that occasionally plagued Saul (cf. I Sam. 18:10; 19:9) was not the spirit of prophecy. It is to be noted that of the *ruah Elohim ra'ah,* the evil spirit that frightens Saul, it is said that it came *el* Saul, to Saul, whereas on the occasions when the *ruah Elohim*

354

caused him to prophecy, as in all cases of prophecy, the preposition is *al.* The prophetic inspiration comes upon a person. It is nonetheless significant that even of the *ruah Elohim ra'ah* it is said that it came to Saul and he "prophesied in the midst of the house." It is reasonable to assume that he did not prophesy, but showed the external signs of prophetic possession by the spirit without any meaningful prophetic message. He acted like one possessed in a rage of mental disbalance. Cf. Hos. 9:7. See also Concluding Notes on this chapter.

23. I Sam. 10:6.

24. Ezek. 11:5.

25. I Kings 22:24.

26. In our opinion II Chron. 20:14 is no exception to the rule. It is true that normally a declaration like that made by Jahaziel would be considered a prophecy; in the light of all the other passages that we have analyzed, however, the statement that the *ruah* of Y came upon him is an indication that his experience was not a prophetic one. It may very well be that Jahaziel was suddenly overcome with a sense of courage and certainty concerning the outcome of one particular confrontation with Ammon and Moab. On that one occasion he might have spoken to the people with the same sense of authority and vocation that also imbued a Jephtah or some of the other Judges in their time. And, indeed, his words are only concerned with the momentary crisis of a threatening war.

CHAPTER 3

1. Gen. 4:26; Ibid. 12:8, 26:25; Deut. 32:3.

2. Exod. 15:3.

3. Isa. 42:8.

4. I Kings 8:41–42.

5. Isa. 60:9; Jer. 3:17. In the light of the text in Jer. in which the same concepts occur as in the one quoted from Isa., we depart from the normally accepted translation of the passage from Isa.

6. Vss. 12–19.

7. Chapter 34:14.

8. Exod. 9:16.

9. I Sam. 17:45.

10. Ps. 54:3.

11. Ibid. 89:25. The Revised Version's "in My name" is a meaningless stereotype. We let the J.P.S. version stand because it may accommodate what we consider to be the right meaning.

12. Vss. 5–9.

13. There are quite a few other passages which illustrate our point. Cf. Pss. 20:2 and the contents of the entire psalm; Ibid. 118:10–12; Zech. 10:12.

14. Chapter 18:10; cf. also Mic. 5:3.

15. Chapter 64:1.

16. 30:27 Unlike the Revised Version or the J.P.S. translation, we refer the description in the text to the name of Y and not to Y himself, as they do. In our opinion the subject of the sentence is "the name of Y"; the text describes the manner of its coming.

17. Chapter 59:19. For our rendering of *ruah Y* as, the wind of Y, cf. our discussion in the previous chapter.

18. Pss. 102:17–18.

19. Isa. 50:10; Zeph. 3:12.

20. Mic. 5:3. The prepositional *bet* in *b'oz* and in *bi'g'on* is instrumental and is, therefore, better rendered as "through," or as "by means of."

21. See also Psalms 135.

22. Cf. Isa. 33:8; 53:3. See also the Hebrew commentary on Hag., Zech., and Mal., by Dr. M. Zer-Kavod, who interprets the expression *hoshve sh'mo* as we do.

23. See the commentaries of Yitshaki and of Kimhi on Prov.

24. Exod. 3:13–15.

25. For the talmudic interpretation see Talmud Babli, Pesahim, 50/a.

26. Isa. 26:8.

27. Pss. 135:13.

28. The J.P.S. edition translates *zikhr'kha* in this line as "Thy name." It assumes then that *shem* and *zekher* are synonyms, which is impossible to maintain. The liberty which it takes with the text is all the more serious, since the theme of the fear of the *name* of Y is introduced a few lines below in the text as a new element which is the result of God's having compassion on Zion. The synonymy between *shem* and *zekher,* which this translation assumes, renders a meaningful interpretation of the psalm impossible. The R.V. is here to be preferred. It has: "and thy remembrance unto all generations."

29. About the meaning of the term, the dwelling place of Thy name, see below in this chapter.

30. While, as usual, we follow in the main the J.P.S. translation, we depart here from it in some essentials. In the J.P.S. translation this psalm is set up in three separated paragraphs, as if it dealt with three different subjects; we believe that it represents a closely-knit entity. It has one theme which is carried through from the beginning to the end. We have set up the text accordingly. Our most important deviation is our interpretation of verse 18. The J.P.S. translation there reads: "Remember this, how the enemy hath reproached the Lord, and how a base people have blasphemed Thy name." Similarly the R.V. has: "Remember this, that the enemy hath reproached, O Lord, and that the foolish people have blasphemed thy name." We do not find this in the text. According to us, "remember this" is addressed to "the enemy that hath reproached God." This is in keeping with the grammar and

syntax of the sentence. The phrase has, of course, meaning only if one acknowledges the difference between name and memorial in the Bible.

31. It certainly does not mean, "But thou, O Lord, shalt endure for ever," as it is rendered in the R.V. It is a great pity that when translators encounter difficulties of meaning, they so often proceed to write their own text.

32. Stylistically, the psalmist expresses his thought in a most ingenious manner. "But Thou, O Y, sittest for ever; and Thy memorial is from generation to generation" is a variation on the more authentic formula, "O Y, Thy name is for ever; and Thy memorial . . . ," which appropriately corresponds to the original formulation in Exodus. By such pointed deviation from the original phrasing the author underlines what is missing in the situation in which he pleads with God. He has replaced the expression of divine activity, "Thy name," with an expression of divine passivity, "Thou sittest." Missing is the name, the name-creating manifestation of divine action.

33. Jer. 32:20–24.

34. Cf. Dan. 9:15; Neh. 9:10.

35. Deut. 26:6–10.

36. To this day every year at Passover the Jew recites at his festive table the words: "*We* were slaves to Pharaoh in Egypt. And Y led *us* out of Egypt." The rabbis gave expression to the ideas we are discussing in the words which have been incorporated into the Passover *Seder* service and are recited in the Jewish home at the *Seder* nights: "In every generation one should consider himself as if oneself had been redeemed from Egypt."

37. Cf. Deut. 28:10; Jer. 15:16; 7:11 and 12.

38. Cf., for instance, I Kings 3:2; 5:17, 19; 8:17, 20; I Chron. 22:6, 18; 29:16, etc.

39. I Chron. 22:5–19.

40. I Kings 8:13. We deviate here somewhat from the J.P.S. edition which has: "A place for Thee to dwell in for ever." The Hebrew does not require as strong an anthropomorphism.

41. Deut. 12:5.

42. The Hebrew, *l'shikhno,* is somewhat ambiguous here. It may refer to God and mean "His habitation," but it may also refer to "His name," in which case it ought to be translated as "its habitation." Since God causes his name to dwell in it, the Temple might well be referred to as *shikhno,* the name's habitation.

43. Deut. 12:11; cf. also ibid. 14:23; 16:2; 11; 26:2.

44. I Kings 8:26–30.

45. Ibid. 8:41–43.

46. Cf. Deut. 18:18–19, 22; I Kings 22:16; I Chron. 21:19; II Chron. 18:15; 33:18; Jer. 11:21; 26:9, etc.

47. Exod. 23:21; Deut. 18:18.

48. Of the priest in the sanctuary it is also said that he serves "in the name

of Y." (Cf., for instance, Deut. 18:5, 7; 21:5.) Of course to serve in the name of Y is not the same as to speak in His name. But that, too, means with His authority. One serves with divine authority only because there has been a manifestation of divine intention and will; as always, such manifestation reveals "a name." To bless "in the name of Y" (I Chron. 16:2; Pss. 129:8) is always an appeal that God may make himself known by acts of providential care, that he may answer a prayer. In the prayer of Solomon we heard that to swear "by Thine altar in this house" meant that God was asked to judge according to the truth of the oath. This is explicitly so stated in the oath between David and Jonathan: "And Jonathan said to David: 'Go in peace, forasmuch as we have sworn both of us in the name of Y, saying: Y shall be between me and thee, and between my seed and thy seed, for ever'" (I Sam. 20:42). "So help me God" is an appeal that God may act in a certain way in a given situation. It is an appeal for a divine manifestation of judgment. The weak form of the prophetic speaking in the name of Y is to come in His name (Pss. 118:26). He who comes in the name of God comes on God's business, represents something which is known to us to be the will or desire of God.

49. We deviate in our rendering from both the R.V. and J.P.S. edition. Our translation is justified by syntax and meaning.

50. See what we said in the previous section about the distinction between name and memorial.

51. We quote the R.V. rather than the J.P.S. translation, though in the essential point of our discussion they are identical, because we prefer its rendering of *am s'gulla* as "a peculiar people" to the latter's "a treasure."

52. The J.P.S. edition translates here correctly and has "glory."

53. Essentially the same as the J.P.S. version.

54. Here, too, since the translator does not know what to begin with the Hebrew *shem,* name, he translates it as memorial. We have shown that *shem* is name and *zekher* is memorial and rather different from name. The phrase, "for an everlasting sign that shall not be cut off" reminds one of the words in Ps. 74 which we discussed in the previous section, "we see not our signs." But this was said of the time when God's name is blasphemed, i.e., the name is not manifest. The "everlasting sign that shall not be cut off" explains the "name." The name will be a sign to be seen. It will be "everlasting," i.e., it will never again fade to a mere memorial. It will remain a name for ever. It is exactly for this reason that the attribute *olam* (ever) is connected with it, as a reminder of the words in Exod., "This is My name forever."

55. II Sam. 7:26; I Chron. 17:24.

56. Deut. 28:10.

57. See, for instance, Gen. 4:26; 12:8; 21:33; 26:25.

58. Exod. 33:19.

59. There is nothing gained by rendering this strange sentence as is done in the R.V. as well as in the J.P.S. edition, as: "and I will proclaim the name of Y before thee."

NOTES

60. Cf. Maimonides, Moreh Nebukhim, I, ch. 54. Rabbinical teaching bases on this text the "Thirteen Attributes."

61. Cf. also Pss. 105:1; I Chron. 16:8. For some mysterious reason, the J.P.S. translation renders the phrase *qir'u bish'mo* in the same kind of context in the Psalms as "call upon His name," but Isa. as "proclaim His name."

62. The translation is from the R.V. The J.P.S. version, instead of "who desire to fear thy name," has "who delight to fear thy name." Undoubtedly, "who desire to fear thy name" is difficult to understand. Nevertheless, *hafes* does not mean to delight, but to desire. The fact that we do not understand a biblical expression does not entitle us to rewrite the Bible.

63. The quotation is from the J.P.S. edition except for this line, for which we accept the rendering of the R.V.

64. Cf. also Amos 9:6 where the same phrase occurs in a very similar context.

65. Cf. Jer. 33:2.

66. For our reason for this form of the translation we refer to what we have said in Chapter 1.

67. It is thus that we understand the meaning of "and perish." Surely, should they really perish, the psalmist could not have continued, "That they may know. . . ." If they perish, they cannot know anymore. Neither do we accept the R.V. rendering, which—basing itself on Kimhi's commentary—changes the subject and translates: that men may know, i.e., learning from the example of those who perished, men will know. We do not accept it, because—quite clearly—the point is being made that they, who at first will be made to seek, will ultimately find, and thus, know.

68. It would seem that for this reason the J.P.S. edition renders the first *ehad,* referring to God, as "One"; whereas the second *ehad,* referring to the name, as "one." We spell both with a capital O.

CHAPTER 4

1. Isa. 6:3.

2. Cf., for instance, ibid. 28:5; 10:16, 33; 19:4; 3:15; 5:9; 14:22–23; 17:3; 22:25; 14:24, 27; 18:7; 19:12; 29:6; 39:5; 48:2; etc.

3. Ibid. 31:1; 30:11 and 15.

4. Ibid. 6:5.

5. For *haya l',* meaning to become, see Gen. 2:24; 18:18; 34:22; Exod. 4:9; II Sam. 12:10; Pss. 31:3; 71:3. Cf. also Ch. 1, "To Become *Elohim* for Someone."

6. The usual translation, his holy name, is inexact. "His holy name" should be rendered in Hebrew: *sh'mo ha–qadosh. Shem qodsho,* on the other hand, the phrase that occurs in the Bible, means, a "name of his holiness." Unfortunately the inexact translation obscures the meaning. See the Concluding Notes on this chapter.

7. As shown above, the term, "the name of YHVH," stands for the manifestations by which God makes himself known.

8. Cf. also Hab. 1:12.

9. Isa. 37:23–32.

10. Ibid. 37:10.

11. Ibid. 45:11–13.

12. See also ibid. 10:20–25.

13. We interpret *mishpat* here in its specific meaning of judgment or punishment. Cf. the discussion in Chapter 5. See also the discussion of *s'daqah* in Chapter 7.

14. See below, Sanctifying God's Name.

15. The syntax here offers some difficulty to the translator. We have departed from the usual translations. However, our argument does not depend on it.

16. Cf., Isa. 43:14; 49:7; and 48:17 to the end of the chapter

17. Only one passage is known to me where the Redeemer is mentioned together with the Lord of hosts. While "King of Israel" does not convey the intimacy of "the Holy One of Israel," it is not difficult to see that "King of Israel and Lord of hosts" may well be indicative of the two-fold function of the Redeemer, which we analyzed.

18. See Ibn Ezra on loc. cit.

19. The Revised Version has here as a clause: "for it is holy," referring holy to the name. This is impossible. *Qadosh hu* cannot mean anything different at this place from what it means at the conclusion of the second section, where it unquestionably refers to God, as the R.V. renders it itself.

20. The term *s'daqah* requires a more exact definition, cf. note 13. The argument in the text, however, is not affected by its traditional rendering as "righteousness."

21. That the way of holiness is the way of the Redeemer is supported by Isa. 35:8: "And a highway shall be there, and a way, and it shall be called the way of holiness." Though it is said of it that "the unclean shall not pass over it," the entire context proves that the unclean there is not a ritualistic but a moral concept. "But the redeemed shall walk there" says the prophet of the way.

22. Exod. 15.

23. We follow the translation of Onkelos, for reasons which will arise from our discussion.

24. II Sam. 15:25.

25. The verb *sh'ag* often expresses the moaning call of sorrow. See Pss. 22:2; 32:3; 38:9.

26. For the passages referred to here and preceding presentation, Isa. 35:2, etc.; 40:2, etc.; 58:8.

27. The Revised Version has here correctly: Proclaim a solemn assembly for Baal. And they proclaimed it.

28. It is rather a pity that the R.V., which renders the passage in II Kings correctly as, "proclaim a solemn assembly," should have in Joel, "sanctify ye a fast."

29. The philological question, whether the original meaning of the word is the religious and ritual or the neutral one, is not very important for this study. Its neutral usage as "marked out," "designated," "assigned to" is the common denominator between the two and thus they confirm each other.

30. I Chron. 23:13; cf. also II Chronicles 7:16.

31. Lev. 19:2.

32. See also Deut. 14:2.

33. Cf. Lev. 11:44–45; 19:2.

34. Exod. 19:6; Lev. 11:44; 19:2; 20:7, 25; 22:31; Num. 15:40; Deut. 26:17–19; 28:9, and the contexts in which they occur.

35. Cf. Rashi's Commentary, loc. cit.

36. J.P.S. Translation. The R.V. has: "and I will not *let them* pollute my holy name any more," which of course is a new text and not the Bible.

37. II Chron. 29:16.

38. There are two passages in Ezek. where this distinction between holy "in Israel" and in the sight of the nations is not as obvious as in the texts quoted. The one is chapter 38:16, where the relevant phrase may well be translated: "When I shall be sanctified in thee, O Gog, before their eyes." However, since God brings Gog into "my land," as the prophet puts it, and it is in God's land that Gog is utterly confounded, the divine act is at the same time one of redemption that reveals that God is holy in Israel. We accept, therefore, the grammatically correct rendering "when I shall be sanctified through thee." See the J.P.S. translation. The other passage is found in chapter 28 (vs. 22). The words we are referring to are: "And they shall know that I am the Lord, when I shall have executed judgments in her, and shall be sanctified in her." This time our translator has "in her" and not "through her," as in Chapter 38. However, the judgment meted out to Sidon is also an act of redemption for Israel. In the same context it is said that the result of Sidon's punishment will be that "there shall be no more a pricking brier unto the house of Israel, nor a piercing thorn of any that are around them, that did have them in disdain. . . ." In keeping with the other unambiguous passages, we would render it here: "and shall be sanctified through her."

39. This is indeed Kimhi's interpretation of the phrase, "Him shall ye sanctify." On the other hand, confer—for instance—Dohin's hopeless struggle with the difficulty to elucidate the meaning of the parallelism.

40. Cf. 2:19; 5:14; 6:9; 7:3, 21; 8:3; 9:14, 16; 19:3; 27:4–5; the prophecies "about the nations" beginning with chapter 46, etc.

41. Cf. 33:11; see also 31: 22; 32:16; 51:13–14.

42. Cf. above, High and Holy.

43. Cf. above, The Holy One and the Lord of Hosts.

44. The J.P.S. translation has: "For their land is full of guilt against the Holy One of Israel"; whereas the R.V. renders it: "Though their land was filled with sin against the Holy One of Israel." The one is as little convincing as the other. *Mi–q'dosh Yisrael* does not mean *"against* the Holy One of Israel." What is more, if in the same verse the same grammatical form occurs three times, it is not possible to render it differently the third time than on the first two occasions.

45. The Holy One and the Lord of Hosts.

46. Cf. also all the other prophecies of redemption in Jer. 31:22; 32:15; 51:13–14. The reference to the present moment of destruction is never lacking.

47. Cf. also the other passages in Zech. 6:12, chapters 8, 9, 16 and their context.

48. High and Holy.

49. Exod. 3:5.

50. Lev. 10:2.

51. Num. 4:15, 20.

52. II Sam. 6:7

53. II Chron. 26:19.

54. The suggestion is made by N. H. Snaith in *The Distinctive Ideas of the Old Testament* (London, 1955), p. 40.

55. I Sam. 6:19.

56. Lev. 10:3.

57. We depart here from the usually accepted interpretation as found in Yitshaki's commentary loc. cit. Cf. what we have said in that account above, Sanctifying God's Name.

58. Cf. above, Holy and Awesome.

CHAPTER 5

1. Deut. 1:17.

2. Num. 27:5.

3. Cf. I Kings 3:11; the R.V. and the J.P.S. translations.

4. Ibid. 3:28.

5. Ezek. 39:21; 5:8–10.

6. Jer. 48:21–47.

7. I Sam. 3:13–14.

8. Pss. 68:6.

9. The R.V. and the J.P.S. edition here are identical.

10. For this interpretation of *s'daqah* see our discussion in Chapter 7.

NOTES

11. This quotation takes, of course, our subject much further than we are at this point prepared to go. Its significance will emerge more clearly when we reach the definition of the biblical concept of justice.

12. Jer. 9:23.

13. Isa. 56:1.

14. Gen. 40:13.

15. Josh. 6:15.

16. Judg. 18:7.

17. II Kings 1:7–8.

18. Ibid. 17:33.

19. I Sam. 8:9; cf. also ibid., vs. 11.

20. II Kings 17:26.

21. The R.V. translates: "For they know not the way of the Lord, nor the judgment of their God." The J.P.S. edition has: "For they know not the way of the Lord, nor the ordinance of their God." Since according to them *mishpat* is different from *derekh* (way) in meaning, they have to introduce into the text the conjunction, nor, which is not found in the Hebrew original and which, in fact, is not in keeping with the Hebrew sentence structure. Both renderings are misrepresentations.

22. The J.P.S. translation renders it correctly as: Hear my voice according unto Thy lovingkindness; quicken me, O Lord, as Thou art wont. And so also in vs. 156 of the same psalm. Whereas the R.V. has: quicken me according to Thy judgment, which is meaningless.

23. We leave *emeth* untranslated because, as we shall show in the next chapter, its translation as truth, especially in this context, is utterly misleading.

CHAPTER 6

1. Deut. 13:15; 17:4; 22:20; I Kings 10:6; 22:16; Jer. 23:28; 26:15; 28:9; Isa. 43:9; Prov. 14:25; Dan. 8:26; 11:2; etc.

2. Zech. 8:8.

3. Pss. 69:14.

4. II Chron 31:20; 32:1.

5. Isa. 39:8.

6. Zech. 8:19.

7. Gen. 24:27, 48.

8. Ibid. 32:11.

9. Exod. 34:6. For the talmudic interpretation see T. B., Rosh Hashanah, 17b.

10. Isa. 22:23, 25.

11. II Sam. 7:16; cf. also I Kings 11:38.

12. Jer. 15:18.

13. Isa. 33:16.

14. In Deut. 28:59 it is said even of plagues and sicknesses that they would be *ne'emanoth,* i.e., steady, enduring, to be counted upon.

15. Isa. 8:2.

16. Prov. 25:13.

17. Neh. 9:8.

18. I Sam. 2:35.

19. Ibid. 3:20.

20. Pss. 78:7–8.

21. Ibid., vss. 36–37.

22. Ibid. 89:29.

23. An interesting comparison is Deut. 28:59 with Prov. 27:6. In Deut. *ne'-eman,* qualifying an object, plagues, means: enduring; in Prov. referring to the action of a friend which wounds, it stands for faithful wounds.

24. Exod. 17:12.

25. Isa. 33:6. We follow here the R.V. which is based on Kimhi's interpretation. *Hosen* is parallel to *emunah* in the sense of steadiness, firmness, strength.

26. Cf. Deut. 28:66–67.

27. II Kings 12:16; 22:7.

28. I Chron. 9:22.

29. It may also be that *emunah* stands for a hereditary office in the sense of its meaning as security or stability, as in the earlier discussed combination with "times." *Emunah,* in this sense, would correspond to a hereditary sinecure.

30. I Sam. 26:23. We left the word *s'daqah* untranslated for reasons which will become obvious in Chapter 7.

31. II Chron. 19:9.

32. Isa. 59:4; cf. Kimhi's interpretation there.

33. Deut. 7:9; for the fuller interpretation of the relation between Y and *Elohim* and *El* in this verse, see what was said on the subject in Chapter 1.

34. Ibid. 32:4.

35. Cf. Chapter 5.

36. Pss. 96:13.

37. Prov. 27:6.

38. Pss. 98:2.

39. Ibid. 92:3.

40. For the midrashic explanation, which is rather close to our analysis, see *Midrash Ekha,* 3, 21; cf. also Yitshaki's interpretation on Pss. 92:3; see also *Tosaphot,* T. B., B'rakhot, 12a, *l'haggid,* etc.

41. Cf. Pss. 19:8; 93:5; 111:7; 119:138.

42. Ibid. 40:11.

43. Gen. 15:6.

44. Exod. 14:31.

45. Jonah 3:5.

46. Ibid. 4:2.

47. Num. 14:11.

48. Cf. also Deut. 1:32; 9:23; Num. 20:12; Pss. 78:32.

49. II Kings 17:14–15.

50. See Chapters 1 and 4.

51. Hab. 2:4.

52. Isa. 11:5.

53. Dan. 10:21.

54. Jer. 14:13; cf. Kimhi's interpretation.

55. Isa. 39:8.

56. Esther 9:30.

57. Josh. 2:12.

58. Isa. 10:20.

59. Judg. 9:15, 16, 19

60. Cf. I Sam. 12:24; I Kings 2:4; 3:6; II Kings 20:3; Isa. 38:3.

61. II Chron. 31:20; 32:1.

62. Pss. 145:18.

63. Cf. Zech. 7:9; 8:16; Ezek. 18:8.

64. Jer. 10:10.

65. Pss. 88:12.

66. Pss. 86:11 and 26:3 may well be explained in the same way.

67. Gen. 24:48; cf. also ibid. 27.

68. Pss. 132:11.

69. See our discussion of this idea earlier in this chapter.

70. Our translation is guided by the syntax of the verse and by our discussion of *mishpat*. *Mishpat sidkekha* is just not "Thy righteous ordinance," but "Thy *mishpat* of righteousness" or "the *mishpat* of Thy righteousness." Cf. Concluding Notes in Chapter 4.

71. Gen. 47:29.

72. Josh. 2:14.

73. Exod. 34:6–7.

74. Pss. 61:8.

75. Ibid. 89:29. See our discussion of the entire passage in the earlier parts of this chapter.

NOTES

CHAPTER 7

1. Deut. 9:4–5.
2. Prov. 11:19; cf. also ibid. 11:4–6; 13:6; 15:9.
3. Ibid. 16:12.
4. Cf. Isa. 16:5; Prov. 20:28; 29:14.
5. I Sam. 26:23.
6. Ibid. 12:6–7.
7. Mic. 6:5; cf. also Judg. 5:11
8. Cf. the R.V. and the J.P.S. translations.
9. Gen. 15:6.
10. Job 35:8.
11. Gen. 30:33.
12. Deut. 24:13.
13. Ibid. 6:25.
14. Pss. 103:17–18.
15. Neh. 2:20.
16. II Sam. 19:29–31.
17. Ibid. 16:4.
18. For other examples of parallelism between *hesed* and *s'daqah,* cf. Pss. 119:40; 36:10–11; 88:12–13.
19. Dan. 9:16–19.
20. It is true that in the same chapter in verse seven we read: "Unto Thee, O Lord, belongeth *s'daqah,* but unto us confusion of face"; but in a similar vein it is also said there, in the same context and in the same mood: "To the Lord our God belong compassions and forgiveness; for we have rebelled against Him" (ibid., vs. 9). In the verses, which we have analyzed in our text, God's *s'daqah* is understood to be motivated by compassion; forgiveness is one of its manifestations. The reference in vs. 7 is to *s'daqah* in the same sense as the reference there to God's compassions and forgiveness.
21. See the R.V. and the J.P.S. translations.
22. See Isa. 45:8; Jer. 33:15.
23. Lev. 19:15; Deut. 16:18; ibid. 1:16.
24. Jer. 11:20; Pss. 9:4.
25. Isa. 11:4.
26. Lev. 19:36; Deut. 25:15.
27. Deut. 16:19–20
28. The context indicates that *yishpot* here is not the future but the continuous presence.
29. Pss. 89:15; 97:2–3.

30. Prov. 1:3; 2:9.

31. Cf. Pss. 94:15; 37:6; Eccles. 3:16; 5:7.

32. Cf. R.V. and the J.P.S. translations.

33. Isa. 60:18.

34. Cf. Jer. 33:15.

35. Isa. 51:1, 7.

36. Exod. 23:7.

37. Gen. 20:4.

38. Amos 2:6; 5:12.

39. Pss. 146:8.

40. Ezek. 23:45.

41. Prov. 29:7.

42. Jer. 23:5.

43. Pss. 37:21; see also ibid. 112:4–5.

44. Prov. 12:10.

45. Mal. 3:18.

46. Ezek. 18:5–9.

47. Exod. 9:27; II Chron. 12:6.

48. Lam. 1:18; cf. also Jer. 12:1; Neh. 9:33.

49. Zeph. 3:5; Pss. 119:137.

50. Pss. 11:7; 116:5.

51. Isa. 45:21.

52. Ibid., vs. 25.

53. Ezra 9:15.

54. Only once do we find *sedeq* qualifying *s'daqah*. In Psalm 119:142, we have: "Thy *s'daqah* is everlastingly *sedeq* and Thy law is *emeth*." Now, as superfluous it would be to state that God's law was true, even more pointless would it be to declare that His *s'daqah* was *sedeq*. Simply, because not only His but everybody's *s'daqah* by definition cannot be anything but *sedeq*. However, as we saw in our discussion of the idea, *emeth* means enduringly reliable. *Emeth* here parallels *sedeq l'olam* in the first half of the verse. As in the case of the Torah the thought expressed is not that the Torah is true, but that it is enduringly valid; so in the case of *s'daqah* the idea is not that it is *sedeq*, but that it is everlasting.

55. Cf. also Pss. 72:2; 89:15; 97:3; Prov. 1:3; Isa. 32:1; I Kings 10:9; Isa. 28:17; 56:1; 59:9, 14; Jer. 9:23; 23:3, 5; Ezek. 33:14, 19; Amos 5:7, etc.

56. *Sedeq* follows on *mishpat* only once in Pss. 119:121, and twice in Eccles. 3:16; 5:7. As to the Pss., see the note in *Minhat Shay*. It may very well be that "I have done *mishpat* and *sedeq*" should be rendered as: "I have done *mishpat* and it was *sedeq*." As to the passages in Ecclesiastes they have in common that they deal with the violation of *sedeq* and *mishpat*. It is not

impossible to theorize why when one deplores the absence of these two, the distortion of *mishpat* should precede that of *sedeq*.

S'daqah precedes *mishpat* in Gen. 18:19; Pss. 33:5; Prov. 21:3. (One or two similar cases we do not consider belonging in this category.) Again these exceptions have one thing in common. They deal with God's evaluation of *mishpat* and *s'daqah*. This may have some bearing on the change in the order of their listing.

57. Isa. 45:13.

58. Ibid. 11:4–5.

59. In one place in the Bible, *sadiq* is used for hero or mighty, without any ethical or religious significance. Cf. Isa. 49:24–25.

Index of Subjects, Names,
and Biblical Passages

far and near, 26; little gods, 33; the Lord of the Universe, 38; function as the Supreme Lawgiver and Judge, 41; the statutes and laws of, 41; concerned about the moral quality of His people, 42–43; a projection of the father image, 46; the image projected, 45; the Creator, the Absolute Sovereign, 50; in providential relationship to man, 50; desire to be *Elohim* for someone, 51; causal nexus between ethical behavior and the knowledge of, 55–59; to know, 56; to know, to love, 57–59; face hidden, 58, 125–27; knowledge of, an existentially transforming influence, 60; knowledge of and about, 62; unconcerned, 94; silent, 101–102; His dignity associated with the destiny of Israel, 117; name shares the destinies of God's people, 118–20; familiarity with, 131–33; oath of, 147–48; holiness, the sustaining and protecting attribute of divine mercy and love, 148; wholly-otherness, 164; unlikeness to anything else, 169; of the deists, 169; transcendent and immanent, 170; the "yearning" of His heart, 172; the oneness of attributes, 174–75, 202; "curbs" His wholly-otherness, 181; the will of, 186; face hidden in exile, 190–91; silent during Israel's exile, 205; *ne'eman*, 265; acts in faithfulness, 266–67; commandments faithful, 271–72; of emeth, 280–81; "charity" toward, 296; The Absolute *Sadiq*, 331; the word of, 334; might and right in, 336; ways with the world, 339–40

Golden Calf, 24–25; sin of the, 65

Goliath, 87–89

Good, the, 347; the idea of, 331, 339; Being and the, 347

Gott Erkennen: Im Sprachgebranch des Alten Testaments, 61

G'burah, equivalent of Shem, 88

Habakkak, 2:4, 276

Hallevi, Y'huda, 65, 219

Hannah, prayers of, 152, 200–202

Haya l', 145

Heilige, Das, 217

Higher Criticism, 7

Hesed ve'emeth, 285–91

Hezekiah, prayer of, 148–49

Hiding of the Face, 125–27, 191

History, the problem of, 339

History, universal, 71; scandalous separation between Being and Value, 348

Holiness, the saving force immanent in creation, 147; God's, 148; God's tragically involved in the destiny of Zion, 173; nearness, and being chosen, 180; of God, "withdrawal" from absoluteness, 181; not ethics, 186

Holy, the, indifferent toward the ethical, 217

Hosea, 2:21, 314, 332; 2:21–22, 57; 10:12, 321, 335; 11:8–9, 147; 12:7, 237; 13:4, 28; 13:16, 68

Hoshvei Sh'mo, 93–95

Ibn Ezra, 360*n*

Imitatio Dei, 242, 252

Inspiration, prophetic, 72, 74

Isaiah, 1:16–17, 229; 1:21, 260; 1:24–25, 142; 1:26, 260; 2:12, 142; 3:1, 142; 5:14–17, 151; 5:16, 150; 6:3, 176; 6:5, 144; 8:12–13, 193; 10:17, 144; 10:20, 143, 278; 11:2, 70; 11:3–5, 71; 11:4–5, 337; 11:9, 55, 12:4–5, 124; 12:5–6, 143; 12:6, 204; 13:3–5, 176; 13:4, 142; 13:13, 142; 16:5, 289, 315; 22:23, 25, 256, 25:4, 90; 26:8, 98; 26:13, 136, 156; 28:23–29, 244; 30:11, 15, 143; 30:18, 237; 30:27, 89; 31:1, 143; 32:16, 332; 33:5, 332; 33:6, 261; 33:16, 257; 33:22, 235; 34:5, 226; 35:8, 360*n*; 37:10, 149; 37:16, 141; 37:23, 197; 37:23–32, 148; 38:17–20, 282; 39:8, 254,

Eliezer Berkovits is chairman, department of Jewish philosophy at Hebrew Theological College, Skokie, Illinois. He received his Ph.D. in 1933 from the University of Berlin, and has been a rabbi in Berlin, Leeds, Sydney, and Boston.

The manuscript was edited by Robert H. Tennenhouse. The book was designed by Sylvia Winter. The type face for the text is Mergenthaler Linotype's Old Style No. 7 based on the early designs of Jensen, Garamond and Caslon; and the display face is Scotch Roman based on English designs of the early 1800's.

The book is printed on S. D. Warren's Olde Style Antique paper and bound in Holliston's Kingston Natural Finish cloth over boards. Manufactured in the United States of America.